Agenda for Progress

Examining Federal Spending

Edited by
EUGENE J. McALLISTER

The Heritage Foundation

Washington, D.C.

Acknowledgments

A study of this ambition could not be completed without the assistance of a large number of people. Although all cannot be acknowledged, some must be. Willa Ann Johnson, Director of The Heritage Foundation Resource Bank, Marvin M. Phaup, and Norman Ture all combined their knowledge of potential authors with considerable enthusiasm for the project. The authors and editor are indebted to numerous expert readers, whose comments enhanced the essays. Special thanks is due to Heritage Foundation staff: Jane L. Kessler and William T. Poole, whose editorial skills grace the entire study; Geoffrey A. Gimber and Sanford Jones, for their proof-reading abilities; and Donald F. Hall and Jamie Cook for their typing support. Leila Marie Lawler and William J. Gribben were also extremely gracious with their time and skills.

The editor's deepest debt is to Richard Odermatt whose devotion to proper usage is matched only by his adeptness with the technical aspects of publication.

Library of Congress Catalog card number 80–85273

ISBN 0-89195-029-X

Table of Contents

Contributors

Eugene J. McAllister is the Walker Fellow in Economics at The Heritage Foundation. He is the author of *Congress and the Budget: Evaluating the Process* (1979).

William Schneider, Jr., an economist with a background in defense policy, is on the staff of the Hudson Institute and is defense analyst for Representative Jack Kemp. He is author of *Food, Foreign Policy and Raw Materials* (1975) and is co-author of *Arms, Men and Military Budgets: Issues for Fiscal Year1981* (1980).

E. Dwight Phaup is Associate Professor of Economics at Union College. He has published numerous technical papers dealing with exchange rates and the demand for imports.

Richard Speier is on the staff of the U.S. Arms Control and Disarmament Agency. He was formerly with the Office of Budget and Management, Evaluation Division, specializing in "big science" and energy issues.

Randall G. Holcombe is Assistant Professor of Economics at Auburn University. He has written several technical articles on estimating the economic impact of an oil embargo.

Gordon S. Jones is an Energy Analyst with the Senate Republican Policy Committee. Previously he was Energy, Environment, and Natural Resources Analyst for Senator Jake Garn, and Director of Special Projects, EPA Office of Pesticide Programs.

Don Paarlberg is Professor Emeritus at Purdue University. He has been Assistant Secretary to the President, Coordinator of the Food for Peace Program, Assistant Secretary of Agriculture and Director of Agricultural Economics. His most recent book is *Farm and Food Policy: Issues of the 1980's* (1980).

Eric V. Robinson, now retired, was for seven years head of the Agriculture Branch at OMB.

Richard F. Muth is Professor of Economics at Stanford University. A member of the 1969 Presidential Task Force on Urban Renewal, he has written extensively on urban economics and housing. His books include *Cities and Housing, The Spatial Pattern of Urban Residential Land Use* (1969), *Public Housing: An Economic Evaluation* (1973), and *Urban Economic Problems* (1965).

Thomas Gale Moore is Senior Fellow and Director of Domestic Studies at the Hoover Institution. A former senior staff economist with the Council of Economic Advisors, he has studied transportation regulation intensively. His publications include *Freight Transportation Regulation* (1972), and *Trucking Regulation: Lessons from Europe* (1976).

Robert W. Poole, Jr. is the President of Reason Foundation and editor-in-chief of *Reason* magazine. His recent book *Cutting Back City Hall* is a guide for privatizing city services.

Eugenia Froedge Toma, Professor of Economics at Loyola-Marymount University, specializes in the economics of bureaucracy, particularly in education. She has written several papers on education and monopoly, and contributed "Government Subsidies, Government Aid, and Private Education" to Richard Wagner, ed., *Government Aid to Private Schools: Is it a Trojan Horse?* (1979).

Dave M. O'Neill is senior staff economist with the U.S. General Accounting Office. His areas of research interest include policy aspects of the labor market, economic growth, and industrial organization.

June A. O'Neill is Principal Research Associate and Director of the Program on Women and Family Policy at the Urban Institute. Previously she was Chief of the Human Resources Cost Estimate Unit, Congressional Budget Office, and Senior Staff Economist with the Council of Economic Advisors.

Jack A. Meyer is Resident Fellow in Economics at the American Enterprise Institute. Previously he was assistant director of the Council on Wage and Price Stability. His essay "Wage and Benefit Trends under the Carter Administration Guidelines" appears in William Fellner, ed., *Contemporary Economic Problems* (1980).

Charles D. Hobbs was Chief Deputy Director of Social Welfare for California, and was one of the principal architects of the California Welfare Reform Program. He has written for several scholarly journals and is the author of *The Welfare Industry* (1978).

Cotton M. Lindsay, Professor of Economics at Emory University, has studied the economics of health care extensively. Among his many publications are *The Pharmaceutical Industry; Economics, Performance, and Government Regulations* (1978, ed.) and *National Health Issues: The British Experience* (1980).

Richard E. Wagner is Professor of Economics at Auburn University. In his studies he has concentrated on the economics of government. He is the author of *The Fiscal Organization of American Federalism* (1971), *Democracy in Deficit: The Political Legacy of Lord Keynes,* (with James Buchanan, 1977), and *Balanced Budgets, Fiscal Responsibility, and the Constitution* (with Robert D. Tollison, 1980).

Stephen J. Entin is staff economist for the Congressional Joint Economic Committee. He is a leading proponent of supply-side economics on Capitol Hill.

Ron Boster is Deputy Minority Staff Director and Senior Staff Economist for the Committee on the Budget, U.S. House of Representatives. Previously he was with the U.S. Department of the Interior and Agriculture, and an adjunct faculty member in the Department of Agricultural Economics at the University of Arizona.

Introduction

In the spring of 1980 Congress searched frantically for $17 billion in budget reductions necessary to produce a balanced First Budget Resolution for FY 1981. After considerable political anguish, and amidst cries of social neglect, the cuts were made, at least on paper.

The interesting aspect of this exercise was not so much that the FY 1981 budget was in balance, a rare sighting which has since proved illusory, but that with total spending of over $611 billion, a 3 percent cut proved so formidable.

The federal budget, the keystone of national economic policy, is a bastion of immutability in a time of flux and inquiry. No longer a reflection of national goals, the inexorable forces of federal spending have become an obstacle to necessary and desired policy changes. The size and ambition of the federal establishment have become, in many ways, an impediment to the successful fulfillment of the basic obligations of a national government.

Since resources are always scarce, the current debate about defense spending, a balanced budget, and tax reform really centers around the allocation process. The promise of greater national security, fewer inflationary pressures, and a more productive and efficient economy cannot be fulfilled without a break from the conventional criteria which have guided political economic thought over recent decades.

This study is an attempt to display the virtues of a market approach to federal spending. Each author inquires, implicitly or explicitly, whether the federal government should engage in the studied activity and, if so, whether current programs are operated in the most efficient manner. Needless to say the total savings from the essays substantially exceeds Congress' 1980 effort. A rough estimate of the FY 1982 impact is a gross cut of $55 billion, or a net (including the defense spending increase of $34 billion) of $21 billion. The difference between the budget as now constructed and the market approach alternatives is perhaps a rough measure of the resources devoted to politics.

The goal however is much more ambitious than a list of possible budget savings. It is hoped that the analyses and conclusions presented here will contribute to both an assessment of the philosophy behind many federal programs and an appreciation of the alternatives. The intent is to demonstrate the tremendous economic and social potential which lies in a different view of the federal budget.

The essays, encompassing the fourteen major budget functions, tax policy, and federal credit programs, are as varied as the authors. Academics, Hill and Executive staff all bring to their tasks a perspective shaped by their experiences. Generally the essays are divided into three parts: a brief introduction, an examination of short-run policies, and less constrained long-term considerations. The FY 1982 figures are based on President Carter's FY 1981 (January 1980) budget. The essays do not consider waste and fraud, travel, or administrative expenses.

The authors were given a free hand. The only qualification given was that they describe not what could be done, but rather what should be done. They have succeeded very well.

Eugene J. McAllister

Editor

National Defense

by William Schneider, Jr.

The nation's defense effort has become a more contentious issue in the past year than at any time since the Vietnam conflict. Unlike the defense debate of nearly a decade ago, no single dimension of U.S. defense investment is the focus of concern.[1] Rather, the dispute reflects divergent perceptions of the nature of the Soviet threat, and the adequacy of our defense effort to meet that threat.

This essay will attempt to summarize some of the major defense issues facing the U.S. during the early 1980s. Although no attempt is made here to formalize a strategy, which indeed must be articulated if U.S. modernization efforts are to have any coherence, the salient features of the Soviet threat are discussed as a means of calibrating the direction and magnitude of the American response. Both programmatic changes in current and proposed Department of Defense programs are discussed, as well as a few organizational and management issues that may have substantial leverage over future cost reduction, and performance improvement, in defense operations.

Soviet-American Defense Investment

Since the mid-1960s, the Soviet Union has engaged in a sustained program of defense investment.[2] The United States, on the other hand, has actually disinvested in defense. Defense expenditures in real terms (inflationary effects removed) are approximately ten billion dollars lower in FY 1980 than they were in FY 1964.[3] As a result, the So-

---

[1] The defense debate(s) of a decade ago were dominated by the ongoing Vietnam conflict, and the decision to develop and deploy an anti-ballistic missile system. The best scholarly review of this debate is B. D. Adams, *Ballistic Missile Defense* (New York: Elsevier, 1971).

[2] These estimates are well documented in public Central Intelligence Agency reports, e.g., *Estimated Soviet Defense Spending in Rubles, 1970–1975* (Washington: National Foreign Assessment Center). A careful study of the consequences of such trends can be found in A. J. Alexander *et al., The Significance of Divergent U.S.-U.S.S.R. Military Expenditure* (Santa Monica: RAND Corporation, March 1979).

[3] Secretary of Defense Harold Brown, *Annual Defense Report for Fiscal Year 1981* (Washington: Department of Defense, 1980).

viet Union now invests 25–50 percent more in defense than does the United States. (The variability reflects differences in dollar/ruble estimates.) In investment accounts (procurement and research and development) the Soviet Union has expended $240 billion more than the U.S. since the late 1960s.[4]

The cumulative effect of more than fifteen years of disinvestment in defense is startling. For the U.S. to "catch up" to the Soviets in aggregate defense expenditure would require more than forty years if the U.S. budget grew at five percent annually. This measure is not wholly satisfactory due to uncertainty about Soviet data, and, more importantly, the failure of such a measure to describe the forces procured by these expenditures, i.e., an efficiency measure. Nevertheless, to the extent that effort is roughly correlated with reward, the expenditure lead the Soviets have accumulated is bound to have an eventual effect on the military balance.[5]

The proposed Carter budget for FY 1982 (based on current press reports) will be $183.6 TOA (Total Obligational Authority). This is substantially below the figure that could be derived from the Ford FY 1978–82 Five-Year Defense Plan (FYDP) when expressed in current dollar terms. Moreover, since the Ford budget did not include the subsequent fuel and military personnel price adjustments, the difference in programmatic effect is even greater. Indeed, over the period of comparable FYDPs (FY 1978–1982), cumulative expenditures by the Carter Administration are $38 billion below that proposed by the previous administration. It must be expected that static measures of military power (numbers of tanks, artillery, missiles, etc.) will continue to show a trend unfavorable to the United States unless current policy is reversed.

In 1977, the Carter Administration pledged to increase defense in-

---

[4] Testimony of the Hon. William J. Perry, Under Secretary of Defense for Research, Development, and Acquisition before the Subcommittee on Defense of the Committee on Appropriations, U.S. House of Representatives, on the Fiscal Year 1981 DoD Budget, March 1980.

[5] So substantial has Soviet defense expenditure grown in comparison to U.S. defense expenditure, that decades would be required to pass before U.S. defense expenditure equaled Soviet expenditure. This can be illustrated in the following manner. If current CIA estimates of Soviet (ruble) defense expenditure growth rates are employed, and we assume that the average real rate of growth for U.S. expenditure will be 5 percent, then:

If S_n and A_n are the Soviet and American defense budgets (after time 0), and G_a and G_s are the American and Soviet budget growth rates (i.e. $S_0/A_0 = 1.50$, and $G_a = 5\%$ and $G_s = 4\%$, then

$$S_n = S_0(1 + G_s)^n, \quad A_n = A_0(1 + G_a)^n$$

For U.S. defense expenditure growing at 5 percent per annum, and Soviet defense expenditure growing at 4 percent per annum, 42 years would elapse before the two defense budgets were equal.

Table 1
National Defense
(in millions of dollars)

Major missions and programs	1979 actual	1980 estimate	1981 estimate
OUTLAYS			
Department of Defense – Military:			
Military personnel	28,407	30,574	31,705
Retired military personnel:			
Existing law	10,279	11,941	13,677
Proposed legislation	–	–	37
Operation and maintenance	36,424	40,852	46,376
Procurement	25,404	27,648	30,497
Research, development, test and			
evaluation........................	11,152	12,933	14,843
Military construction	2,080	2,147	2,053
Family housing	1,468	1,571	1,686
Revolving funds and other	– 201	– 266	– 222
Allowance for civilian and military pay			
raises............................	–	–	1,819
Other legislation	–	–	229
Subtotal, Department of			
Defense – Military...............	115,013	127,400	142,700
Atomic energy defense activities	2,541	2,980	3,386
Defense-related activities:			
Existing law	129	169	362
Proposed legislation	–	– 178	– 203
Subtotal, defense-related activities ...	129	– 9	159
Deductions for offsetting receipts	– 3	– 3	– 4
Total, outlays.....................	**117,681**	**130,368**	**146,241**

Source: The Budget of the United States Government FY 1981

vestment at an annual rate of three percent. To date, however, it has found this commitment a difficult one, due in part to the persistent practice of underestimating inflation. As a result, there has been little real growth in defense expenditure since the Carter Administration took office.[6] Moreover, within Department of Defense accounts there has been an asymmetric loss of purchasing power reflecting the rapidly escalating cost of fuel and the recruitment/retention of military personnel. Surging fuel prices have had the effect of diverting resources from investment accounts to operating accounts. Second order effects from this reallocation of resources has led to reduction in the rate at which new weapon systems are procured. Fewer purchases

---

[6] The failure of the Carter Administration to reach its defense investment objectives due to its persistent underestimate of inflation is described in L. J. Korb, "The FY 1981–1985 Defense Program, Issues and Trends," *AEI Foreign Policy and Defense Review,* Volume Two, No. 2 (1980).

3

then unfavorably affect unit costs due to uneconomic rates of procurement.

Administration attempts to mitigate the effect of inflation by placing a ceiling on cost-of-living allowances for military personnel has contributed to an exodus of skilled personnel previously trained at high cost. The flight of personnel has, in turn, had an adverse effect on the readiness of the armed forces. The result has been a substantial decline in our ability to deploy ships, aircraft squadrons, and ground force units fully ready for war.

THE SOVIET THREAT

The size and character of the Defense budget cannot be evaluated in a vacuum. Beyond some minimum necessary to retain a basic cadre for mobilization, U.S. defense investment must be related to a plausible range of threats. While a full development of character of the Soviet threat is beyond the scope of this essay, a brief description is necessary to appreciate the need for the defense initiatives proposed here.

Military Doctrine

One of the most neglected aspects of Soviet military power is the role of its doctrine in the organizing, equipping, and operating of its armed forces. Simple static comparisons of numbers of weapons and their performance characteristics are not informative because the Soviets use doctrinal concepts that are vastly different from those in vogue in Western armies.[7]

1. *Instrumental view of war:* The Soviets view war, not as a result of a "failure of diplomacy," but as an instrument of policy in the Clausewitzian sense of "diplomacy by other means." War is not a preferred course of action; indeed to the highly cautious Soviet leadership, it is very rarely used to advance Soviet policy objectives, but is one of several alternative means of achieving the ends of the Soviet state.

2. *Emphasis on Mass:* The Soviets view modern war as a brief, but highly destructive conflict. Thus, the Soviets tend to procure weap-

---

[7] See for example Major General F. W. von Mellenthin (former Chief of Staff of the 4th Panzer Army), *Panzer Battles,* (Norman: University of Oklahoma Press, 1956). An important German work analyzing the Soviet assimilation of modern tactical concepts is Major General Eike Middeldorf, *Taktik im Russland Feldzug* (Darmstadt: Ergahrungen und Folgungen, 1956). The studied manner in which the Soviets link their defense policy to military doctrine is poorly understood in detail. A particularly insightful paper on this linkage is contained in J. Erickson, "Soviet 'Command Technology': Problems, Programmes, Perspectives," Defense Studies, University of Edinburgh (mimeo, May 1980).

4

ons in large numbers to offset wartime attrition and gain a margin of tactical superiority over an adversary's defenses. The result is that the Soviets procure forces far larger than their Western counterparts.

3 . *Surprise and Pre-emption:* The Soviets attach great importance to the tactical role of surprise. A component of the Soviet emphasis on surprise is the need to pre-empt a potential opponent. This notion of pre-emption does *not* imply "war-by-calculation"; rather it places considerable emphasis on intelligence collection so that the Soviet leadership can pre-empt an opponent before he can move in a manner which would jeopardize Soviet interests.

4 . *Centralization of Command:* The primacy of the political mechanism in Soviet affairs is a well established principle. Closely related is the tendency to have a highly centralized decision-making and command apparatus. Military initiative originates in higher echelons of command rather than the lower levels as in Western armies.

The Soviets do not make the rigid distinction between nuclear and non-nuclear conflict made in the United States. Rather they distinguish between general war where "all means" of warfare would be employed (including nuclear, chemical, conventional, and para-military) and lesser conflicts that would involve more limited means. When engaged in general war, Soviet military objectives are traditional ones: to destroy the effectiveness of an opponent's armed forces by attacking his command and control apparatus (the primary objective) and limiting potential damage to the Soviet state through attacks on the military forces of an adversary. The notion of making the civilian population the focus of an attack (the operative features of the U.S. "assured destruction" doctrine) is rejected by the Soviets as inadequate to their needs.[8] It is not surprising then to find that Soviet strategic forces emphasize heavy payload missiles capable of delivering accurate, high-yield nuclear weapons since these are needed to destroy hardened military targets including missile silos and command centers.

The Soviet concept of theater warfare also has important differences with its Western counterparts. The Soviets believe that a future conflict will be brief, violent, and highly destructive. Thus, a major tactical advantage will accrue to the side able to take the initiative (i.e., pre-empt). As the Soviets believe a protracted period of industrial mobilization is unlikely — the reverse of the U.S. view — they acquire military equipment in astoundingly large quantities.

---

[8] J. D. Douglass, Jr. and A. M. Hoeber, *Soviet Strategy for Nuclear War* (Palo Alto: Hoover Institution Press, 1979).

5

Deployments

A second dimension of Soviet military power pertinent to the characterization of U.S. military (and budgetary) requirements is the nature of the deployment of Soviet military forces.

The total Soviet force structure includes 4.8 million men under arms plus a large reserve drawn from conscripts who have completed their tour of active duty. Although the Soviet Army is organized into more than 170 divisions, not all are at full strength. More than one-half the divisions are in cadre form and are filled by reservists. As the divisions are fully equipped, even when manned only in cadre form, their availability is relatively high compared to Western armies, which are typically underequipped. In areas of high strategic interest to the Soviet Union, forward-deployed forces are deployed in a high state of readiness (Category I), and are trained for initiating military operations with little warning. This is particularly true in Eastern Europe — the area of the greatest strategic interest to the Soviet Union — where the divisions are equipped and extensive stocks of fuel, ammunition, and spare parts to prevent compromise of mobilizations.[9] Little comfort can be drawn from the nominal states of readiness for individual Soviet divisions. Two Category III Motorized Rifle Divisions (described as having from 25 to 30 percent of their peacetime troop complement) were mobilized from Central Asia for the invasion of Afghanistan in December 1979.

Other areas of significant Soviet deployments are in the Caucasus region north of Iran, Afghanistan (three Motorized Rifle Divisions and all but one battalion of an Airborne Division are deployed along the Iran-Afghanistan border), and in the Soviet Far Eastern Military District along the Sino-Soviet border. The organic mobility of these forces is augmented by the Soviet Air Transport Aviation and the civilian airline, *Aeroflot*.

Soviet Operational Method

The aforementioned elements of Soviet power (its military doctrine, its weapon system characteristics, and the deployment of its forces) coalesce in a "style" of operation of its forces — this "operational method" bears directly on U.S. defense policy choices.

The Soviet operational method, as it pertains to theater conflicts, is based on Soviet initiation of hostilities. Operations are conducted against a relatively narrow front by a massive assault of mechanized infantry and armor formations backed by terrain fire from Soviet ar-

---

[9]See C. N. Donnelly, "Rear Support for the Soviet Ground Forces," *International Defense Review,* Vol. 12, No. 3 (1979), pp. 344–50, and G. Turbeville, "Soviet Logistic Support for Ground Operations," *RUSI: Journal of the Royal United Service Institute,* September 1975.

tillery, ballistic missiles, and tactical aircraft. The primary objective of the Soviet operational method is to break through prepared defenses, disorganize rear areas, cut communications, and paralyze the command apparatus.

Soviet military operations on an intercontinental scale, those involving strategic nuclear weapons, have two objectives: to paralyze the command apparatus and to limit damage through the destruction of an adversary's "means of nuclear attack." Over the past fifteen years, the Soviets have invested sufficient resources to acquire forces necessary to meet most of their doctrinal criteria.

There are several implications of the Soviet operational method for the U.S. U.S. and allied forces must have a capability to sustain a conflict at high levels of intensity. Command-and-control must be flexible and highly survivable. Tactical aircraft must maintain a high sortie rate in the presence of nuclear, chemical, and conventional attacks against airfields and fuel and ordnance storage areas. Soviet naval operations require that U.S. combatants be capable of defending a carrier Battle Group against salvo attacks of scores of cruise missiles (while conducting air and amphibious operations).

Weapon Inventories

The large quantities of Soviet military equipment poses potentially serious problems. The United States, in many areas of weapon design, must wholly offset the Soviet quantitative superiority with a U.S. qualitative advantage achieved through the employment of advanced technology and tactical ingenuity. This is becoming an increasingly difficult task.

One of the consequences of greater cumulative investment in defense by the Soviet Union has been an evolutionary upgrading of the quality of Soviet weapon systems without abandoning the Soviet doctrinal preference for massive procurement. For example, the sophistication of Soviet tactical aircraft since the 1970s has increased to the point where several advanced Soviet tactical aircraft perform their intended mission as well as their American counterparts. This infusion of more costly and sophisticated aircraft in the Soviet arsenal has caused a reduction in the rate of production of combat aircraft, but the Soviets still produce military aircraft at three to four times the annual rate of the United States.[10]

---

[10] See for example, "The Soviet Air Force: An Offensive Posture and Expanding Capability," *Air International,* No. 6, 1976; J. Erickson, "Soviet Theater Forces and NATO Modernization" (mimeo); and Lt. Col. W. Kopenhagen, "Waffensystem Hubschrauber," *Armee Rundschau,* July 1977; the latter essay commenting on the Soviet embracing of helicopters – an area where the U.S. had a unchallenged numerical and qualitative advantage as recently as five years ago.

SHORT-TERM POLICIES

Although the Carter budget estimates for FY 1982 have grown substantially since the first estimates when the FY 1978–82 FYDP was presented, it remains an inadequate response. The growing recognition among specialists that serious shortcomings exist in the American defense posture is unfortunately not matched by a consensus as to the scope of remedial action. At least in part this problem can be attributed to the piece-meal acknowledgement of American vulnerability, *viz.* Secretary Brown's belated observation that U.S. land-based forces will be vulnerable to Soviet attack in the 1980s. In fact, when a significant effort is made to review the Soviet-American military balance on a program-by-program basis, the deficiency in American power results in unsettling estimates of the effort needed to restore the credibility of deterrence.[11]

The estimated defense budget for FY 1982 proposed here (excluding Military Assistance and the Nuclear Weapons program) is $33.7 billion more than proposed by the Carter Administration. This increment will begin to mitigate the protracted neglect of the U.S. defense posture, but will not "solve" the problem.

The very size and urgency of the problem suggests that our defense needs cannot be met simply by appropriating additional funds. Although greater funds will undoubtedly be necessary, they will not be sufficient unless program initiatives are made within the bounds of a well-thought-out strategy. The United States has never sought numerical superiority in a weapon-for-weapon sense, even at the zenith of American military power. A strategy and military doctrine sufficient to deter armed assaults on American interests have made possible the possession of superior military power with forces of modest size. The chasm we now face due to the Soviet accumulation of military power, requires a rethinking of our military posture. Among the issues that must be addressed are basic concerns of strategy and military doctrine, personnel recruitment and retention policy, theater and naval warfare doctrine and tactics, and reserve organization. Although these issues do not directly affect procurement decisions in the near term, they undoubtedly determine those decisions in the long run.

STRATEGIC FORCES

As a matter of budgetary convenience, strategic forces, like other elements of the U.S. defense program, are treated separately. This,

---

[11] There have been two well-informed estimates, however, that address some of the most significant procurement issues: Committee on the Present Danger, *Defense Strategy and Funding for the 1980s* (Washington: Committee on the Present Danger, May 9, 1980), and Capitol Hill Staff Group, *A Program for Military Independence* (Washington: The Institute of American Relations, 1980).

however, should not obscure the necessary unity of our defense posture.[12] The credibility of our strategic nuclear posture affects our general purpose forces as surely as our ability to intervene with general purpose forces affects the integrity of nuclear deterrence. We cannot expect to substantially neglect any major component of our military power without its effects contaminating the efficacy of our defense and foreign policy posture as a whole.

Strategic forces have been the most neglected element of our defense posture for a variety of historical and political reasons. Modernization decisions in the mid-to-late 1960s were deferred due to the high budget priority afforded military operations in Southeast Asia. Subsequent modernization efforts (save for the deployment of multiple independently targetable re-entry vehicles of U.S. ICBMs and SLBMs) were held in abeyance pending the outcome of the Strategic Arms Limitation Talks, negotiations that have served to inhibit U.S. modernization for more than a decade.[13] The failure to modernize has been exacerbated by the sustained Soviet modernization program, which was not influenced by the arms limitation negotiation efforts.

Land-based Forces

The most pressing issue facing the United States concerns the survivability of the land-based ICBM force. Full-scale engineering development of a survivable ICBM, scheduled to begin in FY 1978 was delayed for three years due to arms control optimism and later by White House indecision about the details of the its configuration. In September 1979, a decision was finally made, but it required subsequent revisions to reduce cost and complexity.

The revised proposal would deploy 200 ICBMs in a complex of hardened reinforced concrete shelters, each one mile apart, along a straight road. These shelters would be deployed in the Utah-Nevada area in numbers of 4,600–9,200, depending upon the growth of the Soviet threat. The missile would survive large attacks (up to 15–20,000 re-entry vehicles) because the Soviets would be obliged to attack each shelter in the system to insure completed destruction of the 200 missiles hidden among the shelters. The weakness of the system is its late 1980s deployment schedule (due to the delayed FSED decision) and

---

[12] One of the weaknesses of U.S. policy has been the tendency to treat nuclear conflict as a subject separately from the balance of our defense posture. This practice has led to a devastating lack of realism in the formulation and execution of U.S. policy that has undermined both our defense and arms control programs.

[13] An important statement on the interaction between land-based strategic force modernization and arms control is C. S. Gray, "The Strategic Forces Triad: End of the Road?", *Foreign Affairs*, Vol. 56, No. 4 (July 1978).

Table 2

FY 1982 Strategic Forces Survivability and Modernization Initiatives

Program	Cost
MX Program Acceleration	$1.0 billion
Minuteman II/III Improvements	0.5
B-1 Derivative (enhanced)	0.7
Advanced Penetration Technology	0.5
B-52 Cruise Missile Carrier Acceleration	0.3
Total	$3.0 billion

the costly efforts to confine the system to the limitations of the proposed SALT II treaty.

These problems can be mitigated by acceleration of the MX deployment and elimination of costly complexities imposed by SALT constraints. Pre-emptive land withdrawal legislation, modeled on the Alaska Pipeline legislation, and designed to eliminate bureaucratic delays could permit initiation of shelter construction in FY 1982 so that the first 1,000 shelters could be deployed by FY 1984. Initial deployments could be made without the mobility feature of the current design, although the option should be retained as a hedge against growth of the threat in the late 1980s and 1990s.

A further hedge against an immediate or greater-than-expected threat should be the development of a multiple protective structures basing scheme for the Minuteman III system. This would entail modifications permitting occasional horizontal transport of the missile, as well as a cannister for the missile, which would allow it to be launched from low-cost silos. Even if pre-emptive land withdrawal legislation is enacted, the concurrent development of a *Minuteman* option would contribute to the survivability of U.S. land-based forces when their vulnerability would be most threatened.[14]

Improved performance can be obtained from the existing *Minuteman* force by fitting the *Minuteman III* missiles, now equipped with the low-yield Mark 12 re-entry vehicle, with the higher yield Mark 12A. The appropriate emphasis on attacking Soviet command-and-control targets announced in the Administration's new targeting guidance (Presidential Directive 59) can be supported by modifications of the *Minuteman II*. Equipped with the Advanced Inertial Reference Sphere (AIRS) guidance system and provisions for remote targeting, the *Minuteman II's* high-yield warhead (1.2 megatons) can

---

[14] A description of an alternate *Minuteman* rebasing scheme is described in Paul H. Nitze, "Alternative Launch Point Systems," mimeo, Committee on the Present Danger, Washington, D.C.

be directed against blast-resistant command-and-control targets in the Soviet Union.

Perhaps the most controversial dimension of the land-based element of U.S. strategic forces is the air-breathing component: manned bombers and cruise missiles. Bombers currently carry half the megatonnage in U.S. strategic forces, but have not received the minimum attention necessary for them to be effective over the next two or three decades. The impending obsolescence of the B-52 force (due to air defense improvements, e.g., the SA-10), make an early modernization decision important. However, current proposals offered by the Administration suggest instead the development of yet another bomber, with its potential deployment delayed until the late 1980s or early 1990s, which will be much too late.[15]

If they can be successfully developed, three technological developments have the promise of significantly improving the ability of all manned or unmanned air-breathing delivery systems to penetrate defenses. The first is advanced electronic countermeasures (ECM), which will permit electronic warfare systems to alter their characteristics and confuse radar, regardless of whether or not the performance properties of the radar are known in advance. If such ECM systems can be developed, they will permit enemy radar to be nullified, or severely curtail its use and, thus, greatly improve the probability of penetration of hostile air space.[16]

A second development, whose broad outlines have recently been described by the Department of Defense, involves the use of "passive" (i.e., non-radiating) means to reduce the visibility of cruise missiles and manned aircraft to radar detection. If these techniques (a variety of aerodynamic treatment of the surface of the aircraft) can be successfully "scaled up" to a strategic bomber (260–500,000 lb. gross weight), they could improve the probability of penetration of aircraft at high altitudes, and reduce the vulnerability of cruise missiles to "look-down/shoot-down" radar. While these systems will have limitations (relatively small payloads, and vulnerability to detection by VHF radar and/or advanced signal processing techniques), they will force a substantial investment by the Soviet Union in air defense, thereby diverting resources from strategic attack systems. Short of building a

---

[15] The "track record" on developing strategic bombers does not give much confidence that one could be deployed quickly; the B-70 was canceled in the early 1960s, which was followed by what became the B-1 program in 1963. This was terminated fourteen years later.

[16] Current electronic countermeasures technology (ECM) largely depends upon an understanding of the properties of the hostile radar to permit design of an ECM system capable of "spoofing" the radar either through jamming or other forms of deception. If ECM can be made to "adapt" to the configuration of hostile radar as it is found, traditional penetration techniques (e.g., low altitude flight profiles, high-speed dash, high-g maneuvers, etc.) may be viable for many years in the future.

large-scale ballistic missile defense (BMD) system, or executing a successful pre-emptive strike against Soviet forces, U.S. bombers and cruise missiles are the most important form of damage limitation available to our military forces.

A third technology, now in its infancy, could further enhance the ability of bombers to survive. This is the use of high-powered lasers on bomber aircraft for their self-defense against surface-to-air missiles. Impressive gains have been made in high energy laser (HEL) technology. The large potential power-generation capability could support the operation of an HEL system before the end of the century, and perhaps earlier.

These developments point to the wisdom of multiple approaches to the survivability of the land-based bomber force. Work on cruise missiles, especially second generation versions incorporating passive "stealth" techniques should continue. Resources should also be diverted to the deployment of an "interim" penetrating bomber which is derived from the original B-1 design, but incorporates technology that has become available since the 1977 production cancellation decision. An advanced technology bomber, which will assume the penetration role, should be deployed in the 1990s. The B-1 variant will then assume mixed penetration, cruise missile, and conventional bombing roles. Advanced cruise missiles will augment the effectiveness of both traditional low-altitude manned bombers (with advanced ECM) and advanced high-altitude penetration techniques. The result will be a highly effective force retaining the benefits of a manned nuclear delivery system (recallable, flexible) without incurring the risk of a high rate of attrition in a conflict.

Sea-based Forces

Modernization of the sea-based forces is advancing at so leisurely a pace that the full operational capability (FOC) of the *Trident II* missile/submarine system will not occur until 1999. It is quite likely that the full potential of the remaining elements of the sea-based force will never be exploited. If one converts the cost of the *Polaris* and *Minuteman* programs completed in the 1960s to FY 1981 dollars, the cost of the programs were $40 and $38 billion respectively. Both were constructed simultaneously. In the program advanced by the Carter Administration, modernization of the ICBM force and the SLBM force are sequential efforts. This procedure would be a cost-reducing approach in the short term (although real program costs would remain unchanged), but is not a suitable posture for the threat posed.

The *Trident II* missile is more compatible with the requirements of PD-59 than is the *Trident I*, although the latter is a useful improvement over the *Polaris A-3* and the *Poseidon* currently in the force. Initiation of a significant level of R&D funding in FY 1982 could

Table 3
FY 1982 Modernization of Sea-based Strategic Nuclear Forces

Program	Cost
Trident II (D-5) Missile Development	$0.6 billion
Trident II Submarine acceleration	1.3
Trident I (C-4) Retrofit in *Poseidon*	1.0
SLCM Retrofit in *Polaris*	0.2
Total	$3.1 billion

provide a FY 1989 IOC (Initial Operational Capability) for a *Trident II* missile to be deployed aboard the *Trident* (*Ohio* class) submarines now under construction. *The Trident submarine program should be rapidly accelerated to increase the number of strategic weapons platforms available to the U.S.*

Current Administration plans envision converting only twelve of a potential twenty-four *Poseidon* submarines to accept the more capable *Trident I* missile. This approach has been dictated by the premature enthusiasm for and compliance with the SALT II agreement, as well as President Carter's minimum deterrence preferences. The President's 1979 State of the Union address implied that deterrence could be maintained with a single *Poseidon* submarine.[17] Since the submarine force plays a central role both as a strategic reserve force and as a long range nuclear strike force on behalf of NATO, the modest deployment proposed by the Carter Administration should be adjusted upward to twenty-four *Poseidon* conversions rather than twelve.

Ten of the oldest missile-firing submarines, formerly used to launch the *Polaris* submarines, cannot accommodate the *Trident I* (C-4) missile. These, however, can be usefully employed as launchers for the submarine/sea-launched cruise missile (SLCM). The Carter Administration has proposed restricting SLCM deployments to attack submarines ("hunter/killer submarines") but this would diminish torpedo loading, thereby compromising their attack role. The ten *Polaris* submarines could accommodate five SLCMs per launch tube, or up to 80 per submarine. This would more than double the proposed SLCM deployment and make a much greater contribution to deterrence at both the strategic and theater level. Although important comand-and-

---

[17] According to what is known about the effects of nuclear weapons, a single loading of *Poseidon* warheads could barely cover metropolitan Moscow (900 km^2) with ten lbs/in.^{2} overpressure (approximately the blast pressure necessary to demolish steel/concrete structures) — not 200 cities as was implied by the President's State of the Union Message. See S. Glasstone, *The Effects of Nuclear Weapons* (Washington, GPO, 1977).

Table 4

FY 1982 Modernization of Strategic/Theater C³I Systems

Program	Cost
Airborne Launch Control System	$0.020 billion
Extremely Low Frequency Comm. Syst.	0.025
Expendable Satellite Reconstitution Boosters *(Titan)*	0.100
Survivable C³I Initiatives	0.500
NAVSTAR Global Positioning System	0.040
Spare C³I Satellites	0.250
Total	$0.935 billion

control problems remain unsolved, when successfully completed, the suggested changes will present the most efficient use of our sea-based assets.

Comand-Control-Communications and Intelligence (C³I)

The Command-Control-Communications and Intelligence (C³I) system constitutes the information base upon which the President must make decisions before, during, and after a conflict, as well as the means by which he directs the employment of all military forces under his command. Although Soviet C³I targets have recently attained a high level of priority for American strategic targeting, U.S. C³I facilities have long been a central feature of targeting by Soviet strategic forces.

U.S. C³I in general have been organized with the expectation that a future nuclear conflict would be a brief spasmodic affair in which C³I would play no major role once the conflict began. As a consequence, U.S. command and control facilities, characterized by an extremely low order of survivability, are unable to handle the large volumes of encrypted voice and data traffic associated with managing complex military forces *during* a conflict. Furthermore, the C³I are not capable of providing the President with the kind of information needed to terminate the conflict.

Several developments have made continuation of this posture dangerous. Soviet forces are now able to reliably target U.S. ground- and some space-based (typically low altitude reconaissance satellites) C³I facilities. This threatens to blind the tactical warning of an attack (especially if geosynchronous satellites become vulnerable to Soviet anti-satellite systems) and completely disrupt the advanced communication systems between the President and mobile forces. Numerous major U.S. intelligence systems were compromised by major espionage cases in the past three years. These losses may provide the Soviets with a basis for disrupting the flow of information to the President.

14

The burden of new weapons systems creates a much greater C^3I requirement than the systems they replace (or augment). Cruise missiles and submarines will depend upon satellite navigation systems. Advanced targeting concepts will impose more stringent requirements for communication with mobile forces (e.g., bombers, cruise misile carriers, and submarines) than has heretofore been the case. In addition, there will inevitably be a requirement for real-time information on battle damage assessment (BDA) to fully inform the President about the state of the conflict. It should be emphasized that this somewhat grisly account of the conflict-related needs of the President for a C^3I system does not imply a greater preference for nuclear conflict. It is no more than an important means of assuring the credibility of deterrence by ensuring that the forces could prevail in a conflict if deterrence failed.

Modern C^3I will require not only the technological innovation that has become a characteristic of the American military establishment,[18] but also redundant systems (to hedge against the failure of primary systems), and enhanced "passive means" (concealment, mobility, and hardening) to assure survivability. Included in the requirements are full coverage of all land-based ICBMs, by the Airborne Launch Control System, additional expendable boosters (e.g., *Titan* missiles) to reconstitute satellite systems, development of additional passive means for the protection of C^3I assets, improved communications with deployed submarines (the Extremely Low Frequency Communication system), the production of spare satellites to replace those lost or damaged during the course of a conflict, and systems for improved communications with mobile forces.

Active Defense

The United States has abstained from the active defense against ballistic missiles by the ABM Treaty of 1972, the air defense against manned bombers and cruise missiles by choice, and has made the most timid efforts toward anti-satellite programs in deferrence to the Anti-Satellite Treaty negotiations. The disinclination toward defense is a powerful feature of the Carter Administration and contributes to the low priority attached to research and development in technology suitable for active defense.

---

[18] There is no doubt that U.S. communications/electronics lead the world in sophistication. Many of these have been adapted to military use, but little thought has been given to their survivability in time of war. They are not inherently vulnerable, but U.S. doctrine, especially in the case of nuclear conflict, has been mired in assured-destruction notions of the spasm employment of nuclear weapons. As no thought is given to operating U.S. military forces under circumstances where deterrence has failed, little attention is paid to the post-attack survival of U.S. command-and-control facilities. Thus, U.S. technological sophistication has not been fully exploited in an arena where we possess a manifest advantage.

Despite the reluctance to proceed with a vigorous program of active defense research, the subject remains one of utmost importance to America's long-run security interests. Over the long term, no foreign policy can be effective without a capacity for homeland defense. The technological alternatives to do so have been meager in the past, but will not remain so. The United States will be a position to exploit advanced active defense technology against aerodynamic (aircraft and cruise missiles), ballistic missiles, and space-based threats. The means to do so with respect to aircraft and cruise missiles are already at hand in the form of surface-to-air missiles and manned interceptor aircraft assisted by airborne warning and control systems. Low altitude satellites can be intercepted with current technology by using the SRAM/ALTAIR-3 system launched from an F-15 aircraft. High altitude satellite systems can be placed at risk with technology well within our grasp.

Ballistic missile defense—the most controversial element of any program of active defense—can be described as a three-part problem of ascending technical difficulty. *The first element, protection of hardened strategic forces can be accomplished with technology already identified in the Low Altitude Defense System (LoADS),* now suffering from a lack of official enthusiasm. The second element, protection of urban-industrial areas against a "light" ballistic missile attack (which could be launched by a nuclear power other than the Soviet Union; a worrisome problem if the proliferation of nuclear weapons becomes endemic in the 1990s) could be accomplished by an advanced adjunct to the LoAD system, now being developed in the Homing Overlay Experiment (HOE) program. This system could produce a light area defense of the entire continental United States. The third and technologically most demanding element is the defense of urban-industrial areas against a "heavy" ballistic missile attack. The potential deployment of tens of thousands of re-entry vehicles in the 1990s precludes the use of "traditional" ballistic missile defense technology. *An adequate defense requires a major advance, probably directed energy systems employing high energy lasers or charged particle beam weapons. The vast "payoff" of this technology deserves a greater effort.*

The foregoing litany of vital strategic forces program initiatives additions illustrates the high cost of deferred investment in strategic forces. The proposed effort represents only a portion of the pulse of activity needed to restore the credible U.S. deterrent posture necessary for Soviet-American strategic equilibrium.

GENERAL PURPOSE FORCES

Elements of the U.S. defense posture included in the under-descrip-

Table 5

FY 1982 Active Defense Development/Procurement Initiatives

Program	Cost
F-15 Air Defense Interceptors (20)	$0.6 billion
Patriot Surface-to-Air Missile Batteries (long-lead plus site preparation)	0.6
High Energy Laser R&D Acceleration	0.2
LoADS Acceleration	0.2
E-3A (AWACS) procurement (3 a/c)	0.3
SRAM ALTAIR-3 Anti-Satellite System	0.5
Total	$2.4 billion

tive rubric of "General Purpose Forces" consume the bulk of military personnel and material resources available to the Department of Defense. The destructiveness of modern warfare, combined with the large forces required to achieve a major military objective, magnify the fiscal significance of every decision. The importance of General Purpose Forces (GPF) cannot be overestimated. Because of its crucial linkage in the chain of deterrence, the failure to respond to threats at lower orders of violence increases the risk of nuclear conflict. Threats to American and allied security interests cannot be defended entirely by strategic nuclear power; military power at the local level must be sufficient to prevail.

Since the Vietnam conflict, there has been considerable ambiguity in the development of U.S. GPF. The "lessons learned" from the brief, but violent Arab-Israeli conflict in 1973 came as a rude shock to many observers schooled in the "limited" conflicts of Vietnam and Korea. In the space of a single week, more tanks, armored personnel carriers, and self-propelled artillery were lost than the American arsenal was then able to produce in an entire year.[19] The use of combined arms doctrine (the joint use of mechanized infantry formations with tanks, self-propelled artillery, anti-tank units, and tactical aircraft) in concert with modern technology revealed serious deficiencies in U.S. and NATO expectations about a future theater conflict. This in turn led to a commitment on the part of the U.S. and the NATO nations to improve their defense capability, a commitment which found its expression in a pledge by NATO members to increase their real annual defense expenditure by three percent per year. This effort has flagged in several NATO nations for a variety of reasons, and has been incompletely fulfilled by the United States. The futility of seek-

---

[19] The pace of destruction of advanced equipment was substantial compared to other post-World War II conflicts. See Major General Chaim Herzog, *The War of Atonement* (Jerusalem: Steinmatzky Press Ltd., 1975).

17

Table 6
FY 1982 U.S. Army Modernization Initiatives

Program	Cost
XM-1 Main Battle Tank Program acceleration	$0.225 billion
IFV/CFV Fighting Vehicle System	0.100
Additional 155 mm artillery procurement M-109/M-198	0.135
Division Air Defense Gun (DIVAD)	0.250
ROLAND Surface-to-Air Missile System	0.120
AH-64 Advanced Attack Helicopter	0.020
UH-60 Transport Helicopter	0.480
Total	$1.330 billion

ing to measure defense "output" (the desired result in terms of greater military power) by focusing on an "input" statistic (growth in spending) has been revealed by the fact that the expenditure of several NATO nations (including the United States) conforms to the desired rate only because of an unanticipated increase in fuel prices. *Major deficiencies in the U.S. GPF posture cannot be solved solely through higher rates of investment in military hardware. Organizational and tactical innovation must be linked to technical innovation to make best use of our superior resource base.*[20]

Army

The U.S. Army faces the problem of coping with more than a decade of deferred modernization. Virtually every element of the U.S. combined arms inventory requires modernization, including tanks (the XM-1 to replace the M-60 series), armored personnel carriers (the IFV/CFV to replace the M113), artillery (new towed 155 mm. and an improved 155 mm. self-propelled howitzer), transport and attack helicopters (the UH-60 to replace the UH-1 and the AH-64 to replace the AH-1 series, respectively), field air defense (the Roland surface-to-air missile, and DIVAD self-propelled anti-aircraft gun to replace the *Chapparal/Vulcan* systems currently deployed), and advanced munitions to replace the current inventory of conventional and nuclear munitions.

Although all of the aforementioned systems are currently in production, their production rate has been stretched out to accommodate an

---

[20] This issue is perhaps more crucial than the question of resources as the input of additional sums can be to little avail if they are not wisely employed. Useful discussions of this important and complex problem can be found in E. Luttwak, "The American Style of Warfare and the Military Balance," *Survival,* March/April 1979, and S. L. Canby, *Tactical Airpower in Europe: Airing the European View* (Santa Monica: Technology Service Corporation, July 1976). Tactical/operational questions are likely to be as important in the 1980s as are the resources and equipment provided to the armed forces.

arbitrary budget ceiling. As a result, modernization for most combat units and reserve components will be delayed for many years. Long-term logistical problems can be expected with multiple systems deployed without a common set of spare parts. Moreover, protracted procurement schedules forces uneconomic rates of acquisition, thereby increasing costs. The emphasis must be on expanding production facilities, not only to meet higher rates of production for the modernization of U.S. active and reserve forces, but also to provide a production base to support wartime surge requirements. With few exceptions, the Army's modernization plan lags simply because of inadequate spending.

The U.S. tank program (XM-1) should be enhanced to produce 300 tanks per month on a surge basis, rather than the programmed 150 units. Production of the Infantry/Cavalry Fighting Vehicle System (IFV/CFV) should be increased to a target production rate of 1,200 units per year (achievable by FY 1983 or 1984). Similar FY 1982 production rate increases in other major Army procurement items are needed to reduce overall system acquisition costs and to accelerate modernization of active and reserve components.

It has been argued that the U.S. needs an increase in the number of active divisions from the current level of sixteen divisions to twenty-one or twenty-four divisions.[21] This step would be very costly in terms of both Military Personnel expenditures and the O&M burden of several additional active units. *A preferable course would be to increase the number of reserves if the Army Reserve and National Guard structure is modified to increase unit and individual proficiency with a higher order of readiness.* Then a cadre system could be used, analogous to the Soviet Category III divisions which are kept at 25–35 percent of full strength, but are able to be filled swiftly with suitable reserves. In any case, even a twenty-four-division force would not be adequate to meet the magnitude of the threat posed by a major conflict with the Soviet Union. Ample reserves (along the lines of the Israeli, Dutch, West German or South African models) are the best means of augmenting a forward deployment of active forces and should be the preferred mode of readiness for U.S. Army GPF.

Navy and Marine Corps

The Navy and Marine Corps have suffered an acute identity crisis under the attempted formulation of U.S. foreign and defense policy objectives. The Carter Administration sought to reduce the role of naval forces in American strategy. Evidence of the extent of this effort

---

[21] As the Soviets have more than five times as many divisions deployed, each with a similar measure of combat power (although the large support structure of U.S. forces gives a division more sustaining capability), this will be insufficient to meet the threat without addressing the problem of the reserves.

is best measured by changes in funding for the naval shipbuilding program. The final Ford defense budget (FY 1978) five-year shipbuilding program proposed the construction of 157 vessels, the Carter Administration cut the figure to only 83; a number insufficient to even sustain the 450-ship Navy described by the Chief of Naval Operations as a "one-and-one-half ocean Navy for a three ocean commitment." Extrapolation of the Carter shipbuilding program would reduce the Navy to 350 ships by the end of the century.

The reduction in shipbuilding has been paralleled by a reduction in the rate of procurement of naval aircraft, the cutting edge of U.S. power projection ashore. The Navy requires an annual rate of procurement of 325 aircraft merely to meet attrition through accidents and replacement of obsolete aircraft. Yet, the average annual procurement has been less than 150 for the past three years. As a result, the atrophy of the U.S. Navy's ability to support U.S. security interests abroad has reached grave proportions.[22]

Subsequent to the seizure of U.S. diplomatic personnel in Iran by a government-sponsored mob, the rhetorical (but not budgetary) posture of the Administration has changed. In his 1980 State of the Union message, the President declared the Persian Gulf to be a "vital" American interest. To date, no new programs have been advanced which would enable the Navy to meet such a commitment.

Major shipbuilding initiatives should include long-lead time funding for a new nuclear-powered aircraft carrier (CVN). The conventionally powered ORISKANY should be recommissioned to augment inadequate U.S. attack carrier assets. U.S. sea-based firepower could be rapidly augmented by recommissioning the four mothballed battleships, beginning with the NEW JERSEY. Suitably modified, this vessel could increase the firepower of an aircraft carrier battle group sixty times. The aft sixteen-inch gun battery can be removed and replaced with a cruise missile "farm" of 320 nuclear and conventional cruise missiles. *Increased rates of procurement of the CG-47* Aegis *guided missile cruiser are needed to increase the air defense assets of the fleet,* which is otherwise almost totally dependent upon the embarked aircraft of the attack carriers. The multiple threats posed from submarine, surface vessel, and air-launched cruise missiles dictates a swifter introduction of *Aegis* ships to the fleet.

New shipbuilding innovations are needed to speed the introduction of vertical/short take-off and landing (V/STOL) aircraft to naval operations in peripheral theaters where the adversary lacks sophisti-

---

[22] The principal means of projecting U.S. power in the past three decades has been with naval air power, yet this element is in the most jeopardy from underfunding. Alternative means of projecting U.S. power require a basing infrastructure that must either be secured in advance through diplomatic means, or in a time of crisis when resources are most seriously stretched.

Table 7

FY 1982 Navy and Marine Corps Modernization Initiatives

Program	Cost
Aircraft carrier long lead (CVN)	$0.3 billion
Oriskany recommissioning	0.3
Battleship modernization (BB-62)	0.22
SSN-688 submarine	1.4
CG-47 *Aegis* Cruiser	0.8
Mine Countermeasures Ship	0.08
Fleet oilers (TOA)	0.25
LSD-41 (Marine Corps support)	0.26
Total (Shipbuilding)	$3.41 billion
A-6E Attack aircraft	0.35 billion
EA-6B Electronic Warfare A/C	0.2
F-14 Fighter	0.7
CH-53E helicopter (Marine Corps)	0.2
SH-60B helicopter	0.6
P-3C Maritime Patrol a/c	0.12
E-2C Early Warning a/c	0.11
Total (Aircraft)	$2.28 billion
AIM-7F/M air-to-air missile	0.08
Phoenix air-to-air missile	0.2
SM1/2MR surface-to-air missile	0.09
SM2-ER surface-to-air missile	0.12
CAPTOR mine	0.08
Mark-48 Torpedo	0.09
Mark-46 Torpedo	0.06
Total (Ordnance)	$0.72 billion
Total (Navy/MC)	$6.41 billion

cated air defense and land-based strike aircraft. *Such innovations should include a new class of light aircraft carriers and the introduction of hydrofoils and/or surface-effect ships for strike, escort, anti-submarine warfare, and fleet air defense.* If these ships can be successfully developed, they could improve the ability of the Navy to conduct operations in remote theaters distant from areas of a major Soviet threat. Such innovations could reduce the long-term requirement for a greater number of larger ships of conventional design.

The inadequate inventory of combatant vessels is accompanied by a similar shortage of support vessels as well. The Navy has only three mine countermeasure ships (MCMs) in its inventory. Fifteen are required to meet current conditions. Initial procurement of the remainder should begin in FY 1982. Although the Navy is now obliged to operate on a permanent basis in the Persian Gulf region, the Administration has failed to request suitable numbers of fleet oilers (TOA) for replenishment of combatants at sea. (Vessels to support Marine amphibious operations have received inadequate funding.) *Pending the*

21

availability of more advanced ships, additional LSD-41 class ships should be procured to meet the amphibious support requirements of the Marine Corps.

The Marine Corps has traditionally been "short-changed" in access to first-line weapon systems for its ground forces. Shortages of mundane items such as anti-tank weapons, small arms, and tracked combat vehicles undermine the ability of the Marine Corps to conduct opposed landings in areas of the world where sophisticated Soviet-supplied equipment is abundant.

A critical shortage exists in Navy tactical aircraft. The inherent danger of carrier-based operations causes losses in aircraft due to attrition through accidents. Further losses occur through the phasing out of over-age aircraft. As a consequence, the Navy requires the procurement of 325 aircraft per year simply to have sufficient aircraft for its existing carrier force. In FY 1981, for the third consecutive year, the Carter Administration proposed to procure only slightly more than one-third the number needed.[23] As a result, the backlog in tactical aircraft requirements is substantial. It does, however, have the potential advantage of permitting more economical procurements of these aircraft, if the quantity order is larger.

Navy requirements for long-range attack and defense operations place a high premium on surface-to-air and air-to-air missiles. Yet, these are in short supply in the Navy inventory, thereby compromising the ability both to defend the fleet and to attack land and sea targets at long ranges. Although the missiles in the U.S. inventory are highly capable, there are insufficient quantities to meet operational requirements. The sixty *Phoenix* air-to-air missiles used on the F-14 fighter are sufficient for only a single day of combat. Similarly, procurement of the Mark 48 Torpedo has been constrained by manipulation to the target set it is designed to attack so that sufficient torpedoes are available for only a single loading of each attack submarine in the current inventory—hardly enough to sustain a protracted conflict or to cope with the unanticipated demands of modern war.[24]

The cumulative backlog in ships, aircraft, and munitions is so large that it is unlikely that sufficient funds can be diverted in a short period of time (two-to-three years).

---

23 Reductions in the number of replacement aircraft being procured has caused a reduction in the number of aircraft per squadron (e.g. 10 A-6s rather than 12 per squadron), and virtually eliminated "spares" for wartime attrition. As the Administration has sought to close production lines for currently operational aircraft (e.g. A-6, EA-6, A-10, etc.) the time consuming and costly process of production lines restarts seriously inhibits our ability to mobilize in a time of military need.

24 The calculation of "requirements" for ammunition appears driven by budgetary rather than operational requirements. Entire classes of ships have been eliminated from the target list, for example, to permit a reduction (and eventual closure of production) in torpedo requirements.

Table 8
FY 1982 U.S. Air Force Modernization Initiatives

Program	Cost
F-15 fighter	$1.65 billion
F-16 fighter	0.6
A-10 attack aircraft	0.6
AWACS (E-3A)	0.45
KC-10 Tanker aircraft	0.5
KC-135 re-engining	0.05
C-130H tactical transport	0.24
CRAF acceleration/modification	0.10
Total (aircraft)	$4.19
Maverick precision guided munition	0.05
AIM-7F/M air-to-air missile	0.20
AIM-9L/M air-to-air missile	0.03
High Speed Anti-Radiation Missile	0.08
Total (ordnance)	$0.36 billion
Total (Air Force)	$4.55 billion

Air Force

The problems of modernization and readiness in the Air Force parallel those of the other services. The role of the Air Force should be viewed (save for the special case of strategic forces operated by the Air Force) as an integral element of the overall scheme of land warfare. Tactical airpower provides local air superiority and a source of mobile "artillery" in support of the operations of ground combat forces.

During the course of the past decade, the scope of the land warfare battle has changed considerably, and with it, the threat posed to U.S. tactical air operations. Although there is a considerable amount of pertinent detail, the problem can be summarized briefly. Over the past few years, changes in the composition of Soviet ground forces have shifted the air defense of Soviet divisions primarily into the hands of the anti-aircraft missiles and guns of the division itself. The Soviet tactical air force has shifted its emphasis to the ground attack of mobile formations (fixed targets are attacked by ballistic missiles). Therefore, U.S. tactical air power must not only support engaged U.S. ground combat forces and their immediate air space, but must also defend targets deep in rear areas formerly unavailable to short-range Soviet tactical aircraft. The high density of air defense in the vicinity of Soviet ground forces makes traditional bombing and strafing tactics too dangerous. There is thus a need for weapons capable of delivering their munitions out of range of Soviet ground-based air defenses.

Moreover, as the number of secure forward air bases available to the U.S. Air Force diminishes, the importance of rapid deployment to a crisis area through strategic airlift grows. Yet, the growth of military airlift has not kept pace with the requirement. *One of the most promising means of meeting this shortage — the use of wide-bodied commercial aircraft in the Civil Reserve Air Fleet (CRAF) program — should be fully exploited.*[25] It is possible to convert the aircraft to carry both passengers and cargo though at the cost of greater weight and drag. A government subsidy would be required to make the modification attractive to commercial carriers. Moreover, it is feasible to install a refueling probe on commercial aircraft, modified to permit the more than 400 wide-bodied aircraft in commercial service to contribute to the strategic airlift role. While such a program is not cost-free, it is far less costly than a dedicated Air Force fleet of similar size. By exploiting a "natural" advantage of U.S. industry, the commercial aircraft industry, the U.S. can gain some of the advantage inherent in its superior resource base.

Like the Navy, the Air Force also suffers from inadequate quantities of critical air combat and strike munitions to sustain a period of protracted conflict. Hence, essential munitions should be procured in numbers sufficient to augment the low estate to which the sustainability of combat has fallen.

Military Personnel and Military Retirement

The recent operation of the military personnel system has undermined the ability of the armed forces to recruit and train sufficient volunteers for both active and reserve forces. The failure to adjust salaries adequately for inflation has severely damaged recruitment and reenlistment efforts. To simply restore FY 1976 real income will require an additional appropriation of $6 billion.[26] *In the short term, there is no viable alternative but to raise military compensation.*

However, as is discussed elsewhere in this essay, major reforms will be needed if we are to have sufficient personnel. *In addition to changes in the military recruitment and retention system, a greater emphasis on reserve forces is essential.* Successful reserve systems, such as Israel, South Africa, and the Netherlands, are available to serve as models from which useful lessons can be drawn. The focus of such reform is to have a readily mobilizable asset (reserves) to support forward-deployed active forces. Such a system already exists in the Air Reserve and the Air National Guard, but the unique problems of the

---

[25] The CRAF concept is a viable one if suitable compensation can be provided to commercial operators for the additional costs of military-compatible features on civil transport aircraft. A refueling probe could be fitted to all U.S. commercial aircraft for $3.5–5.0 million per aircraft, greatly increasing the operational flexibility of the U.S. civil air fleet to augment the specialized military airlift capacity.

[26] See testimony of Hon. Robert Piere before the Subcommittee on Defense, Committee on Appropriations, U.S. House of Representatives, on the FY 81 Defense program, June 1980.

24

Army make the development of innovative solutions of the problem an essential task.

The Military Retirement system is a costly relic of earlier times in which the relatively short careers attributable to demanding physical requirements dictated a preference for deferred, not current, compensation. Today, only 15 percent of the force has demanding physical requirements. Since the retirement commitment is of a contractual nature, only long-term solutions can affect its cost. Changes in retention policy will serve to reduce the potential retirement liability in future years. Additional changes could differentiate between retirement programs to reflect the reality of military service under contemporary conditions. New accessions could be provided with a choice between retirement benefits and current income. Experience with the all-volunteer force suggests that most individuals not inclined toward a military career prefer current income, a preference which could serve to reduce the high cost of the DoD retirement program.

Operations and Maintenance

Operations and Maintenance (O&M) expenditure is central to the readiness of the armed forces. It provides the training in upkeep of the physical plant as well as in operational equipment, and the supply of combat consumables essential to the ability of the armed forces to conduct military operations. O&M has been appropriately described as the most important component of defense expenditure without an outside constituency. The growth in O&M expenditure (other than fuel costs) has been only about one-fifth that of procurement in recent years. In an environment of competing political objectives of "real growth" in defense expenditure and constrained federal budgets, the more visible items of procurement — ships, aircraft, missiles, etc. — have received the benefits of additional defense investment. The resources to operate and maintain the forces have not kept pace, thus leaving advanced equipment inoperative for lack of sufficient O&M funds to employ them.

The lack of adequate readiness funding has not only affected maintenance of major equipment, it has reduced training (due to inadequate fuel supplies), depleted war reserve stocks, and left a vast backlog of deferred maintenance. The shortage of O&M funding has had a serious effect on both our readiness for war as well as our ability to sustain a conflict.[27]

Illustrative of this point is the proposed procurement of the Multiple Launch Rocket System. This system provides a modern multiple

---

[27] Testimony before the House Appropriations Committee, *op. cit.*, on O&M funding has disclosed significant shortages in fuel necessary to provide sufficient flying hours to assure air crew combat proficiency.

rocket launcher on a tracked vehicle, able to provide saturation fire against massed enemy troop and vehicular concentrations. The proposed procurement includes 130,000 rockets, a number sufficient for a Corps-sized engagement of only *four* days. Unless the production complex is at a sufficiently high state of readiness to resume production of rockets without delay, shortages would render the system useless during a conflict. Similar shortfalls exist in most advanced munitions including air-to-air missiles, precision-guided weapons, and advanced artillery munitions. Since these advanced munitions are intended to provide the numerically inferior U.S. forces with the tactical advantage, we gain little from our technological superiority. Press reports indicate that when the aircraft carrier NIMITZ returned from a nine-month deployment to the Persian Gulf, it met the EISENHOWER, its replacement in the region, in the Indian Ocean to turn over her load of *Phoenix* air-to-air missiles. There are insufficient missiles in the U.S. inventory to simultaneously support deployment on two of the Navy's most advanced ships. While these illustrations are considerably more dramatic than most (perhaps qualifying as "horror stories" rather than a genuinely representative selection), the shortage of mundane items does jeopardize our ability to sustain a conflict. The ammunition deficiency now exceeds $20 billion. The backlog in deferred maintenance, inadequate fuel, and spare parts for war reserves and training probably exceeds $40 billion.

In the face of such awesome gaps, it is clear that no reasonable peace-time expenditure is likely to mitigate such a backlog quickly. *A ten-year "get-well" program would require a $6 billion annual add-on to planned O&M expenditure, but is perhaps the only sufficient time period in which a solution to the problem can be considered viable.*

There are several steps which could be taken to mitigate some of the most pressing readiness problems. *One which should be taken is to seek additional allied assistance on base maintenance and support throught the Host Nation Support Program.* Very substantial backlogs in European air base maintenance could be reduced if U.S. allies took a greater share of the burden in NATO. The unique burden borne by the United States in the Persian Gulf almost dictates such recompense.

A partial substitute for filling large war reserve inventory backlogs would be to improve the state of industrial readiness. Encouraging greater allied acquisition of ammunition from the United States to meet their NATO ammunition requirements (even if storage was in the U.S.) could assist in keeping production lines in the U.S. "hot".

Finally, a "buy-out" of the O&M backlog should be given high priority. Immediate requirements include increasing inventories of critical ammunition for forward-deployed units, increasing the flying hour and steaming days program to improve the level of troop training, and

Table 9
FY 1982 Initiatives for Military Assistance

Program	Cost
Military Assistance Program	$0.50 billion
International Military Education and Training	0.05
Foreign Military Credit Sales	1.2
Total	$1.75 billion

increasing procurement of spares for first line combat and transport aircraft.

Military Assistance*

Military Assistance programs, although financed outside the Department of Defense budget, are an integral part of our overall defense effort. However, for a variety of reasons, the military assistance effort has borne little relationship to the objectives of our defense effort; indeed it has frequently been managed at cross-purposes. Reduced to a somewhat oversimplified characterization, the fundamental flaw in military assistance, including foreign military sales, has been its use to support a wide variety of diplomatic ends that only occasionally appear directly related to U.S. defense objectives.

The Carter Administration military assistance budget requests have been approximately $100 million annually ($104.4 million in FY 1981). A total of sixty-three nations receive military assistance in some form (including training), but assistance is typically denied to friendly nations under direct assault.[28] Recent examples include Nicaragua, and the Angolan and Afghan guerillas. An illustration of the extremes is the Carter Administration's refusal to issue the United Kingdom a license to purchase U.S.-made handguns for a police organization.

The most important unmet military assistance needs are in Turkey and the Republic of Korea. Both nations have large and professionally competent standing armies. For very different reasons, neither has received the appropriate assistance or access to the U.S. defense market. The modernization of the armed forces of these two nations could contribute very significantly to meeting U.S. diplomatic objectives in the regions they represent at a modest fraction of the cost of direct U.S. involvement.

---

*functionally included in International Affairs.

[28] See *Foreign Assistance and Related Programs Appropriation Bill, 1981,* and the *Report* appended to the bill by the Commiteee on Appropriations of the U.S. House of Representatives.

27

When the United States does embark on a major military assistance effort, there is a tendency to overemphasize U.S. tactics and organizational doctrine—a strategy which does not necessarily enable the recipient to meet the regional threat, or to contribute significantly to its alliance interests with the U.S. Perhaps the worst example was the aid program to Iran; the best is the U.S. aid program to Israel. In the former case, an attempt to transplant American advanced technology into an armed force unable to exploit it actually diminished the effectiveness of their military forces. In the case of Israel, a maximum of participation by the Israelis in military assistance planning, and suitable modification to local needs has made Israel the most effective recipient of American military aid. With a force one-seventh the size of her adversaries, Israel's military power dominates the region, a situation which accrues to the benefit of American policy.

American military assistance programs should be restructured (a) to insure their congruence with American foreign policy interest, and (b) tailored to meet local conditions. It will be of little benefit to the United States to provide artillery and armored vehicles to a Central American ally attempting to cope with a Soviet-sponsored insurgency when police-related assistance and mobility equipment may be of more benefit.

Perhaps the most politicized dimension of our foreign assistance effort has been the growth restrictions placed on the Foreign Military Sales program. The Carter Administration made the reduction in foreign military sales a major policy objective. The result has been an arbitrary reduction in the scope of the program, limiting access to a few major buyers. Israel has been the principal beneficiary ($500 million of the $747 million recommended by the House Appropriations Committee for FY 1981). There remains however a long list of nations, with which we have an undeniable security interest (e.g., Korea, Morocco, Taiwan), but which cannot purchase the desired equipment.

The Foreign Military Credit Sales program should be the major (and preferred) component of our military assistance effort. When suitably integrated with U.S. training assistance, it can be the most effective vehicle for providing friendly nations with the ability to meet their defense requirements in a manner supportive of American foreign policy.

Further, nations providing U.S. access rights to airfields and port facilities should have a priority claim in seeking access to the U.S. defense market through the FMS program. Such access can markedly increase the effectiveness of U.S. forward defense in regions of the world where a large Subic Bay (Philippines)-type infrastructure does not exist.

Table 10
FY 1982 Modernization of the Nuclear Weapons Complex

Program	Cost
Oralloy Production Restart	$0.010 billion
Plutonium and Tritium Production Restart	
(Savannah River)	0.020
Munclear Weapons Test program (accelerated)	0.300
Weapons Laboratories (LASL, LLL, Sandia) Upgrade	0.070
Deferred Maintenance on Weapons Production Facilities	0.300
New Plutonium Production Complex	0.200
Total	$0.900 billion

Nuclear Weapons Production Complex*

Since the post-World War II reorganization of the nuclear weapons program, the production and development of U.S. nuclear weapons has been outside the Department of Defense. The Department of Energy, successor to AEC, funds the development and production complex.

The production facility has become so run down that a shortage of sufficient fissile material is inevitable. Nuclear weapons testing has declined by 70 percent since the 1960s, and shortages of critical nuclear materials now are a constraint on nuclear weapons modernization.[29]

As an arms control measure, President Johnson stopped the production (in 1964) of oralloy, a weapons grade material, in hopes that the Soviet Union would benefit by the example. Soviet oralloy production has increased steadily since 1964, enabling the Soviets to meet the demands of their own nuclear weapons modernization program. There remains no justification for sustaining our self-defeating posture. Excess capacity now exists at U.S. gaseous diffusion plants (due to Administration restrictions on the export of nuclear fuel for civilian power reactors) which should be used for the nuclear weapons program.

Shortages of weapons-grade plutonium and tritium are a particularly serious matter for the modernization of U.S. weapons, especially for theater use. *In the short term, the production reactors at Savannah River should be restarted. An additional production reactor will be needed as well.* The most economic solution would be a dual-use reactor that could produce electrical power for sale to the civilian market

---

*functionally included in Energy.

[29] See Hearing before the Procurement and Military Nuclear Systems Subcommittee of the Committee on Armed Services, U.S. House of Representatives, *Coordination of Department of Energy/Department of Defense Nuclear Weapons Materials Requirements,* June 18, 1980.

as well as to produce needed plutonium and tritium for the weapons program.[30] *The Purex reprocessing facility, employed to produce weapons-grade plutonium, is in need of modernization and expansion to meet the demands of the weapons already authorized for production or advanced development during the 1980s.*

During the course of the 1970s, the nuclear weapons R&D effort has undergone very substantial retrogression in personnel, purchases of laboratory equipment and computers, and a weapons testing program. Much of the decline is attributable to the Carter Administration's intense opposition to the development of new nuclear weapons.

The nuclear delivery systems which the Administration supported, including the MX, the air-launched cruise missile, the ground/sea launched cruise missile, the Pershing II tactical missile, the Trident, and the 203 mm. artillery shell, have strained the ability of the entire weapon complex to meet production requirements. The low weapon production rates of the early 1970s resulted in the attrition of the experienced production personnel now needed to meet requirements. This experience points to the futility of allowing wide swings in support for the nuclear weapons program. The time and resources associated with a re-start effort inevitably are greater than would have been the case had a prudent capability been sustained throughout the decade.

An organizational issue which has not been addressed, despite three reorganizations of the federal government's energy program, has been the role of the nuclear weapons program. Historically, the weapons program has been embedded within the U.S. energy research program. For three decades the arrangement has been a successful one, primarily because of a unique institutional arrangement for the weapon laboratories (Los Alamos Scientific Laboratory, Lawrence Livermore Laboratory, and Sandia Laboratory) which has protected their independence in a quasi-competitive atmosphere. Transfer of these functions to the Department of Defense (logical as such an arrangement appears) would be unsatisfactory due to the probable attempt to "rationalize" the weapons research program into a single integrated laboratory staffed by civil servants. However, the present arrangement is unlikely to continue to be appropriate in the future. the DoE has major bureaucratic and budgetary responsibility for federally-sponsored energy development programs and regulatory activities which deflect significant management attention from the weapons program. *As a consequence, the most useful course would be to create a new sub-cabinet agency or commission to manage the nuclear weapon development and production program.* Similar budgetary and legislative oversight arrangements as now exist could be maintained,

---

[30] *Ibid.*

but with the prospect for improved management attention for the program.

LONG-TERM CONSIDERATIONS

From a security perspective, the past fifteen years have been both dismal and dangerous. No one can assert with confidence what effect a continuation of U.S. defense trends of the late 1950s and early 1960s would have had on Soviet behavior and their willingness to bear the defense burden they now carry. Expressed in FY 1981 dollars, we spent three times the current figure on strategic nuclear forces, while maintaining a Navy twice as large as the one we have today. It is safe to assert, however, that the task of "catching up" with the Soviet military power would not have been nearly as great as it is now likely to be.

Regrettably, what has been done cannot be undone, and because of this, the United States faces a profound strategic problem. The U.S. can no longer fulfill the commitments which heretofore have been inextricably linked with the security of the U.S. and our allies. So awesome is the task that almost any analyst finds defense planning for the 1980s a daunting task. So large is the effort that it seems unlikely that sufficient resources will be available to simply replicate a larger scale version of our current force posture.

New approaches to our defense posture are required to improve the utilization of the resources available in the 1980s. This is not to argue that more resources are not needed – they are essential – but merely doing "more of the same" is neither likely to address the military threat we face, or be available in sufficient time to affect the political-military balance of the 1980s.

The remainder of this essay will seek to provide illustrative suggestions for alternative approaches to achieving greater military capability per dollar invested than is now the case. As is the case with any substantial change from current practice, it is easy to overstate achievable benefits due to a host of institutional, political, or other exogenous factors. It is hoped, the impact of even partial achievement will be positive nevertheless.

All-Volunteer Force Reforms

Since 1973, the United States has relied on volunteers to meet its military personnel requirements. Although there is considerable dissatisfaction with the All-Volunteer Force (AVF), both in the officer corps and in the Congress, there is no early prospect of resuming conscription in a peace-time context. Yet there is little doubt that the AVF as currently managed will not meet U.S. defense requirements in the 1980s without very significant increases in cost. As U.S. defense needs in other areas will be competing for substantial funding, it is important to find the means to improve the effectiveness of the AVF without increasing its cost.[31]

Modified Recruitment and Retention Policies

The change wrought in the mode of entry to the Armed Forces by the adoption of the AVF has not had a significant impact on the remainder of the military manpower system. The low budget cost/high turnover conscription system has simply been replaced by a high budget cost/high turnover volunteer system. The U.S. needs to shift to a longer service force to reduce the economic burden of the AVF and to increase the productivity, and hence the effectiveness, of the AVF. *To do this requires two measures: First, increase the average term of the first enlistment and second, curtail re-enlistments.* These reforms would be important for several reasons.

- While a longer initial term of service (five to eight years rather than three as is currently the case) would entail higher costs to induce enlistees to volunteer for a longer initial term of service, it would reduce annual accessions by nearly one-third.

- Nearly one-fifth of the Army is currently absorbed directly or indirectly in the training base. This high ratio is made necessary by the demands of a high turnover force. Reduction in accessions brought on by longer initial tours of duty would have a major impact on the size and cost of the training base. Additional troops would be freed for regular duty permitting greater combat power in the Army by increasing the "teeth to tail" ratio.

- Current policy of short initial tours makes it necessary to pay substantial re-enlistment bonuses to minimize turnover. This is not only costly, but it encourages a swelling of the retirement rolls, where unfunded liabilities exceed $300 billion today. A preferred system would reduce retention of first-term enlistees to 10–20 percent for the non-commissioned officer ranks, reducing the costly retirement liability which is a consequence of current retention policy.

- To the extent that length of service is a proxy for "productivity" in the armed forces, the longer-term force will be more effective than its shorter-term counterpart. Even in the combat arms where the potential gains from productivity are less apparent than in the support services the greater emphasis on small-unit tactics

---

[31] A comprehensive set of suggestions for increasing the effectiveness of the AVF is contained in S. L. Canby, "The Military Manpower Problem," in *Arms, Men, and Military Budgets* (New York: Crane, Russak, 1978).

associated with limited conflicts makes small gains in combat arms productivity a high-leverage item.

- Today nearly one-third of the Army's budget is consumed by Operation and Maintenance (O&M) expenditure. O&M is largely driven by peace-time training activities. With a high rate of annual accessions made necessary by a short-term force, O&M is diverted from war readiness functions to entry-level training. Moreover, extensive company-level training imposes a costly burden of wear-and-tear on operational equipment.

The potential long-term saving from the full implementation of the above reforms is $10–12 billion. However, even a partial implementation of such a program could have a considerable impact on the cost and performance of the AVF.

Multi-Year Training

The high turnover of the current structure, particularly in the Army, makes it necessary to conduct training on an annual cycle. *If turnover can be significantly reduced through lengthened first-term enlistments, the training cycle could be shifted to a two- to three-year period.* Once entry level training objectives have been met, unit equipment need not be used to save for periodic refresher training. Emphasis could then shift to battalion and higher level maneuver training where obsolescent equipment could be employed without significant loss of training value. This will avoid using modern unit equipment with savings associated with reduced utilization of advance equipment.

Additional benefits of multi-year training are that training quality and readiness are increased while maintenance cost is reduced. To fully exploit the benefits of multi-year training implies a fundamental change in U.S. policy from individual replacement to unit replacement. There are operational advantages to both approaches, but in view of the need to sustain a large standing army for forward defense the unit replacement approach merits consideration. The Soviet Union employs a similar system which in part accounts for its ability to procure such a large inventory of weapons.

Reserve Force Reorganization

Although the U.S. maintains a standing army large by historical standards, it is insufficient to meet the threat posed by Soviet military power. Short of mobilization, it is unfeasible for the U.S. to match Soviet deployments or force levels. U.S. active duty forces should be organized for foward defense with additional increments of combat power to reside in well prepared reserve forces.

Since conscription was abandoned in 1973, the reserves, particularly

33

of the Army, have suffered from declines in personnel strength, unit equipment, and readiness. Yet, current and forseeable circumstances require a far greater component than exists today.

1. Post-1973 recruitment incentives have been inadequate to induce sufficient volunteers and to retain current reserve strength. As a result, we face the unwelcome circumstance of having neither sufficient forces-in-being to meet current need, nor do we have an adequate reserve structure to overcome these deficiencies.

2. There also is some interaction between the content of Reserve or National Guard training and the willingness of individuals to volunteer. Surveys of Reserve and National Guard personnel are frequently critical of the training program and the lack of suitable modern equipment.

Moreover, the lack of readiness of many Reserve and National Guard units implies a protracted period of training in the event of mobilization, further diminishing the incentive on the part of the active forces to afford the reserve forces a higher budgetary priority.

A useful model of reserve force reorganization exists, in the Dutch RIM (*Rechstreeks Instromend Mobilisabel*) system.[32] Dutch reservists generally perform better in major military competitions in NATO than active forces from any nation. Although there are important differences between the circumstances facing the Netherlands and the United States, the RIM system could be applied to U.S. forces. The RIM system is one ideally suited to a relatively small active duty cadre supplemented by a larger reserve force. The RIM system trains recruits (conscripts in the Dutch case) to the desired level of individual and unit proficiency at the company level. Immediately after the unit completes its training cycle, it is placed on leave *in toto* with its entire set of unit equipment.

Unit integrity and the training and experience the individual soldiers gained as a unit is retained rather than lost through dispersal. The RIM system bears an important resemblance to the militia system that was the primary vehicle of mobilization in the United States during the 19th century. Recruiting done on a regional or local basis could facilitate the maintenance of a high order of unit proficiency. Wartime dispersal of platoon-sized units drawn from a local company-sized unit could diminish the potential for regional or local inequities in bearing the burden of combat.

Improving readiness and capability of the reserve structure is essential if the U.S. is to be able to meet the military threat it faces without mobilization. *In the absence of an early upgrading of the reserve*

---

[32] See S. L. Canby in *Priorities in U.S. Defense Policy* (Washington: American Enterprise Institute, 1979).

structure, it will be necessary to raise five new active Army divisions. This costly alternative will still be inadequate to meet the threat without an adequate reserve base. Indeed, it will absorb resources which could otherwise be used to improve the reserves. The average annual cost of maintaining an active Army division is $2.7 billion. Though the marginal cost of raising a division is somewhat less, the higher cost of competing in the civilian market for additional manpower could impose a cost of $5–7 billion to raise active duty strength by five divisions. These resources, properly applied in the modernized reserve structure, could vastly improve the ability of U.S. forces to cope with the Soviet threat.

MISCELLANEOUS MANAGEMENT AND FORCE STRUCTURE IMPROVEMENTS

Light Infantry Improvements

The U.S. needs to augment the combat power of its ground forces, not only to fulfill the traditional responsibilities in Europe, but to increase its ability to move swiftly into troubled areas where American interests are threatened. Today, U.S. "light infantry" units, its five infantry divisions and two airborne/air assault divisions have been somewhat cynically described by analysts as being "too light [in firepower] to fight, and too heavy to move." Programs are currently in place, though funded at a modest pace to improve the heavy and mechanized infantry components of the force with a new main battle tank (the XM-1), and advanced armored personnel carrier (the Fighting Vehicle System/XM-2/XM-3), modified self-propelled artillery and multiple rocket launchers, etc. The areas of the world where U.S. forces may be engaged in the future (such as the Persian Gulf region) do not lend themselves to the insertion of "heavy" ground forces. The burdensome logistics of U.S. armored or mechanized infantry division is a factor inhibiting their swift delivery to a troubled region, particularly when no basing structure exists.[33]

The most effective solution would be to increase the capability of U.S. light infantry divisions. To do so would require an emphasis on the maneuver of forces rather than reliance on firepower. This would include the introduction of light tanks (14–16 tons compared to the 60-ton M-60/XM-1 series), wheeled vehicles (such as the *Commando* vehicle currently used only in Military Policy battalions) for firepower as well as mobility, and small helicopters.[33] Equipment of this type can

---

[33] The burden of heavy mechanized equipment is so great that to transport a single mechanized infantry division from the continental United States to the Persian Gulf would require all U.S. C-5A and C-141 military airlift aircraft for nearly fourteen days to complete the airlift.

35

be more easily transported in large numbers over great distances by heavy lift transport aircraft. This would enable the U.S. to intervene swiftly with sufficient local firepower and "presence" to dominate the early stages of a conflict. Such an approach could be useful from several perspectives. First, it would improve the combat effectiveness of U.S. forces, reducing the need to increase authorized strength. Second, it would diminish airlift requirements relative to the case where heavier units would have to be transported, making the current and projected U.S. airlift capability a more effective contributor to U.S. defense. Third, it would preserve heavy equipment (tanks, APCs, self-propelled artillery, etc.) for use in Western Europe where the Soviet deployments are most threatening. Fourth, with the logistically less burdensome unit equipment of light infantry divisions, the number of maneuver battalions could be increased (due to the smaller logistics "tail"). It would also create the possibility of raising the cadre divisions filled by reservists — thereby increasing the overall force structure at low cost.[34]

Multi-year/Multi-Source Procurement

Defense procurement practices have become a wasteful response to the rigidities of defense budget procedure. These rigidities in turn have had an adverse effect both on the ability of the armed services to acquire the equipment it needs at minimum cost, and the vitality of the industrial base to support peacetime procurement and wartime mobilization requirements. The problem is a complex legal and bureaucratic tangle that will not yield a quick solution. The evidence accumulated in recent years, however, makes clear the high-cost consequences of current practice. Unit cost of major tactical warfare systems (e.g., aircraft, ships, tracked vehicles, air defense fire units, etc.) has increased rapidly as the armed services have sought to keep production lines "warm" for all current acquisition programs. To fit such a procurement strategy within declining budgets over the past decade, annual quantities procured have declined significantly. This has reduced the responsiveness of the industrial base to a mobilization contingency (clearly revealed in the 1978 Joint Chiefs of Staff exercise, *Nifty Nugget*), without providing the armed services with sufficient quantities of equipment to replace obsolescent systems. Both unit and total program costs have risen an average of 69 percent without favorably enhancing U.S. military power.[35]

[34] The development of innovative tactical/operational concepts can interact with the procurement process to permit the introduction of equipment that would have significant military effectiveness in selected circumstances at lower cost than would be the case if total dependence were placed on conventional equipment.

[35] The FY 1981 budget request for tactical aircraft was a particularly serious example of this phenomenon. Virtually all aircraft were being procured at uneconomic rates, e.g., the unit cost of the F-18 "light-weight" fighter exceeded the cost of the far larger F-14 due to uneconomic procurement practices.

The adverse consequences of DoD procurement practices can only be eliminated by a major overhaul of the acquisition system. *Procurement of economical quantities of military hardware and equipment can be facilitated by instituting a practice of multi-year purchases.*[36] Such a proposition would serve to stabilize the industrial base (thereby improving its ability to respond to a mobilization contingency) by having an acquisition quantity known for several years in advance. This would permit the adjustment of the scale of the industrial plant to avoid extremes of excess and under capacity, thereby facilitating DoD procurements at the most economical rate.

The mobilization base can be expanded as well if multi-year procurements are integrated with a program of multi-source acquisition of high volume items. A good illustration of the failure of the present system is the planned acquisition of the Multiple Launch Rocket System. The MLRS is a much needed system, but present plans call for the acquisition of only 130,000 rockets from a single manufacturer. This quantity is sufficient for only four days of combat at currently estimated munition consumption rates. If the manufacturer develops his production plant only to most efficiently meet the current DoD demand, it is unlikely that such capacity will enable him to meet a stressful wartime contingency. Multiple source procurement would facilitate wartime mobilization, and maintain competitive pressure on prices that could serve to reduce total program cost, while permitting a larger peacetime procurement.

The DoD weapons acquisition system needs to be changed to reduce cost and improve force readiness. While adoption of multi-year/source procurement would reduce long-term system acquisition cost, it would not necessarily diminish the lengthy development and production cycle. The major source of the lengthy cycle is an unreasoned fear of concurrent development and production. The time-consuming sequential process stretches the time from development to deployment on major systems to seven-to-ten years.[37] Although the introduction of more concurrency into DoD procurement would create the additional costs of adjustments to production units after the development program was completed, these costs would be more than offset by more rapid procurement and the reduction of the logistics burden of retaining obsolescent equipment in the inventory. Of the fifty-four major systems now acquired by DoD, cost growth is esti-

---

[36] This practice now involves only lump sum appropriations for the naval shipbuilding program where the entire amount required is appropriated in a single year even though the expenditure may be spread out over five or more years.

[37] Wartime programs are characterized by overlapping development and procurement, a process which normally requires post-production retrofits, but results in far more rapid introduction of new systems to the field. Offsetting reductions in training and maintenance costs (by not having to field two systems, one old and one new for an extended period of time) will serve to reduce the adverse effects of concurrent development and procurement.

mated to be $96 billion above the $139.1 billion originally thought necessary to procure the systems.[38] The most significant factors inducing the cost growth is stretched-out rates of procurement which occasion later payments and higher cost due to the inflation, and uneconomic rates of procurement. The prospects thus exist for multi-billion dollar saving in the DoD acquisition process.

There are powerful legal and bureaucratic obstacles to achieving significant savings in the U.S. defense program, but the magnitude of the effort required to rebuild U.S. defense makes it desirable that institutional barriers be reviewed if they impose an impediment to the ability of the U.S. defense posture to meet the threat posed during the coming decade. Without such an effort, substantial additional resources will be needed to meet the needs of the 1980s.

Defense acquisition cannot be effective in isolation. The ability of the U.S. defense establishment to produce the necessary stream of modern weapon systems demands a modern and productive economic system. The effectiveness of the armed forces themselves require the personal interest and attention of Congress and the Commander-in-Chief. None of these important dimensions of our defense posture respond directly to resources invested, yet without them, the investment of a vast fraction of our national treasure will gain very little.

---

[38] General Accounting Office, *Digests of Major Weapon System Reports,* various issues, 1979 and 1980.

2

International Affairs*

by E. Dwight Phaup

The great rule of conduct for us in regard to foreign nations is, in extending our commercial relations to have with them as little political connection as possible. George Washington, Farewell Address, 1796.

In his commentary on the Farewell Address, Richard B. Morris suggested that the "Great Rule" enunciated by George Washington represented a reasonable standard for the needs of the nascent nation, but went on to imply that Washington himself would have recognized that the Rule would not apply to a larger, more powerful country in a technologically-advanced age.[1] Clearly, Washington's Rule has been abandoned and the scope of governmental expenditures on international affairs has been broadened, especially over the past three-and-a-half decades. But given that these expenditures have departed so dramatically from the levels implied by Washington's advice, what principles or rules now govern federal spending for international affairs?

In exploring that question, this essay reaches three main conclusions:

- there currently is no clear, underlying set of principles which guide international affairs expenditures; rather, rhetorical flourishes notwithstanding, most program spending occurs on an *ad hoc* basis without a clear delineation of precisely what benefits are likely to accrue to the American taxpayer;
- a set of rules for directing and assessing international affairs expenditures, which rests on the same foundation as those that should guide domestic spending programs, can be established; and

---

*Military assistance is treated under Defense.

[1] Richard B. Morris, on George Washington's "Farewell Address 1796" in Daniel J. Boorstin (ed.), *An American Primer* (Chicago: University of Chicago Press, 1966), pp. 208-10. In the same volume, Dumas Malone makes a very similar argument (p. 217) in commenting on Thomas Jefferson's First Inaugural Address 1801" in which Jefferson advised the nation to seek "peace, commerce, and honest friendships with all nations, entangling alliances with none."

- the adoption of such a set of rules would significantly alter the current level and scope of international affairs expenditures.

To assist in developing these themes, let us first review the nature of current spending programs for foreign affairs (Table 1).

Foreign Economic and Financial Assistance

The first and largest expenditure category is for Foreign Economic and Financial Assistance, which encompasses the multilateral and bilateral foreign aid programs of the U. S. The mission of these programs is to provide humanitarian assistance to the needy abroad, encourage economic development and promote U. S. foreign policy.

The International Development Cooperation Agency (IDCA) is the result of a recent administrative re-organization in which several aid programs — most notably the Agency for International Development (AID) — were placed under the supervision of a single director. Other programs incorporated in the IDCA include the Institute for Scientific and Technological Cooperation, the International Fund for Agricultural Development (a multilateral lending program), and the Overseas Private Investment Corporation. The latter is a U. S. government corporation devoted to providing loans, insurance, and advisory services for U. S. firms wishing to construct facilities in developing nations. Hence, the IDCA includes an amalgam of bilateral aid and multilateral aid programs to foreign nations, plus support services for some U. S. companies investing abroad.

The multilateral development banks include the World Bank group and several regional banks which provide loans (some of a concessional nature) to qualifying member nations.

Although the purpose of P.L. 480 (food program) is ostensibly to provide humanitarian and development assistance, it should be mentioned that this program also serves as a mechanism for the disposal of U. S. "surplus" agricultural production arising from the Department of Agriculture's price support efforts. Other programs are, for the most part, self-explanatory.

While the United States has provided aid to foreign nations on a somewhat erratic basis for most of this century, a surge in aid programs occurred in the years immediately following the Second World War. First directed to assist the redevelopment and reconstruction of the war-devastated nations of Western Europe, U. S. foreign aid more recently has concentrated on the economic development of Third (and Fourth) world countries.[2] Despite this particular shift in beneficiaries,

---

[2]For example, in 1950, aid through the European Recovery Program and to occupied areas represented over 80 percent of total expenditures on international affairs while aid for developing countries was negligible. Twenty years later, the proportions were nearly reversed, with almost 70 percent of foreign affairs spending being devoted to aid for developing nations.

40

Table 1
International Relations
(in millions of dollars)

Major missions and programs	1979 actual	1980 estimate	1981 estimate
OUTLAYS			
Foreign economic and financial assistance:			
International Development Cooperation Agency	1,374	1,575	1,737
Multilateral development banks	683	926	966
Public Law 480 — Food aid	976	1,169	1,153
Peace Corps	94	104	116
Economic support fund/Peacekeeping operations	1,755	2,040	2,056
Refugee assistance	166	468	534
Offsetting receipts and other	− 304	− 308	− 349
Subtotal, foreign economic and financial assistance	4,743	5,974	6,212
Military assistance:			
Grant military assistance	140	195	150
Foreign military training	28	26	28
Foreign military sales credit	640	540	515
Relocation of facilities (Israel)	31	411	318
Offsetting receipts and other	− 276	− 275	− 260
Subtotal, military assistance	563	897	751
Total, foreign aid	**(5,306)**	**(6,871)**	**(6,963)**
Conduct of foreign affairs:			
Administration of foreign affairs	785	867	927
International organizations and conferences	495	487	535
Other	30	35	39
Subtotal, conduct of foreign affairs	1,310	1,389	1,501
Foreign information and exchange activities	465	544	569
International financial programs:			
Export-Import Bank	200	1,054	1,230
Foreign military sales trust fund (net)	− 1,434	1,200	—
International commodity agreements	—	—	5
Other	354	− 568	− 566
Subtotal, international financial programs	− 879	1,687	669
Deductions for offsetting receipts	− 110	− 90	− 89
Total, outlays	**6,091**	**10,401**	**9,612**
MEMORANDUM — Attribution of Federal Financing Bank outlays			
Overseas Private Investment Corporation	− 4	− 7	− 7
Foreign military sales credit	1,293	2,420	1,990
Export-Import Bank	—	50	350

Source: The Budget of the United States Government FY 1981

there was, at least through the mid-sixties, a consistent design which fashioned U. S. foreign policy and perhaps the bulk of its economic assistance to other nations: the policy of containment.[3] This is not to argue that humanitarian and other concerns were not also a motivating force behind U. S. aid, but the apparent "selectivity of U. S. altruism" does suggest that foreign policy considerations were dominant.[4]

Yet, as Kindleberger noted, "discouragement with foreign aid set in during the 1960s. Economic development was stubbornly slow. Aid achieved little growth, less gratitude, few political objectives."[5] That discouragement which continued to some extent through the seventies is reflected in the rather modest growth in foreign assistance expenditures over the past decade. As Table 2 illustrates, real non-military assistance to foreign nations expanded by just 36 percent between FY 1972 and FY 1979; the Table also indicates that non-military aid as a percent of total governmental expenditures has remained at roughly 1.5 percent (with a noticeable dip in the middle of the decade).

Table 2 also mirrors a shift in the mechanism by which U. S. aid has been disbursed. Specifically, since the late 1960s and early 1970s, the proportion of aid provided through multilateral arrangements has grown relative to bilateral aid. This change is in part due to announced efforts by donor nations to "de-nationalize" aid, but is also reflective of the Nixon administration's emphasis on "New Directions" where bilateral aid was to rely more heavily on self-help projects and private investment. Perhaps even more importantly, the shift is in response to greater militancy on the part of recipient nations which view aid from the developed nations as an entitlement involving no implicit or explicit obligation to the donors.

Conduct of Foreign Affairs

The U. S. government has, of course, been involved in international affairs since the founding of the Republic. Chief among its traditional activities has been the conduct of foreign policy through the State Department and related agencies. Funds allocated for this category

---

[3] See, for example, the testimony of C. Fred Bergsten in the Hearings before the Subcommittee on International Economic Policy of the House Committee on International Relations, *United States Foreign Economic Policy Objectives,* 94th Cong., 1st Sess. (1975). For an interesting treatment of the origins and development of the containment policy, see the interview with George F. Kennan and the companion articles by Charles Gati and Chalmers M. Roberts in *Foreign Policy,* No. 7 (Summer 1972).

[4] For empirical estimates of the determinants of U.S. (and other) aid flows, see Paul Isenman, "Biases in Aid Allocations Against Poorer and Larger Countries," *World Development* 4 (1976), pp. 631–41. Also, see R. D. McKinlay, "The Aid Relationship: A Foreign Policy Model and Interpretation of the Distribution of Official Bilateral Economic Aid of the United States, the United Kingdom, France and Germany, 1960-1970," *Comparative Political Studies,* 11 (January 1979), pp. 411–463.

[5] Charles P. Kindleberger, "U.S. Foreign Economic Policy, 1776–1976," *Foreign Affairs,* 55 (January 1977), pp. 395–417.

Table 2
U.S. Non-military Foreign Assistance Authorizations
(in millions)

	Multilateral		Bilateral***		Total		Total as Percent of U.S. Government Outlays
	Current Dollars	Constant Dollars*	Current Dollars	Constant Dollars	Current Dollars	Constant Dollars	
1972	484	484	2,972	2,972	3,456	3,456	1.49%
1973	865	818	2,522	2,385	3,387	3,203	1.37%
1974	934	805	2,143	1,848	3,077	2,653	1.14%
1975	758	597	2,945	2,326	3,703	2,923	1.14%
1976**	1,116	833	4,643	3,469	5,759	4,302	1.25%
1977	1,385	975	4,583	3,232	5,968	4,207	1.48%
1978	2,166	1,425	4,642	3,061	6,808	4,486	1.51%
1979	2,769	1,668	5,023	3,026	7,792	4,694	1.58%
Pct. Change 1972–79	472%	245%	69%	2%	125%	36%	

Source: Adapted from House Committee on Foreign Affairs, *Congress and Foreign Policy – 1979* (Washington: GPO, 1980), Tables 1A and 1B.

Notes: *Base year = 1972
**Includes transition quarter
***Includes economic support and food assistance

($1.5 billion estimated for FY 1981) primarily involve salaries and expenses for the foreign service and support personnel, and operation and maintenance of consular buildings and similar facilities abroad.

Expenditures for memberships in international organizations and conferences ($535 million), however, are of relatively recent vintage and include the assessed contributions of the U. S. to such diverse organizations as the U. N. and its affilitates, NATO, the Arms Control and Disarmament Agency, and a host of others devoted to such far-ranging purposes as weather monitoring, trade negotiations, disease control and consultation about the production and marketing of a number of agricultural and mineral commodities.

Foreign Information and Exchange Activities

Foreign information and exchange activities ($569 million) mainly involve the operations of the International Communication Agency which include the provision of cultural centers and libraries, academic exchanges, Voice of America broadcasts, and similar efforts to disseminate information about the United States, its people and policies.

International Financial Programs

International Financial Programs for the most part concern the operation of the Export-Import Bank. The Eximbank dates to the mid-thirties, when it was designed to promote trade with selected nations. It later evolved into a program to promote U. S. exports in general by providing direct loans, loan guarantees and insurance to the export customers of U. S. firms. In recent years, however, there has been much more emphasis on justifying the Eximbank and its expansion in order "to meet officially supported export credit competition" from abroad.

Finally, it should be noted that the data in the tables presented here do not always fully reflect the total involvement of the U. S. government. For example, the Eximbank is subject to certain limitations on its loan and guarantee programs which are not listed in the budget appropriation or outlay data; nor are the Bank's cumulative loans and guarantees listed. The Carter administration has projected that the balance of Eximbank loans and guarantees at the end of FY 1981 will total $14.4 billion and $7.95 billion, respectively. Direct loans provided through the Economic Support Fund are also subject to a limitation, but not a budget authorization; yet, by the end of FY 1981, such loans will climb to $5 billion. Similar techniques are employed in treating that portion of U. S. capital subscriptions to the various multilateral development banks (MDB) which is not paid-in, but remains "callable." These contingent liabilities for American taxpayers would increase by about $1.1 billion under the Carter administration's proposals for FY 1981.[6]

This brief review of International Affairs should convey some impressions of the size, variety and even inconsistent nature of federal spending in this area. On the one hand, there are the bilateral aid programs over which the U. S. maintains close control and, on the other, there is the trend toward increased emphasis on aid through the relatively uncontrollable MDB's. Policy pronouncements suggest that private sector forces can play a larger role in development goals, yet the government repeatedly interferes in the private market. Food aid programs are touted as serving humanitarian purposes, but seem designed mainly to assist domestic agricultural interests. Media campaigns are launched to present the high purposes and aspirations of the United States when simultaneously aid expenditures are disbursed to regimes which have little apparent regard for democratic institutions and other principles espoused by the U. S. It is hardly surprising, therefore, that Hans J. Morgenthau was moved to comment: "The United States... has been in the business of foreign aid for more than two decades, but it has yet to develop an intelligible theory of foreign aid that could provide standards of judgement for both supporters and opponents of a particular measure."[7] And Morgenthau's sentiments have been echoed since, as by Harald B. Malmgren who remarked: "The fact is that there is no coherent, over-all foreign economic policy" in the U. S.[8]

In the next section, a framework for providing such standards and constructing a coherent policy is presented and applied to current international affairs expenditures.

Framework and Application

A Basis for Governmental Action

Traditional justifications for governmental expenditures are based on the notion that governments have a responsibility to provide "public goods" and to discourage undesirable or promote positive nonpecuniary externalities.[9] Public goods are characterized by the traits of non-excludability and independence-in-consumption. Non-excludability simply means that once a good is produced, it becomes prohibitively expensive to deny the good to those individuals who benefit

---

[6] See the *Appendix to the Budget for FY 1981* (Washington, D.C.: GPO, 1980).

[7] Hans J. Morgenthau, "A Political Theory of Foreign Aid," *American Political Science Review*, 56 (June 1962), pp. 301–309.

[8] Harald B. Malmgren, "Managing Foreign Economic Policy," *Foreign Policy*, No. 6 (Spring 1972), pp. 42–63.

[9] For a clear discussion of the concepts involved, see Robert H. Haveman, *The Economics of the Public Sector*, 2nd ed. (New York: John Wiley and Sons, 1976).

from it but are unwilling to pay for it. The provision of defense-related goods is a standard example. By independence-in-consumption, we mean that the consumption of the good by one individual does not diminish the amount of the good available to others. Highways (up to some congestion point) are an often-noted example (although non-payers could theoretically be excluded) as are defense goods (where exclusion is much more costly). Because of the difficulty of appropriating a return on the provision of public goods, the private sector sometimes fails to produce them. Hence, if these goods do have economic value, a case may be made for their provision by the government.

The standard model of firm behavior in a private, competitive market concludes that the production of a commodity will expand until the expected private marginal benefits (or revenues) derived from production are equal to the expected private marginal cost of production. There may be instances, however, where the marginal social costs (MSC) or marginal social benefits (MSB) of some activity diverge from the marginal private costs and benefits; that is, not all costs or benefits are "internalized" by the firm or otherwise accounted for by the market mechanism. In these instances, the level of production generated by private decision-makers may involve non-pecuniary externalities, where the MSB is greater than the MSC (and the good, from a societal perspective, is underproduced) or where MSB is less than MSC (and the good is overproduced). Then, it may be contended that a legitimate role of government is, in some fashion, to encourage or discourage the production of the relevant commodity.

The existence of public goods or externalities is not, however, a sufficient condition for governmental involvement. Frequently, the private sector can still generate arrangements to effectively treat both phenomena. For example, private associations and more clearly delineated property rights will sometimes be fully adequate in providing a resolution of these conditions without further governmental participation.[10]

Collective action through the government may, however, be required in some situations. The concept of "foreign policy," for example, does meet the standards of being a public good and it is unlikely that the private sector could fully serve to provide that type of public good. Consequently, the formation and execution of foreign policy is in the venue of the government.

Having said this, a caveat is in order. Specifically, perfunctory appeal to the concept of foreign policy does not establish a *carte blanche*

---

[10] Gordon Tullock, in his *Private Wants, Public Means: An Economic Analysis of the Desirable Scope of Government* (New York: Basic Books, 1970), provides a description of how private arrangements can work in certain cases involving public goods or externalities. See, especially, Chapter 6.

for governments to pursue any and all measures without some standards of justifiable expenditures. Rather, to justify particular foreign affairs programs, clear and operational statements of the purposes of U. S. foreign policy and of how particular measures may coincide with those policy goals are required.

As discussed earlier, such clearly-defined and operational statements seem to be rare indeed. Nonetheless, certain minimum standards seem intuitively evident. For example, the taxpayer should be able to have a reasonable expectation that foreign affairs programs will generate some benefit which clearly accrues to the citizens of the U. S. (and which would not otherwise be provided through private arrangements); i.e., international affairs spending should involve a *quid pro quo* relationship. Further, there should be some assurance that a given program is not obviously dominated (in terms of efficiency) by some alternative program. And, finally, the program should not be counter-productive or ultimately inimical to U. S. interests.

In short, international affairs spending can and should be judged on the same basis as domestic spending programs. Public goods or non-pecuniary externalities, which cannot be accommodated by the private sector, should be at stake and there should be reasonable assurances that the taxpayer will derive a clearly-defined benefit.

Inappropriate Reasons for Foreign Aid Spending

Current international affairs expenditures, especially those for foreign aid, appeal to more than foreign policy considerations. Aid for humanitarian and economic development are frequently cited as separate and independent justifications for government involvement. Because of the pervasiveness of such claims, both of these alleged justifications should be considered in more detail.

Humanitarian Aid

First, consider the notion that humanitarianism is a self-sufficient basis for foreign aid and, for the moment, assume that humanitarianism can be regarded as a public good. Even when this much of the case is conceded, as was emphasized above, public good status alone (or purity of motive) does not automatically admit the legitimacy of government involvement. Only if private sector arrangements do not provide opportunities for humanitarian behavior or gestures is a potential role for the government established.

Clearly, private arrangements for such actions are plentiful. Numerous private foundations, religious organizations, and secular associations provide humanitarian assistance to peoples abroad. According to one estimate, based on the responses of 700 organizations reporting to the Department of Commerce, private and voluntary organizations contributed an annual average of $815 million (exclusive of some governmental funds channeled through these agencies) to overseas aid.[11] Additionally, since salaries and other costs associated with this aid were frequently far below the levels paid by governmental agencies, the size of private sector contributions relative to those of the government is understated by the above data.

Further, if the terms "humanitarian" or "altruistic behavior" imply actions taken with no expectation of compensation or obligation for the beneficiary, the idea that there can be a market failure or an "undersupply of voluntary humanitarianism" involves both a redundancy (how can humanitarianism not be voluntary?) and a contradiction in terms. When governments employ taxation to coerce or force the population to undertake "humanitarian" expenditure programs, the contradiction is more evident still, especially when the expenditures are openly opposed by taxpayers. That such opposition is present is clear from a series of opinion polls. For example, the Roper poll reported that around 70 percent of the respondents in surveys taken between 1971 and 1977 (the latest date for which information was available) thought that the U. S. government was spending too much on foreign aid. A separate survey by Yankelovich, Skelly and White in late 1978 revealed similar findings: 72 percent of the registered voters sampled felt that foreign aid expenditures were excessive.[12]

It can be argued that if the public were better informed about the "needs for foreign assistance," sentiment would shift to favoring additional aid. While a casual review of "public service" announcements and advertisements seems to belie the notion that the public is underinformed, Burns W. Roper sees increased attention to foreign aid programs as having very different effects. He writes that despite a "negative public attitude towards (foreign aid),...it has probably managed to survive in reduced form because of the public apathy about foreign affairs. Given the lopsided negative sentiment about foreign aid, the program would probably have been killed long ago if foreign affairs and hence foreign aid were a burning issue to the American public."[13] Given the attitudes of the American public and the coercive aspects of taxation, the official aid program seems to have all the humanitarian aspects of armed robbery.

It must be admitted that the surveys did not appear to differentiate between aid for altruistic versus other purposes and it might be argued that public opinion would favor the former. Yet, it is precisely aid of a humanitarian nature in which private associations specialize. In addi-

---

11 John G. Sommer, *Beyond Charity: U.S. Voluntary Aid for a Changing Third World* (Overseas Development Council, 1977), pp. 6–8.

12 Burns W. Roper, "The Limits of Public Support," *The Annals of the American Academy of Political and Social Science,* 442 (March 1979), pp. 40–45.

13 *Ibid.,* p. 45.

tion, the many different private organizations with different areas of emphasis (e.g., child care, disaster relief, food aid, etc.) provide the individual donor with more control over the type of aid he wishes to give. This, in itself, represents a convincing argument that pure humanitarian aid is better provided through the private sector than through government programs. Moreover, private organizations are widely believed to be much more effective in "person-to-person" or humanitarian aid than is the government.

To summarize, there are no shortages of private arrangements for individuals or corporations to contribute to humanitarian purposes abroad. The notion that governments can provide humanitarian aid — in the proper sense of the phrase — is clearly contradictory. As was discussed above, there may be foreign policy reasons for government becoming involved in aid programs which resemble humanitarian assistance — that is, a legitimate foreign policy may involve altruistic-type gestures — but, to repeat, there is no justification for humanitarianism *being* U. S. foreign policy. *Thus, to the extent that governmental expenditures provided for humanitarian purposes* per se *can be identified and separated from the foreign assistance program, they should be eliminated.*[14]

Economic Development

From the perspective of the American taxpayer, developmental projects or programs are not public goods nor do they involve non-pecuniary externalities. If economic aid to developing nations ultimately gives rise to cheaper consumer goods in the U. S. or new markets for domestically-produced commodities, these effects are fully reflected in relative prices. *Consequently, aid for development* per se *does not satisfy the criteria for justifying governmental intervention and it, too, should be discontinued.*

Those who defend aid for development purposes on its own merits argue that there are private market failures in the supply of credit to finance various projects abroad. Specifically, they contend that the private capital markets generate sub-optimal amounts of loanable funds for development and hence there is a role for government action. There are several problems with this position. First, such arguments rarely define what an optimal level of financing would be and, moreover, they represent a misunderstanding of how the capital markets operate. The standard "failure" argument is that the private mar-

---

[14] Again, see the sources in fn. 4 for evidence on the extent to which U.S. is apparently motivated by humanitarian concerns. For related studies, see William R. Cline and Nicholas P. Sargen, "Performance Criteria and Multilateral Aid Allocation," *World Development*, 36 (June 1975), pp. 383-91 as well as Leonard Dudley and Claude Montmarquette, "A Model of the Supply of Bilateral Foreign Aid," *American Economic Review*, 66 (March 1976), pp. 132-42.

kets are willing to lend for development projects only at very high (in some cases, prohibitively high) interest rates because of both economic risks (the project has a relatively high probability of failure) and political risks (returns may be blocked by government foreign exchange regulations or changes in political regimes may result in expropriation or reneging on the commitments of "discredited" former officials). Such observations are true but they do not represent evidence of market failure. To the contrary, they indicate that the private markets are operating effectively since higher rates of interest are the means by which scarce funds are allocated and lenders are compensated for assuming higher levels of risk. When governments, by contrast, supply credit for projects at rates of interest below those which otherwise would be provided by the private market, it is the government which introduces an inefficiency — by redirecting capital away from other ends which have a higher social return or equal social return but involve less risk.

Why, then, do the private markets not devote more resources to developing nations or provide credit at lower interest rates? Röpke provides an insightful answer:

> Many underdeveloped countries refuse to satisfy the conditions necessary for a voluntary flow of capital from the West. They reserve to themselves all sorts of rights and devices, such as taxation, expropriation, exchange control, expulsion of foreign technicians, company law discrimination, and so on, and they refuse to pay in interest, dividends and salaries the price without which no capital aid can be offered even in the most favorable case....

Röpke goes on to point out that

> Those...countries which, by their policies and principles in economic and social matters, create the necessary conditions — the right climate — for private investment, obtain Western capital through the market.... The others, which do not create these conditions, have no right to complain about the consequences....If (a country) sets its policies by the lodestar of nationalism and socialism and persists in doing so, it must pay the price. If it does not want to pay the price, it must alter its policies.[15]

A very similar sentiment was expressed more recently by Charles P. Kindleberger, Professor of Economics at MIT, in testifying before a House Committee about private investment in developing countries (LDCs) and whether the government should subsidize or insure such investments.

> If the LDCs want more foreign investment, they will have to create a climate in which such investment can flourish. If they fail to create such a

---

15 Wilhelm Röpke, *A Humane Economy: The Social Framework of the Free Market,* (Chicago: Henry Regnery Company, 1960 and 1971).

climate, they will not succeed in attracting capital, technology, management and the like....Let MNCs (multinational corporations) bear the risks, realistically appraised, and let LDCs reflect on the repercussions of whatever actions they take....The Cocoyoc Declaration of UNCTAD calls for LDC self-reliance. Here is a good place to start.[16]

The essence of these comments is, of course, that there is no market failure in the provision of capital for development purposes to the LDCs. Rather, capital flows which are smaller than some individuals would subjectively prefer are a result of the market's assessment of conditions in and largely created by potential recipient countries. Hence, there is no reason for the U. S. taxpayer to carry the burden of subsidizing or offsetting those conditions; to provide such subsidies is, at best, a form of charity for which private sector arrangements are, in any case, already available.[17]

SHORT-TERM POLICIES

Multilateral Development Banks (MDBs)

The U. S. government is a member of several multilateral development banks including the World Bank group — the International Bank for Reconstruction and Development (IBRD), the International Development Association (IDA) and the International Finance Corporation (IFC) — and several regional banks — the Inter-American Development Bank (IDB), the Asian Development Bank (ADB) and the African Development Bank (AFDB) as well as the concessional-lending Development Funds associated with the regional banks (e.g., the AFDF).

Actual expenditures on some of these organizations appear rather modest, but those expenditures understate the potential liability which the memberships impose on the American taxpayer. The commitment of the U. S. is in the form of a promise to provide "callable capital," which requires congressional authorization, but not appropriations. Table 3 compares estimated appropriations with the estimated increase in contingent liabilities arising from memberships in the MDB for FY 1981. (Note that the table refers only to the projected increase and not to the cumulative levels of callable capital which have emerged over the years.)

It is acknowledged both by defenders and opponents of U. S. membership in the MDBs that the primary disadvantage of membership is that once funds are promised or pledged, the U. S. government has lit-

---

[16] Testimony before the Subcommittee on International Economic Policy of the House Committee on International Relations, *United States Foreign Economic Policy Objectives,* footnote 3, above.

[17] Another consideration relevant here is that it is by no means clear that the developing nations can always usefully absorb capital inflows far in excess of the levels provided by the private markets.

Table 3
Estimated Budget Appropriations and Limitations for MDBs
(FY 1981; in millions of dollars)

	Appropriation	Limitation on Callable Capital
International Bank for Reconstruction and Development	20	180
International Development Association	1,080	–
International Finance Corporation	–	–
Inter-American Development Bank	370	636
Asian Development Bank	136	227
Asian Development Fund	–	–
African Development Bank	18	54
African Development Fund	42	–
Total	1,666	1,097

Source: Appendix to Budget for FY 1981, pp. 79–83.

tle or no control over the use of those funds. It is the bureaucracy of the individual banks that determines in which countries and for what amounts projects will actually be funded. Although the U. S. representatives do vote on the recommendations for funding made by the staffs of the MDBs, there is no assurance that the U. S. can prevent a particular loan or grant from being made. Indeed, in the five months from October 1977 through February 1978, the U. S. voted to deny a loan or grant under consideration by the MDBs on ten different occasions; yet, in every case the loan or grant was made.[18] Given such obvious lack of control over the activities of the MDBs, it is clear that the first minimum standard of what taxpayers should reasonably expect from aid expenditures — some identifiable return on their tax dollars — is grossly violated.

What then are the alleged advantages, if any, to membership in the MDBs? Government spokesmen have identified several possible benefits.[19] A list would include the following: 1) the MDBs have been flexible in responding to new "needs" such as programs for agricultural and energy development; 2) they contribute to the economic development of and alleviation of poverty in the LDCs; 3) they maintain highly competent staffs; 4) the aid they provide ultimately results in an increased demand for U. S. goods and in a supply of raw materials for the U. S. economy; 5) they represent a forum for a continuing North-

---

[18] *U.S. Participation in Multilateral Development Institutions,* Hearings before the Subcommittee on International Development Institutions and Finance of the House Committee on Banking, Finance and Urban Affairs, 95th Cong., 2nd sess. (1978), pp. 96, 258–260.

[19] See, for example, the statements made by Richard N. Cooper, and C. Fred Bergsten, and the reprinted remarks of W. Michael Blumenthal in *U.S. Participation in Multilateral Development Institutions, op. cit.*

South dialogue; 6) they tend to de-nationalize foreign aid or provide it through apolitical organizations; and 7) they provide for a more equitable distribution of the burden for aid among the developed nations.

Clearly, the first five alleged advantages are by no means unique to a multilateral aid program. Flexibility, contribution to development, competence, expansion of markets and opportunities for "dialogue" are all available through bilateral aid programs.

Since foreign policy is inherently political, and since aid can be justified only on the grounds of contributing to foreign policy objectives, it is not desirable even to attempt to de-politicize aid. De-nationalization of aid is a clear disadvantage of the MDB approach. In any case, congressional witnesses are anything but consistent on this issue. While asserting the benefits of de-nationalized aid at one point, at others they explain why the U. S. must contribute more to the MDBs in order that we may have greater influence in promulgating U. S. policies. The proponents of the MDBs cannot have it both ways: if the U. S. wants to influence others through its foreign policy, then it should rely on the more controllable bilateral aid programs; if it does not want to politicize aid, then it should not be in the aid game at all.

The final argument — that the MDBs encourage other nations to bear their fair share in aid programs — relies on the *non sequitur* that if the U. S. does not provide funds for aid, neither will other nations. Other developed nations have records of supplying assistance to the developing countries which are as long or longer than that of the U. S. When they perceive it to be in their best interests to provide foreign aid, surely they will do so without further prompting from the U. S.

The U. S. should begin to reduce its role in the MDBs with the ultimate aim of withdrawing altogether. This need not mean the end of the development banks, however. As Wilson Schmidt has convincingly argued,[20] a strong case can be made for moving the MDBs into the private sector. Their very modest default experience, competitive average returns, and highly diversified portfolios suggest that they could continue to tap private capital sources and become viable, independent international intermediaries. Since to a large extent they behave in this manner already (except for their concessional lending and grants which are the most obvious candidates for absorption into bilateral programs in any case), it is puzzling that national governments feel compelled to support them at all.

If the development banks were shifted into the private sector, the budget savings for FY 1982 would be over $500 million (not including the reduction in contingent liabilities). The concessional programs of the IDA and development funds could be scaled back over, say, a five

---

[20] Wilson E. Schmidt, "Rethinking the Multilateral Development Banks," *Policy Review,* Fall 1979, pp. 47–61.

year period, with the associated savings either transferred to bilateral programs or phased out altogether. In the latter case, the FY 1982 saving would be about $225 million (or one-fifth of total FY 1982 expenditures).

International Development Cooperation Agency (IDCA)

The IDCA is the result of an effort to bring several of the bilateral and multilateral assistance programs under a single management. The major program for which the Director of the IDCA has responsibility is the Agency for International Development (AID). In turn, the AID program is the principal mechanism through which U. S. bilateral aid is disbursed.

Having earlier argued that bilateral development programs are superior to multilateral approaches does not imply that the bilateral programs are easily defended. Again, the problem is in having few standards for judging the effectiveness of aid expenditures. Of course, selected examples can be mustered either to defend or attack the AID program, but such an approach is not useful for an analysis of aid expenditures in general; instead, we will consider some of the preconceived notions which underlie aid expenditures.

Those views are embodied in part in the following causal chain: aid promotes economic growth and social stability, stabililty and growth lead to the development of democratic institutions, and democratic regimes will associate themselves with and work for (at least not against) the same principles of freedom held by the U. S.[21] Unfortunately, this chain is weak at almost every link.

First, there is no guarantee that aid or infusions of capital will lead to development. It has already been established that if conditions were ripe for the productive and remunerative use of capital in developing nations, then the capital would automatically flow from private sources. Here, we can simply note again that there are numerous political, social and cultural factors involved in creating a climate for capital investment and for some nations, not even unlimited infusions of capital by governments will generate the appropriate pre-conditions.

Even more clearly, development need not result in social stability. Rapid economic growth, by definition, implies change and with it some instability. It is because of such inevitable change that some observers argue that the ruling elites in certain nations, in an attempt to maintain the *status quo,* will often act to minimize the chances of economic development and instead direct aid inflows into highly visible, if relatively useless, infrastructure projects. Further, when develop-

---

[21] This "causal chain" is repeated frequently. For a sharp criticism of it see Hans J. Morgenthau, "A Political Theory of Foreign Aid," *op. cit.*

ment is forced, it is often with unforseen or undesirable consequences (to which the Iranian experience may attest).

Finally, American aid has simply failed to "win us friends," who are committed to either democratic ideals or support for other U. S. policies. Indeed, U. S. aid has, in several well-known instances, been concentrated on regimes with little respect for democratic principles. When such governments fall or come under attack, then, rightly or not, the U. S. is frequently implicated. To that extent, some aid expenditures are clearly counter-productive.

These considerations suggest, *inter alia,* that aid expenditures should involve some characteristics of a contractual arrangement. In making aid expenditures, it should be made clear what the U. S. hopes to gain and what it expects of the recipients. Of course, some will contend that aid proffered in return for some purpose of the U. S. is not aid at all — it is bribery or worse. Perhaps, but what is the alternative? To provide aid and merely hope for the best? The citizen, again, has a legitimate claim for some accounting for his tax dollars and some assurance that the best interests of the nation are unambiguously and tangibly served by aid spending. Introducing more of the attributes of open bargaining and voluntary exchange makes clear and explicit to all what expectations are involved and hence leaves less room for disappointment.

Accordingly, until the ultimate purposes of bilateral aid can be operationally defined and some reasonable probability of attaining those purposes can be made, *aid expenditures should certainly not be increased and careful attention should be given to reducing them.* Although estimates of the impact on the budget of a contractural approach to aid provision are difficult to make, it seems highly probable that a large share of current foreign aid spending is inconsistent with that approach.

Other programs monitored by the IDCA include U. S. contributions to certain multilateral agencies such as the International Fund for Agricultural Development and the United Nations development program. As multilateral aid agencies, the same objections apply as to the MDBs — viz., they are less controllable than and possess no special advantages over bilateral aid programs. *To the extent that the expenditures associated with these programs can be justified, they should be made part of the U. S. bilateral aid agencies.*

The final program which falls under the aegis of the IDCA is the Overseas Private Investment Corporation (OPIC). The OPIC provides loans, loan guarantees, advisory services and "insurance against the political risks of expropriation, war, revolution and insurrection, and the inconvertibility of local currencies" to U. S. firms considering investing directly in developing nations.[22] The OPIC currently does not require budgetary appropriations.

The OPIC is among the most egregious examples of inappropriate intervention by the U. S. government which passes under the guise of "international affairs." The Corporation involves none of the characteristics of a public good since its benefits accrue directly and solely to U. S. multinational corporations (and firms unwilling to meet OPIC's terms can be excluded). There are also no non-pecuniary externalities involved since the benefits of the Corporation's activities are all private in nature. Finally, private markets are more than capable of providing precisely the same services at market-clearing prices. *OPIC does not meet the usual standards for appropriate government action and should be abolished.*

Let us consider two more examples of programs falling under the heading of "Foreign Economic and Financial Assistance": food aid under P. L. 480 and the Economic Support Fund/Peacekeeping Operations.

Whatever the merits of food aid, the case against it is elegantly simple: there is nothing that food aid can do that cash grants (of an equivalent value) cannot do as well or better. Ultimately tilting the case for cash grants are two considerations. First, food aid is not always essential for economic development, and more importantly, it may in fact hinder development. Increases in food aid will depress the relative price of food in the recipient nations and hence discourage the production of locally-grown agricultural products.[23] In this way, too, the developing country becomes more dependent on outside aid as it becomes less able to provide for itself. Second, food aid is primarily a function of the availability of "surpluses" (at government-guaranteed support prices) in the donor nations. As a result, the volume of food aid can fluctuate significantly, not because of the needs of the developing nations, but due to the vagaries of market conditions in other places. Food aid as "surplus" disposal will frequently mean that the type of foodstuffs provided are inconsistent with the dietary preferences or nutritional requirements of the recipients. In short, food aid supplied by the U. S. government is primarily for the convenience of the U. S. agricultural sector (which also explains why one of the major proponents of food aid is the U. S. agricultural lobby). Equally evident is that the American citizen bears a double burden in providing such aid: first as a taxpayer whose dollars are employed to purchase

---

[22] From an advertisement for OPIC's services "How to Prevent Yourself When You Venture Overseas," in the *Wall Street Journal,* October 3, 1980, p. 15.

[23] For a broad, balanced review of food aid programs, see S. J. Maxwell and H. W. Singer, "Food Aid to Developing Countries: A Survey," *World Development* 7 (1979), pp. 225–47.

"surplus" food stocks and second as a consumer who must then pay higher prices for food.

Therefore, food aid from the U. S. should be phased out. Where aid is justified from a foreign policy perspective, cash grants should be employed. With the grants, the recipient nations can choose to purchase food if they desire, but are not forced to do so. If food purchases are preferred, then the developing nation has greater control over the volume and type of food best suited for its purposes. If the recipient countries have other, more pressing requirements, then cash grants allow them to satisfy those.

The last type of foreign assistance to be discussed is for the Economic Support Fund/Peacekeeping Operations. Expenditures under this category primarily involve payments to Israel and Egypt related to U. S. efforts to seek peace in the Middle East. Peaceful relations between Egypt and Israel would seem to be in the best interests of both those nations and, as such, would not normally require subsidization by the U. S. But if an attenuation of tensions between these nations involves the loss of other sources of support, "refereeing" expenses, costs of territorial transfers and the like, then the net internal benefits they derive from peace may be less than the net benefits to all countries including the U. S. Middle East peace can generate positive externalities for the U. S. and hence expenditures for maintaining or promoting that peace are justifiable. Notice that such expenditures for these purposes also provide the *quid pro quo* aspects of aid discussed earlier.

Conduct of Foreign Affairs

Expenditures under this category include the "Administration of Foreign Affairs" and expenses for memberships and related activities in "International Organizations."

The first of these categories, which involves the operation of the Department of State in forming and executing foreign policy, is clearly consistent in principle with legitimate government activities. However, merely because a specific activity falls under the "Administration" heading does not automatically confer legitimacy. For example, one consular activity is to provide services to U. S. firms which have trade arrangements with or production and distribution facilities within foreign nations. Such programs of the State Department are not easily defended since their benefits accrue exclusively to specific firms. Either the firms should purchase such services in the private markets, or from the State Department itself. Certainly, there is no reason for the taxpayer-at-large to subsidize such programs when the beneficiaries are so clearly-defined and "excludable." Consequently, *com-*

mercial services provided to specific firms should be discontinued or placed in a market setting.

U. S. participation in various international organizations and conferences could serve the foreign policy interests of the U. S. To the extent that law, the codification of standards for behavior, and the peaceful adjudication of disputes possess public good characteristics, U. S. membership in agencies seeking international agreements in these fields can be justified.

Yet membership in some international organizations, especially those engaged in providing economic and technical assistance to developing countries, is subject to the same complaint previously leveled against the MDBs. In many organizations (and in particular those associated with the U.N.), the United States exercises little control over the use of funds and thus forfeits its abilty to insure that the taxpayer's resources are employed with a reasonable probability of generating benefits to the U. S.[24]

In addition, other agencies are involved in programs that could well be handled in the private sector. The International Seed Testing Association, the International Cotton Advisory Committee, and the International Center for the Preservation and Restoration of Cultural Property not only sound as if they could be private trade and philanthropic associations, but they should be. Support of organizations devoted to the specialized aims of national or international vested interest groups falls outside the proper province of government support. *The U. S. might encourage private support by reducing its subsidization of these types of organizations.*

Export-Import Bank (Eximbank)

The Eximbank provides loans, refinancing of export credits, loan guarantees and insurance to promote U. S. exports. Such activities are usually claimed to be required in order to overcome limitations in private sector export financing and to offset the credit subsidies given foreign exporters by their governments.

To justify this program of government subsidies, it must be demonstrated that either public goods or non-pecuniary positive externalities are involved with export sales. In this case, the additional argument that the government must intervene to overcome market failures due to high transaction costs is also invoked. As will be seen, none of the above possibilities can survive even a cursory review.

First, exports *per se* are not public goods. The benefits of export sales accrue directly to those who sell their products abroad; the prin-

---

[24] For an evaluation of U.S. membership in such organizations, see the Committee on Government Operations, U.S. Senate, *U.S. Participation in International Organizations,* February 1977.

ciples of non-excludability and independence-in-consumption are obviously as irrelevant for export sales as they are for the sale of goods on domestic markets.

There are also no non-pecuniary externalities involved. Increased export sales may have secondary or tertiary effects elsewhere in the economy, but these repercussions are fully reflected in relative prices. That is, if export sales increase the demand for certain types of labor or capital, and on that basis are regarded as "favorable" or "good," those who supply such factors will be rewarded through the market mechanism in the form of higher relative prices. Since the higher relative prices would automatically attract more resources to these markets, there is no reason for governments to further subsidize them. In short, the market in such cases provides the rewards and additional governmental support is not required.

The argument that the private credit markets "fail" is based on the belief that banks or other financial intermediaries are unable or unwilling to make relatively long-term loans to foreign firms or governments (which frequently do borrow from or have their loans guaranteed by the Eximbank). Banks are asserted to avoid such loans because they are "too risky." Alternatively, banks may be unable to make large loans because of statutory constraints limiting the size of any given loan or set of loans to a particular borrower.

The last charge is the weakest. To the extent that a given loan is too large for one bank to cover alone, the loan can be syndicated among several banks. Indeed, this is a very common practice any time unusually heavy demands are placed on the credit markets by a given borrower.

Further, there is no evidence of market failure in large, long-term loans. As Steven E. Plaut recently pointed out, the U. S. credit markets "routinely finance risky ventures," including the Alaskan pipeline.[25] The case for government financing of exports, in fact, rests on some very strange arguments. For example, according to a CBO Staff Working Paper, "The quantity of funds demanded for the financing of long-term capital goods exports is greater than the quantity supplied by the private capital market, and Eximbank narrows the gap by increasing the supply of funds available."[26] The obvious question which such arguments neglect to ask is at what interest rate will the demand be greater than the supply? Certainly not at an equilibrium rate, by definition. But if Eximbank steps into the market and offers loans at below the market's equilibrium rate, then of course there will be a

---

[25] Steven E. Plaut, "Export-Import Follies," *Fortune,* August 25, 1980.

[26] Congressional Budget Office, "The Export-Import Bank: Implications for the Federal Budget and the Credit Market," Staff Working Paper (Washington, D.C.: GPO, October 1976), p. 11.

private market "shortage." We are in the peculiar position of having the government artifically lower interest rates and create a condition of excess demand so that it can justify its presence *because* of the existence of excess demand! By this reasoning, the government could justify supplying literally every product which the private sector now produces: just lower prices below equilibrium levels, and watch the shortages develop. In this sense, government is not the solution, it is the problem.

Perhaps the real argument is that the market-clearing interest rate is "too high" and should be lowered by the government. This argument is meaningless, wrong, or both, for it fails to establish any objective criteria about what the "correct" interest rate is and why the market rate is "wrong." Market interest rates must be examined in light of risk premia and the real cost to the borrower. If risks are relatively large, lenders should be compensated for assuming them; certainly, risk-reduction in this case is not a public good and therefore risk-related costs should not be shifted to the taxpayer. Further, it is well-established that relative national interest rates for comparable assets are correlated with the expected rate of change in the relevant exchange rate. If the dollar is expected to depreciate relative to, say, the Japanese yen, U. S. rates will be higher than Japanese rates, but the borrower expects to purchase dollars in the future with relatively fewer resources. The real expected costs of borrowing in Japan or the U. S. are the same when the appropriate markets are allowed to operate.

Since government intervention via the Eximbank cannot be justified using the normal criteria, the intervention must involve some kind of income redistribution. The winners in this exercise in income transfer are foreign firms and goverments which are able to borrow at below market interest rates. But who are the losers?

A burden does exist and it is placed on every individual, business, or state and local municipality which must compete with the federal government for a share of the private credit market. The Eximbank ultimately raises funds in the private capital markets and thereby increases the costs of borrowing for everyone else. Thus, the redistribution is from individuals, local governments and small businesses to corporations and governments abroad.

One final concern expressed by proponents of the Banks is that "something must be done" about the U. S. balance-of-payments deficit and the Eximbank at least serves that purpose. This concern is unnecessary and misplaced. It is unnecessary because changes in the exchange rate are sufficient to restore equilibrium to the external account. Fears that export-credit subsidies abroad will displace U. S. exports are, for the same reason, unnecessary. Any successful attempt by foreign governments to subsidize their exports will ultimately be offset by an exchange rate adjustment, so that their efforts are largely self-defeating. It is also misplaced because balance in the external sector does not require that exports and imports be equal. A demand for dollars abroad for use as a reserve or vehicle currency will generate, in equilibrium, a capital account surplus to offset or finance a trade imbalance.

No justification exists for the Eximbank and it should be discontinued or allowed to operate as a private concern with no ties whatever to the U. S. government. The savings for FY 1982 would involve over $3.75 billion. Even more importantly, however, by removing this and other mechanisms through which the government and its agencies raid private capital markets, borrowing costs for the private sector would be lowered.

LONG-TERM CONSIDERATIONS

As Stephen D. Cohen remarked, "in studying international economic policy or foreign policy, it is insufficient to say that the United States seeks global prosperity in the former and seeks to protect and enhance its security in the latter policy area. Such generalizations afford very little predictive power concerning policy specifics."[27] Yet many of the usual justifications for government spending in international affairs rely precisely on the various types of platitudes against which Cohen cautions us. The result has been a patch-work of programs which frequently either fall outside the province of legitimate government action or fail to provide the taxpayer with a reasonable assurance of a clearly-defined payoff.

This essay has suggested that international affairs expenditures can and should be subject to the same scrutiny and criteria which should be employed in assessing domestic expenditures. This approach to the budgetary process relies on the well-known precept that government action is required only when public goods or externalities which cannot be provided or accounted for by private sector arrangements are involved.

Although foreign policy considerations can fit this criterion, mere appeal to the concept is not a sufficient condition for proceeding with any given international affairs expenditure. The taxpayer is entitled to an accounting of precisely what the citizen of the U. S. stands to gain from a particular spending program and the probability of actually realizing that gain.

It is no answer to respond that whether a given program will ultimately and clearly serve U. S. interests is unknowable. If appeals to

---

[27] Stephen D. Cohen, *The Making of United States International Economic Policy* (New York: Praeger Publishers, 1977), p. 29.

61

the notions of securing and cultivating international friendships, of having a presence in important geographical locations and/or of recognizing the growing interdependence of the world economy are to be more than mere cant, then expected benefits *must* be calculated. If the calculation is difficult (or its results embarrassing) for current programs, then that is an indictment of the current programs and not of the principle that the taxpayer deserves an accounting.

By developing a contractual approach to, say, foreign aid, the necessary identification of spending benefits is emphasized and made more explicit. To dismiss this approach as unbecoming or crass bribery is to miss its point. The "purchase of votes" in international fora is not the potential here. Rather, it is the promotion of positive externalities and the attenuation of negative externalities. If the cessation of hostilities between two nations friendly to the U. S. is in this country's best interest and can be facilitated by U. S. financial assistance, then the benefits of such spending are clear. If nuclear proliferation among developing countries generates undesirable externalities, then U. S. aid can justifiably be tied to the recipient nation's acceptance of test-ban treaties and the like. Even if human rights is the concern, then specific programs to encourage the respect for those rights can be linked as a precondition to aid.

The contractual approach is not coercive or threatening to the sovereignty of other countries nor does it involve mere wishful thinking on the part of the U. S. government. Instead, it simply presents other countries with a choice which they are free to accept or reject. But again, and more importantly, it provides a much-needed connection between expenditures and benefits for taxpayers — they are entitled to no less.

3

General Science, Space, and Technology

by Richard Speier*

In a study filled with accounts of federal program failures, it is refreshing to find an area filled with spectacular successes — space and general science. Federal programs have put men on the moon, achieved closeup observations of most of the planets in the solar system, developed such practical applications of space as communications and remote sensing, revealed information about the smallest constituents of matter, and developed knowledge of incalculable future importance about the basic functions of living things.

At present, total annual spending in the United States for research and development is approximately $60 billion. Of this about half comes from the federal government, largely going for R&D in the areas of national defense, energy, and health. This essay will not examine R&D in those three areas but rather will focus on more "basic" research in the areas of space and general science — research that frequently cannot be associated with immediate end uses.

The intent of this essay is not so much to evaluate the merits of particular programs but instead to develop a framework through which federal research efforts might be evaluated. Nevertheless, we will examine some programs closely and suggest some budget changes. A salient feature of federal research is that it is "controllable"; it can be adjusted from year to year with no drastic near term effects on the nation as a whole.

The General Science, Space and Technology function consists of the entire budgets of the National Aeronautics and Space Administration (NASA), the National Science Foundation (NSF), and the General Science and Research and the Basic Energy Sciences programs of the Department of Energy (Table 1). Funding in these areas has increased rapidly, approximately 25 percent over the last two years. Some 75 percent of the money goes to NASA with nearly half of that ear-

---

*The views expressed in this essay are those of the author. They should not be attributed to any institution.

63

Table 1

Space and General Science Programs Discussed in this Essay
(Budget Authority in $ Millions)*

	1979	1980	1981
National Aeronautics and			
Space Administration			
1. Space transportation system			
(a) Space shuttle	1,638	1,886	1,873
(b) Space flight operations	300	447	810
(c) Expendable launch vehicles	74	71	56
2. Space science			
(a) Physics and astronomy	283	337	439
(b) Planetary exploration	183	220	180
(c) Life sciences	40	44	50
3. Space and terrestrial applications			
(a) Space applications	275	332	382
(b) Technology utilization	9	12	13
4. Aeronautics and space technology			
(a) Aeronautical research and technology	264	308	290
(b) Space research and technology	107	116	115
(c) Energy technology	5	3	4
5. Tracking and data acquisition	300	332	359
6. Construction of facilities	148	156	120
7. Research and program management	934	1,006	1.047
NASA total	4,559	5,270	5,737
National Science Foundation			
1. Research and related activities			
(a) Mathematical and physical sciences	209	226	264
(b) Astronomical, atmospheric, earth, and			
ocean sciences	212	218	241
(c) U.S. Antarctic program	51	56	63
(d) Ocean drilling programs	12	20	27
(e) Biological, behavioral, and social sciences	155	167	182
(f) Engineering and applied science	110	112	137
(g) Scientific, technological, and inter-			
national affairs	24	26	29

marked for a single development, the space shuttle and the associated preparation for its flight operations.

Other NASA activities include the development of spacecraft to observe objects at unprecedented distances in the universe, to explore as yet unobserved aspects of the sun and other planets, to develop practical uses of space—including communications, remote sensing, and manufacture of materials in space—and to improve technology applicable to aircraft and spacecraft.

The National Science Foundation supports a large number of relatively small research projects, generally undertaken by universities. More than 90 percent of its activities relate to research projects, with the largest single programs involving astronomy facilities, ships for exploring the ocean and its floor, and a continuing U.S. scientific

Table 1 (Continued)
Space and General Science Programs Discussed in this Essay
(Budget Authority in $ Millions)*

	1979	1980	1981
(h) Cross directorate programs	17	26	52
(i) Program development and management	55	61	61
2. Science education activities			
(a) Scientific personnel improvement	33	32	35
(b) Science education resources improvement	29	24	24
(c) Science education development and research	12	15	18
(d) Science and society	6	8	9
3. Special foreign currency appropriation	4	6	6
NSF total	927	994	1,148
Department of Energy			
1. General science and research			
(a) Life sciences research and nuclear medicine applications	41	42	49
(b) High energy physics	297	325	359
(c) Nuclear physics	93	105	116
2. Basic energy sciences			
(a) Nuclear science	29	32	35
(b) Materials sciences	94	97	100
(c) Chemical sciences	55	65	85
(d) Engineering, mathematical, and geosciences	17	21	31
(e) Advanced energy projects	4	5	8
(f) Biological energy research	4	6	9
(g) Program direction	2	2	2
DOE total	636	701	784
Grand total, space and general science	6,122	6,965	7,669

*This table and Table 2 are the only ones in this study to express budget figures in terms of budget authority rather than outlays. This is due to the absence of detailed outlay figures in published documents.

presence in Antarctica. Some 8 percent of NSF's funding goes for the development of scientifically trained manpower, including assistance to individuals and institutions.

The Department of Energy, with a budget for general science and basic energy sciences that is two-thirds as large as the NSF budget, sponsors a variety of small research projects concerning energy and nuclear physics and a large research program (nearly half of the DOE total) in high energy physics. The high energy physics program involves the operation of three large facilities in the San Francisco Bay area, the Chicago area, and the eastern Long Island area. At each of these complexes, machines which cost hundreds of millions of dollars accelerate subatomic particles to nearly the speed of light; the collision of these particles with other matter releases subatomic debris, the study of which sheds light on the fundamental laws of matter.

Since matter is everywhere, it might seem that high energy physics would have wide practical applications. On the contrary, except for some possible applications of accelerator technology, the processes studied involve conditions so extreme that they seem applicable only to phenomena occurring in the smallest subatomic distances or under the most remote astronomical circumstances. As far as we can foresee, the $359 million high energy physics program is, like astronomy and space exploration, the accumulation of knowledge for its own sake — with no immediate practical benefits in sight. However, regardless of its practical applicability, exploration of the very large and the very small is of interest, is indeed one of the most outstanding products of our civilization for many who follow such matters, and is therefore a "benefit."

While the appropriateness of the federal role in many activities has been subject to dispute, there is a remarkable unanimity of support for a federal role in space and general science. Activities subsumed under space and general science in many cases produce net benefits for the nation, yet in many cases they would not be undertaken under present institutional arrangements without federal funding. Some forms of science, e.g., activities closely related to the development of marketable products, are undertaken by the private sector because their benefits can be captured. The patent/copyright/trade secret system allows the researcher to control the use of knowledge he has developed and therefore to pay for his research through transactions in the market place. However, more basic research such as the understanding of the behavior of matter or of the processes governing living things cannot effectively be patented, copyrighted, or kept secret. Thus, the researcher is not able to gain the exclusive use of beneficial knowledge that he may develop and is not able to charge a price to those who wish to use the benefits. This "nonappropriability of benefits" of basic scientific knowledge has in recent years become the strongest justification for acceptance of a federal role in space and general science.

Given the two outstanding features of the space and general science programs — the federal successes in the area and the justification for the federal role — why should we be concerned about the budgets for these programs? Is there room for improvement?

SHORT-TERM POLICIES

There are two broad criticisms to be made of the federal government's conduct of the space and general science program: (1) *The federal government gets overly involved in the detailed choice of inputs to these programs, with consequent inefficiencies.* (2) *The federal government funds too much of the program itself rather than sharing*

66

the funding and the decision-making with other beneficiaries. To highlight these problems Table 2 illustratively restructures the budget for space and general science. The same $7.7 billion of programs that were displayed in Table 1 are now rearranged according to categories: inputs to science, programs where commercial applications are relatively apparent, programs where commercial applications are not foreseeable, and overhead and unallocated programs.[1]

Note that 40 percent of the space and general science budget goes for "inputs to science." This is not the procurement of scientific knowledge; it is not even the procurement of research designed to produce that scientific knowledge. Rather, it is the procurement of some input that is used in the research process. That input may be the transportation to orbit of a spacecraft that will be used for research, the training of people in scientific skills so that they later can undertake research, or the preparation of isotopes that will be used for scientific research or for medical treatment. These inputs are products or activities that are fairly clearly distinguished from the research process itself. An additional $231 million of construction and operation of high energy physics facilities could be added to the list of "inputs," but such activities are close enough to the research process that — for this illustrative purpose — we choose not to include them.

Commercial applications which are relatively apparent constitute somewhat more than 15 percent of the space and general science total. Improved technology for communications, for remote sensing satellites, and for aircraft are NASA activities that fit this description. Research with engineering applications, research already partly sponsored by industry, and development of techniques of science education are examples of NSF activities in this category. In DOE, research applicable to medical practice or to the production or conservation of energy fall into this category.

The third category is research where commercial applications are not foreseeable. This includes activities where the benefits may not be "practical" but rather are cultural, exploratory, or adventuristic, as in the space science activities of NASA that explore the planets and the universe, the astronomy activities of NSF, and the high energy physics program of DOE. It also includes research where the potential beneficiaries in society are so uncertain that we cannot identify commercial entities with a disproportionate interest in the research. This could include most NSF research (although a finer grain analysis would undoubtedly assign more of that research to the "commercially applicable" category) and life sciences and basic nuclear physics research (too basic to be sponsored by the nuclear power industry) in DOE.

---

[1] The distinctions that we are going to discuss are broadly applied. They are possibly inappropriate in some instances, especially when one gets into the fine structure of the programs.

Table 2

**Space and General Science Programs Illustratively Categorized
by Federal Role**
(Budget Authority in $ Millions)

	FY79 Actual	FY80 1/80 Plan	FY81 1/80 Proposal
Inputs to science			
1. NASA			
(a) Space transportation systems	2,012	2,403	2,737
(b) Tracking and data acquisition	300	332	359
2. NSF			
(a) Scientific personnel improvement	33	32	35
(b) Science education resources improvement	29	24	24
(c) Cross directorate programs, special facilities instrumentation	6	8	20
3. DOE			
Nuclear sciences, isotope preparation	7 (est)	8	9
Inputs total	2,387	2,807	3,185
Commercial applications relatively apparent			
1. NASA			
(a) Space and terrestrial applications	284	344	395
(b) Aeronautics and space technology	376	427	410
2. NSF			
(a) Engineering and applied science	110	112	137
(b) Cross directorate programs, industry/university cooperative research	5	7	20

Federal Support For Inputs To Research

When the federal government purchases documented research results, it is procuring the output of the research process, scientific knowledge. When it gives a contract or grant to a principal investigator — along with funding for assistance, equipment, and overhead — to undertake research that may later produce documented results, it is procuring research activity as an input to the process of producing knowledge. When the federal government funds manpower training, facilities, materials, or transportation services that may later be used in a research project that may someday produce knowledge, it is intervening far below the output end of the process of producing knowledge. At such a level of input funding, and at lower levels, there are wide varieties of alternative investment patterns.

	FY79 Actual	FY80 1/80 Plan	FY81 1/80 Proposal
(c) Science education development and research	12	15	18
3. DOE			
(a) Nuclear medicine applications	16 (est)	18	20
(b) Most basic energy sciences	198	221	251
Commercially applicable, total	1,001	1,144	1,251
Commercial applications not foreseeable			
1. NASA			
Space science	505	601	668
2. NSF			
(a) Most research and related activities	722	783	880
(b) Science and society	6	8	9
3. DOE			
(a) Life sciences research	25	24	29
(b) High energy physics	297	325	359
(c) Nuclear physics	93	105	116
Non-commercial, total	1,648	1,846	2,081
Overhead and unallocated			
1. NASA			
(a) Construction of facilities	148	156	120
(b) Research and program management	934	1,006	1,047
2. NSF			
Special foreign currency appropriation	4	6	6
Overhead, total	1,086	1,168	1,173

The federal government is less effective than the market at making complicated low-level investment decisions. Federal choices will undoubtedly be tainted by the administering agency's self-interest and the wider political considerations that are inevitable in any significant resource decision.

Space Shuttle

An excellent illustration of the pitfalls of federal intervention at too low a level is the space shuttle. The shuttle is a re-usable space launch vehicle capable of taking off vertically, placing large payloads in an orbit close to the earth, if necessary retrieving spacecraft that require maintenance, and landing like an airplane on designated runways. Scheduled to make its first orbital flight in 1981 and to gradually replace almost all expendable U.S. launch vehicles over the next four years, the fleet of four or more space shuttles will return the United States to an era of manned space activity; every shuttle will be flown by a human crew.

The federal government, of course, has always been responsible for launching U.S. spacecraft. This has been done with so-called expendable launch vehicles that have typically cost far less than the spacecraft they were carrying and that have made some space applications so economically attractive as to justify private sector reimbursement of the federal government on a "full cost recovery" basis for launching commercial satellites.

The decision to turn toward a new generation of much more expensive launch vehicles, vehicles that could be re-used, was made in 1969 when President Nixon decided to terminate the Apollo mission. At the same meeting, due in part to the survival instinct of the NASA Office of Manned Space Flight, preliminary development of the space shuttle was approved. The next two-and-one-half years saw a growing level of development activity. In mid-1972, the Administration committed itself to the full fledged development and deployment of the space shuttle.

The economic argument for the space shuttle was that it could lower the cost of space launches by re-using most of the launch vehicle hardware. Other arguments concerned possible savings from bigger, simpler payloads and from refurbishment of inoperable payloads. However, miniaturization technology and rapid payload obsolescence have reduced these arguments to minor importance. It was also asserted that the shuttle's reliability would eliminate spacecraft losses resulting from launch failures of expendable vehicles. However, the reliability of the shuttle has yet to be determined, while the reliability of expendable vehicles is high, is privately insurable, and can be further increased if economically justified.

At some level of space operations launch savings could justify the shuttle's development cost, at that time estimated in 1971 at slightly more than $5 billion. In 1971, NASA forecast an average of 57 shuttle flights per year for the first 13 years of the program. NASA's own evaluation contractor, Mathematica, Inc., reduced this estimate to 46 flights per year. By 1980, NASA reduced its forecast to an average of 41 flights per year "for planning purposes"; however, during the five-year period for which NASA plans are somewhat firm, the predicted flight rate never rose above 30. Later in this essay, we cite a shuttle development cost in excess of $10 billion with average savings per launch in the area of $15 million. Under these circumstances, a shuttle launch rate of 67 per year would be required just to "pay" 10 percent interest on the development cost.

Moreover, there were other alternatives besides the shuttle or the present stable of expendable launch vehicles. For about one-tenth of the shuttle development cost a high confidence family of large, unmanned boosters could be developed, such as the Titan III L. The upgraded Titan III family of vehicles could send larger payloads to orbit than could the shuttle, as much as 125 thousand pounds vs. about 65 thousand pounds. The upgraded Titan III had only modest disadvantages. It was projected to cost on average approximately twice as much as the shuttle per launch for the limited number of launches where such a large booster was required. The upgraded Titan III could not transport men to and from space or retrieve payloads from space — a capability of disputed value — except with the additional development of a glider spacecraft that would raise the Titan's development cost to approximately half that of the space shuttle.

The space shuttle program has had its difficulties. Its initial operational capability has slipped several years. The vehicle's payload capability has declined, requiring an additional, disposable engine ("thrust augmentation") to be fitted onto the vehicle's disposable fuel tank. Ceramic tiles, designed to prevent the vehicle from burning up on re-entry, have fallen off during air transportation of the vehicle — requiring a costly and time consuming project to remount thousands of individually computer designed tiles. The U.S. space program, which until now has been immune to the failure of any one launch vehicle or family of launch vehicles, will by the mid-1980s be putting all its eggs into a very few baskets. As few as four shuttle launch vehicles will carry virtually all of the U.S. civilian, commercial, and military payloads into space. The crash of one of them will reduce the size of our fleet by as much as 25 percent. A determination at some point that the vehicle is unsafe for human crews could result in a "generic shutdown" (to use terminology from the nuclear reactor industry) and ground virtually all U.S. space activities. At least two recent reviews of the shuttle program have called for warnings to the President that the shuttle does not offer the safety margins required in the Apollo program. The Defense Department and NASA plan to maintain the capability of producing expendable launch vehicles until they have confidence in shuttle operations; this will further increase the total cost of U.S. space activities.

Table 3 compares indicators of the relative economics of the space shuttle and expendable launch vehicles. The FY 1981 budget for the space shuttle is nearly $2.7 billion plus whatever the foreign, commercial, and DOD costs will be for their minor parts in the system development. By contrast, the total cost of the expendable vehicles to be launched during FY 1981 will be some $600 million. According to NASA the space shuttle will save one-third to one-half of the launch vehicle costs compared to the cost of expendables. When this fraction is applied to the FY 1981 expendable costs, the savings from the shut-

Table 3

Space Shuttle Versus Expendable Launch Vehicles

	Shuttle		Expendables
1981 cost ($ million)			
NASA, NOAA, Commercial, Foreign	2,683 + ?		214
DOD	?	(approx.)	400
Total	2,683 + ?	(approx.)	600
Price for comparable payloads to synchronous orbit with specified expendable vehicles versus shuttle ($ million)			
Delta	10.9		22.0
Atlas Centaur	26.3		38.0
Titan/IUS	50.3		75.1
Development cost (millions of 1971 $) for shuttle versus upgraded Titan III			
1972 estimate	5,150	(approx.)	500
1980 estimate	6,185		N.A.

tle turns out to be some $200–300 million per year. On the criterion of a private sector rate of return (at least 10 percent a year), this savings can hardly be expected to justify the upwards of $2.7 billion for the single year FY 1981 shuttle budget, much less the shuttle's total development cost. That cost, according to NASA, is some $6.2 billion in 1971 dollars—about 20 percent above the original estimate. In 1981 dollars this would become more than $10 billion. The present value of this development cost will be even greater in the year when the space shuttle will start producing its anticipated $200–300 million in annual savings. Moreover, it is not clear that the shuttle development program will stop with NASA's predicted expenditure of $6.2 billion in 1971 dollars. Further overruns and program slips are a clear possibility, if not a likelihood. Just as the Apollo team resisted being disbanded, the shuttle development teams will want to continue their activity; an $11 million advanced program in NASA is already looking at the possibilities for follow-on efforts.

Federal officials talk in terms of a commitment to finish the shuttle development and procurement, but the wisdom of this commitment is not clear. *An early item of business for the federal government should be a re-examination of the economics and the institutional arrangements for space transportation.* In spite of the received wisdom that there is no turning back on the shuttle commitment, the alternatives should be reviewed thoroughly and soon. Alternatives to be examined should include a discontinuation of the shuttle program, a variable mix of shuttle and expendable launch vehicles, and the possible development of a new expendable vehicle. Gross shuttle costs are now on the order of $3 billion per year. Resumed production of expendables would cost several hundred million dollars per year, with a new unmanned expendable development adding no more than a few hundreds of millions to this annual figure. Consequently, the early net savings from terminating the shuttle program are approximately $2 billion, more than one-quarter of the space and general science budget.

A longer-term approach would be for the federal government to turn the space transportation business over to the private sector and to purchase space transportation services as necessary for research and national defense activities. Competing firms would develop, produce, and operate launch vehicles, similar to the way that many firms under federal and private contracts now produce and operate space satellites. The launch facilities and the tracking and data acquisition system would be sold or leased to the private sector. (Private management of tracking and data acquisition would probably result in a system of user charges — a real efficiency improvement.) The federal government would still have a role, required by the Outer Space Treaty, of assuring that space launches did not carry weapons of mass destruction or interfere with other space activities, and that third parties suffering damage from a space launch would be compensated. But, otherwise, the investment decision as to what mix of launch vehicle types to develop and operate would be left up to the private sector.

There is a strong indication that the private sector has both the willingness and resources to continue to improve and to develop space vehicles, as justified by the market. A current example is the private commercial development of a Solid Spinning Upper Stage (SSUS), designed to take small payloads from near earth orbit to geosynchronous orbit. Some private firms have already expressed an interest in taking over the space transportation business.

The National Science Foundation

At a lower budget level the National Science Foundation funds inputs to the research process. As a residue of its activities in the 1950s and 1960s, when the dominant concern of the agency was "the scientific manpower pipeline," NSF proposes to spend $59 million in FY 1981 on the improvement of scientific personnel and scientific education resources and an additional $20 million for facilities and instruments for institutes of higher education with science programs.

In the past, however, the federal government has made some bad guesses on tinkering with "manpower pipelines." It overstimulated the production of teachers and doctors in the face of contrary demographic trends, resulting in a "glut" of trained professionals with associated unemployment, low salaries, and demands for further federal subsidies.

NSF not only continues to experiment with the "pipeline" but identifies new objectives far afield from the production of knowledge: "To identify and encourage the talented, particularly minorities, women and the physically handicapped, to participate more fully in the study of the sciences, mathematics and engineering. . . . To improve the quality of science by stimulating and increasing the competitiveness of scientists for federal research support in states that are now relatively less able to compete successfully." We would suggest that the nation's research effort would not suffer if the science agencies allowed market forces to determine who, where, and how many people entered scientific careers. *It appears that NSF's $80 million of input programs — the goals of which appear to be equity toward women, minorities, the handicapped, low performance states, etc. — are so inefficient in terms of lowering the cost of desirable federal research that the program could be terminated with net savings almost equal to the program's total funding.*

Commercially Applicable Research

The fact that knowledge is commercially applicable does not guarantee that private firms or individuals will have the incentive to develop that knowledge. New principles of aerodynamics may have widespread commercial benefits but prove impossible for the researcher to patent, copyright or keep secret. The existence of such a phenomenon is widely taken to justify a federal role in R&D that will ultimately produce commercial benefits.

However, this phenomenon can be overstated. The private performer of research need not capture all the benefits in order to have the incentive to undertake the research; he need only capture enough benefits to encourage his own investment in the research process. A recent study suggests that this may happen a significant fraction of the time.[2] Of twenty-one innovations studied the social rate of return was positive for nineteen. Of these nineteen innovations the social rate of return was higher than the private rate of return for eighteen. Taken on its face this statistic would support those who advocate a vigorous federal role in the funding of innovation since in the overwhelming majority of the cases the private innovators did not appear to capture all of the benefits. However, of those nineteen innovations with positive social returns, the private rate of return was 20 percent or greater for sixteen of them. Consequently, there was a substantial incentive to undertake the research in over 80 percent of the cases — in spite of the private inability to capture all of the benefits.

These statistics may not be representative of the kind of knowledge and innovation generated by federally funded research. But they do suggest the first of three measures that should be considered with

---

[2]Tewksbury, Crandall, and Crane, "Measuring the Societal Benefits of Innovation," *Science* 209 (August 8, 1980) 658–662.

respect to the types of commercially applicable programs identified in Table 2: *a federal review of such programs with consideration given to backing out of them entirely and leaving their funding to the private sector. The criterion for such a federal backout should be that the benefits of an innovation are sufficiently appropriable to the firm developing it (through patents, copyrights, trade secrets, or even early entrance into the market) that the private sector has enough incentives to decide whether to invest in the innovation.* The criterion should *not* be that the private sector would actually develop the innovation; some innovations yield such a low return on investment that no entity — private or public — should waste resources on them. A particular area in which application of this criterion should result in substantial federal backout is NASA's program for aeronautical research and technology.

In some cases — perhaps in the majority of cases in Table 2 — the argument will be made that the benefits of research are insufficiently appropriable by the private performers of the research. In that case the federal government should consider a second measure: *redesigning the rules of "capturability" so that the private sector can appropriate an adequate share of the benefits.* This can certainly be done in some cases in the commercial uses of space. The federal government could enforce temporary exclusive rights to innovative uses of space that were developed by private researchers at their own expense or to remote sensing information obtained at private expense. NASA is making a start in this direction as part of the $22 million (FY 1981) program on materials processing in space. Under a "Joint Endeavor," NASA and a private firm will develop a process of continuous-flow electrophoresis in space to produce medical substances in quantity and purity beyond those available from current ground-based facilities; as an incentive the private firm will possess certain exclusive rights to the process. More moves in this direction, with funding turned entirely over to the private sector, are to be encouraged.

Research Associations

The third proposal for modifying the federal research role starts with the recognition that many types of knowledge, while not appropriable by a single individual or firm, are largely capturable by industries. *In such cases the federal government should attempt to share the cost of the research with firms in the industry, forming "research associations" for the purpose of conducting specific research projects or types of research.* Depending on the value of the research and the benefits that can be captured by the industry as a whole, a large part of the research cost could be borne by private industry. Although we describe the benefits of research that would be funded by research associations as being capturable by an "industry," membership in a research association need not be restricted. Foreign firms, foreign

75

governments, non-profit organizations, and even interested individuals could and should be encouraged to contribute.

There are two objections that are generally raised with respect to the research association concept: the free rider problem and concerns about oligopolies. The free rider problem is that, with scientific activities that cannot be protected by the patent/copyright/trade secret system, a firm or other entity can secure the benefits of the research without contributing to the research association. What then is the incentive to contribute?

The classical answer to the free rider problem is the contingent contribution: a research project would only be undertaken if enough total funds were raised; if enough funds were not raised, the contributions would be returned to the donor. Such an arrangement maximizes the influence of individual contributions on the conduct of the research even though it does not entirely eliminate the free rider problem. It appears that the mechanism of contingent contributions can go a long way toward eliminating the free rider phenomenon and toward extracting from each beneficiary a donation approximately equivalent to the value of the research to that beneficiary. This is indicated by experimental research done with individuals, not firms, and conducted by Peter Bohm in Sweden approximately a decade ago.[3] A more mundane effect will further reduce the intensity of the free rider problem: Normal delays in dissemination of research results will give an advantage to research sponsors who have continuous access to the scientific activity.

The oligopolistic concern does not have as clear cut an instrument for dealing with it, but that may not be as much of a problem. One can hypothesize that firms joined together in a research association could conspire to retard innovation in an industry. This hypothesis implicitly asserts that direct government funding of research could not be influenced in such a manner. All of these speculations are open to question. The dynamics of a research association — usually conceived as an independent research organization such as a university financed by separate entities such as industrial firms — may not be conducive to retarding the most promising research proposals. Direct government financing of research is not necessarily the answer to avoiding oligopolies; governments have been captured before by private sector interest groups. At any rate, it is not proposed that we immediately place all possible research into research associations. A period of experimentation and mixed types of research support — some by government, some by research associations, and some turned entirely over to the private sector — is the only realistic way to make major long-term

---

[3]Peter Bohm, "Estimating Demand for Public Goods: An Experiment," *European Economic Review* 3 (1972) 111–130.

changes. Finally, an industrial conspiracy to retard an innovation that offered very large benefits would encourage some firms, perhaps foreign firms, to break ranks with their colleagues. The breakaway firms would try to capture such (often large) benefits as exist for being the first to introduce an innovation.

Beginning in FY 1974 NSF funded an experimental program based on one version of a research association. In the program for "industry/ university cooperative research" NSF and a number of industrial firms jointly fund research at a specific university. Figure 1 shows the relative funding that the NSF program was able to attract from industry in the most successful of these research centers, the Polymer Processing Program at MIT. The figure compares the ratios of industry to government support for the research association, for another MIT department, and for MIT as a whole. The program was

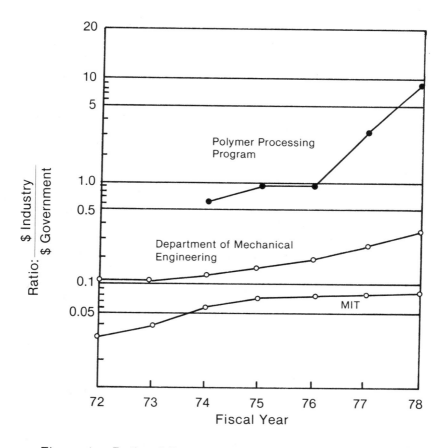

Figure 1.   Ratio of Research Funding: Industry/Government.

so successful that at the end of five years of funding NSF was able to discontinue government support entirely. Some other cooperative research centers have been moderately successful and some have failed entirely, but such is the nature of experiments.

The NSF cooperative program includes a number of specific features that would not necessarily be desirable in most research associations. In the NSF program the government is involved in decisions on the nature of the research and on the funding distribution between government and industry. *It would be preferable to at least experiment with a research association where the government's role in these decisions was minimized, i.e., where the industrial firms and the performers of the research themselves would decide the nature of the research and where the government would share the funding by some automatic mechanism.* One automatic mechanism would be an auction where funds went to the research associations offering the highest matching ratios relative to the government funds.

The danger with too much governmental involvement in research decisions, including the decision with respect to funding ratios, is that the government tends to become locked into specific projects that thereafter live or die on the basis of government decision. The British, for example, for many years sponsored research in conjunction with industry associations at a fixed matching ratio of funds; ultimately the British found themselves locked into research with such low priority partners as the lace and glue industries. An auction-type mechanism that removed the funding decision from the government would, it is hoped, allow unproductive types of research to die as a result of lack of industrial support.

A second possible difference between most research associations and the NSF program is that the NSF limits the performers of the research to universities. This is understandable since NSF regards the universities as its special interest group, but it unnecessarily excludes as performers of research other non-profit or even profit-making institutions. Some constraints on the performer might be appropriate; for example, it might be desirable in a research association to try to avoid unnecessary subsidies by insisting that the research be performed in an institution that was effectively separate from the firms sponsoring the research.

Another feature of uncertain value in the NSF program is the provision allowing the firms sponsoring the research to gain patent or other proprietary rights to the research results. On the one hand, it is desirable to have "capturability" provisions that minimize the federal role in research funding. On the other hand, allowing patent rights runs the risk of having the government subsidize research that could just as well be financed entirely by the private sector, given that enough benefits are capturable to allow such instruments of exclusivity as patents.

78

The government's interest in sponsoring scientific research, as we have discussed above, is in funding those areas of activity where the benefits are not capturable. Certainly the inclusion of patents and other property rights for sponsoring firms reduces the "free rider" problem, but we have discussed other inducements for firms to participate in research associations. One study of the NSF program has found that negotiations of patents and proprietary rights can be a "barrier" to cooperation;[4] it would appear that the effect of patents on the ability to organize research associations is not entirely positive.

One last difference between NSF's industry/university program and possible future research association arrangements is all important: the NSF program is too small. A serious research association program should make substantial inroads into the $1.25 billion of federal research, identified in Table 2, for which commerical applications are relatively apparent. NSF's $20 million program displayed on Table 2 is less than two percent of this total.

Research With No Forseeable Commercial Applications

What about research for which there may be no foreseeable dollar benefits to be captured—such research as high energy physics, astronomy, and space exploration? People do want to learn about the universe, so such research is worth funding at some level. The benefits of such research are in no way confined to the United States, and this observation leads to a suggested method for adjusting federal funding of such research: *international cost sharing.*

Some projects such as the manned lunar landing are such a visible source of national pride that politicians may prefer to keep the entire effort a national one. But is it necessary for the United States alone to fund the positron electron project (PEP) "to keep its forefront physics research program highly competitive with comparable European facilities"? Why not share the funding and the access to research facilities with, for example, the Japanese, who have no comparable program?[5] Indeed, why not invite into the funding process some of the OPEC nations, who can thereby invest some of their surplus funds in a commodity that can never be expropriated—knowledge? Many of the "big science" projects most suitable for cost sharing exhibit economies of scale; by modifying the hardware, twice as many experiments may be done with a given high energy physics facility or space exploration instrument at less than twice the cost. Consequently, the researchers of

---

[4] R. M. Colton, "An Analysis of the National Source Foundation's University-Industry Cooperative Research Centers Experiment," National Technical Information Service, Springfield, Virginia, 1979.

[5] The Japanese will fund a portion of $20 million detector being developed for use at the Fermilab facility, which cost upwards of $300 million to construct. This is a desirable step, but far from substantial cost sharing.

many nations can gain more knowledge per hundred million dollars by pooling their research activities.

There is a practical barrier to international cost sharing. The scientists of various nations frequently try to use the "threat" of being surpassed by other nations as one of the major levers for larger research budgets. The Nixon Administration explored on several occasions the possibility of international cost sharing in "big science." In each case the scientific community strongly discouraged initiatives with respect to programs already underway. The scientific community was, however, always willing to consider international cost sharing as a means of securing funding on the next big project. To help secure approval for the space shuttle, NASA successfully negotiated to have Europe develop a "spacelab" module at a cost approximately one-tenth that of the basic shuttle development. The most successful area of international cost sharing appears to be the joint development of payloads for NASA's space science program; substantial shared efforts are underway for such projects as the Galileo Jupiter spacecraft, the International Solar Polar Mission, and various spacelab experiments. But in most cases the research community has successfully resisted the effort to remove nationalism from basic research. Substantial international cost sharing has yet to occur on a major U.S. high energy physics or ground-based astronomy installation.

It should be understood that international cost sharing works two ways. The U.S. will sometimes find it beneficial to buy into foreign projects, especially if economies of scale are possible.

Research with no foreseeable commercial applications could be abandoned entirely, but it would not be in the interest of modern civilization to do so. A characteristic of research with no foreseeable objective is that it can be slowed down at no known economic penalty (except increased costs for changing one's mind and accelerating the research soon thereafter). *The stretchout of expensive undertakings, such as new accelerator projects or spacecraft development, can save hundreds of millions of dollars in early years while the U.S. seeks to negotiate international cost sharing.* Closing one of the three high-energy physics complexes could save on the order of $100 million per year.

LONG-TERM CONSIDERATIONS

This section discusses long-term approaches to improving the output orientation of federal research sponsorship, to spreading the sponsorship of research among the beneficiaries, and to increasing the value to the nation of federally sponsored research.

A Federal Prize Program

Is there any way the federal government could pay for completed research, based on the value of that research to the nation, and leave to the private sector the decisions on what research to perform and what mix of inputs to use? There is at least one way: prizes. Prizes have been an instrument for inducing scientific progress for centuries; the ship's chronometer was developed as a result of a large prize offered by the King of England for the creation of an instrument that could allow accurate navigation. More recently, a man-powered aircraft was developed partly under the stimulus of a large prize offered by a British philanthropist.

Prizes can be prospective or retrospective. If the government has the foresight to specify desirable innovations in advance, it can offer prizes for their development and await the course of events. In those cases, however, where the government cannot predict the most useful course of scientific activity, it can offer large prizes—and, importantly, much larger numbers of smaller prizes—for the most useful innovations which have been completed and their value verified.

The purpose of a federal prize program should be to reward private innovative activity—that is, activity conducted without substantial federal support—that produces substantial benefits not capturable by the innovator. A serious prize program must be large and long-term; this is necessary to attract private risk capital into the research process in the hopes of eventually garnering a prize that will justify the investment. The lack of an appropriate scale and long-term commitment was one of the failings of the Nixon Administration's abortive attempt to formulate a program of "Presidential prizes." The funding was to have been a few million dollars per year, which merely irritated the scientific community by threatening to water down the currency of such standards as the Nobel Prizes.

NSF currently has two programs that might be described as "prize" programs: the Waterman Prizes for outstanding achievement and the "master grant program" that provides long-term funding for researchers with demonstrated records of accomplishment. Both of these programs are so small that they cannot be expected to change the structure of incentives for scientific activity. On the other hand, it cannot be expected that the government will jump into a full blown multibillion dollar prize program without first experimenting on a smaller scale. It may be appropriate, therefore, to focus prize programs on relatively discrete areas of scientific research and even there to keep a mix of prize and grant/contract funding of research during a multiyear period of experimentation. The potential efficiency improvements of output funding of research are so great, and the reduction of red tape for researchers is so promising, that long-term experimentation with a prize mechanism is worth the most serious planning and analysis.

Philanthropy

Earlier, we proposed research associations as instruments for internalizing some of the benefits of investing in scientific knowledge. With knowledge, as with other public goods, there is always the problem of free riders, individuals or institutions that can gain the benefits of the public good without paying the cost. We referred to Bohm's experiments, which suggested that a well designed arrangement of contingent contributions could substantially reduce the free rider problem and could draw from contributors donations closely matched to the value to them of the activity being funded. In the early 1970s the Corporation for Public Broadcasting experimented with and adopted such a mechanism to fund the creation of public television programs.

Experiments with the design of contingent funding mechanisms can easily be conducted on a small scale and would offer potential benefits not only for the support of scientific research but also of other public goods. What we are talking about is philanthropy, efficient philanthropy designed to organize voluntary actions to fund collective activities at a level commensurate with the total value placed on them by members of society. The development of such techniques for efficient philanthropy deserves real attention and effort as a major long-term hope for reducing the coercive role of government.

Institutional Innovations

The two instruments we have just discussed, prizes and efficient philanthropy, are themselves examples of innovations that require research. They are not hardware innovations or technical innovations as are most scientific developments that are federally funded. We might call them institutional innovations, and the process of developing them institutional R&D. In the opinion of this writer, institutional R&D offers at least as great a potential for benefits to modern civilization as does technical R&D. An example of institutional innovation is congestion fees as a low-technology means of improving transportation. Congestion fees could include special charges for driving in an urban area during rush hours or for using an airport during peak periods. Such fees would shift some traffic to less congested hours, would shift other traffic to vehicles that create less congestion (buses, large aircraft), and would discourage other traffic altogether. *The federal role in researching such an innovation would be to develop a theoretical and practical understanding of how to apply the innovation and to help fund controlled experiments (undertaken by communities in the case of congestion fees) to bring knowledge of the innovation up to the point where other potential users could decide whether to adopt it on their own.*

Some areas that are ripe for institutional experimentation and innovation include:

- price mechanisms, e.g. time-of-day prices for efficiently rationing energy use, congestion prices as a low-technology means of improving transportation, and futures markets for efficiently guiding investments of a long-term nature;
- property rights such as transferable effluent rights as a means of limiting pollution;
- bonds or other insurance mechanisms for effectively compensating members of society for the consequences of dangerous activities while not stifling society with overregulation;
- competition instead of government enforced monopolies in such areas as cable television and electric power generation; and
- buyout mechanisms for ending bad government programs by having the beneficiaries of such changes compensate the losers.

The federal government should play a role in sponsoring such institutional research — albeit an efficient and minimal role that in the end may reduce its own coercive powers.

4

Energy

by Randall G. Holcombe*

Federal energy policy is remarkable in a number of respects. Most obvious is its rise from relative obscurity in fewer than ten years; what was only a few years ago a scattering of energy programs throughout the federal bureaucracy has become the Cabinet-level Department of Energy. The growth in the energy budget function reflects this rise in prominence. Whether the energy crisis is the "moral equivalent of war" is still being debated, but it does appear to be the financial equivalent. Federal energy expenditures in 1979, five years after the 1973–74 OPEC oil embargo, were $6.9 billion, and are projected to reach $13.4 billion in FY 1982, an increase of 96 percent in just three years.[1] By comparison, national defense expenditures increased by only 57 percent from 1964 to 1968, during the war in Vietnam.[2] The growth of the federal energy budget has been a direct result of the oil embargo of the winter of 1973–74 and the energy crisis mentality that resulted.

Another unusual aspect is that the Department of Energy has generally been viewed as an adversary of the domestic producers. By contrast, the Department of Agriculture is the ally of the agricultural community, the Department of Labor is the ally of labor, and the De-

---

*The author gratefully acknowledges information, research assistance, and comments from Milton Copulos, Lora Prtichett, Arthur Randol, and Richard Speier.

[1] Source: FY 1981 Budget (submitted January 1980). These figures include the U.S. Synthetic Fuels Corp., an off-budget entity for financing synthetic fuels (discussed later in the essay), but do not include the Rural Electrification and Telephone Revolving Fund. The budget for this fund is projected to more than double, from $2.5 billion in FY 1979 to $5.3 billion in FY 1982.

[2] Source: Annual U.S. Economic Data, May 1980, prepared by Federal Reserve Bank of St. Louis. The 1964 defense budget of $49.0 billion was lower than the two previous years, and the 1968 defense budget of $76.9 billion was the highest during the war.

[3] Regulation, of course, has had its effects in other areas of the economy as well, but the adversary relationship appears to be especially narrowly focused in energy policy. Two interesting views on regulation are Paul Johnson, "Sick Man of the West," *Policy Review* 14 (Fall 1980), pp. 125–139, and J. R. T. Hughes, *The Government Habit* (New York: Basic Books, 1977).

partment of Education is the friend of the educators.[3] Compare, for example, the Department of Agriculture's price supports for farm products with DOE's price ceiling on energy, both at the wholesale and retail levels. As price controls, allocation plans, and other regulations have hindered the private production of energy,[4] DOE has attempted to fill the void with federally-funded energy development.

One might well expect that an agency that has grown so rapidly would have some growing pains. The more fundamental questions surrounding DOE, however, do not concern administrative details, but whether its activities are justified. Federal energy expenditures are especially vulnerable to criticism since the United States throughout its history has enjoyed inexpensive and abundant energy without the assistance of a Department of Energy. In fact, Milton Friedman has suggested that our national energy policy is contributing to the causes — not the solutions — of our energy crisis.[5]

The situation today is very different from ten years ago, and the American economy is having to adjust rapidly to the change. The two major problems are higher prices and increased dependence on foreign sources.[6] Federal energy policy is not directed to the problem of higher prices. To the contrary, the so-called windfall profits tax, is really an excise tax that will increase energy prices.

The reduction of oil imports is the primary goal of current energy policy. Given the changes in the energy situation and the tremendous growth in federal spending, it is necessary to determine whether the energy expenditures are really in the national interest or whether federal programs are merely efforts to solve the problem by throwing money at it.

An important justification for the federal role in energy is to enhance national security through reduction in dependence upon foreign energy supplies. This is a rational goal, particularly in light of the unstable political climate of the Middle East. Programs that cannot be justified on national security grounds must then be justified on the basis of their economic costs and benefits.

This analysis will present an overview of the U.S. energy budget, examine the issue of national security in light of this overview, and, finally, provide a detailed examination of the energy budget function.

---

[4]See William A. Johnson, "The Impact of Price Controls on the Oil Industry: How to Worsen an Energy Crisis," in Gary D. Eppen, ed., *Energy: The Policy Issues* (Chicago: University of Chicago Press, 1975), for a lucid account of the effects of government regulations on the energy problem.

[5]Milton Friedman, "Blaming the Obstetrician," *Newsweek,* June 14, 1979, p. 70.

[6]See R. Holcombe, "Causes of the Energy Crisis," *Oil & Gas Tax Quarterly* 29, no. 1 (September 1980), pp. 139–150, for additional discussion.

Table 1
Energy
(in millions of dollars)

Major missions and programs	1979 actual	1980 estimate	1981 estimate
OUTLAYS			
Energy supply:			
Promotion of domestic production:			
Synthetic fuels promotion:			
Existing law......................	—	155	53
Proposed legislation..................	—	12	16
Biomass (proposed)...................	—	50	41
Solar bank (proposed)...............	—	29	130
Research, development, demonstration and applications:			
Solar..............................	437	617	656
Other renewable resources..............	509	537	645
Fossil:			
Existing law......................	740	931	939
Proposed legislation.................	—	50	50
Nuclear fission:			
Existing law......................	1,207	1,269	1,048
Proposed legislation.................	—	− 100	200
Other technology.....................	671	583	608
Direct production (net):			
Uranium enrichment...................	43	245	105
Petroleum reserves...................	− 350	− 443	− 1,823
Power marketing.....................	1,643	1,564	1,825
Subtotal.........................	4,900	5,499	4,493
Energy conservation:			
Technology development	176	246	278
Conservation grants	76	336	481
Utility oil use reduction (proposed)..........	—	1	22
Public information and others.............	—	11	34
Residential and commercial conservation (proposed)	—	14	357
Subtotal	252	608	1,172
Emergency energy preparedness:			
Strategic petroleum reserve:			
Existing law	1,021	767	1,294
Proposed legislation	—	3	11
Subtotal	1,021	770	1,306
Energy information, policy, and regulation:			
Energy information and policy	82	127	144
Regulation:			
Federal Energy Regulatory Commission ...	50	70	76
Economic Regulatory Administration	82	172	176
Nuclear Regulatory Commission..........	309	307	476
Alaska gas pipeline inspector	—	9	25
Administrative expenses (Department of Energy)...........................	219	261	314
Subtotal	742	946	1,211
Deductions for offsetting receipts	− 59	− 72	− 74
Total, outlays.......................	**6,856**	**7,751**	**8,107**

Source: The Budget of the United States Government (January 1980).

Energy Supply

The most important category in the energy budget from the standpoint of financial commitment is energy supply, which comprises 55 percent of the function. In addition, the U.S. Synthetic Fuels Corporation, is an off-budget item designed to promote the production of synthetic fuels.

The major subcategory within energy supply is research and development, which is intended to support long-term high-risk research and to develop support for solar, geothermal, and nuclear technologies. Also included are outlays to demonstrate and apply energy technology. The Carter Administration requested funds in its FY 1981 budget to establish a 300-acre facility for the Solar Energy Research Institute in Golden, Colorado.

Also included in energy supply is the promotion of domestic production entirely through biomass and solar bank energy production. Since these technologies are not now economically feasible, what is called the promotion of domestic production is closer in character to research, development and implementation than its name would imply. The budget does not allocate funds to promote the domestic production of economically cost-effective fuel sources such as petroleum, natural gas, coal, and nuclear power.

The direct production of energy is also included in the energy supply. This is composed of uranium enrichment, sale of oil from the Naval petroleum reserves, and power sales, mostly from the Tennessee Valley Authority. That costs exceed revenues in this category is due primarily to the costs of construction of nuclear power plants for TVA.

Energy Conservation

The second major energy budget category is energy conservation; at $1.2 billion it comprises about 14 percent of the total budget. This is largely self-explanatory and includes funds for technology development, conservation grants, and other programs.

Emergency Energy Preparedness

The single item in this rubric is the strategic petroleum reserve (SPR), a proposed one billion barrel reserve of crude oil to be stored primarily in salt domes in Louisiana and Texas. In the event of a future interruption of oil imports, this reserve could be used to replace the lost oil. The SPR is the largest item within the energy budget in which actual production can be clearly compared with planned output. Measuring the performance of the SPR against the DOE's own cost and timetable estimates shows that construction of the SPR is costing more than originally estimated and is behind schedule.

Energy Information, Policy, and Regulation

The final major budget category is energy information, policy, and regulation. There is good reason to examine this closely, since most energy regulation hinders rather than promotes the production of energy and thus is in conflict with the energy supply mission. However, the budget of the Nuclear Regulatory Commission, the largest single item under this subheading, should probably remain untouched. Aside from any practical benefits that might be produced, a prominent NRC has the potential to do much to lessen the public uneasiness over the future of nuclear power in the United States.

This overview provides a background against which the major programs of supply, conservation, emergency preparedness, and information, policy, and regulation can be examined in greater detail. However, the national security argument is so fundamental to the development and justification of current energy policies that the value of existing and proposed programs cannot be fairly assessed without an appreciation of the importance of national security issues.

SHORT-TERM POLICIES

Reducing Oil Imports for National Security

The oil embargo of 1973–74 not only caused dramatic economic dislocations, but also illustrated how vulnerable the United States is to oil import interruptions that could be initiated by potentially hostile foreign governments. The costs of our vulnerability could come in two forms: the potential damage to the economy from another embargo and the possibility that foreign governments could influence the United States, particularly with regard to foreign policy, by using the threat of another oil embargo. Although this latter cost is not easily measured in dollar terms, it is real, nonetheless, and policy options for minimizing this cost should be examined.

If a unifying principle can be found behind the energy budget, it is to reduce oil imports so that the United States will not be vulnerable to the whims of unpredictable suppliers. The strategic petroleum reserve is obviously aimed at reducing the potential damage from a possible future embargo, and many of the information, policy, and regulatory programs have the same goal. The energy supply portion of the budget primarily finances development of alternate fuel sources and technologies that will reduce petroleum use and imports through substitutes for oil. Conservation efforts, while geared to energy in general, are especially oriented toward oil. The Carter Administration proposed a major effort aimed at reducing oil use by electric utilities. Such a move may reduce oil use, but it will undoubtedly increase the use of coal, so that the program, while its goal is consistent with an energy policy designed to reduce oil imports for security reasons, is not really conservation at all, but merely substitution.

The nation's energy problem is neither that it is consuming too much nor that it is producing too little, but rather that, as a result of the levels of consumption and production, it is importing more oil than is prudent. Current policy addresses this problem only indirectly through the encouragement of domestic production and conservation. A more direct approach would be to raise the cost of imports. The problem is not that oil imports are undesirable, but that oil importers impose a cost on the rest of society in the form of increased political vulnerability. The importers, however, have no incentive to take account of this cost. The problem is, in economic jargon, an externality, and the economist's classic response to this is to tax the importers. The importers and consumers who create the political costs would then have an incentive to take these costs into account and therefore avoid them.[7]

Formal economic analysis demonstrates that such a tax would provide the optimal incentives to reduce imports through conservation, increased domestic energy production, and the development of cost-effective alternative energy sources.[8] The most obvious result would be to make imported oil more expensive to oil suppliers than domestic oil, and thus to create an incentive to produce domestic oil and a disincentive to import. Suppliers would import if the cost of imported oil plus the tax was less than the cost of domestic oil. The tax should be equal to the perceived political costs of imported oil (a plan for setting the tax is outlined below), so that oil would only be imported as long as it was more valuable than the costs associated with increased political vulnerability. Importers would then have an incentive to import the optimal amount of oil when all the costs associated with imports are considered. They would still have the option of importing as long as they found it worthwhile to pay the political costs as reflected by the tax.

The oil import tax also has the benefit of providing incentives for cost-effective conservation efforts, whereas government spending programs leave open the possibility of using tax dollars to finance conservation programs that cost more than they are worth. One need only compare the size and fuel economy of automobiles today with those of 1973 to see consumer response is an extremely effective method of conservation. Changes in thermostat settings, insulation, and other

[7]See R. Holcombe, "Taxation and Energy Policy," *Oil & Gas Quarterly* 24, no. 2 (December 1977), pp. 224–233, proposed this oil import tax, and explains it in more detail.

[8]See William T. Baumol, "On Taxation and the Control of Externalities," *American Economic Review* 62 (June 1972), pp. 307–322.

energy-saving measures are less visible but equally dramatic. Domestic energy consumtion today is approximately the same as it was before the 1973–74 oil embargo, even though before the embargo it was growing at a rate of over four percent each year.[9] This conservation has been a result of consumer response — not expensive Department of Energy programs.

Implementing the Tax

The first year, a tax of $2 per barrel could be imposed on all imported oil; each succeeding year, the tax would be increased by $1 per barrel unless the administration specifically decided that the increase would not be appropriate. To insure that domestic producers would continue to have at least the same incentives to search for and produce alternatives to imported oil, this tax would never be decreased. The gradual increase in the tax would give domestic producers and consumers time to adjust to the changes in import prices caused by the tax. This simple proposal would provide the optimal incentive structure for reducing oil imports in the most cost-effective way.[10]

A principal advantage of this tax is that it provides the proper incentives for reducing oil imports without spending tax dollars. It would both reduce the amount of bureaucracy needed to administer energy policy and raise money for the Treasury. This additional money could be used to help balance the budget or to lower other taxes.

These are two policies superficially similar to the oil import tax whose fundamental difference should be mentioned. The first is a quota on oil imports, as once existed. A quota would have the effect of reducing imports, and thus would raise the domestic price of imported oil. Those firms that would be able to import oil would buy it at the world market price, but once imported its value would be higher due to the quota's restrictions. Import licenses under a quota system would be a valuable asset, but would be granted at no cost to the importers. A more equitable system would be to sell the import licenses at a fair price. In effect, this is precisely what an import tax would do, since the right to import would have to be purchased through the tax.

A second policy is a retail tax, such as the proposed 50¢ per gallon gasoline tax. Unlike an import tax, a retail tax would not discriminate between imported and domestic oil, and so would discourage domestic production as well as imports. Since domestic oil is generally more ex-

---

[9] See R. Holcombe, "The Economic Impact of an Interruption in United States Petroleum Imports: 1975–2000" (Center for Naval Analyses Research Contribution 245, November 1974).

[10] Some imports could be exempt from the tax, if they came from reliable suppliers under contract. For example, Canadian oil might be exempted. This plan is similar to that presented in the author's "Taxation and Energy Policy," cited above.

pensive to extract, a retail tax could conceivably increase the amount of oil imports.

The United States should adopt an oil import tax as the primary response to the potential political costs associated with imported oil. Since this tax deals effectively with national security needs, other energy programs would have to be justified on the basis of a purely economic cost-benefit analysis. A program that could not pay for itself cannot be justified as an appropriate part of the federal energy budget. With this in mind, a closer examination of the major components of the energy budget is in order.

Energy Supply

Promotion of Domestic Production

The budget for promotion of domestic production provides grants, loans at terms more favorable than market terms, or purchase guarantees for solar, biomass, and synthetic fuels.

As a general principle, tax dollars are not allocated cost effectively when used to subsidize the direct production of energy. If the output was worth the cost, the private sector would find it profitable to produce the energy without government assistance. It is interesting to note that the funds for promotion of domestic production are all allocated for energy sources that have not been demonstrated to be cost-effective. No money is spent on promoting the domestic production of petroleum or nuclear power. In fact, in these proven areas, government regulations and controls actually hinder domestic production.

Another problem is that subsidies provide an unfair competitive advantage; unsubsidized energy sources may be discouraged. A case in point stems from the development of the Tennessee Valley Authority. While the benefits of TVA are generally known, there may have been some significant and almost invisible costs associated with rural electrification. Before TVA there was a growing windmill industry, with government assisted electrification; the industry was virtually eliminated, and windmill technology has shown almost no advance. One cannot know what would have happened if TVA had not been subsidized, but it is obvious that the windmill industry was hurt, and that development of a renewable energy supply was halted. This reinforces the general principle that will be invoked throughout this section: the government should not subsidize the direct production of energy.

Synthetic fuels production is allocated $69 million in FY 1981, but government expenditures are scheduled to increase dramatically in FY 1982 with the expansion of the Synthetic Fuels Corporation. The Corporation is an off-budget item that will promote the production of synthetic fuels through loans, pricing agreements and purchase guarantees, and which is allocated $2.4 billion in FY 1982. The synthetic fuels to be subsidized are primarily oil shale and coal liquefication projects. There is also some potential for producing liquid fuel from natural gas. *As just noted, there is no justification for supplementing the market to support energy production, and the subsidy to synthetic fuel producers should be eliminated. The same criticism applies to the biomass budget, which provides outlays and loans to convert grain, farm residues, and other biomass into synthetic fuels.*

The Carter Administration's proposed solar bank, within the Department of Housing and Urban Development, would provide subsidies to lenders who make long-term, below-market-rate loans to finance the use of solar energy systems. *This approach should also be abandoned; taxpayers should not be forced to pay for energy systems that cost more than they are worth.*

Research and Development

Research and development has been a traditional governmental function and is one of the more easily justified expenditures within the energy budget. Basic research is characterized by uncertainty, and successful research may yield general benefits not appropriable by the researcher. While particular programs may be questioned, energy R&D should be continued. Implementation programs, called demonstrations and applications, are more questionable. Aimed at promoting programs that Congress would like to see commercialized, demonstration and application projects are much more open to political manipulation. There is always the possibility that today's politically popular programs may fall into disfavor in the future. Thus, there is no guarantee that such a project would be completed.

A case in point is the Clinch River breeder reactor, a joint government and industry demonstration project begun in 1969.[11] The technology has been developed, and $800 million has already been spent on the project; yet it cannot be completed because the Carter Administration has not allowed license proceedings to begin. Approval has been withheld not because the reactor is infeasible, but because it will produce weapons-grade nuclear fuel. Other countries operating or building breeder reactors at present are the Soviet Union, Britain, France, and West Germany. Without passing judgment on President Carter's decision (the United States could, of course, allow other countries to develop the breeder reactor technology and then purchase foreign-made reactors), the point is that a political decision has halted this project in mid-stream, and the same fate could befall other dem-

---

[11] Information on this project is from the Comptroller General's Report to Congress, "U.S. Fast Breeder Reactor Program Needs Direction" (September 22, 1980), and the "1980 Progress Report: Clinch River Breeder Reactor Project," published by the Project Management Corporation.

onstration projects. *While R&D is worthwhile, the implementation budget should be drastically reduced.*

It should be noted, however, that because of the very real national security issues surrounding nuclear technology, there is better reason for the government to engage in implementation of nuclear energy than other energy sources. The budget for FY 1982 allocates $858 million to nuclear fission, but the Carter Administration has proposed to cut this figure by $36 million. In light of the special technological and security considerations in nuclear energy, the proposed cut should not be made. There are however some areas of the nuclear budget that should be examined closely. One is the liquid metal fast breeder reactor. By March 31, 1981, the President must decide on authorization for a breeder reactor demonstration project, larger than the one at Clinch River, that is now estimated to cost about $3 billion. The press of time will allow little opportunity for a thorough study, but it is likely that the project is not an effective investment.[12] *A cost-benefit analysis would probably show that R&D money would be better spent to develop the technology of light water resources.* Another area that deserves close scrutiny is the reprocessing program, although this is a relatively small area in FY 1981 budget — only $11 million.

Cuts should be made in the demonstration and application portion of the solar budget, which is $196 million out of the $656 million proposed by the Carter Administration for the FY 1982 budget. This would leave $460 million available for solar R&D. Budget increases are projected in the other R&D categories for 1982, but the overall recommendation is to provide level funding, achieved by phasing out implementation programs. There is the potential — although it is not examined here — for selling the promising implementation programs to private firms.

Direct Production

The final category in the energy supply budget is direct production, which includes uranium enrichment, sale of oil from the Naval petroleum reserves, and power marketing, of which the largest example is TVA. The general philosophy of these programs is in line with the goal of increasing domestic energy supply. While an audit might turn up places where money could be saved — particularly in the uranium enrichment program — the recommendations given here are those proposed by the Carter Administration for FY 1982. In the longer term,

---

[12] There have been several studies which have concluded that the breeder reactor will not be economically feasible until around the year 2020 or beyond. See "Nuclear Strategy of DOE," April 1979 and "Nuclear Proliferation and Civilian Nuclear Power: Report of the Non-Proliferation Alternative Systems Assessment Program (NASAP)," June 1980.

there is the possibility in this area for the government to divest itself of these assets, although an examination of that possibility is beyond the scope of this study. The recommendations given here would reduce the FY 1982 energy supply budget 26 percent below the FY 1981 level.

Energy Conservation

Energy conservation is an area in which governmental activity is difficult to justify. Higher prices give every energy user the incentive to conserve, and the proposed oil import tax would provide a special incentive to conserve imported oil. Money should be spent on conservation only when the cost can be recovered through future energy savings. Spending more than a dollar to save a dollar's worth of energy is not conservation — it is waste. The profit motive provides the right incentives for cost-effective conservation measures in the private sector. After all, insulation was not invented by DOE, and higher energy prices have certainly done more to encourage more insulation, more fuel-efficient automobiles, and other conservation measures than the government's energy policies.

The most easily justified energy expenditures are those that involve the development of new conservation technologies. Such investments are focused on projects with technical risks and long lead times. These projects are justified on the same grounds as the basic R&D expenditures under energy supply. Successful innovations will have the dual effects of lowering energy costs and providing the incentive for private sector R&D.

A gradual reduction in technology development expenditures will allow a continuation of some existing programs and thus facilitate their transfer to the private sector. The recommended FY 1982 budget of $250 million, which is 10 percent below the FY 1981 budget, should be adequate to continue the promising programs until private support can be obtained.

The remaining items in the conservation budget will cost more than they will return. Conservation grants are earmarked to low-income persons and public or non-profit institutions. Since the price system already provides the incentive to spend up to a dollar to conserve a dollar's worth of energy, these grants spend more to conserve than the value of the energy conserved. If there is concern about the burden of energy expenditures on low-income individuals, a better approach would provide the poor with cash payments, and let them decide whether it is better spent on energy conservation or something else. This same criticism applies to the residential and commercial conservation program, since that money would subsidize conservation investments, and thus would lead to an overinvestment in conservation.

The utility oil use reduction program suffers from the same weakness: more will be spent to conserve than the conservation is worth. This program is primarily geared toward shifting from oil to other fuel sources — most notably coal. Electric utilities already possess the incentive to reduce their use of oil when it is cost-effective, so additional spending will not only use taxpayers' dollars unwisely, but will also tend to increase utility bills as well.

The public information program (which proposes to spend $34 million in a national advertising campaign using television, magazines, radio, and newspapers) could also be dropped. While this is a small item, the money would probably buy more oil than the amount it would save if it were used to disseminate information.

Tax credits for conservation should be abolished for the same reason as grants for conservation. Individuals already possess the incentive for cost-effective conservation measures. Tax credits add to those incentives and thus encourage conservation that is not cost-effective.

Emergency Energy Preparedness

The Strategic Petroleum Reserve (SPR),[13] a stockpile of oil that could be used in the event of another oil embargo, is budgeted for $1.3 billion in FY 1981, $2.9 billion in FY 1982, and $4.0 billion in FY 1983. Planning for the SPR began in 1975, and it was originally authorized to store between 500 million and one billion barrels of oil. The initial cost-benefit analysis calculated the optimal size to be 500 million barrels and estimated that such a reserve could be in place by 1982 at a cost of between $7.5 and $8.0 billion.[14] Since that time, the cost estimates have drastically increased and the fill schedule has been slowed. Storage costs that were originally estimated at less than $1 per barrel rose to $3.50 per barrel by early 1979.[15] Incredibly, even as the price of oil was rising and therefore making the SPR less economical, the Department of Energy expanded the proposed size of the reserve from 500 million to one billion barrels.

The oil will be stored primarily along the gulf coast, and 91 million barrels of crude oil have already been placed in salt domes in Louisiana and Texas. Plans have been made to place the oil in such a manner that it can be channelled into the existing distribution system with a minimum of loss and delay. The pumps to retrieve the oil were not operating during the spring of 1979, so none of the oil in place at that time was available for use during that disruption. While the oil already stored could presumably be retrieved now, no oil has been placed in the SPR since the spring of 1979, largely because Saudi Arabia has

---

[13] Emergency standby rationing programs for gasoline and other petroleum products are being developed, but this funding has been included in the energy information, policy, and regulation budget, and is discussed in the next section.

[14] *Strategic Petroleum Reserve Plan* (Public Law 94–163, Sec. 154), December 15, 1976.

[15] *Energy Policy* (Washington: Congressional Quarterly, April 1979), p. 72.

made it clear that it does not want the SPR completed. In light of the political problems, cost overruns, and technical delays, it is certainly time to reassess the original cost-benefit analysis that first justified the SPR.

If another oil embargo were to occur in early 1981, if it were to be the same magnitude as the 1973–74 embargo, and if it were to last six months, the economic cost to the United States would be about $39 billion.[16] Taking this as the expected loss from a typical embargo, the question is whether this threat justifies the cost of the SPR.

The SPR, as it is currently planned, cannot be justified based upon realistic expectations concerning future embargoes, and the program should be terminated. A major change that has occurred since the original cost-benefit analysis (that could only recommend storage of 500 million barrels) is that the price of oil has risen tremendously. The original cost-benefit analysis estimated the price of oil to be under $12 per barrel, and oil is now selling for around $30 per barrel. If one billion barrels of oil worth $30 per barrel were stored, the opportunity cost would be $3 billion per year, assuming a conservative 10 percent interest rate. The interest cost alone makes the SPR a questionable investment. Consider this simple scenario.

Assume an oil embargo occurs every ten years, and a one billion barrel SPR is stored. The storage for ten years costs $47.7 billion, and the estimated cost of a six-month embargo is $39 billion. Even a 500 million barrel SPR would cost $24 billion over ten years, exclusive of construction and administrative costs. In addition, it is unlikely that the economy would suffer no harm even if the SPR were built, so the SPR would not save the entire $39 billion in the hypothetical embargo costs.

Further compounding the cost problem is the uncertainty surrounding the SPR. The DOE has not yet devised a use plan for the reserve. Without such a plan there is a distinct possibility that an embargo could be initiated and terminated before the debate about whether the SPR oil should be drawn down, who should get the oil, and at what price is concluded.

The partial cost figures just given illustrate that expected embargoes would have to occur fairly frequently for the SPR to be justified. A policymaker who expects frequent embargoes (perhaps as often as every five years) could argue in favor of the SPR, but it does appear that if an embargo were expected once every ten years the SPR would not be justifiable.

Some supporters argue that the SPR is valuable even if it is not used

---

[16] This figure is calculated from the model presented in R. Holcombe, "A Method for Estimating the GNP Loss From a Future Oil Embargo," *Policy Sciences* 8 (1977), pp. 217–234.

because it will act as a deterrent to future embargoes. OPEC would be less likely to stage an embargo if the U.S. were prepared. The reverse is probably true: OPEC would be more likely to embargo with an SPR than without one. One important factor in the likelihood of an embargo is the high price of oil. With oil selling at ten times its 1973 price, an oil embargo now would cost the embargoing nations ten times as much in foregone revenues as the 1973–74 embargo. A six-month embargo, for instance, would mean the loss of six month's worth of oil revenues if no SPR were in place. If an SPR were in place, oil could be used from the reserve to replace embargoed oil, but after the embargo, the SPR would surely be refilled. This would mean that the purchase of oil would only be delayed six months, since after the embargo normal purchases of oil plus the oil to refill the SPR would be shipped from the embargoing nations.

In fact, the embargoing nations may even make money on an embargo. The demand for oil is inelastic, meaning that purchases of increased quantities will result in much higher prices, and the higher prices after the embargo (caused by the demand for SPR oil) could more than compensate the embargoing nations for a temporary revenue loss. The SPR may actually encourage embargoes since with the SPR the oil revenues would not be lost, but simply deferred. This would make oil embargoes a more attractive tool for political manipulation.

The bottom line is that under plausible circumstances, the SPR cannot be justified even when only the cost of oil to fill it is considered. Given its large expected cost, its uncertain construction schedule, and the uncertainties about how DOE would use the stored oil if another embargo were to occur, the program should be terminated.

Energy Information, Policy, and Regulation

Energy information and policy fulfills two distinct roles: information collection and policy formation. The Energy Information Administration collects, analyzes, and forecasts information on reserves, consumption, imports, and other factors. The collection of information is critical both in evaluating energy policy and in the private sector. The Office of Policy and Evaluation is charged with the development of the National Energy Plan, the formulation of basic energy policies and program strategies, response to topics of congressional and presidential concern, and similar issues of policy formation. The Office of International Affairs cooperates with foreign governments in the development of energy policy and analysis. While the scope and philosophy of energy policy may need re-evaluation, the government certainly needs to develop an energy policy. Thus, the $140 million recommended for FY 1982 is the same as the Carter Administration's proposal.

The Federal Energy Regulatory Commission (FERC) dates from the Roosevelt Administration and is the oldest regulatory body concerned exclusively with energy matters. The FERC has had a significant role in the direct regulation of natural gas since this began in 1954. Currently, it is responsible for implementing the Natural Gas Policy Act. A recent positive step has been the approving of a phasing-out of natural gas price controls, which is consistent with an energy program designed to reduce imports. *Since its duties are essentially price fixing, an impediment to production, the FERC should be abolished.*

The Economic Regulatory Administration is responsible for price and allocation regulations, some aspects of the Fuel Use Act, and the development of the standby gasoline rationing plan. As a result of its administration of the price and allocation rules, the ERA is the center of considerable controversy. Many critics have charged that it is unfairly biased against industry and tends to promulgate undecipherable regulations. A 1979 Office of Management and Budget report lent considerable support to this criticism when it gave the Department of Energy the poorest rating in an assessment of federal regulations, accusing DOE of "...hastily issuing poorly analyzed regulations that have grown into a tangled, confused and error-filled mess...." Such regulations have a negative effect on production, which is clearly opposed to the national interest.

In September of 1981, the price and allocation controls will expire, eliminating a major portion of the ERA's responsibility. If its other regulatory activities were ended at that time, its only remaining responsibility would be the standby allocation plan, which has been plagued with difficulties from the beginning and would undoubtedly cause more problems than it solves.

DOE has been working on a gasoline allocation plan since its inception as the Federal Energy Office in 1973. The present version is to distribute ration coupons based on car ownership. Hardship applications, which would entitle recipients to more coupons, would be considered by—of course—an enlarged bureaucracy. Coupons could be bought and sold legally. ERA is currently working on a similar plan for the allocation of diesel fuel.

In the event of another embargo, automobile owners would purchase some gasoline at lower (controlled) prices, but would have to pay the market price (controlled price plus the cost of a rationing coupon) for any additional gasoline. Owners of automobiles would thus receive a windfall profit by getting rationing coupons at no cost. But taxpayers have already been paying for years to finance the design of this scheme and will continue to do so under the proposed budget. A better plan is to save the tax dollars and do away with the allocation plan. Unfortunately, one of the important lessons that went unlearned after the last embargo is that mandated allocation plans make things worse, not better.

In summary, the Energy Regulatory Administration should be abandoned, thereby saving taxpayers both the cost of tax dollars to finance it and the additional cost of regulation. Price controls and mandated allocation plans make matters worse, and it is senseless to spend tax dollars to design a system that will misallocate resources.

The Nuclear Regulatory Commission is responsible for regulating the siting, construction, and operation of all civilian nuclear reactors. Additional NRC responsibilities include the regulation both of nuclear fuel storage and radioactive waste disposal. While there are considerable doubts about the long-term future of nuclear power, at present it is a proven technology with the greatest short-term potential for producing cost-effective energy to replace imported oil. Thus, it is important that there be an effective and visible NRC capable of winning the confidence of the public.

The Recommended Budget

This analysis finds that $4.5 billion for FY 1982 would be the ideal energy budget, and the method recommended to realize this goal is to allocate the desired budget level to each category and add $2 billion in transitional funding to phase out those areas scheduled to be cut. These funds could be used to meet prior commitments that the government has made and to finish projects nearing completion. *Indeed, under this plan DOE could be eliminated as a Cabinet-level agency, with its remaining components being returned to the agencies from where they came. The elimination of DOE as a single agency would insulate somewhat the ongoing R&D effort from short-term public policy issues.*

In addition to the transitional funds, anticipated revenues from the oil import tax are included in Table 2. The $5.1 billion in revenues assumes a $2 per barrel tax on 7 million barrels of imports per day. The net cost of the recommended energy programs is $1.4 billion, a $12.9 billion reduction, or over 90 percent below the estimated FY 1982 cost.

LONG-TERM CONSIDERATIONS

This essay was written specifically as part of a budget study, but since basic energy policy issues dictate the shape of the budget, it would be useful to take a wider view. The nation's current energy policy is not geared toward solving domestic energy problems, but toward encouraging expenditures in unproven and uneconomical energy sources while discouraging the production of domestic oil, natural

Table 2
Energy
(in millions of dollars)

Major missions and programs	1982 estimate	1982 recommended
OUTLAYS		
Energy supply:		
Promotion of domestic production:		
Synthetic fuels promotion:		
Existing law	*	0
Proposed legislation	60	0
Biomass (proposed).	45	0
Solar bank (proposed)	146	0
Research, development, demonstration and applications:		
Solar	674	460
Other renewable resources	678	645
Fossil:		
Existing law	1,374	
Proposed legislation	50	
Nuclear fission:		
Existing law	858	989
Proposed legislation	− 36	858
Other technology.	872	608
Direct production (net):		
Uranium enrichment.	214	214
Petroleum reserves	− 2,324	− 2,324
Power marketing.	1,867	1,867
Subtotal	4,478	3,317
Energy conservation:		
Technology development	309	250
Conservation grants	648	0
Utility oil use reduction (proposed).	979	0
Public information and others	54	0
Residential and commercial conservation (proposed)	504	0
Subtotal	2,494	250
Emergency energy preparedness:		
Strategic petroleum reserve:		
Existing law	2,912	
Proposed legislation	14	
Subtotal	2,926	0
Energy information, policy, and regulation:		
Energy information and policy	140	140
Regulation:		
Federal Energy Regulatory Commission . . .	77	0
Economic Regulatory Administration	134	0
Nuclear Regulatory Commission.	474	476
Alaska gas pipeline inspector	36	36
Administrative expenses (Department of Energy).	325	261
Subtotal	1,186	913
Deductions for offsetting receipts	− 74	
Total, outlays.	**11,010**	**4,480**

Table 2 (Cont.)
Energy
(in millions of dollars)

Major missions and programs	1982 estimate	1982 recommended
Off-Budget Item:		
Energy Security Corporation	2,500	0
Tax Credits for Energy Conservation	739	0
Total Energy Program Cost	14,249	4,480
Revenues from Oil Import Tax	0	– 5,110
Recommended Transitional Funds	0	2,000
Total	14,249	1,370

Source: The Budget of the United States Government FY 1981.

gas, and nuclear power, all of which have the proven ability to produce energy. Our best policy is to develop our proven strengths, rather
than hindering their development and emphasizing unproven energy
sources.

The cornerstone of the proposals in this chapter is the oil import
tax, actually proposed by President Nixon in April 1973, about six
months before the 1973–74 embargo, specifically to control the level
of imports. The oil import tax would reduce imports, increase conservation and domestic petroleum production, and encourage the development of alternative energy sources, but only when they are
economically justified. The role of government should be to emphasize research, collect information, and formulate policy.

The most immediate priority in energy policy is to eliminate the
tangle of government regulations, such as price controls and other disincentives, that inhibit domestic energy production. An excellent case
is the so-called windfall profits tax on the oil industry, which is really
an excise tax on oil. It is not in the national interest to place an extra
tax burden on an energy producing industry. Similarly, price controls
on natural gas that date back to 1954 also hinder the domestic production of energy. The key to any successful energy policy must be the restructuring of incentives so that private enterprise is able to profit
from the production of energy.

The goals of the U.S. energy policy should be to reduce oil imports,
at a minimum cost to the nation, and to create an incentive for importers to take into account the political costs they impose on the nation. These goals can best be achieved by:

1. Restructuring government rules and regulations to provide an incentive for domestic energy production; and

2. The imposition of an oil import tax to discourage imports.

In its zeal, the government has tried to solve the energy crisis by spending, but poorly conceived policies have aggravated rather than helped the energy situation. Milton Friedman observed, "There is an energy crisis because the government has decreed that there shall be one."[17] The proposals in this essay would provide a foundation for a more sensible energy policy and save the taxpayers billions of dollars at the same time.

---

[17] Friedman, *op. cit.*, p. 70.

Natural Resources
and the Environment

by Gordon S. Jones

At about $13 billion, the Natural Resources and Environment function is neither the smallest nor the largest piece of the federal pie. It is, however, a substantial amount of money, and is, more significantly, a piece of the pie that is "controllable," in that it is not obligated on the basis of open-ended formulae, carrying over from year to year. The function contains those government programs which have to do with the management of the natural resource base on which the nation depends for its raw materials, its energy, and for its quality of life.

The bulk of expenditures now being made for natural resources and environmental protection are unnecessary. Through the elimination of those programs which do not involve third party costs (or at least returning them to the states for administration) substantial savings can be achieved. Furthermore, the application of economic incentives and constraints, such as users' fees and effluent taxes, will increase efficiency, while at the same time reducing federal spending.

The programs of Natural Resources and Environment fall into five missions: (1) Pollution Control and Abatement; (2) Water Resources; (3) Conservation and Land Management; (4) Recreational Resources; and (5) Other Natural Resources. This last, catch-all mission includes the U.S. Geological Survey, mapping activities, oceanic and atmospheric programs, and general function revenues from oil and gas leases. Royalties and fees charged for other services provided by the government are also included in this mission. Its budgetary impact is relatively small, and its revenues exceed its costs slightly. It will not receive major consideration in this essay. Also, for purposes of this essay, Mission 4, Recreational Resources, will not be considered separately, but as part of Mission 3, Conservation and Land Management.

Pollution Control and Abatement

The pollution control and abatement programs of the federal government are of fairly recent vintage. The environmental activism of

Table 1
Natural Resources and the Environment
(in millions of dollars)

Major missions and programs	1979 actual	1980 estimate	1981 estimate
OUTLAYS			
Pollution control and abatement:			
Regulatory and research programs .	938	991	1,106
Oil and hazardous substance liability fund (proposed)	–	–	45
Oil pollution funds:			
Existing law	13	31	19
Proposed legislation	–	–	– 13
Sewage, treatment plant construction grants	3,756	3,900	3,950
Subtotal, pollution control and abatement.	4,706	4,922	5,107
Water resources:			
Existing law	3,897	4,214	4,118
Proposed legislation	–	–	3
Subtotal, water resources	3,897	4,214	4,121
Conservation and land management:			
Management of national forests, cooperative forestry and forestry research	1,536	1,662	1,755
Management of public lands	395	448	444
Mining reclamation and enforcement	48	114	158
Conservation of agricultural lands .	559	572	562
Other, including offsetting receipts .	– 654	– 541	– 673
Subtotal, conservation and land management	1,884	2,256	2,245
Recreational resources:			
Land and water conservation fund .	600	451	489
Urban recreation grants	*	74	74
Operation of recreational resources	913	938	936
Subtotal, recreational resources.	1,513	1,463	1,499
Other natural resources:			
Existing law	1,273	1,366	1,449
Proposed legislation	–	–	19
Subtotal, other natural resources.	1,273	1,366	1,468
Deductions for offsetting receipts	– 1,183	– 1,445	– 1,622
Total, outlays.	**12,091**	**12,776**	**12,819**

*500 thousand or less.
Source: The Budget of the United States Government FY 1981

the 1960s and 1970s produced the Environmental Protection Agency (created by Executive Order in 1970) and legislation authorizing EPA to regulate pollutants and polluters directly. Major legislation has been passed providing regulatory authority for air, water, pesticides and other toxic substances, radiation, noise, and solid wastes. EPA also administers a program of grants to local communities designed to help them cope with the problems of disposing of waste water. The National Environmental Policy Act of 1969, which created the Council on Environmental Quality, established a framework under which environmental protection is carried out, but did not establish a major budgetary program that need be considered here.

EPA's regulatory activities are of two distinct types. The more common programs (air and water pollution control) set absolute limits on the amount of pollutants that are permitted to enter the environment. Strategies are devised to prevent increments of clean air and water from being used up, and regulations are promulgated forcing polluters to reach the standards set. Noise, radiation, and solid wastes are also subject to this approach to environmental regulation.

Pesticide and toxic substance regulation are radically different. In these programs, the substances themselves are registered as safe and effective, and the details of their use specified by federal permits. EPA activity in this area is similar to the traditional regulatory activity of such agencies as the Food and Drug Administration and the Consumer Product Safety Commission.

Although all EPA programs are theoretically cooperative programs, operated in conjunction with and through the agencies of the several states, they are, in fact, among the most "federal" of all government programs, widely recognized as being imposed from the top down.

The water and sewer grant program consists of a cost-sharing program with local governments to assist them in treating water at the back end of the use cycle: after it is dirty. Prior to passage of the Clean Water Act in 1972, there was a small program under which costs were shared equally. Under the Clean Water Act, the federal share was increased to 75 percent, despite widespread predictions that the change would lead to inevitable waste. Waste has, in fact, been the result. In 1972, EPA projected the total lifetime cost of the program to be about $12.6 billion (the National League of Cities estimate was $21 billion higher). Although $34 billion has already been spent, the additional costs of completing the program are now estimated to be well over $100 billion.

Initial funding levels for the water and sewer grant program were set at $5 billion for the first year, $6 billion the second, and $7 billion the third. Only half that much was actually provided, until a lawsuit by the City of New York forced the release of the balance, leading to a $9 billion appropriation in a single year. Since then, the annual level of funding has settled at $3 to $3.5 billion a year.

Although the local share of these projects is set at 25 percent, in practice, most of the cities and towns receive state assistance as well, so that they sometimes pay as little as 5 percent of the actual construction costs. The grants are for construction only, with no money available for actual operation of the plants.

Water Resources

The public works programs involve the development of the nation's water resources and their management for the provision of water and water transportation. These programs are conducted primarily by three agencies of the federal government, located in three separate departments.

The Army Corps of Engineers is the oldest of the agencies charged with water resource development. Civil works programs planned and carried out by the Corps date back to 1824. The program of the Whig Party included the development of the economic infrastructure (though the Whigs would not have called it that) by the national government. The immediate task was the construction of dams, canals, harbors, locks, and other structures necessary to convert the nation's rivers and coastal waters into transportation highways. The Army was at hand, with its corps of trained engineers, and it received the mission.

The mission remains in effect today. The Corps plans and executes construction projects designed to provide flood control benefits, to expedite transportation and to lower its costs, to provide water for municipal, industrial, and recreational use, and to enhance the environment both for its own sake and for the benefit of fish and wildlife. The Corps also assists state and local governments with environmental protection and pollution abatement.

In the West, the nation's dam builder is more likely to be the Water and Power Resources Service, formerly the Bureau of Reclamation,[1] located within the Department of the Interior. Created in 1902 for the purpose of helping reclaim spring runoff in the arid West for use in irrigating land otherwise too dry for agriculture, the operations of the Service are restricted to the seventeen contiguous western states and Hawaii.

Corps undertakings are primarily for flood control, but may include some irrigation projects. The situation is reversed with Water and Power Resources: the primary benefits are intended to be irriga-

---

[1] Popular disaffection with "bureaucrats" and "bureaus" has led to a number of name changes of this sort in recent years.

tion, but may include flood control, electric power, and recreation, as ancillary benefits. The Service operates and maintains about fifty hydroelectric facilities, and has under construction another thirty or so projects designed to develop additional water for the West.

The third of the water development agencies also concentrates its efforts in the West. The Soil Conservation Service, located within the Department of Agriculture, came into being in 1935, and is designed to promote the agricultural capability of the nation through the construction of soil erosion control and irrigation facilities. The Service is divided into almost 3,000 conservation districts, which cover the entire United States, and which provide technical assistance to landowners, in addition to major flood control and erosion control projects. The bulk of the Service's activities are in rural areas, and the Service has thus assumed a substantial role in rural development.

Corps of Engineer projects are essentially provided free, at least when flood control and navigational benefits are their expressed aim. When irrigation benefits are involved, some reimbursement is required. The same is true with respect to Water and Power Service projects, and Soil Conservation Service projects. However, the payback formulae and schedules vary widely and arbitrarily. There are, in fact, dozens of different schedules. Two identical projects might be paid back in radically different ways, over different time periods.

Conservation and Land Management

The nation's public domain consists of 762 million acres of land,[2] about one-third of the total on-shore land mass of the fifty states. In addition, the federal government retains control over the mineral rights on 63 million acres of land previously sold or given to private owners or state governments.

Although virtually all federal agencies own small amounts of land, most of them have only "acquired land," which is land purchased from private owners or local governments for the specific purpose of carrying on the work of the agency. The "public lands" are conceptually different, consisting for the most part of land in federal ownership because of cession from states or other nations, conquest, or purchase from foreign governments. The vast bulk of this public domain is managed by four land management agencies.

The Bureau of Land Management (BLM), located within the De-

---

[2] The actual size of the public domain is lost in a maze of definitions as to provenance, management, reservation of rights, maintenance of easements, and so on. The numbers in the text give an idea of the magnitudes involved, but they understate the impact of federal land ownership. Because much state and private land is totally surrounded by federal land, in a "checkerboard" pattern, federal management practices essentially dictate state and private practices, and access to state and private lands is often controlled by the federal land manager.

partment of the Interior, is the largest of the land management agencies, controlling about 470 million acres. The primary management function of BLM is the allocation of grazing rights on the land, and its maintenance and protection for the purpose of grazing. BLM land is also open to mineral and energy production under the 1872 Mining Act and various other mineral and energy leasing acts. About 14,000 operators graze sheep, cattle, and horses on the public range under the provisions of the 1934 Taylor Grazing Act. Grazing is allowed on over 250 million acres of BLM land (and on substantial acreage in the National Forests, wilderness areas, and National Parks, under different statutes). Mining activities are conducted on about 6 million acres of BLM land.[3]

The National Park Service (NPS) is also located within DOI. By definition, lands administered by the NPS are not managed for multiple use.[4] They are largely withdrawn from mineral entry, cannot be grazed under normal Taylor Grazing Act procedures, and are not ordinarily open to energy exploration and development. Park Service lands are set aside primarily to provide for natural and unspoiled recreation. For that reason, they are funded under the Recreational Resources mission. The lands managed by the NPS are among the most spectacular in the nation. The Service administers 326 "units"[5] which include thirty-nine National Parks and thirty-one recreation areas. Total NPS holdings are 23.3 million acres. The Service even operates bookstores, such as the one at the National Visitor's Center in Washington, D.C.

The Fisheries and Wildlife Service (FWS), formerly the Bureau of Sport Fisheries and Wildlife, is the third major land management agency within DOI, and is responsible for 26.6 million acres of land, most of which are in National Wildlife Refuges and Ranges. Although other compatible uses are not prohibited, the management priority is the single objective of wildlife preservation and enhancement.

In addition to its land management responsibilities, the FWS also includes the Office of Endangered Species. Although this office has a relatively minor direct budgetary impact, the indirect costs it imposes on industry and the public at large are considerable.

---

[3] The raw numbers of acres touched by mining activity vastly overstates the actual impact of mining. With the exception of strip mining activity (not the rule in the West), mining is compatible with most other uses of the land.

[4] The concept of "multiple use" is somewhat nebulous. The multiple uses include, but are not limited to, recreation, grazing, mining, logging, preservation, wildlife protection, and habitation.

[5] A Park Service "unit" may include more than one reservation or holding. For example, the National Capital Area Unit includes separate national monuments (Washington, Lincoln, Jefferson, etc.) within the Capital, Arlington Cemetery, the National Visitors' Center, and so on.

The last major land management agency is the National Forest Service (NFS) and it is not located within DOI, but within the Department of Agriculture. The responsibility of the NFS is to manage the timbered lands of the United States for the sustained yield of timber and wood fiber. Sustained yield management is not incompatible with other uses, such as recreation, grazing, and mining, and Forest Service lands are classified as multiple use lands. The Forest Service manages 186.9 million acres of such lands. Obviously some of these management functions result in revenues to the government, the most important of these being lease sales and royalties from gas, oil, and minerals, grazing fees, and timber sales.

SHORT-TERM POLICIES

Pollution Control and Abatement

The federal government's regulation of the environment has produced classic illustrations of institutionalized political conflict. It has undeniably produced some improvement in air and water quality. The question is whether more could have been achieved with less cost to the economy, in monetary terms, and to the body politic in terms of institutional stress.

Regulatory and Research Programs

When Congress chose, at the urging of the environmental community, to adopt a set of absolute standards for air and water pollution, it guaranteed a long and difficult political battle. Faced with the political fact of absolute standards, industry invested substantial effort in defeating, delaying, and modifying the standards. Industry's response was predictable and predicted. It was cost-effective to fight, given the massive investment that would have been required to achieve the required clean-up.

Detroit's ten-year battle with EPA is only the most publicized of the struggles. During the ten years since Congress first set auto emission standards, those standards have been relaxed several times, and substantially modified. In fact, it has been argued, cars are no cleaner now than they would have been in the absence of the standards.[6] In the meantime, the auto industry has had technology and timetables thrust upon it, and been forced to tool and re-tool as trends in pollution control have changed.

The costs of this tooling and re-tooling are not direct expenditures of the government, and they do not show up in budget figures (except as a line item for the relief of Chrysler Corporation). Nevertheless,

---

[6]See, for example, Howard Margolis, "The Politics of Auto Emissions," in *The Public Interest,* Fall 1977, No. 47.

they are real costs to the taxpayer in his capacity as consumer. The magnitude of the costs involved may be judged from a single requirement of the Clean Water Act. The Clean Water Act requires that, by 1985, the nation's industry will have eliminated all discharges of pollutants into the nation's waterways. The goal is, of course, nonsense, and it is a measure of the realism of the nation's lawmakers that it was written into statute. The cost of attaining this chimera was estimated in 1975 as $320 billion.[7] Again, that is a cost to the consumer, but not to the taxpayer.

When the Congress undertakes re-authorization of the Clean Air and Water Acts in the 97th Congress, some form of effluent tax (tax on emissions) should be adopted to replace the outmoded and inefficient technique of absolute standards. Effluent standards have the merit of being applicable to all companies, rather than simply to the largest; they enlist the creative energies of America's entrepreneurs on the side of clean-up rather than on the side of procrastination; and they produce revenue. Besides permitting a drastic reduction in the size of the EPA regulatory structure, the entire budget of EPA could be funded out of the fees or taxes imposed. In addition, costs to industry and consumers would be lower. Charles Schultze and Allen Kneese reported in 1975 that a strategy of effluent taxes could produce the same levels of clean-up at one-fifth the cost.[8] A recent EPA-commissioned study estimated that similar control levels for certain automobile emissions could be reached for one-tenth to one-fourth the cost through use of market incentives.[9]

EPA's other regulatory programs are harder to justify. It is difficult to see what the national (as opposed to individual and local) interest is in noise pollution. Certainly there is an interest in a quieter environment, but it is difficult to defend national noise standards. To the extent that government has a function in regulating noise, local government is obviously better equipped to make the kind of flexible response required.

The noise control program does illustrate that the clamor for federal regulation is not all from the environmental community. Industry, in an effort to attain some predictability and uniformity, is often the strongest proponent of federal pre-emption. However, the costs of the federal regulatory apparatus, while relatively small, are still significant, and industry has managed to cope with a complex

---

[7] Allen V. Kneese, and Charles L. Schultze, *Pollution, Prices, and Public Policy.* (Washington, D.C.: Brookings Institution, 1975), p. 21.

[8] *Ibid.*, p. 23.

[9] "An Analysis of Alternative Policies for Attaining and Maintaining a Short-Term NO_2 Standard," Mathtech, Inc. (1980). The final report is to be completed by the end of 1980.

local regulatory structure before. *All federal noise programs, with the exception of some minor informational functions, should be eliminated, and the local governments left free to adopt standards in response to their local conditions.*

The case for federal solid waste programs is even less persuasive. While air and water pollution, existing in fluids, are by definition general problems, the same is not true of solid wastes. These are purely local matters, which can be handled perfectly well by local governments. *Again, EPA should perhaps act as a clearinghouse for information and technology, but its direct regulatory functions should be eliminated.*

The federal government does have a role in the regulation of radioactive materials, as the result of legislation adopted at the beginning of the nuclear age. Barring some modification in that national policy (which is not recommended here), that responsibility will continue. Nevertheless, it is not clear that the bifurcation of responsibility between EPA and the Nuclear Regulatory Commission (NRC) is necessary or desirable. *EPA's nuclear responsibilities should be transferred to the NRC.*

The remaining EPA regulatory functions are in pesticides and toxic substances. In both cases, EPA is wrestling with impossible tasks. The variety of chemicals used in the United States is enormous, and their regulation by a single agency impossible. It is, moreover, presumptuous. Many of the states have been regulating pesticides for as long as fifty years. All of them had regulatory programs of some kind before Washington got into the act. The United States Department of Agriculture, through its extension agents, carried out a program of providing localized advice to users and growers, a program which generally assured safe usage without danger to consumers or to crops.

This flexible system was wiped out with a stroke by a system of federal registration of pesticides with specific products tied to specific crops and specific pests.[10] The result has been a tremendous increase in the costs of registering pesticides, tremendous delays and backlogs in registering products and uses, and virtually universal violations of the law. It is, for example, a violation of federal law for a homeowner to use a mildew spray on his roses if the product is registered only for use against mildew on tomatoes.

The costs of registering a pesticide are now so great that smaller

---

[10] The Department of Agriculture registered pesticides prior to the creation of EPA, but the regulatory effect was on the manufacturer, not on the individual user. It was a violation of law to sell an unregistered pesticide (in interstate commerce), but using a pesticide in an unregistered manner was not a violation. Additionally, the states maintained extensive registration programs of their own, registering thousands of pesticides for intrastate use. Those state programs are now virtually obsolete.

companies cannot afford them. Competition is thus reduced. The consumer's choice is further reduced by the unavailability of pesticides for "specialty crops." These are crops grown in such limited quantities that the costs of registering pesticides for use on them cannot be recouped by the manufacturer. The specialty crop must go unprotected, the law must be broken, or the government must undertake the registration. None of these alternatives is particularly satisfactory.

The preference for federal action is ideological and political. *EPA's pesticide regulatory functions should be returned to the states and to the Department of Agriculture, from whence they came. The problem of pesticide runoff is a water pollution problem, and should be handled not through the registration/regulation process, but through effluent charges under the water pollution control program.*

The regulatory budget of the Environmental Protection Agency is about $1.6 billion. Proper allocation of these functions between federal and local levels of government, the transfer of radiation programs and a limited pesticide program to other agencies would save most of that amount in FY 1982. The remaining air and water protection programs would be financed by the effluent taxes which would constitute the new regulatory mechanism. Because the environment budget is spread among all of the EPA programs, more definite estimates of budget savings are not possible.

Sewage Treatment Plant Construction Grants

The components of the sewage treatment grant program seem to have been assembled for the purposes of wasting the taxpayer's money. Because the local share of the expense is never more than 25 percent, and often much less, there is no incentive to economize on design of the plants. Consequently, the tendency has been to build plants with capacity far in excess of what is required, using the most expensive construction techniques. In addition, the sophistication often built into the plants makes them difficult to maintain and to operate.

Since 1973, a total of $34 billion has been expended on this program, but only $5.2 billion worth of plants have been completed. For the completed plants, the operating downtime rate is 62 percent, clear evidence that the nation has under construction an enormous herd of white elephants.

Building plants more complicated than necessary has other pernicious side effects: the plants take too long to build. That fact alone assures massive cost overruns, since time is the most expensive construction factor. The relatively small appropriation is spread over such a large number of plants under construction that each moves ahead only a little each year. The manner of financing, coupled with an inflation rate of 12–18 percent, guarantees cost escalation, and accounts for a part of the rise in the "needs assessment" from $12.6 billion when the program began to over $106 billion today. EPA now projects that, at a $4.5 billion annual appropriation,[11] it will take twenty-six years to complete the construction of only the highest priority treatment plants. It is obvious that this projection will also slip.

Other serious budgetary pressures are at work on the grant program. One proposal is to permit the funds to be used to build water supply facilities, as well as waste treatment facilities. Another is to permit the funds to be used for environmental cleanup, such as for PCBs spilled in the Hudson River. If these initiatives succeed, the potential for expansion of the program is virtually limitless, and the impact on the taxpayer obvious.

One pressure has already been yielded to. Although the construction of facilities used for the treatment of industrial wastewater is permitted by the Water Pollution Control Act, municipalities were originally required to recover the costs from the benefitting industry. That requirement has now been removed. Until it is restored, the taxpayer will continue to subsidize industries which are often perfectly solvent and profitable.

Some immediate remedies for the problems of the construction grant program are obvious: cost-recovery for industrial services; strict limitations on the kinds of facilities that can be built with the grants; and, as a hedge against wasteful plant design and construction methods, an increase in the local share. *A more radical solution would involve the adoption of a repayment contract, or the elimination of the program altogether.* This is, in fact, the proper course. The program is simply a mechanism for cross-subsidization, since virtually every community has waste water treatment problems. No costs are reduced by the cross-subsidy. In fact, as has been seen, costs are substantially increased. Every municipality has an incentive to extract the maximum grant from the common treasury. Elimination of this program now would save the taxpayer more than $3.5 billion per year, beginning in 1982.

Water Resources

The construction of major water projects by the federal government is an enormously expensive endeavor. A single project, the Central Arizona Project in the Salt River Basin, is now expected to cost $1.8 billion, or $750 for every man, woman and child in Arizona. The project will keep water costs low enough that the citizens of Pheonix can continue to water their lawns with culinary water.

In a similar undertaking, costs are escalating so rapidly on the Central Utah Projects that the annual appropriation for continued work is

---

[11] Actual appropriation levels have been running at just about $13 billion per year.

less than the annual increase in total project costs. Apparently, the project will never be finished. The project directors have already started looking for new funding mechanisms. If they succeed, the price of water in Salt Lake City will remain unrealistically cheap: water that costs $2 in Utah costs as much as $13 in Pennsylvania.

The Tennessee-Tombigbee Canal, a proposal to connect the Tennessee River at Pickwick Pool with the Gulf of Mexico at Mobile, Alabama, which would essentially duplicate the already existing Tennessee-Ohio-Mississippi waterway, is projected to cost as much as $4 billion. Charges and countercharges fill the air when this project is debated on Capitol Hill. One side claims a cost/benefit ratio of slightly over 1.0 (does that include benefits from an unauthorized section of the proposal? Does it include benefits for a company that has now gone out of business? No one knows); the other side produces figures showing that the cost/benefit ratio is really 0.23 to 1.00.

The controversy over these and a hundred other projects like them is wasteful, expensive, and time-consuming. Given the nature of our political system, it is unlikely that a definite solution could ever be achieved. Water construction programs are plagued with an inherent inefficiency, and an intractable problem of declining institutional support. The agency which carries out the construction of the project is also the agency which conceives of the project, designs it, moves it through the political process to authorization, and then shepherds it annually through the appropriations minefield. Projects are pushed according to the priorities of the agency, and not according to the priorities either of the nation as a whole or even of the specific constituency which will benefit from the project.

It is certainly time to explore alternative ways of accomplishing water development. Most important is the need for a mechanism for determining whether or not individual projects are worth their costs. Inevitably, that means the adoption of market tests of the costs and benefits of projects. There is no theoretical reason why government should build dams, dredge harbors, or dig canals.

Although such projects as the Tennessee-Tombigbee are massive and expensive, they are certainly not beyond the capability of private finance. (A consortium of pipeline and energy companies currently is putting together a financing package for the construction of a natural gas pipeline from the North Slope of Alaska to the American Midwest, the largest construction project in the history of the world. This pipeline is expected to cost more than $12 billion, far more than the most expensive water project, and yet it is to be built entirely without public funds.) The beneficiaries of the Tenn-Tom will be specific individuals and companies; the region is a secondary beneficiary, and the nation a beneficiary only at distant remove. There is no compelling federal interest in the construction of this project, or any other project designed to assist navigation for private individuals.

The federal government should immediately adopt a requirement for payback for the capital costs of navigational waterway construction. Administration of the repayment would be accomplished through a regional waterway authority, which would assess waterway user fees.* Under legislation adopted in the 95th Congress, users of the navigation system already built and operated by the Corps of Engineers on the Mississippi River began paying into a waterway trust fund on October 1, 1980. The payments are raised by a tax on fuel set at 4¢ per gallon initially, rising to 6¢ per gallon after one year. At this rate, the tax will produce only about 10 percent of the construction expenditures of the Corps for upgrading and maintaining the system. This is a beginning, but it is obvious that the waterway authority will have to find other funds to assure that the general taxpayer does not continue to pay for a waterway system which benefits primarily specific individuals.

In addition to the capital subsidy, the operating costs of this system are borne entirely by the federal taxpayer. *It is essential that actual users of the systems (including pleasure boat operators) begin to pay the costs of operation through a system of lockage fees, congestion fees, and other user charges.* The operating subsidy in the federal budget now totals $950 million per year, which could be saved outright. The waterway authority should eventually replace the federal government as the operator of the system.

What is true for navigational water projects is true in no small measure for reclamation water projects in the West, although reclamation projects are repaid. Their costs are not beyond the ability of private enterprise to finance, and their current rates of subsidization permit water and services to be sold to the public at unrealistically low prices. A number of specific steps should be taken immediately.

(1) *The agency planning the project must be separated from the agency carrying out the construction and operation of the project.* This step would eliminate the conflict of interest outlined above, and would do much to rebuild public support for those projects which are necessary.

(2) *Local jurisdictions should plan and set priorities.* So long as funding is almost entirely federal, that ideal is unattainable. The local share of water projects should be increased, giving local government more say in setting priorities and introducing incentives to save money.

An increase in the local share of water project funding would not necessarily permit a substantial cut in the present federal construction budget. The single most expensive factor in project development is the cost of time and inflation. If the federal government is going to continue to fund water projects, the present levels of federal spending, about $4 billion per year, should be maintained, even if local spending is increased to a similar level.

In the meantime, there are some institutional reforms which would improve efficiency and reduce costs at least marginally.

A superior solution is to fund all projects now under construction totally in one year, thus discharging the federal commitment. All new projects should be built by consortia of local governments, without federal participation. The one-year, FY 1982 cost of this recommendation would probably be about $20 billion, but the federal government would be able to save $4–5 billion annually thereafter. Similar treatment of the Soil and Conservation Service irrigation projects would save another $500 million annually.

If the federal government is to retain a dam-building function, one agency, not three, should be responsible. Consolidation of the construction function would allow regularization of the payback schedules. *The myriad of payback schedules and cost-sharing formulae now in existence should give way to a single schedule,* at a somewhat higher level than at present, as already noted. A 50–50 percent split would most nearly harmonize the principles of local responsibility and federal assistance.

Conservation and Land Management

The present pattern of land ownership by the federal government is, in a manner of speaking, an historical accident. Land management is not one of the functions of the federal government outlined in the Constitution. Throughout most of the nation's history, no one contemplated or advocated a large-scale, permanent land management function for Washington.

Government has always owned land, of course. The land west of the Thirteen Colonies was originally thought to belong to the colonies individually, as their boundaries extended westward. As the nation came into existence, those western territories, amounting to 237 million acres, were ascribed to the national government. The Louisiana Purchase of 1803 brought almost 530 million acres of land and water into federal ownership, and other cessions and purchases brought in another billion acres or so.

About two-thirds, then, of the land mass of the United States was at one time "owned" by the federal government. Obviously, half of that land has been disposed of. The disposition began immediately, as unsettled land west of the original colonies began to be transferred to states as they, in turn, came into existence. In 1806, for example, the United States received title to what were then western territories of North Carolina; in 1846, that same land became the State of Tennessee. Land in federal ownership was also transferred to individuals, as

118

the prairies were opened to settlement under homesteading laws designed to encourage the westward expansion of the nation.

This federal policy of disposing of unsettled, unreserved[12] land continued until 1976. The passage of the Federal Land Policy Management Act (FLPMA) in that year provided the Bureau of Land Management with its "organic act," and institutionalized the permanent federal ownership of land other than the reserved lands of the National Forest and Parks.[13]

The formal change reflected, as formal changes usually do, a shift in the public perception of the federal government's responsibilities towards the land area of the United States. The change had taken place over time, and by 1970, when the Public Land Law Review Commission made its report, its recommendation that "the policy of large-scale disposal of public lands reflected by the majority of statutes in force today be revised" provoked few cries of outrage.[14] Public land ownership had acquired a constituency more powerful than the land-use interests.

The bureaucracy of the federal land management agencies was itself a prime component of this constituency, as was a growing and influential environmentalist/preservationist movement. This latter group includes many opposed to growth, production, and consumption on philosophical and selfish grounds.[15]

Today it is widely believed that the lands which remain in the public domain are the undesirable lands, so dry that neither state nor individual will take them. This view is both false and costly.

Demand for land west of the 100th meridian has been constant since the early 1800s. It has not been disposed of because a Congress ill-acquainted with the West always imposed unrealistic conditions of

---

[12] "Unreserved" lands are those not dedicated to some specific use, such as National Forests or Parks, wildlife refuges or monuments. In practice, the "unreserved" lands are lands managed by the Bureau of Land Management, although under the Roadless Area Review and Evaluation, vast acreages of BLM land have also been withdrawn from multiple use.

[13] This Act passed by unanimous consent during the final moments of the 94th Congress, and could have been stopped by the objection of a single senator.

[14] *One Third of the Nation's Land: A Report to the President and to the Congress by the Public Land Law Review Commission,* GPO (1970) p. 1.

[15] See, for example, William Tucker, "Environmentalism and the Leisure Class," *Harper's,* December 1977; John Baden, *et al.,* "Environmentalists and Self-Interest: How Pure are Those Who Desire The Pristine?" in John Baden, ed., *Earth Day Reconsidered,* (Washington, D.C.: The Heritage Foundation, 1980); Thomas W. Hazlett, *The California Coastal Commission and the Economics of Environmentalism* (Los Angeles, International Institute for Economic Research, 1980); Bernard J. Frieden, "The New Regulation Comes to Suburbia," *The Public Interest,* No. 55, Spring 1979.

size and operation on the land. The land could not be used in the most economic fashion, and so was either unclaimed or abused.[16]

There is no question that the vast bulk of the public lands could have been disposed of profitably, and to the advantage of all citizens, had Washington been willing to adopt a realistic attitude towards conditions in the semi-arid West, and permit the land to be disposed of in blocks large enough for grazing or farming.[17] John Wesley Powell surveyed the nation's land in 1878 and recommended disposition of the range lands to private owners as a way of preserving its quality.[18]

The present situation is unsatisfactory to all parties. The land remains in public ownership, but private parties are permitted to use it. Since the land is potentially productive, with proper management, the federal government is subjected to political pressures by the ranchers to upgrade the land to its potential. The costs of that work are borne by the taxpayers at large, while the benefits accrue to the permittees.

Furthermore, the discretion public land managers have in use allocation results inevitably in political conflicts. The conflicts appear in every aspect of land use, from allowable cut on the national forests to the number of animal unit months permitted on the range, from the amount of coal that will be leased to the type of bids that will be accepted on oil and gas lands, from wilderness withdrawal to special use permits for cabins.

It is government policy, for example, that the use of coal in the production of electricity and process heat should be increased. This policy has been repeatedly stated by every president since Richard Nixon first called for a doubling of our coal production. It has been cast into legislative form several times. Yet despite this national commitment, it is apparent that the 200 billion tons of coal on the federal land will remain there. No new leases for federal coal have been issued since 1971.[19] It is true that coal companies already have under lease about 18 billion tons of coal on federal lands, but this coal was leased before passage of strict mining and combustion standards. It may not be minable, and may not be burnable.

---

[16] Thadis W. Box, *The Arid Lands Revisited,* Utah State University Honor Lecture (1978), p. 13.

[17] *Ibid.* See also *An Economic Evaluation of the Transfer of Federal Lands in Utah to State Ownership,* Utah Agricultural Experiment Station (1980) pp. 5–34.

[18] *Ibid., passim.*

[19] In the last few months a few small leases have been issued, permitting the Carter Administration to claim that "the embargo has been lifted." These leases are inconsequential in terms of new coal under lease, and it remains to be seen whether large-scale leasing will be resumed. EPA's rejection of Utah International's request for leases on the Alton Coal Fields in Utah, without any indication of what could be done to present an acceptable plan, gives us a clue to the future.

The inability of the government to issue new leases is largely a product of environmental activism. Under the terms of a legal settlement reached between the National Resources Defense Council (a leading environmentalist group) and the Department of the Interior, NRDC must approve any new lease of federal coal.[20] Legislation regulating surface mining has been so expanded by regulations issued by the Office of Surface Mining that the state role in mining regulation has disappeared and mining itself been seriously impaired. The situation is so widely recognized that the Senate has twice passed legislation *repealing the regulations* while leaving the law intact.

Politics, rather than economics, is the rule in range management practices as well. One of the duties of the Bureau of Land Management is the maintenance of the range. To do that, the Bureau limits the carrying capacity of the range through a system of grazing permits issued to certain ranchers. In some cases, these permits have been issued to the same families for generations.

The ranchers do not have a property right *per se* in a geographically limited portion of the range. Therefore, they have no real incentive to protect that range. If they can squeeze an extra cow onto the range the marginal benefit is theirs, the marginal cost is spread among all ranchers and, indeed, the United States taxpayers, the ultimate owners of the land. The result is, as was predicted by John Wesley Powell, the deterioration of the rangeland.

Another result is rancher pressure on the BLM to rehabilitate the land and thus increase its carrying capacity. To some extent this can be done. Much of the rangeland is covered by native plants such as pinion juniper which are not suitable for grazing. By linking two huge Caterpillar tractors together with a length of chain and driving them through the brush, the juniper can be swept off. The cleared land can then be seeded, probably with crested wheat grass, to provide improved forage for more cows.

The problem with this ingenious scheme is that it very often costs more than it is worth. If the land were privately owned and maintained, the owner would find that it would cost him more to chain the land than he could hope to recover from the increased sales of beef. The rancher wants his permit land chained only because he does not have to pay for it. The chaining continues (though it is now under serious environmental and economic attack) because the ranchers can organize politically and persuade the BLM to pay for the operation.

Other political conflicts in land management are invited by provi-

---

[20] *NRDC v. Hughes,* 474 F. Suppl. 148 (D.D.C. 1978). Specifically, in a stipulation to the proceeding issued February 25, 1978 (Civil Action No. 75-174) it is agreed that no lease applications will be processed except those which Interior and NRDC "mutually concur would cause the least environmental impact."

sions of FLPMA allowing any person or agency to nominate BLM land for designation as an "area of critical environmental concern" (ACEC). Since this is a very nebulous concept, it is read expansively by the environmental community. Following nomination, extensive evaluation is required, during which the ACEC is managed essentially as a wilderness. The potential for delay is obvious, as is the requirement for additional management personnel and the accompanying increase in budget authority for BLM.

Conflicts similar to those in the grazing permit program arise in the management of timber on the National Forests. While timber grows rapidly on the western slopes of the Cascade Mountains, it grows very slowly in the higher reaches of the Uintahs. Small timber operations can survive in the Uintahs, but the value of the timber does not approach the value of the trees left standing for recreational use. The government does not even recover the costs of holding timber sales. Yet logging continues on the Uintahs, under political pressure from the timber industry. We can expect that pressure to continue since the logger receives no benefit from trees left standing for recreation. What timber he can harvest under political protection produces a marginal benefit to him. The lost recreational value (and the cost of the timber sale) is spread among the "owners" of the National Forest, or at least among users of the forest.

The Park Service is similarly caught up in political conflicts. The National Park System originally was to include representative types of geological formations, ecosystems, and climatic conditions, in a kind of geographical zoo. The goal of representativeness has largely been achieved, but in the meantime it has been supplemented by a more ambitious goal, that of setting aside for single use as much land as possible.

The vast majority of a typical National Park is not developed and thus is not accessible to the day-visitor. For instance, the road that leads into Zion's National Park in Utah reaches only 3 percent of the park. The rest of the park, including some of the most beautiful scenery, is accessible only by foot or horseback. The result is severe overcrowding in the developed area, with attendant damage to the resource.

The Park Service reaction is interesting. Rather than expanding the developed zone (which could be done fairly easily with roads out to park overlooks from Kolob Mountain or Navajo Lake), the Service has in recent years tried to eliminate the existing visitor facilities, and has proposed banning all private vehicles from the park. Subsidized mass transit would replace them. At the same time the rest of the park would be placed in "wilderness" classification and thus kept undeveloped and virtually inaccessible permanently.

The Park Service pursues a similar course even in areas which are required by law to be open for development, such as National Recreation Areas. Congress has designated NRAs as suitable for multiple use, including the development of visitor facilities, grazing, mining, etc., but the Park Service continues to manage them very much as if they were single-use National Parks. The Service resists requests for additional development, seeks restrictions on existing facilities, and proposes large sections of NRAs for formal wilderness designation, which would eliminate any multiple use forever.

These examples illustrate why the current pattern of land ownership and management in the "public lands states" generates political conflicts. The most obvious expression of the conflict is the Sagebrush Rebellion, a movement designed to achieve for the western states a larger measure of autonomy and control over their resources. The Rebellion takes many forms, including legislation calling for the transfer of ownership and control of all or some of the federal lands to the states within which they are located.

Taking a different approach, several states have passed legislation asserting title over all or part of the federal domain within their boundaries, and suits have been filed in federal courts seeking to force a transfer through legal or constitutional channels. Most recently, the citizens of Alaska approved a referendum calling for the establishment of a commission to study whether twenty-one years of statehood has been a good thing for Alaska, and to consider alternative forms of association with the United States.

The Sagebrush Rebellion is not the only example of political conflict over land-use issues in the West. There is also an internal struggle within the Executive Branch. Older BLM agents and Forest Service rangers have long been dedicated to the "use" ethic which pervaded the land management agencies in the 1940s and 1950s. The newer agents and, more importantly, the top-level political appointees who direct their work, represent the "preservationist" ethic of the 1960s and 1970s. The obvious potential for conflict is being realized. When the superintendent of the Glen Canyon National Recreation Area and local officials carefully worked out a management plan providing for substantial development and multiple use access (quite within the law), that plan was pointedly and completely rejected by political appointees in Washington.

These political conflicts have budgetary impacts. To the extent they produce expensive land management activities, such as chaining or seeding, and the conduct of uneconomic timber sales, the general taxpayer subsidizes certain users of the public domain. To the extent land withdrawals restrict access to critical energy and mineral supplies, consumers as a whole are penalized for the benefit of the limited number of people who can "consume" the withdrawn land.

It is evident that the political problems (and their budgetary costs)

123

flow inevitably from the dislocation between land ownership and land use. If the land is going to be preserved, if costs are going to be related to benefits, a closer fit betweeen those who benefit from land use and those who bear the costs must be designed.

Control of the federal lands should be given to local governmental units better suited to make judgments about the best use of the land. The disposal need not be absolute. For instance, the federal government could retain certain access and recreational rights over the land, much as mineral rights are now often reserved. Or, certain components of private ownership could be transferred to private owners, giving them a stake in the physical preservation of the resource.

The possibility can best be illustrated with respect to grazing rights. If the right to graze a specific parcel of the public range were "sold" to a rancher, and were his to hold in perpetuity, or to sell or transfer to others, he would have an incentive to conserve the resource. Under current practice, his incentive is to overgraze, since he obtains the marginal benefit without the marginal cost. Some states have already implemented such a system, with remarkable success. The entire cost of range rehabilitation could thus be saved, and the land would be devoted to its best use.

Some years ago, Milton Friedman suggested that National Parks be sold to private owners—perhaps to the Sierra Club. This is an excellent suggestion. In view of the overcrowding at many of its parks, it is obvious that they could support themselves as economic enterprises. Of course, the uses for which the Sierra Club wishes land withdrawn (backpacking and wilderness experience) are not always the same as the uses which produce overcrowding at Yosemite, Yellowstone, and Zion's. But the relative unattractiveness of backpacking and wilderness survival to the average American (especially in the arid terrain of Utah and Arizona) illustrates on whose behalf land withdrawals are being made.

The total land management budget of the federal government is just over $4 billion per year. It is very difficult to ascertain exactly how much of that could be saved by immediately beginning to transfer land management functions away from the federal government. Nevertheless, it does give us an idea of how much could be saved annually over the medium- to long-run by more closely aligning land ownership with land management responsibilities.

To achieve a rapid and orderly transfer of the resources, the land management budget should be cut by $400 million for each year of the next ten years. At the end of ten years, the federal government would no longer have land mangement functions.

LONG-TERM CONSIDERATIONS

The recommendations of this essay are directly contrary to the policies prevailing in Washington, and those that are anticipated for the near future. For example, Congress has before it now a proposal for a massive program to clean up chemcial waste dumps, oil spills, and deal with other aspects of hazardous substances.* The Environmental Protection Agency is already developing the framework to manage this new program.

Despite this initiative, the 97th Congress will have an opportunity to undertake a redirection of the nation's course in pollution control. Both the Clean Air Act and the Clean Water Act will come before the 97th Congress for re-authorization.

In considering these attitudes and programs, it is essential that the Congress distinguish between those involving substantial externalities, such as air and water pollution control, and those which do not, such as the clearing and seeding of rangeland. Where externalities are involved, it is important that economic principles be used, to keep costs and dislocations as minimal as possible.

Even where substantial externalities are involved, the 97th Congress should consider where the third parties are located. It is evident, for instance, that those adversely affected by noise pollution are those close to the source of the noise. Local government is perfectly capable of internalizing the costs of noise pollution; in fact, is likely to be much more capable than the federal government. Even in such cases as National Forests, it is not clear that national action is required to internalize costs. There is evidence that most users of the forest resource do not come from great distances, but live within a hundred miles or so of the forest. The greatest gains in efficiency can very likely be made by decentralization, by permitting the states to regulate and manage wherever that can possibly be done. The preference for federal action is irrational, and is the source of mismanagement and waste.

Given the political realities of America in the 1980s, it may be wishful thinking that the recommendations of this essay will be adopted. But even if they are not, the principles on which they are based can be asserted, and can affect the public debate, and the management of the government, for the better.

Finally, while the Natural Resources and Environment function is only about $13 billion, it is clear that its impact on the economy is far greater than that. It is essential that Congress be forced to consider that fact, and that the costs of legislation on individuals and the private sector be considered during debate in the House and Senate. The

---

*This "Superfund" bill was adopted at the time this study was going to press.

125

recommendations of this essay would save the government about $10 billion in direct costs; the reduction in the federal regulatory burden would be at least five times that. And these savings would come with no attendant loss in pollution control efficiency. What would accompany them would be a substantial increase in the output of needed energy and minerals, and better management of local pollution abatement problems.

6

Agriculture

by Don Paarlberg and Eric V. Robinson

Astonishingly, in a functional breakdown of the federal budget, the activities that come under the heading "Agriculture" constitute only 16 percent of the Department of Agriculture budget. In other words, 84 percent of the Department's activities are primarily non-agricultural. The overwhelming majority of the activities of the Department of Agriculture are in areas added in recent years: food programs, housing, environmental initiatives, service to rural areas and the like. These "new agenda" activities have an extremely tenuous relation to the historic mission of the Department of Agriculture, which is to serve the farm people and to increase efficiency in the production of crops and livestock.

Congress has planted the "new agenda" programs in the Department of Agriculture and under the jurisdiction of agricultural committees. This was done largely because of the aggressive attitude of the agricultural committees in the Congress, who wanted control of these new activities both to influence their content and to use them as carriers to win non-farm votes for the historic farm legislation. These programs have taken root and grown rapidly. The organizational form has developed in spite of the efforts of the executive branch to establish the "new agenda" items elsewhere. Two recent Secretaries of Agriculture, Clifford M. Hardin and Earl Butz, tried unsuccessfully to give the food programs to the Department of Health, Education and Welfare.

The Office of Management and Budget prefers a functional rather than a departmental approach, as does Congress in its budget deliberations. For example, three departments help develop our water resources, while four agencies in two departments are involved in the management of public lands. The functional approach aggregates like activities, despite their different departmental homes, and so permits better analysis.

This review of Agriculture is on a functional basis. The major budgetary load of USDA is elsewhere: the Food Program in Income Se-

Table 1

Agriculture
(in millions of dollars)

Major missions and programs	1979 actual	1980 estimate	1981 estimate
OUTLAYS			
Farm income stabilization:			
Price support and related programs:			
Existing law	3,572	2,792	1,697
Proposed legislation	—	—	359
Federal Crop Insurance Corporation:			
Existing law	− 8	27	27
Proposed legislation	—	—	93
Agriculture credit insurance fund	1,017	238	− 1,020
Other programs	43	40	41
Unallocated salaries and expenses	226	188	193
Subtotal, farm income stabilization	4,850	3,286	1,389
Agricultural research and services:			
Research programs:			
Existing law	524	524	538
Proposed legislation	—	—	1
Extension programs	273	262	276
Marketing programs	64	81	81
Animal and plant health programs	230	254	261
Economic intelligence	133	149	163
Other programs	56	59	61
Unallocated overhead	115	90	99
Offsetting receipts	− 55	− 66	− 65
Subtotal, agricultural research and services	1,340	1,353	1,416
Deductions for offsetting receipts	48	− 3	− 3
Total, outlays	6,238	4,636	2,802
MEMORANDUM — Attribution of Federal Financing Bank outlays			
Agricultural credit insurance fund	5,045	2,946	2,487

Source: The Budget of the United States Government FY 1981

curity; Rural Development in Community and Regional Development; the Forest Service in Natural Resources and Environment; and Public Law 480 (Food aid) in International Affairs. But what is left is considerable: $2.8 billion in FY 1981.

The agriculture function consists of two main divisions, one more that 100 years old and the other approaching its fiftieth birthday. A brief resume of the Department's history will be instructive.

From the time of its founding in 1862 to the year 1933, the purpose of the Department was clear: to engage in research and education on behalf of the farm people, and help them to increase production and improve efficiency. The mission was philosophically in keeping with Jonathan Swift's famous quote from *Gulliver's Travels:* "Whoever could make two ears of corn or two blades of grass to grow upon a spot of ground where only one grew before would deserve better of

Table 2

Table 2
USDA Budget for Research and Education (Outlays) 1930 –1979
(millions of dollars)

	1930	1940	1950	1960	1970	1979
Education (Extension)	9	19	32	64	124	273
Agricultural Research Service	—[1]	—[1]	104	172	267	330
Total Research and Education			136	236	391	603
Research and Education as a percent of total USDA outlays			5	4	4	2

[1]Prior to establishment of the Agricultural Research Service, outlays for research were carried within various other agencies of USDA.

mankind and do more essential service to this country than the whole race of politicians put together."

A small degree of regulation was provided to help the markets work better. The effort was market oriented, based on the idea that individual farmers, if given good information, were capable of making wise decisions within the framework of an open competitive system.

The original mission of the USDA, which we call the "first agenda," was and is cooperative with the states and counties. The State Experiment Stations and the State Extension Services are keys to the system. The budget for this mission grew rapidly but never took on the mushroom growth characteristic of the "agendas" which followed. (Table 2)

The effort was phenomenally successful. In its 100 years, the Department of Agriculture has helped produce more technological advancements than in all the previous years since Biblical times. Food production has risen, efficiency has increased, living conditions on American farms have improved, the social status of farm people has risen, and the consumers have been able to buy an improved diet with a smaller proportion of their incomes. The overall wholesomeness of the diet is attested by the virtual disappearance of such nutritionally-associated diseases as rickets, beri-beri, scurvy, and goiter. The efficiency of agricultural production was so enhanced that American agriculture achieved comparative advantage over agricultural production elsewhere in the world. This occurred while the non-farm sector steadily lost its competitive position in comparison with other countries. Earl Heady of Iowa thus appraised the experience: "The United States has had the best, the most logical, and the most successful program of agricultural development anywhere in the world."[1]

The research and education effort of the USDA provides most of its

[1]Earl O. Heady, "The Agriculture of the U.S.," *Scientific American,* September 1976, p. 107.

assistance to the larger, better-off farmers.[2] Much of this is inherent in a system which is voluntary and cooperative. But to some extent, the work can be re-oriented so as to broaden its base. The current emphasis on what is called the "structure issue" has produced an effort to redirect research and education so as to provide a better balance.

The second major division of the agriculture function consists of the commodity programs and related activities. These programs involve governmental decision-making with respect to price and production of such crops as corn, wheat, and cotton. During the 1930s, the Great Depression brought low prices and severe difficulties for farm people. Surplus stocks of grain and cotton piled up as demand declined. Here was a situation with which historic farm policy — programs of research and education — could not cope. The dominant explanation for the low prices was the farmers had produced too much. A new function, drastically altered, was laid on the Department of Agriculture: it was to reduce production of farm products so as to raise prices received by farmers and thus increase farm income. This undertaking, together with associated activities, became the "second agenda." It did not fit well with the first.

First Agenda Research and Education	Second Agenda Commodity Programs
pro-farmer	pro-farmer
full production	restricted production
individual decision making	group decision making
belief in markets	mistrust in markets

Both the old and the new initiatives unequestionably belonged in the Department of Agriculture and were so placed. They have operated side by side for nearly fifty years as uneasy partners: one pushes practics that increase production, the other applies restraint. One bears down on the accelerator; the other rides the brake. Needless to say, this gives a rather jerky ride and poor economy.

Experience with the second agenda was less clear and more controversial than was the case with the first. Price supports and production controls increased farm income, especially in the early years, and quieted what might otherwise have been a farm revolt. The effort was effective in helping cope with the income drop associated with the Depression. But, like most government programs, the effort became institutionalized. The Depression gave way to the farm prosperity of World War II, which in turn gave way to a post-war technological

---

[2]Extension Service, Science and Education Administration, USDA, *Evaluation of Economic and Social Consequences of Cooperative Extension Programs* (Government Printing Office, January 1980; 620–220/SEA-3622), p. 152.

Table 3
USDA Budget (Outlays) for Commodity Programs, 1940 –1979
(millions of dollars)

	1940	1950	1960	1970	1979
Total outlay for the Commodity Programs	605	2,122	3,657	5,325	9,424
Commodity Programs as percent of total USDA outlay	43	72	67	54	16

revolution. Agricultural conditions were vastly improved. But the Depression-born program continued much in its earlier form.

The commodity programs have had adverse side effects, which only gradually became visible.[3] They widened the income gap within agriculture, priced us out of markets, increased the cost of food to consumers, helped big farms to cannibalize the small ones, increased the price of land and made it harder for young people to start farming, misallocated resources, involved loss of freedom, and increased costs. Anticipated outlays for price support and related activities in fiscal 1982 are estimated at $2.1 billion.

Beginning about fifteen years ago, in large part because of the above difficulties, there was a moderate but discernable moving away from the commodity programs. Since 1965, each agricultural act written into law by Congress has shown an identifiable movement toward greater reliance on the market and less on government. Commodity programs now constitute a small proportion of the Agriculture Department activities. (Table 3)

In the sixties, a "third agenda" came into existence which was a reflection of the social disturbances of that time. The "Great Society" and the "War on Poverty" gave rise to programs whose laudable purpose was to help disadvantaged people such as producers and consumers of food who, without government assistance, would be in deep difficulty. Rural Development and the food programs were the chief manifestations of these concerns. As had been said, the congressional committees were successful in establishing these undertakings in the Department, despite the apprehensions of the agricultural establishment. The third agenda people have — or are suspected of having — an anti-farm bias.

The budget for the third agenda grew exponentially. The cost of supplying food to low-income people increased, in actual dollars, from $475 million in 1962 to $13.4 billion in 1980. By mid-1980, one person in eleven was receiving food stamps. The Department of Agriculture became, in fact if not in name, a Ministry of Food. Rural de-

---

[3]Don Paarlberg, *Farm and Food Policy* (Lincoln: University of Nebraska Press, 1980).

131

velopment experienced a similar growth. By fiscal 1981, the "third agenda" took up the overwhelming share of the USDA budget.

As has been explained, the third agenda programs are taken up by other authors in this study, in connection with other functions. They are mentioned here, however, of necessity. The agricultural function cannot be explained without reference to them.

Some of the activities of the Department of Agriculture have provided the rationale for adding new off-setting missions, in USDA and elsewhere.

- Production-stimulating effects of research and education have led to production-restricting efforts of the commodity programs.
- Price supports for farm products have increased the retail price of food and helped make the case for the Food Stamp Program.
- Subsidies for irrigation have hastened the depletion of ground-water reserves and laid the basis for government assistance in the necessary transition to dryland farming.
- Subsidized upstream drainage has led to subsidized down-stream flood control.
- Price-boosting activities of USDA have led to staff increases for the Council of Wage and Price Stability, whose charge is to hold down prices.
- Dairy price supports have attracted foreign manufactured dairy products to our shores and made necessary a program of import controls.
- The commodity programs have encouraged the production of wheat, cotton, and sorghum on hazardous lands and contributed to the need felt for programs to relieve the effect of drought and flood in these areas.

Thus a growing government feeds on itself, growing even more. The public deserves government programs that do more than offset one another.

Mangement of any activity, whether private or public, is exercised chiefly through the financial discipline, a fact known by every businessman, politician, lobbyist, or bureaucrat. Thus, these questions regarding agricultural programs focus on the budget.

This essay accepts the basic presumption of the first agenda: if given the facts, farmers and consumers are usually able to make wise decisions about the use of their resources; the market is generally a useful institution; and the efforts of government should be addressed to improving the functioning of the market rather than supplanting it.

SHORT-TERM POLICIES

Price Supports and Related Matters

Deficiency Payments

This alternative is offered as a means of transferring part of our decision-making out of the public sector and into private hands. Political acceptability of these proposals is not the decisive element, though that has been considered. In statistical terms, a cut of this magnitude probably lies about two standard deviations from what is most likely; a $3.3. billion cut has perhaps two or three chances in 100 of being enacted. Even though the patient may be unwilling to take the cure, diagnosis and prescription are still worthwhile.

If farm prices of corn, wheat, cotton, barley, and grain sorghum fall below specified (target) levels, the government is required to make payment to farmers equal to the difference between the market price and the target level. Assurance to farmers with respect to price targets is open-ended. Changes in crop yields or in demand conditions could double these outlays, cut them in half, or eliminate them altogether. In such circumstances, a budget is more of an outlook statement than a financial discipline.

The purpose of the deficiency payments is to increase farm income. The justification for this effort is the alleged handicap experienced by farm people. In the absence of price supports, agriculture would purportedly be the only major unprotected sector in an otherwise protected economy. This vulnerability is believed to carry with it an economic penalty which the payment program attempts to redress.

There is considerable doubt about the economic penalty of farming. Per capita incomes of farm people in recent years have averaged about 90 percent as large as per capita incomes of non-farmers. However, the average net worth of farm families is about twice as high as that of non-farm families.[4]

Payments are on a per-bushel or per-pound basis. Thus, they are regressive. In 1978, a farmer in the top 10 percent bracket received, on the average, fifty times as much money from the government as did the farmer in the lowest 10 percent.[5] Equity between farm and non-farm people is the rationale of the program. But equity within agriculture is somehow set aside. Average farm income is increased by adding many dollars to those already well-off and adding little or nothing to

---

[4] Thomas A. Carlin, and Linda M. Ghelfi, "Off-Farm Employment and the Farm Sector," *Structure Issues of American Agriculture,* USDA, ESCS, Agricultural Economic Report 438, 1979, p. 272.

[5] James D. Johnson, Milton H. Erickson, Jerry A. Sharples, and David H. Harrington, "Price and Income Policies and the Structure of Agriculture," *Structure Issues of American Agriculture,* November 1979, pp. 174–184.

those on the low end of the income scale. The average is raised by increasing the dispersion that makes up the average.

Increasingly, government payments are income supplements: no performance is required for eligibility. In these circumstances, large payments to wealthy farmers are inequitable. The huge payments make it possible for large farmers to absorb the smaller, thus speeding the disappearance of farmers with limited resources.

To at least in part alleviate the above distortions, the budget for deficiency payments should be halved for FY 1982 and thereafter. To achieve the $432 million savings would require substantive legislation. The reductions in target prices would be a long step toward a market oriented agriculture.

The question may be asked, "Why not eliminate the deficiency payments altogether?" The answer given here is that net farm income in today's agricultural economy is highly volatile, and a cushion at a conservative level can have a good overall effect. Reduction of the payments to half their recent value is admittedly arbitrary but has a certain rough logic.

Payment Limitation

Currently, there is a limit on the amount of money which a farmer can receive from the government under the commodity programs. This limit is $50,000, a figure which is too high. Fifty thousand dollars is an amount equal to approximately twice the average family farm income in the United States. In 1978 only about 4 percent of the program participants were affected by the limitation. A top one percent of the farmers receive 29 percent of the benefits.[6]

The payment limit should be reduced from $50,000 to $10,000. The saving for fiscal 1982 is estimated at $100 million. The lower limit would reduce the government's bias toward large farms and thereby slow the absorption of smaller farms. Public acceptance of a program which can help stabilize the farm income would be enhanced.

Commodity Loans

Commodity loans are intended to increase and stabilize prices received by farmers. They date from the beginning of the commodity programs in 1933. They are non-recourse loans; that is, no recourse is available to the lender (the government) if the farmer defaults on his loan. The government lends, say, $2.25 a bushel on a farmer's corn crop. If the market price goes above $2.25, the farmer sells the corn, repays the loan, and pockets the difference. If the market price falls below $2.25, the farmer turns the crops over to the government in full

---

[6]General Accounting Office, *Changing Character and Structure of American Agriculture: An Overview,* Staff Study, USDA, Washington, D.C., 1978, p. iii.

repayment of the loan. When markets are weak, as has often been the case in the past, the government thus acquires a large inventory. The effect is to keep the market price, in most cases, from falling below the loan level. If the loan level is kept modest, so that the market clears most of the time, harmful market price gyrations can be dampened to the advantage of farmers and nonfarmers alike. The danger comes when the loan level is raised so high as to price our products out of the markets, pile up commodities in government hands, require deep cuts in production, necessitate controls on imports, and incur heavy government cost. In other words, the objective of stabilizing prices is in the public interest; the objective of increasing them is not.

It appears likely that the dangers of excessively high loan levels have been avoided for the 1980 crop. Both recent and projected prices for the 1980 crop are above the loan rates, even after the increases announced by the President in late July.

As with target payments, changed crop yields or changed demand conditions could greatly modify the outlays under the loan program. If more money is needed to make good on promises to farmers, the money is provided, no matter what the budget says. The USDA then goes to Congress to ask for reimbursement for net realized losses.

The strategy proposed for the years ahead is to set the loan rates at modest levels. If political pressures result in excessively high current loan levels, these levels should be held while inflation escalates market prices out of the danger zone. If, over a period of years, loan rates could be set so that the market clears two years out of three, loans could be helpful both to farm and nonfarm people. Changes in both substantive legislation and administrative decisions would be required to bring about this recommended policy modification.

Interest Rates

The Commodity Credit Corporation (CCC) provides loans for a variety of programs. The rate of interest usually is subsidized. The purposes are several: to encourage farmer holding of farm products, to provide incentives for certain activities such as the building of storage facilities, and to increase exports. All of these loans have as their ultimate objective the increase of farm income. There is great latitude for administrative decision regarding interest rates.

In the spring of 1980, a farmer could borrow from the government at 9 percent interest to build grain storage, while credit from the bank for the same purpose would have cost him about 14 percent. This subsidized credit went disproportionately to the big farmers who could pay a competitive interest charge, but of course preferred the subsidized rate.

Some of the programs involved in the Commodity Credit Corporation loans, such as encouragement for farmer-holding crops, are in the public interest. They deserve encouragement and merit a measure of subsidy. The difficulty comes when the rate of subsidy becomes excessive.

The government should continue to offer these loans, but the farmers should pay an interest rate one percent above what the Treasury charges CCC. The result would be an annual saving estimated at $200 million. Effectiveness of the programs would not be significantly reduced.

Dairy Program

The law requires the government to support the price of milk at 80 percent of parity. This is done by supporting prices of manufactured dairy products (butter, cheese, nonfat dried milk). Eighty percent of parity is substantially above what would otherwise be the market price. During the present year, the dairy program will cost the government $1.3 billion. There are several adverse effects of the program, in addition to the heavy cost: it stimulates excessive milk production, attracts foreign dairy products to our shores, encourages uneconomic production of non-dairy supplies of fat and protein, and increases the price of dairy products to consumers.

The dairy cow is a potent political symbol. Campaign contributions made by organized dairymen are capable of generating votes for high price supports. Periodically, these high supports get the industry and the government into trouble. This is one of those times.

The required level of price support should be reduced from the present 80 percent of parity to its previous level, 75 percent. Both Republican and Democratic Secretaries of Agriculture have pursued this objective, but have been unsuccessful. If this reduction could be achieved, budgetary costs could be reduced by an estimated $300 million annually.

Established at a proper level, the dairy price support program could provide a helpful degree of market stability at reasonable cost. The problem arises from setting the support too high. Some latitude exists for administrative decisions. But changes in substantive legislation would be required to bring about the changes recommended here.

In addition to the previously mentioned savings, $407 million would be saved by eliminating Disaster Payments, as will be demonstrated in the following section. All the foregoing items are under items are under the heading Price Support and Related Activities. Total savings under this category would be $1,440 million. Costs would be cut by two-thirds (Table 4).

Crop Insurance

In 1974, the Congress enacted a Low-Yield Disaster Program which provided payments to farmers whose crops were severely damaged or destroyed by drought, flood, frost, hail, or other disasters. This in ef-

Table 4

Summary of Reductions, Price Support and Related Activities:

Deficiency payments	$ − 436 million
Disaster payments	− 407 "
Interest rates	− 200 "
Dairy program	− 300 "
Payment limitation	− 100 "
Total	$ − 1,443 million

fect provided farmers with crop insurance without the need to pay a premium. Compensation to farmers under this program has ranged from $555 million in FY 1975 to an estimated $630 million in FY 1981.

While this program has helped alleviate some genuine hardships, it has had adverse side effects:

- *Bad resource use.* Crops have been planted on land that is disaster prone and wind and water erosion have resulted.
- *Misuse of the program.* Some farmers, when weather or other prospects were adverse, have gone through the motions of planting a crop, primarily in order to receive disaster payments.
- *The Crop Insurance Program has been undercut.* Since 1958 the USDA has had a Crop Insurance Program, involving the payment of premiums. The availability of free "insurance" has undermined this program and reduced participation in it.

The Department of Agriculture has proposed a nationwide crop insurance program that would combine the insurance provisions of the Federal Crop Insurance Act and the Low Yield Disaster Payment programs to protect producers of agricultural products against loss.

Under the Administration's original proposal, the insurance program was to replace the disaster program. However, the Administration afterwards agreed to support legislation which will give producers a choice of free disaster payments or subsidized insurance at a 40 percent level for the 1981 crop (not later crops). This will result in disaster payments in 1982.

The crop insurance subsidy should be reduced to 25 percent and disaster payments eliminated. Savings would be $90 million. Changes in substantive legislation would be required to accomplish the program modifications recommended here.

The question may be asked, "Why subsidize crop insurance at all?" The answer is that without subsidy, premiums would be so high that participation would be very low. Then in the event of disaster, affected farmers would demand — and likely would receive — open-handed, hastily-administered assistance that would be more costly than a modestly-subsidized insurance program.

Agricultural Credit

Agricultural loans are made to farmers who present acceptable evidence that they cannot obtain credit elsewhere. These are of three major kinds: farm ownership loans, farm operating loans, and emergency disaster loans. Emergency disaster loans are estimated at $2 billion in 1981 and 1982.

In FY 1981, farm ownership loans are estimated at $870 million. Interest rates were at 10 percent, except for low-income borrowers who paid not more than 6 percent. Terms for guaranteed loans were negotiated. Operating loans were expected to total $875 million. Interest rates ranged from 6 percent to 10.5 percent; as with ownership loans, terms for guaranteed loans were negotiated by lender and borrower. An insured loan may not exceed $200,000 and a guaranteed loan may not exceed $300,000. These limits are roughly equal to the average value of farm operating units in the United States.

Funds disbursed to farmers under this loan program are offset by "selling" these loans to the Federal Financing Bank. In fiscal 1982, it is anticipated that there will be $943 million of such loans. The effect of this operation is to make the budget appear much less than in fact it is.

There is a substantial subsidy involved. Interest rates are much less than the inflation rate so that the real cost of the borrowed money was negative. Understandably, under these circumstances the demand for loans was very great.

The original objective of the program was to strengthen and sustain the family farm system by helping promising young farmers who were short of capital. Farm plans were worked out with the borrowers, and supervisors helped the operators carry out these plans. The repayment record was good.

In part, this original concept continues. But the size of the loans has increased rapidly. Personnel ceilings for the responsible agency, Farmers Home Administration, have limited the amount of supervision, and the program is now little more than a form of cheap credit. Certification as being unqualified for commercial credit has been developed into a high art. The interest rate is so low that it is difficult to "graduate" borrowers from the program when they have advanced to the state at which they can meet commercial credit standards. And it is extremely difficult to close out farmer borrowers when the loans go bad. On September 30, 1979, 6 percent of the farm ownership loans and 19 percent of the operating loans were delinquent.

Total commitments to guarantee new loans should be reduced by half. The limits for both insured and guaranteed farm ownership and farm operating loans should also be cut in half. The amount of the subsidy is reduced. The effect will be to direct a greater share of the agency's effort to those in real need, to scale back the rate of growth in this problem-prone program, to reduce government competition with

Table 5

Agriculture Function Budget Outlays, FY 1982
(millions of dollars)

	Base (rounded)	Changes (rounded)	Alternative Budget
Price support and related	2,160	− 1,440	720
Crop insurance	150	− 90	60
Agricultural Credit[1]	1,500	− 1,865	− 365
Research	550	+ 30	580
Extension	300	+ 25	325
Animal and plant health	280	+ 15	295
Economic intelligence	170	+ 10	180
Other	430	−	430
Total	5,540	− 3,315	2,225

[1]Includes $943 million off-budget outlays of the Federal Financing Bank.

the private sector, and to cut budgetary outlays below where they otherwise would be. The volume of new insured loans would be reduced by $1.9 billion. Such is the momentum of the program that even with these drastic cuts total volume would continue to grow and the government's contingent liability would experience a further increase. The existing volume of loans is so great and the terms of the loans so long that even the sharp decrease in new loans would permit some growth in total loan volume.

To bring about the changes recommended here, changes in the substantive legislation would be required. Action by the appropriations committees could help, as could strong administrative action.

Agricultural Resources and Services

Research, extension, animal and plant health, and economic intelligence are addressed primarily to the improved functioning of a market oriented agriculture. They are held to approximately a 5 percent increase to offset in part the effect of inflation. Other activities, which are chiefly administrative, are left unchanged.

Reduction and Recasting

Total outlays for the agricultural function should be cut by $3.3 billion, or 60 percent (Table 5). While such a cut would, in the short run, reduce the incomes of some better-off farmers, it would have certain advantages. It would reduce the income gap within agriculture; result in better utilization of resources; check the drift toward super-large, corporate-type farms; and limit the competition of government with private enterprise.

As has been noted, a small part of the savings sought could be achieved through administrative action. A somewhat larger share could be accomplished in the appropriations process. The overwhelming portion would require changes in legislation. Program reductions are not easy, and a reduction of this magnitude would be very difficult. These programs are written into law, institutionalized in a series of operating agencies, provided with budgets, staffed by established government workers, and supported by powerful lobby groups. In government, these are the certificates of longevity. Nevertheless, changes would be in the public interest and the time for making them may now be better than it has been for some decades.

LONG-TERM CONSIDERATIONS

The body of this essay focuses on the budget for the agricultural function for fiscal year 1982 and therefore is short-term in its focus. Longer-term goals, however, are necessary in the formation of public policy. And longer-term goals cannot be achieved unless they are enunciated and supported. The Department of Agriculture must rediscover its "first mission": to engage in research and education on behalf of farm people, helping them to increase production and improve efficiency. Commitment to this mission has been diluted by devotion to the second (commodity programs), and by emergence of the third (help for those believed to be in special need).

Farm people use more land and water than any other group. There is concern about the manner in which these resources are used, and their sufficiency for coming generations. Congress should re-examine policies with regard to farmer stewardship of these resources, and with respect to its own resource-related programs. Prevailing practices and programs were generally laid down when these matters were perceived differently; their appropriateness to modern and prospective conditions should be reviewed.

Increased agricultural productivity has been the source of much of our past progress in the United States. There has been an inclination to assume that agricultural productivity will continue to increase. More real resources should be committed to agricultural research and education, both in the basic and applied fields. The whole profile of research and education should be reviewed, including private and tax-supported. The adequacy of the inputs should be appraised, priorities should be lifted up, and resources committed thereto.

Agriculture, once a "way of life," is becoming industrialized. There are side effects of an economic, social, and political nature. Some by-products of the modern trends are generally viewed as advantages. Some are seen as hurtful. Most are difficult to appraise. Some may be amenable to change and other appear to be inexorable. Congress should consider what kind of agriculture is desired and review its program as they relate to the public purpose.

The world's population continues to grow. The greatly increased

140

numbers of people in the developing countries of Asia, Africa, and Latin America need larger amounts of food. Some of this will be imported from the United States and other suppliers, but much of it will have to be grown in the countries themselves.

The Department of Agriculture and the Land Grant Colleges possess a larger body of scientific agricultural knowledge and a larger number of agricultural scientists than any other agency in the world. As American agriculture progressed, successful institutional arrangements were developed involving research, education, transportation, processing, merchandising, credit, tenure, and food aid. With appropriate modification, these institutions are being adapted to the needs of the developing countries.

Agricultural capability is an asset which we have, which our friends need, and which our rivals lack. From 1933 to recent times, this asset was generally looked on as a liability. It is time for reappraisal. Congress should examine the United States' capability to help the people of the developing countries meet their food needs. The rather modest effort at technical assistance in agriculture which characterized the past thirty years may be amenable to expansion, to the advantage of ourselves and the people overseas.

7

Commerce and Housing Credit

by Richard F. Muth

The section of the budget called Commerce and Housing Credit is a curious conglomeration. On the one hand, it provides funding for a number of agencies whose aim is to safeguard our monetary system. Among these are the Comptroller of the Currency, the Federal Deposit Insurance Corporation (FDIC) and similar organizations. Although one might find fault with specific actions taken by these agencies, controlling the monetary system is an essential function of government in society. The FDIC, in particular, has eliminated banking "panics," which were so destabilizing in the 19th and early 20th centuries. On the whole, then, such programs are clearly legitimate functions of government.

At the other extreme stand obvious boondoggles. Subsidies to the U.S. Postal Service are principally subsidies to bulk mail advertising and the delivery of periodicals by mail. There is no good economic reason to subsidize one form of advertising over others, or advertising over other forms of commercial activity. To the extent that subsidizing periodicals would be desirable, direct subsidies as opposed to subsidized mailing costs are economically more efficient. Likewise, loan guarantees to the Chrysler Corporation have little to recommend them. Though such guarantees may temporarily increase employment and prevent other disruptions by reducing Chrysler's borrowing costs, their principal effect is to perpetuate an inefficient management and subsidize the corporation's stockholders. Even if some possible public purpose were served by such guaranteed loans — Lockheed, after all, is an important defense contractor, part of whose problems resulted from inflation-generated real price reductions on government contracts — direct subsidies would be economically more efficient than subsidies to Chrysler's borrowing costs.

The area between the obviously valid and obviously invalid programs in the Commerce and Housing Credit section of the budget is inhabited principally by various housing programs. Housing has long

Table 1
Commerce and Housing Credit
(in millions of dollars)

Major missions and programs	1979 actual	1980 estimate	1981 estimate
OUTLAYS			
Mortgage credit and thrift insurance:			
Department of Housing and Urban Development:			
Mortgage purchase activities (GNMA) ..	225	1,036	− 351
Mortgage credit (FHA)	193	148	− 70
Housing for the elderly or handicapped .	459	700	700
Department of Agriculture − rural housing programs	184	1,806	− 958
Federal Deposit Insurance Corporation ...	− 1,218	− 1,450	− 1,500
Federal Home Loan Bank Board.........	− 488	− 479	− 602
National Credit Union Administration....	− 30	173	− 32
Subtotal, mortgage credit and thrift insurance	− 677	1,935	− 2,813
Postal Service.........................	1,787	1,677	1,593
Federal Financing Bank	−	− 253	− 188
Other advancement and regulation of commerce:			
Small business assistance	674	719	869
National Consumer Cooperative Bank	−	36	161
Technology utilization	212	243	268
Economic and demographic statistics	214	648	317
Other:			
Existing law	354	471	517
Proposed legislation	−	−	− 12
Subtotal, other advancement and regulation of commerce	1,454	2,118	2,121
Deductions for offsetting receipts	*	− *	− *
Total, outlays....................	2,565	5,476	712
ADDENDUM			
Off-budget Federal entities:			
Postal Service:			
Outlays.....................	− 891	178	1,606
Federal Financing Bank:			
Budget authority	16,050	22,006	23,937
Outlays.........................	13,172	16,408	16,316
MEMORANDUM − Attribution of Federal Financing Bank outlays			
Rural housing insurance fund	2,930	1,852	4,889
Federal Financing Bank (net interest and capital transfers)	− 110	159	72
Small business assistance	68	169	166

*$500 thousand or less.
Source: The Budget of the United States Government FY 1981

been of special concern in this country. Beginning in the early 1930s, a great variety of programs to improve the housing of Americans have been undertaken by the federal government. Housing credit programs are those which seek to reduce the cost to individuals of acquiring housing on the private market principally by reducing borrowing costs. The more inportant of these programs will be treated in the second section of this essay after an appraisal of the general issues bearing on the desirability of such programs. The third and final section will offer some suggestions as to what types of programs would be preferable to our current ones.

General Issues

There are two principal ways in which housing credit programs might operate to reduce private housing costs. One consists of measures which seek to increase the supply of funds for mortgage lending in private markets. The other consists, essentially, of paying part of the private cost of borrowing. This critique will first inquire whether it is socially desirable to reduce the cost of mortgage borrowing through either of these mechanisms.

Increasing the Supply of Mortgage Funds

Since the establishment of the Federal National Mortgage Association (FNMA or Fanny Mae) in 1938, the federal government has sought to increase the supply of funds for mortgage loans. This is done by borrowing from the private sector, either by selling bonds directly to private individuals or firms or indirectly by selling bonds to the Treasury. The proceeds of these bond sales may then be used to make mortgage loans directly or, more commonly, to buy mortgage loans already made by private lenders. To the extent that such operations increase the number of mortgage loans made, the market interest rates on such loans would decline. Their decline would, in turn, reduce the financing costs of individual homeowners or the rental payments for rented housing necessary to cover the landlord's financing costs.

It is frequently, though somewhat naively, supposed that the dollar volume of mortgage lending increases by an amount equal to the amount of new funds provided by the operations just described. A critical examination, however, suggests that they are at least partially offset by changes in the amount of other private lending. The sale of bonds to the public in order to acquire the funds to support new mortgage loans causes the prices of bonds to decline and their yields to rise. An increase in the number of mortgage loans made reduces the yields on such loans. If, prior to the government operation, private lenders viewed bonds and mortgages as equally attractive, bonds would be more attractive than mortgages following the government operation. Presumably, private lenders would then make fewer mortgage loans and buy more bonds. The volume of mortgage lending would increase by the amount of the government operation only if the amount of private lending made is completely insensitive to changes in relative yields.

In fact, there is strong reason for believing that something approximating the reverse is the case. Over relatively short periods of time the yields on mortgages and on bonds of various kinds tend to move closely together. In the long run the differential yield of conventional first mortgages over, say, the Moody's Aaa bond yield or the yield on long-term Treasury bonds may change in response to changes in any of a variety of underlying conditions. But over the course of a recession and the subsequent recovery from it the yield differential on the two kinds of securities is remarkably constant. This suggests that the private sector as a whole would reduce its mortgage lending and increase its purchase of bonds, largely to offset the effects of government supported purchases of new mortgages. In a very real sense, government attempts to increase the supply of mortgage funds is rather like borrowing from Peter to pay Peter.

Paying Part of the Interest Cost

Although attempts to increase the supply of mortgage funds may have little lasting effect upon mortgage interest costs, other actions of government may make borrowing cheaper. Indeed, by making it easier for private lenders to sell off mortgage loans held in their portfolios, FNMA and the Government National Mortgage Association (GNMA) increase the attractiveness of mortgage investments. Consequently mortgages became more attractive relative to bonds and other investments at given yields, and mortgage yields fall relative to the yields on other assets. By using resources to make mortgage loans more marketable and by incurring the cost of doing so, the government is in effect paying a part of the borrower's financing cost. Specific programs which reduce mortgage yields will be presented in the next section.

At first glance, it seems like a good thing to make borrowing cheaper. But lower borrowing costs have two side effects. First, lowering borrowing costs makes certain ways of providing housing cheaper. For instance, aluminum siding has a higher initial cost than other forms of exterior finishing for houses but requires less frequent painting and other forms of maintenance. With a fall in borrowing costs, the annual payment a homeowner must make to cover the cost of aluminum siding falls relative to the cost of financing and maintaining other forms of exterior finishing. More homeowners, no doubt, would choose aluminum siding as borrowing costs fall. Part of the impact of lower interest rates, then, is simply to increase the capital expenditure on dwellings of a given size. Only a part of the increased volume of mortgage lending increases the amount of housing (the number of dwelling units or the square feet of living area per dwelling).

Reducing borrowing costs reduces the annual payment a family would have to make to acquire a dwelling of any given size. With housing cheaper families presumably would consume more housing. However, using more of the nation's fixed productive capacity to produce more housing necessarily means, except during recessions, that fewer of all other goods and services are available. As the consumption of food, clothing and furnishing declines and that of housing increases, the value of additional housing declines relative to the value placed upon additional food, etc. A larger kitchen is worth less if there is less food to prepare in it. Part of the effect of lowering borrowing costs is simply to alter consumption choices. It does not enhance total welfare.

Are Borrowing Costs Too High?

The two side effects of lower borrowing costs — borrowing more for a given sized dwelling and reducing the value placed upon housing relative to other kinds of consumption — may be either good or bad. The answer depends upon whether the yield or return on capital used to produce housing is greater or less than that on capital used to produce other goods. If the yield on capital used to produce housing is higher than the yield on other kinds of capital, shifting capital away from the production of other goods to housing increases the national income. This is because the additional output given up to obtain housing is less than the value placed on additional housing. Conversely, if the yield on housing capital is less than the yield on capital used to produce other goods, lowering borrowing costs and thus using more capital to produce housing results in a net loss.

There are reasons which might be cited to suggest that too little capital goes into the production of housing. These are certainly outweighed, however, by two features of our tax system which together suggest that the gross yield on capital used to produce owner-occupied housing is only about half that on capital used in the corporate sector of our economy. The corporate sector uses roughly two dollars of equity capital (funds raised by the sale of stock and retained earnings) for every dollar of borrowed capital. The return to the latter is paid in the form of interest, which is deducted from income before tax to arrive at a taxable income. To earn 8.5 percent, the approximate real return on capital after payment of all but personal income taxes, a return of 17 percent must be earned on equity capital (assuming a corporate tax rate of 50 percent). Corporations thus must earn a return of 17 percent on two-thirds of their capital and 8.5 percent on the rest, or

147

almost 14 percent, to pay out 8.5 percent after paying the corporate income tax. Capital used in the unincorporated sector, however, need earn only 8.5 percent to pay out 8.5 percent before personal income taxes. Owner-occupied housing, of course, belongs to the unincorporated sector.

Moreover, unlike other capital used in the economy, no personal income tax is paid on the return to capital used in the owner-occupied housing sector. Homeowners are allowed to deduct mortgage interest and property taxes paid in calculating taxable income but are not required to include the rental value of their home in gross income, as they would have to if they rented the home to someone else. If the tax on additional income is 20 cents per dollar, an 8.5 percent return before payment of personal taxes is equivalent to a return of 6.8 percent after tax. Homeowners would be willing to invest additional capital in their home so long as it yields more than this amount. Consequently, one would expect capital invested in owner-occupied housing to yield 20 percent less than other forms of capital and, indeed, only about half the yield of capital used in the corporate sector.

Matters become even worse during inflationary periods, as currently. Interest rates rise as lenders build in an inflation premium to protect the real value of the stream of repayments. Though the additional interest payments made on mortgage loans reflect a repayment of part of the capital originally loaned, as interest these payments are tax-deductible. In inflationary periods, then, the cost of capital in sectors such as housing which depend heavily on debt financing is reduced relative to capital costs for other sectors. Even in the absence of inflation, however, because of the corporate income tax and the personal tax treatment of income from owner-occupied housing, capital invested in owner-occupied housing yields substantially less income than capital invested in the corporate sector of our economy. For this reason, there is little rationale for programs which further reduce borrowing costs to homeowners. Doing so merely leads homeowners to use capital less productively and withdraws capital from the production of commodities consumers value more highly.

SHORT-TERM POLICIES

Programs which seek to increase the supply of mortgage funds for private lending are likely to have little lasting impact on private mortgage interest rates. A variety of governmental activities, however, may reduce directly the rates of interest mortgage borrowers must pay. Whether these actions are desirable or not depends upon whether the return to capital invested in housing exceeds or is less than that on capital invested elsewhere in the economy. Insofar as owner-occupied

148

housing is concerned, there is strong reason to believe that the return on capital is only about half that earned in the corporated sector of the economy. Consequently, programs designed to reduce the borrowing costs of homeowners have little to recommend them.

It is now appropriate to examine the nature and likely effects of principal housing credits programs.[1] These are programs of GNMA, the Federal Housing Administration (FHA), the Farmers Home Administration (FmHA), and so-called tax expenditure programs related to housing. The last refer to tax revenue losses resulting from tax provisions such as the treatment of income from owner-occupied housing, described above.

Government National Mortgage Association

GNMA is a "spin-off" of FNMA. The latter was established by the FHA in 1938 to provide a secondary market for the then-new FHA mortgages. In its early years it was a net buyer. In 1948, FNMA was authorized to purchase VA mortgages from private lenders, while in 1970 it acquired the authority to purchase conventional mortgages as well.

FNMA's nature changed considerably in 1954. Under the Housing Act of that year, it was authorized to purchase so-called Section 220 mortgages. The latter are mortgages made on housing in urban renewal areas on liberalized terms, in effect "special assistance" for such housing. The 1954 Housing Act also divided FNMA into three distinct parts: secondary market operations, special assistance functions, and management and liquidation of the portfolio of mortgages previously acquired. Later, FNMA's special assistance operations were expanded to include the purchase of Section 221 (d) (3) mortgages for moderate income rental housing in 1961 and Section 221 (h) low-interest loans to non-profit organizations for rehabilitation and resale of homes to lower-income families.

The Housing and Urban Development Act of 1968 produced still more changes. Under this Act, FNMA became a federally chartered, privately owned corporation. The President, however, appointed five of the fifteen directors and HUD was given power to regulate certain aspects of its operations. The new FNMA retained only the secondary market function of its predecessor. The primary motive for the change in FNMA, one suspects, was to make the federal budget look smaller.

GNMA was organized as a wholly owned federal corporation to carry out the special assistance as well as the management and liquida-

---

[1] For an excellent summary of housing credit and other programs see U.S. Department of Housing and Urban Development, *Housing in the Seventies, A Report of the National Housing Policy Review* (Washington, 1974), to which I have referred at several points in preparing this section.

tion functions of the old FNMA. Its special assistance functions, financed by funds authorized by Congress and provided by the Treasury, included buying loans made under the Section 235 (low-income homeowners) and Section 236 (renters subsidy programs, housing for the elderly), and others.

Like FNMA, GNMA tries to increase the supply of funds for mortgage lending. It does so through the use of so-called pass-through securities. These are securities sold principally by mortgage companies as an alternative to selling mortgages directly to institutional investors, such as pension funds and life insurance companies principally. The investor receives monthly payments of principal and interest and any prepayments of mortgages backing the pass-through securities. As such, there would seem to be little difference between the sale of pass-throughs and the mortgages themselves, apart from how the accounts are kept. GNMA, however, guarantees the pass-throughs for timely payment of principal and interest.

Pass-through securities are unlikely to have much permanent impact on private mortgage interest rates. To the extent that pension funds buy these securities rather than bonds, bond yields would rise. In addition, if the proceeds of the sale of pass-throughs were used to make additional mortgage loans, private mortgage yields would fall, and bonds would become more attractive relative to mortgages. Other lenders, therefore, would have the incentive to make fewer mortgage loans and buy more bonds. GNMA's guarantee, however, works directly to reduce the private market yield on mortgages used to back the pass-throughs. By reducing the risk of loss to holders of pass-through securities, they became more attractive to hold. Institutional investors would thus pay higher prices for pass-through securities, and mortgage companies would make mortgage loans at lower interest rates than otherwise. GNMA's guarantee, then, amounts to the federal government paying part of the borrowing cost for mortgage loans used to back pass-through securities.

GNMA's other major activity is the so-called tandem plan. GNMA purchases FHA-insured mortgages (see below) under various subsidized housing programs. The mortgages purchased are then resold to FNMA or other investors at a lower price which, presumably, reflects the market valuation of these loans. Tandem plan purchases reduce mortgage yields below the market yields and, hence, lower the borrowing costs of the owner of the mortgaged property. This directly reduces the housing cost of certain homeowners. Under most government subsidized housing programs, rentals charged tenants are limited to an amount dependent upon income, for instance 25 percent. The government then pays the balance of the maximum rental the landlord may charge. Under these programs tandem purchases are merely a means of reducing the explicit rental subsidy payment made by the government under the subsidized housing program.

On the whole, there is little to justify the activities of GNMA. To the extent GNMA's activities reduce the interest cost of home-owners, as under the Section 235 program, they seem clearly unjustified. Even for renters, there is no strong reason to suggest the return on capital invested in housing is higher than for other sectors of the economy, and because of a variety of other government subsidies it is probably smaller. Reducing borrowing costs merely serves to use capital wastefully in producing housing and further to reduce the value consumers place on additional housing. To the extent that GNMA's activities serve to reduce borrowing costs on subsidized housing programs, they tend to cover-up the true expenditure made under these programs.

GNMA should be immediately directed to issue no new insurance for pass-through securities. Since the insurance program does not create any direct federal outlays, aside from administrative costs, the budget impact would be negligible.

A second desirable step would be to eliminate the tandem purchase program. Tandem purchases are not only poor economics, but deceptive budgeting. Budget savings will not be immediate because much of the current outlays are dictated by past obligations. A savings of $400 million is likely for FY 1983.

Federal Housing Administration

The FHA was created in 1934 by the National Housing Act to insure privately-made mortgage loans. Most observers feel that it was instrumental in making the fully amortized, relatively long-term (20-to-30 year) loan the standard mortgage instrument in the post-war U.S. FHA insurance implies that a lender's loss is reduced should the loan go into default. A lender would incur legal and administrative costs in foreclosing on a defaulted loan and obtaining possession of the mortgaged property. But he would not suffer from any decline in the value of the mortgaged property below the unpaid balance of the loan, as he would on an uninsured loan. FHA loans are thus more attractive than they would otherwise be, and lenders make them for lower interest rates. These loans reduce borrowing costs for certain homeowners, thus increasing the number of families who own homes and leading them to consume more housing.

The kinds of loans FHA would insure, defined in particular by the size of the loan and the maximum ratio of loan to property value, have changed frequently in the post-war period. For much of this time, however, conventional loans were made by private lenders for up to 70 percent of the value of a property, while FHA-insured loans were made for up to 90 percent. As an alternative to an FHA loan, for

151

which an insurance premium of one-half of 1 percent is charged, a homebuyer might make a 70 percent conventional first mortgage loan and a 20 percent second mortgage loan. (Rates on second mortgage loans were typically twice first mortgage rates.) Borrowers making FHA loans instead presumably found them cheaper. Since there is no reason to believe that the market-imposed interest rates are too high given the riskiness of conventional loans and the resource costs of making and insuring them, one must conclude that FHA insurance also amounts to the federal government paying part of a homeowners' borrowing cost. Given the fact that capital invested in owner-occupied housing would yield only about half what it yields in the corporate sector, there is little reason to induce more capital into home ownership through FHA loans.

Indeed, given the development of private mortgage insurance in the 1970s, FHA loan insurance seems largely unnecessary. In the 1970s, 80 percent conventional loans have become quite common, and conventional lenders frequently loan up to 90 or even 95 percent of a property's value, where permitted by the regulatory agencies, if these loans are privately insured. Rates charged by private mortgage insurance companies are roughly half those charged by the FHA, though, unlike FHA, private companies insure only a fraction of the top of the loan. Since the private market now does more cheaply what FHA once did, there is little reason for continuing FHA mortgage insurance.

Since the mid-1950s, the FHA has also been charged with operating special insurance programs as an adjunct to other housing subsidy programs. Most noteworthy of these was the infamous Section 235 program. The latter enabled low- and moderate-income families to purchase houses financed by FHA-insured loans at interest rates as low as 1 percent per year, with the federal government paying the balance of the interest required by a private lender. In the early 1970s large numbers of such loans were defaulted on, and charges of corruption by FHA officials were rampant.

The program was clearly ill-conceived. While the Section 235 program reduced the borrowing costs of acquiring a home, it did nothing to reduce the cost of maintaining it or to increase the incomes of the recipients. Lower-income families usually had little equity in their homes. When unexpected, expensive repairs became necessary or when the family's income was lower than anticipated, the cheapest course of action was frequently to default on the mortgage and give up the home it financed. Quite generally, reducing borrowing costs, as in the Section 235 program, is inferior to direct housing subsidies. The proceeds of the latter can be used to meet either mortgage payments or the cost of unexpected repairs. If made to vary inversely with current income received, such subsidy payments would help solve the problem of unanticipated decreases in income.

There thus seems little reason to continue FHA special insurance programs, either. Like GNMA's tandem program, these programs serve to hide part of the costs of other housing subsidy programs. *Therefore, the FHA should be directed to stop making new FHA-insured loans.*

Farmers Home Administration

FmHA provides essentially the same services for rural persons as the alphabetical agencies already discussed do for urban dwellers. Created by the Housing Act of 1949, FmHA borrows from the Treasury to make direct loans and insures loans made by private lenders. In somewhat similar fashion to the Section 235 program just discussed, FmHA pays part of the interest cost on loans to low-income rural families. Since the nature of these activities is fundamentally the same whether performed for the urban or for the rural population, FmHA programs are subject to essentially the same shortcomings as their urban counterpart programs are. *The Farmers Home Administration should cease making direct and guaranteed loans for rural housing.*

Tax Subsidies

In addition to the programs already described, the federal government seeks to reduce housing costs of private families and individuals through several tax subsidies. By so doing, the Treasury incurs a cost in lost revenue, which in turn means higher taxes for everyone else if a given level of expenditure is to be maintained. By and large, the effect of these tax-breaks is to reduce the capital costs of housing, with the unfavorable side-effects described earlier. Because of the corporate income tax, from which owner-occupied housing is exempt, these tax-breaks are expecially harmful.

By far the most important of tax expenditure programs for housing is the tax treatment of income from owner-occupied housing. As was described earlier, by not requiring the inclusion of the imputed rental value of owner-occupied housing as taxable income but allowing deductions for mortgage interest and property taxes paid, the cost of capital for owner-occupied housing is reduced by 20 percent. In part, so doing leads homeowners to invest more capital in dwellings of any given size with no improvement of their housing. Moreover, since capital costs are perhaps three-fourths of housing costs, the price of housing to homeowners is reduced by about 15 percent. Part of this price reduction causes homeowners to consume more housing with no improvement in their well-being. The tax treatment is estimated to result in a revenue loss of about $25 billion, by far the most important quantitatively of the programs discussed in this essay.

153

The tax treatment of income from owner-occupied housing is the most perverse subsidy scheme imaginable. Most homeowners tend to be middle- and upper-income families, and so the benefits of the subsidy go disproportionally to these families. In addition, the extent of the tax-saving and housing price reduction increases as the taxpayer's income does. This is partly because the additional tax paid on additional income rises as income does and partly because the fraction of taxpayers who itemize deductions, and thus benefit from the subsidy, also rises with income. One would be hard-pressed to find anyone who would endorse such a subsidy scheme if paid as a straight cash subsidy. Paradoxically, the latter would be less objectional on purely economic grounds, for it would increase the benefit to subsidy recipients at the same cost to everyone else.

The other principal tax expenditures for housing are various ways of taxing capital gains at less than ordinary rates. Assets other than housing receive such breaks as well, but not surprisingly they are especially important for owner-occupied housing. For some years, homeowners have been able to defer tax on capital gains from the sale of a house if another is purchased within eighteen months. Recently, homeowners have been allowed a one-time exemption of the first $100,000 of capital gain at age 55 or older. The only justification for the latter is the fact that valuing acquisition cost at historical cost during inflationary periods means that nominal as well as real capital gains would be taxed; the former in effect represents a capital levy. The deferral and exemption from capital gains taxation also reduces capital costs and housing prices to homeowners and benefits higher- (at the expense of lower-) income households. As such, there is little to recommend the tax treatment of capital gains from housing.

LONG-TERM CONSIDERATIONS

The conclusion of this essay is that housing credit programs are boondoggles, just as post-office subsidies or loans to Chrysler. Whatever good these programs might do can be done better by other approaches.

Forms of Assistance

What programs should replace housing credit programs? The answer depends upon the purpose of the subsidy. The principal aim of most housing credit programs is to improve the housing of the American public, especially the lower-income population. For this purpose, *a direct housing subsidy such as a rent certificate program would be more suitable.* Eligible families would receive certificates or vouchers. Renters could use these certificates for partial or total payment of rent for private rental dwellings. Certificates for homeowners might take the form of stamps of small denomination like food stamps. These could be used not only for making mortgage and property tax payments but also for maintenance and operation. In this way, the economic waste which results from subsidizing capital inputs only would be avoided.

But is it desirable simply to try to improve people's housing? Though obviously important, housing is only one item of consumption upon which people's well-being depends. Improving people's housing does improve people's well being. But, as pointed out earlier, a part of the effect of a housing subsidy is merely to reduce the valuation people place on additional housing as compared with other kinds of consumption. If the value of the rent certificate described earlier were given in cash the recipient could spend it as he wished and his well-being would be increased at least as much. If he desired to spend the whole of the subsidy on housing, he could do so. If he preferred to spend only part of the subsidy on housing and the rest on other things, as most recipients doubtless would, it is presumably because he considers himself better-off doing so.

The direct benefits of housing subsidies are thus no greater and almost certainly smaller than the benefits of income subsidies. Why, then, have housing subsidies at all? There are only two possible answers. One is that there are indirect benefits — benefits which accrue to others than the subsidy recipient. It is widely believed that such indirect benefits of housing subsidies are indeed significant, and such beliefs were important sources of support for the initial establishment of the public housing program and others. It would be far beyond the scope of this essay to attempt a careful evaluation of them. I have done so elsewhere[2] and concluded that such effects are negligible. A second reason for providing housing rather than general income subsidies is that families and individuals consume too little housing for their own good. Such an argument, of course, is pure paternalism. Though certainly a subjective assessment, there is no room for paternalism in a free society. *Not only housing credit programs but all housing programs should be replaced by programs designed to increase the funds available for private spending of whatever kind the recipient wishes.*

Tax Revision

Personal income tax provisions are sometimes justified as improving the housing of the American public. These provisions, however, share the same shortcomings as credit programs. By reducing capital

---

[2]*Public Housing, An Economic Evaluation* (Washington: American Enterprise Institute, 1973), Ch. III.

costs relative to the costs of maintenance and operation, part of the subsidy is simply wasted. Unlike other housing programs, which are aimed at low- and moderate-income families, tax provisions for owner-occupied housing provide benefits mainly to higher-income families. This last, alone, would seem sufficient reason for eliminating them.

The simplest way to tackle the differential taxation of income from owner-occupied housing would be to disallow deductions for mortgage interest and property taxes paid on new owner-occupied homes.[3] The principal advantage of doing this is that it would be relatively easy to implement and could thus be done fairly quickly. A great disadvantage of this method, though, is the fact that the implicit return on the homeowner's own or equity funds invested in the home—the difference between market value of the home and the outstanding indebtedness on it—would remain untaxed. The implicit return on equity funds would be relatively small on newly financed homes initially, since mortgages typically account for 80 to 90 percent or even more of a home's purchase price. If recent trends of market value appreciation continue, however, the return on equity funds would grow over time.

A more satisfactory, longer term reform, therefore, would be to require the homeowner to include the implicit rental value of the home as income subject to tax and to allow deductions for maintenance and certain operating expenditures. The greatest difficulty would be in insuring accuracy in the reported rental value. A reasonable way to determine this rental would be for the Internal Revenue Service to determine and publish the average ratio of assessed to market value of single-family homes. The taxpayer would then divide the latest assessed value of his home by the assessment ratio for his jurisdiction. Market value so determined could then be multiplied by a ratio, also determined by the IRS, of imputed rental value to market value. The taxpayer would be allowed the option of reporting a lower value, subject to justification by special circumstances. Calculating implicit income in this way would be no more difficult or less accurate than current calculations of deduction for state sales or gasoline taxes paid. One other problem is that such a change in the tax laws would result in capital losses. To avoid these, homes which are owner-occupied as of

---

[3]The recommendations which follow are based upon the presumption that income will remain the basis for federal taxation. They are directed at eliminating the differential taxation of income from owner-occupied housing and other real assets under the current system of income taxation. If the bases of federal taxation were changed, the appropriate treatment of owner-occupied housing might well be different.

Editor's Note: See Stephen J. Entin's essay on tax policy for a discussion of the tax treatment of owner-occupied housing under a consumption-based tax.

the date of enactment of the change could be exempted from the new tax provisions.

As was discussed earlier, problems also arise with respect to taxation of capital gains on owner-occupied housing. Failure to tax them has essentially the same effects as provisions which reduce taxes on current income. In principle, one would want to tax real capital gains at the same rates as ordinary income. Nominal gains — gains in dollar values resulting purely from changes in the value of money — should not be taxed at all. Depreciation — the reduction in the value of an asset such as a house associated with its use during a certain period of time — should be related to its replacement cost during that period of time.

An appropriate way to tax capital gains, therefore, would be as follows. Take latest market value, calculated as above, minus current relative to last year's value of an appropriate general price index[4] times last year's market value. This amount would then be added to the implicit rental value whose calculation was described above for inclusion in taxable income. The price inflator could be supplied by the IRS to the taxpayer. Though somewhat complicated, the calculation would certainly be no more difficult than calculating one's deduction for medical and dental expenses currently.

Corporate Income Tax

Even if the reforms suggested earlier in this section were all adopted, new capital invested in owner-occupied housing would yield a return only about half as large as that in the rest of the economy. This is because of the corporate income tax, whose effect was discussed in the first section. *Serious consideration should thus be given to eliminating the corporate income tax.* This, of course, is a complicated question, one which is far beyond the scope of this essay. The corporate income tax, however, is a serious obstacle to the equilization of the return to capital in different uses. The latter is clearly a desirable state of affairs for a free market economy. Yet the corporate income tax certainly leads to a much greater departure from a desired state than all the housing credit programs taken together.

---

[4]The consumer expenditure implicit price deflator would probably be best for this purpose.

8

Transportation

by Thomas Gale Moore

Government involvement in transportation has a very long history. Construction of bridges, roads, and port facilities has long been recognized as an important function of the state. Adam Smith in *The Wealth of Nations* wrote:

> The third and last duty of the sovereign or commonwealth is that of erecting and maintaining those public institutions and those public works, which, though they may be in the highest degree advantageous to a great society, are, however, of such a nature, that a profit could never repay the expence to any individual or small number of individuals, and which it therefore cannot be expected that any individual or small number of individuals should erect or maintain. . . .

> It does not seem necessary that the expence of those public works should be defrayed from that public revenue. . . . The greater part of such public works may easily be so managed, as to afford a particular revenue sufficient for defraying their own expence, without bringing any burden upon the general revenue of the society.[1]

In recent decades, the federal government has subsidized all the major forms of transportation. Railroad subsidies, however, go back to the large land grants in the 19th century. More recently the government has been involved in direct subsidies of rail passenger transportation, freight transportation in the Northeast and a subsidy program for selected roads. Government funding of highways can be considered aid to trucking and bus transportation. Some air carriers have received direct government subsidies since at least the 1930s. The construction and maintenance by the government of harbors, docks, and canals have helped significantly barge lines and shipping interests. Direct subsidies have been provided for our merchant marine since 1936.

Depending on the political popularity of various forms of transpor-

---

[1] (New York: Random House, The Modern Library, 1937), pp. 681–682.

tation, these subsidies have waxed and waned. During the 1960s and most of the 1970s, there were attempts to increase user fees and to reduce subsidies for airlines and motor carriers. Railroads received little in the way of government aid from the time of land grants in the second half of the 19th century until the 1970s. Until the post-World War II period, mass transit was mainly a private enterprise activity. Federal aid for mass transit did not start until the mid-1960s and was small-scale and mainly for capital projects until the 1970s. Federal expenditures on mass transit projects are now second in size only to highway expenditure (Table 1).

Regulation

With government subsidies have come government regulations. Except for basically private transportation (such as the individual automobile), part or all of every mode has been regulated in terms of entry, price, and quality. Generally, the objective of this regulation has ostensibly been to promote the particular form of transportation. In practice it has served to increase the profitability of the medium. In each case regulation has attempted, not necessarily successfully, to cartelize the industry.

There has been much disagreement over the intended goals of the Interstate Commerce Commission (ICC); nearly all scholars believe that the railroads pushed for the legislation in order to increase their own profitability. Attempts to cartelize the railroad industry often broke down, with the result that many railroad executives wanted a government agency to enforce their cartel rules. Other interests had different objectives, with the result that the original legislation was not a coherent piece but one that represented conflicting viewpoints.

Trucking regulation was established at the state level in the late 1910s and early 1920s in order to protect railroad interests. Federal legislation did not come until 1935 and then reflected both railroad interests and those of major trucking companies. Water carrier and freight forwarder regulation followed in the early 1940s. Each additional regulation appears to have been designed primarily to enhance the effectiveness of the original and increase the railroads' profitability.

With the development of air carriers in the 1920s and 1930s came federal aid in the form of subsidies for carrying mail. These subsidies in turn stimulated entry and increased competition for passengers. The regulation of air carriers originated in 1938 with the stated objective of fostering the industry. This was taken by the regulators as a mandate to cartelize the commercial airline carriers.

Even though the Federal Maritime Commission approves collusive

160

Table 1
Transportation
(in millions of dollars)

Major Missions and Programs	1979 actual	1980 estimate	1981 estimate
OUTLAYS			
Ground transportation:			
Transportation energy initiatives (proposed):			
Public transportation capital investment	–	50	425
Auto-use management	–	50	180
Fuel economy standards	–	–	4
Cooperative automotive basic research	–	–	8
Highway improvement and construction	6,759	7,116	7,045
Highway safety	733	1,243	1,465
Mass transit	2,542	2,712	2,801
Railroads:			
Existing law	1,962	2,321	1,756
Proposed legislation	–	–	40
Regulation	67	79	84
Subtotal, ground transportation	12,064	13,571	13,808
Air transportation:			
Airways and airports......................	2,850	3,124	3,297
Aeronautical research and technology	443	532	554
Air carrier subsidies	72	94	87
Regulation	27	30	29
Subtotal, air transportation	3,392	3,779	3,967
Water transportation:			
Marine safety and transportation	1,424	1,570	1,728
Ocean shipping	543	668	590
Regulation	10	12	12
Subtotal, water transportation	1,977	2,250	2,330
Other transportation........................	93	102	109
Deductions for offsetting receipts	– 67	– 70	– 55
Total, outlays..........................	**17,459**	**19,631**	**20,159**
ADDENDUM			
Off-budget Federal entity:			
U.S. Railway Association:			
Budget authority	59	68	71
Outlays	89	68	68
MEMORANDUM – Attribution of Federal Financing Bank outlays			
Railroads	– 25	305	241

Source: The Budget of the United States Government FY 1981

agreements on freight rates for ocean shipments by granting antitrust immunity, the most important "regulatory" devices to protect the merchant marine are the cabotage laws and the cargo preference laws. The cabotage laws, which go back to at least the early 19th century, provide that goods and passengers moving between U.S. ports must be carried in U.S. flagships. Since U.S. flagships are defined as ships constructed in American shipyards and manned by American crews, this provision provides a significant subsidy to those special interests. Cargo preference laws also aid the American merchant marine by restricting certain classifications of cargo to U.S. bottoms. For example, the Military Transportation Act of 1904 requires that all military cargos be carried in U.S. flagships or vessels owned by the United States. Under a 1934 congressional resolution half of all exports financed by the Export-Import Bank must move in U.S. bottoms. The Cargo Preference Act of 1954 mandates that at least half of cargos financed with foreign aid must be carried in vessels of U.S. registry. The subsidies to the merchant marine in these programs are hidden in the military and foreign aid budgets and in the cost of Export-Import Bank-financed shipments. While these subsidies are wasteful and should be eliminated, this would require a change in the laws.

Since the National Traffic and Motor Vehicle Safety Act of 1966, the automobile industry has become increasingly regulated. In 1968, controls on auto exhaust emissions were imposed. More recently the Congress has required manufacturers to meet specified fleet gas mileage standards. While the cost of these regulations is small for the government, the burden on the automobile industry is huge. General Motors, for example, has estimated that it spent over $8 billion in a six-year period, 1974–1979, to meet regulatory standards.[2]

With certain exceptions, the trend towards regulating the transportation industries reversed in the 1970s. Air cargo and air passenger deregulation bills were passed by Congress in 1977 and 1978. The partial deregulation of trucking and railroads followed in 1980. There has been no significant move towards deregulation of the merchant marine, nor has there been anything more than an extension of the time given the automobile industry to meet safety, environmental, and fuel economy standards.

It is necessary for the government to cease regulating and cartelizing the transportation industries, and it should eliminate subsidies. Transportation companies are large, mature enterprises that can survive and prosper without federal aid.

The next section evaluates each federal government program dealing with transportation. The evaluations are based on the benefits derived from the program, whether the activity is an appropriate government function, and, if so, whether the program should be handled at the local, state, or federal level. The basic criterion for judging if an expenditure is appropriate is whether the market could handle

---

[2] *1980 General Motors Public Interest Report,* "How Government Monitors our Performance," April 7, 1980, p. 115.

the problem as well as the government. If there are major externalities from a program that a market solution cannot adequately internalize, then the expenditure is judged to be a proper government function. In addition if users of government-provided facilities pay the cost of the facilities and a suitable private alternative does not exist, then the program is justified.

If a program is appropriate for the government, then what level of government should administer it? As a rule, it is better to run all programs from the most local jurisdiction that permits the externalities to be adequately handled. Thus mass transit systems are clearly local while certification of airline pilots is an appropriate federal role.

SHORT-TERM POLICIES

In the sections below each government program dealing with transportation is described and analyzed. Recommended obligations for FY 1982 and 1983 are given (Table 2). With the exception of the Civil Aeronautics Board figures, the estimates for FY 1983 can be taken as long-run projections of the appropriate level of government outlays. After 1985, the CAB should be totally abolished, but some of the subsidies must be transferred to the Department of Transportation, because they are guaranteed for ten years under the Airline Deregulation Act.

Ground Transportation

Federal Highway Administration

The federal highway construction program has been mainly a user-financed system. The Highway Revenue Act of 1956 provides for the proceeds of federal taxes on gasoline, trucks, buses, trailers, tires, inner tubes, diesel fuels, and some other minor user's taxes to be paid into a Highway Trust Fund. This trust fund is drawn upon to pay for the construction of a federal highway system, primarily the interstate system. The interstate highway system was designed to be a road program that tied together every state. Users were to pay for it so it would not be a burden to the general taxpayer. While there may be a question about whether each class of users is paying an appropriate share, there seems little doubt that highway users are paying their way. The Office of Management and Budget estimates that receipts from the tax on users during FY 1981 will amount to about $8.2 billion, while appropriations for highway construction will be $7.9 billion, and the total appropriation from the Highway Trust Fund will be slightly greater than $8.2 billion.

Of the total Federal Highway Administration estimated budget for FY 1981, $3.9 billion is for the interstate system, $2 billion for rural

Table 2

Table 2
Transportation
(in millions of dollars)

Major Missions and Programs	1981 estimate	1982 recommended	1983 recommended
OBLIGATIONS			
Ground Transportation:			
Highway improvement and construction	7,192	7,200	5,200
Highway safety	2,113	1,800	1,800
Mass transit	3,915	1,000	0
Energy Saving Program	1,222	0	0
Railroads	1,908	312	0
Automobile energy initiatives (proposed):			
Use Management		0	0
Fuel Economy Standards ⎫			
Cooperative automotive basic ⎬	278	0	0
research ⎭			
Regulation	85	40	0
Subtotal, Ground Transportation	16,713	10,352	7,000
Air Transportation:			
Airways and Airports	3,410	3,000	550
Aeronautical research and technology	572	0	0
Air carrier subsidies	86	84	84
Regulation	29	29	29
Subtotal, Air Transportation	4,097	3,113	663
Water Transportation:			
Marine Safety and Transportation	1,821	1,906	2,006
Ocean Shipping	587	0	0
Regulation	12	0	0
Subtotal, Water Transportation	2,420	1,906	2,006
Total obligations	23,230	15,371	9,669

and small urban highways, $1.2 billion for urbanized area highways, just under $1 billion for bridge construction, and $0.8 billion for safety. Broken down by purpose, $1.8 billion goes for highway safety-related projects, such as bridge construction, elimination of highway hazards and roadside obstacles, pavement marking demonstration projects, and rail-highway crossings. The remaining $7.2 billion is spent on actual construction and major maintenance of the highways. Federal highway expenditures currently are limited to construction projects. *Legislation should be passed to permit the use of these funds for maintenance of the interstate system.* Moreover, at the moment the Highway Trust Fund does not cover all federal expenditures. *Either these expenditures should be reduced and shifted to the state level or the taxes for the Highway Trust Fund should be increased to cover these expenditures.*

The primary source of Trust Fund revenue is from the federal gas tax, which currently is four cents per gallon. While the nominal value of the tax has not been changed since it was imposed in 1956, its real value has been sharply reduced, by nearly two-thirds, due to inflation. The remaining portion of the interstate system is largely urban freeways which are the most expensive to construct. However, since construction of the interstate highway system is 93 percent completed, large sums of additional money will not be needed. It is not adequate funding that is holding up completion but political disputes over the location and desirability of the freeways.

Congress reduced the authorization for highway construction for 1982. It would seem desirable at least to restore the previous level of funding, $9 billion, until the interstate system is finished. At that time a reduction would be possible. Funding then would be aimed at maintaining the existing network of highways. *A one-cent a gallon tax increase would raise about $1 billion in extra revenues for the trust fund, bringing total annual receipts to around $9 billion.* For subsequent years about $2 billion less can be spent because the interstate system will be virtually completed.

The National Highway Traffic Safety Administration

While the Federal Highway Administration spends some money on safety-related programs, mainly providing money for building safer highways or upgrading existing ones, the other large highway-related agency, the National Highway Traffic Safety Administration (NHTSA), is concerned exclusively with safety. NHTSA's primary function is mandating safer vehicles and driving; it is budgeted to spend about $300 million on this task in FY 1981.

The congressional purpose in establishing NHTSA was to reduce the number of highway-related fatalities. Federal regulation of the safety of automobiles began with the 1966 National Traffic and Motor Vehicle Safety Act which required, among other things, that new cars be sold with seat belts. At that time highway fatalities were running about 50,000 per year. Fatalities continued to rise until they hit a peak of over 56,000 in 1972. The reduction in driving due to gas shortages and higher prices, in combination with slower highway speeds, has lowered fatalities to about 50,000.

Notwithstanding the large number of fatalities, there are considerable reservations about (1) the role of government in mandating safety and (2) the appropriate level of government regulating safety. Certain regulatory requirements protect only the occupants of a vehicle; others protect pedestrians or other vehicles and their occupants.

165

Requiring good working brakes, prohibiting drunk driving, mandating adequate lights for night driving, all protect parties other than the driver and his passengers. Such safeguards reduce externalities and therefore are desirable. Given that a governmental role is desirable for reducing these externalities, should it be done by the states or the federal government? Since state governments can take into account local driving conditions, local public concerns, and respond better to local public wishes, this type of regulation should be left to the states. Most driving is intrastate and, therefore, there appears to be no reason why the federal government should be doing this regulating.

Federal requirements for safety devices that reduce the risks to occupants of vehicles are even more questionable. If a consumer wants seat belts, collapsible steering columns, or padded dashboards, the consumer can buy them. The consumer can weigh the costs of the improved safety against the consumer's preferences for reducing automobile driving risks. As a result, there does not seem to be any significant reason why the federal government should be regulating automobile safety.

NHTSA also has been given the task of regulating automobile energy consumption through gas mileage standards. There is no reason for such prescriptions. It is true, due to other federal regulatory programs, petroleum products have been under-priced. The remedy for that is not more regulation but decontrol of energy prices. That is being implemented, at least for oil.

The National Highway Traffic Safety Administration, therefore, should be abolished. This would save around $300 million per year for the federal government. It would also provide significant benefits to the auto industry and to consumers. The main cost of NHTSA is not the federal cost but the significantly higher prices consumers must pay for vehicles as a result of its regulation.

The Urban Mass Transit Administration

In the mid 1960s the federal government appropriated a small amount of aid for the construction of major mass transit projects. This assistance has grown rapidly and now includes operating subsidies as well. In FY 1981, the government plans to spend a little less than $4 billion. This is part of a long-range spending program of $52 billion in the 1980s.

On the surface, urban mass transit would appear to be a local responsibility. Many urban transit projects are confined to one state; even those that involve more than one state are primarily local in nature. There would appear to be no good reason why the federal government should impose taxes on the nation as a whole and then transfer the money back to a particular community for a project that will have only local benefits.

Many observers would argue that no government, at any level, should be involved in building mass transit systems. If a transit system is worth building and operating then users should be able to pay for the system through the fare-box. This argument makes good sense if users are faced with paying the true marginal cost of other forms of transportation and housing. But in most cases auto travel, especially rush-hour travel, is not charged its true opportunity cost. Rush-hour automobile use imposes large congestion costs on users; air pollution in urban areas is aggravated by commuter traffic; excess highway capacity may be built to handle commuter traffic. In many urban centers it is difficult, if not impossible, to charge drivers for the costs they create. Unless the city is an island, like New York, it may not be possible to charge tolls for the use of highways into the city. Parking taxes can be levied, but employers can reduce the cost of such taxes through employer-supplied parking spaces, which in practice may be difficult to tax. As a net result, if those commuting by car cannot be charged the costs they impose on others, a program of subsidizing transit may be a third best. However, that still does not justify subsidies from the federal government.

Therefore, the federal government should reduce its expenditures for mass transit quickly and discontinue them as soon as possible thereafter. Because of contracts that local transit boards may have entered into under the understanding that the federal government would cover most of the cost, it would be unfair immediately to stop funding these projects. A transition fund of $1 billion should be adequate for FY 1982.

Federal Railroad Administration

The main goals of the Federal Railroad Administration (FRA) are to aid railroads in this country, subsidize rail passenger transportation, and run the government-owned Alaskan railroad. Historically railroads in this country have been private corporations. Because of onerous regulation, a shift in the composition of the national product—from basic heavy commodities to services and high technology products—and the development of an efficient nationwide trucking system, the railroads have been in a serious decline for decades. A declining industry naturally attempts to reduce capacity to meet the lessened demand, but for the railroads this has been bitterly opposed by communities, businesses, and industries that feared a loss of rail service.

From the point of view of both economic efficiency and the taxpayer, the government should get out of the railroad business. It should eliminate the regulation of the railroads that prevents them from putting their business on a sound economic footing. Once that is done there is no excuse for continuing the large subsidy programs that are now part of the budget.

Under the Administration's 1981 budget, the FRA plans to spend $465 million on improving the Northeast Corridor rail line and $354 million on assistance to the nation's railroads and offer $133 million in a loan-guarantee program. It also budgeted $975 million for grants to Amtrak. *All of these programs should be eliminated.* There is no justification for spending the taxpayers' money on subsidizing a private business. The railroads could and should take care of themselves and after deregulation they will be able to do so.

Amtrak no longer should be subsidized. In the past Congress has insisted on federal support for rail passengers. There is no reason except nostalgia for aiding passenger transportation. For long distances, airlines are more efficient; for short distances, either the bus or the private car is more economical. It is possible, but far from certain, that rail passenger traffic can cover its costs in the Boston-New York-Washington corridor. If the Northeast Corridor operations cannot be made profitable, they should be shut down with the rest of Amtrak.

While the Alaskan railroad costs the government only about $10 to $12 million a year, there is no reason for the federal taxpayer to cover this loss. The railroad itself should be sold either to the private sector to run on a profit-making basis or to the State of Alaska, if they want it.

The Alaskan Railroad should be given $12 million for FY 1982 and zero thereafter. Likewise, Amtrak should be authorized $200 million for FY 1982 and zero thereafter, and the nation's railroads should be granted $100 million as wind-up assistance and zero for subsequent years.

Automobile

The Carter Administration proposed a new program to provide grants of $250 million in FY 1981 to state and local governments in order to achieve energy-saving alternatives to the use of single-occupancy automobiles. Subsidizing alternatives to automobiles to save energy makes no economic sense. Provided auto users are paying the appropriate cost of driving, there is no reason for subsidizing alternatives, whether mass transit or other schemes. Recently the Administration initiated a timetable for deregulating crude oil prices in the United States. When this is fully implemented in the fall of 1981, auto users will be paying world prices for crude, which are certainly not too low. The plan for alternatives to the private car faces the same objections as mass transit discussed above. There could be reasons

168

why some communities may feel the need to subsidize alternatives to commuting by automobile; there is no reason why the federal government should be involved.

The fuel economy standards improvement program is part of this initiative and would cost the government $22 million. The automobile manufacturers already have ample incentives to carry on research in this area and no federal subsidies are needed. The program also calls for spending $55 million in FY 1981 on cooperative basic automobile research with the car manufacturers. The auto companies are capable of financing their own research and no government handouts are necessary or desirable.

Ground Transportation Regulation

The Interstate Commerce Commission regulates most large interstate motor carriers, railroads, and some water carriers. This regulation in the past has been very anticompetitive and has imposed large costs on the public. While the budget of the ICC is only $85 million in FY 1981, its regulation leads to significantly higher freight charges and also increases other transportation costs. In 1980, Congress enacted truck and rail deregulation bills which partially reduced the scope of federal controls.

The ICC should be put out of business entirely. Numerous studies have shown that surface freight transportation regulation imposes large costs on the American public.[3] While total deregulation would not result in a perfectly competitive industry, the transportation system would be much more competitive and efficient under deregulation than with the current controls. A transition budget of $40 million for FY 1982 would be desirable.

Air Transportation

The Federal Aviation Administration

The mission of the Federal Aviation Administration (FAA) is to insure the safety of commercial and general aviation. This is handled by licensing pilots and aircraft and by maintaining an elaborate air traffic control system. In addition the FAA provides grants to airports for construction and improvements, conducts and funds research, guarantees aircraft loans, and also operates the two Washington, D.C., airports. The Airport and Airway Trust Fund, which is estimated to take in $2.6 billion in FY 1981, covers about three-quarters of the total

---

[3]See, for example, Thomas Gale Moore, *Freight Transportation Regulation* (Washington, D.C.: American Enterprise Institute, 1972), and Ann F. Friedlaender, *The Dilemma of Freight Transport Regulation* (Washington, D.C.: The Brookings Institution, 1969).

FAA budget. Since the FAA provides some benefits for military aircraft, there is a justification for paying a small part of the budget out of general revenues.

A careful study should be made of whether the beneficiaries of FAA — commercial airlines, air freight carriers, general aviation, military air operations — are paying their fair share. It is likely that general aviation (private pilots, corporate jets, etc.) is not covering the costs attributable to its operations. A small private plane landing at a busy commercial airport can impose significant costs on other airplanes, especially by delaying a large commercial airplane filled with business personnel or vacationers.

While aircraft users appear to be covering about 75 percent of the airway and airport expenses that the FAA incurs, the method of raising the funds is inefficient and not conducive to economizing. The Carter Administration proposed that the receipts of the Airport and Airway Trust Fund in the 1981 budget come mainly from taxes on tickets (74 percent), fuel *ad valorem* tax (8 percent), the waybill tax (5 percent), aircraft/avionics tax (8 percent), and the international passenger tax (5 percent). Nearly 80 percent of the tax receipts of the trust fund comes from commercial airline passengers directly.

It would be preferable to shift, at least in part, from taxation of passengers to taxes levied on landings and takeoffs. Such taxes should be scaled to reflect the relative costs to the FAA of handling the aircraft and the costs imposed on other airway users due to congestion. These costs depend mainly on the time of day. Thus, a large commercial plane landing during peak hours should pay a much larger landing charge than a small plane landing at an off-peak hour. A general aviation aircraft that is landing during peak hours and forcing a large plane into a holding pattern should pay a relatively high landing cost, one that reflects the costs imposed on the FAA and on other aircraft. This would encourage general aviation to use alternative airports or to schedule their operations for non-peak hours, saving resources for all.

These landing charges, however, should be levied by the local airport, which in turn would reimburse the FAA for its costs in maintaining the air control system. Thus, ideally much of the FAA budget should be shifted to local airports, with the exception of that portion which reflects services provided to the military and those expenditures which increase aviation safety generally but cannot be attributed to any given airport. For example, the certification of pilots, planes, and equipment is primarily a federal function and should be covered by user charges at the national level.

About 60 percent of the FAA budget goes for operating the traffic control system ($1.1 billion), maintenance of the traffic control system ($0.6 billion), installation and material services ($0.3 billion), and administration of a flight standards program ($0.2 billion). The next largest part of the budget is for grants-in-aid for airports ($0.7 billion). The third major expenditure of the FAA is for facilities and equipment ($0.35 billion).

With the exception of the administration of the flight standards program and the enroute air traffic control system, the expenditure for operations by the FAA should be covered appropriately by landing fees, since these charges are essentially for maintenance and operation of aircraft control. The airport grants are for runways and other airport related facilities and are properly a cost that should be borne by the local airport authorities. Except for outlays for airport traffic control towers, all other spending under the category of facilities and equipment is of a general interstate nature that should be covered at the federal level.

In summary, landing and takeoff fees levied by airports should cover most of the traffic control operations, maintenance, and installation ($2 billion) plus any expenditures on air traffic control towers ($70 million). *The airport grant program should be abolished. The administration of flight standards and medical programs should be covered by licensing fees imposed on pilots, aviator technicians, and aircraft ($250 million).* Expenditures on facilities, equipment, and operation of the air route traffic control centers, flight service facilities, air navigation facilities, research, engineering, and related outlays, which total something over $300 million, are appropriately a federal cost but should be covered with taxes levied on the industry.

The FAA spends about $50 million annually to run National Airport and Dulles Airport. The FAA should sell both airports to the highest bidder. This would insure that the properties were operated at the highest value use.

Since by FY 1983 only about $300 million would remain of the FAA budget to be covered by existing user charges, passenger ticket taxes should be abolished or lowered to cover only the costs of the enroute air traffic control system.

Aeronautical Research and Technology

The National Aeronautics and Space Administration spends about $500 million on research and development of the civilian and military air transportation system. Primarily, the objective of this program is to maintain U.S. leadership in aeronautical technology. There is no good justification for the federal government to spend money on this program. It is actually likely to divert skilled talent from potentially profitable development into projects that are politically favored. Consequently, it may actually erode our leadership, not strengthen it. Even if the money were well spent, it is not something that the tax-

should be financing. The aircraft companies can finance their own research. *The program should be abolished.*

Air Carrier Subsidies

The Civil Aeronautics Board spends $58 million to subsidize local service carriers, $7 million to subsidize regional carrier operations, $7 million to subsidize Alaskan operations, and $13 million to subsidize "essential air service." The last was established to protect small communities that feared a loss of air service with deregulation. While none of these subsidies is worthwhile, and, on a strict economic basis, all should be abolished, proposing their abolition may not be worth the cost; it would also renege on the implicit bargain struck to achieve airline deregulation. Moreover, it would open up the whole question of airline deregulation and might result in reregulation.

Since the amounts are small, subsidies should be maintained for the next ten years as the law requires.

Airline Regulation

The Congress has enacted an airline bill that will totally deregulate the airlines by 1983 and abolish the Civil Aeronautics Board by 1985. *The schedule is inadequate, and thus funding should continue at the current level.*

Water Transportation

Marine Safety & Transportation

This program reflects primarily the efforts of the Coast Guard to protect the coasts, to aid navigation, and to increase maritime safety. Of the total $1.8 billion Coast Guard budget, nearly $1.2 billion is allocated for operations. This is spent on search and rescue, aids to navigation, enforcement of laws and treaties, marine safety, marine environmental protection, marine science and polar operations, and military readiness. Ninety-five percent of these funds provides benefits to the public for safety and police activities; the rest is spent on basic research. While these programs should not be reduced in size, the Coast Guard could reduce the burden on the taxpayer by charging for some of its services. For example, in the case of search and rescue missions, the individuals aided should be billed for the cost of the rescue. While certainly the victim will not be able to reimburse the government in all cases, wherever possible it should be done.

To increase marine safety, the Coast Guard sets standards and procedures for navigation, licenses personnel, administers a recreational boat safety program, and enforces federal regulation of the merchant marine industry relating to the construction and alteration of merchant vessels. *For many of these activities the Coast Guard should charge fees.* Recreational boats should be licensed, with the proceeds going to support the Coast Guard activities.

Ocean Shipping

The Maritime Administration provides subsidies of about $200 million annually for the construction of U.S. flagships in U.S. shipyards. It also provides subsidies of about $350 million for the operation of U.S. flagships. *These subsidies are completely unwarranted and should be abolished.* We could and should purchase transportation in the cheapest market, which means foreign constructed ships operated with foreign crews. It costs half as much or less to construct a ship in some foreign shipyards as in an American one. It also costs half as much or less to operate the ship with a foreign crew. These subsidies primarily benefit shipyard workers and American merchant marine personnel, who are heavily unionized, relatively high-income workers and are significant contributors to congressional and senatorial campaigns.

It is sometimes argued that the merchant marine program is necessary for national defense. On the basis of World War II experience this does not seem likely. In a very short period of time after the outbreak of hostilities, new shipyards were constructed and were turning out "liberty ships." New crews were quickly trained to man these ships. *If it were felt that an existing merchant marine were necessary, it would be cheaper to buy twice as many ships built in foreign yards for the same resources and mothball them here. They would then be immediately available for use in time of war.*

Federal Maritime Commission

The Federal Maritime Commission (FMC), like other regulatory bodies dealing with transportation, has assumed a mandate to cartelize its industry. In the main the Commission gives antitrust immunity to restraints of trade. It spends much of its effort on attempting to prevent "illegal rebating." *The FMC should be abolished, as it performs no worthwhile function. At the same time the cabotage laws that restrict shipping between U.S. ports to only U.S. flagships should be repealed.*

LONG-TERM CONSIDERATIONS

The philosophy behind the recommendations for the transportation function is described in the quote from Adam Smith in the first section. The government may need to provide a certain infrastructure that the market cannot efficiently produce, but it should attempt to collect from users the cost of doing so. Also, where possible the government should structure its taxes or fees so as to charge the user with the costs of such activity. This will encourage the user to economize and will improve the efficiency of the economy.

Much of the transportation system is in the nature of a public good, or at least it would be very inefficient to use the market to provide the service. For example, it would be conceptually possible for private entrepreneurs to build and maintain the highway system. But the cost of collecting tolls every time a driver turned from one road to another would be a heavy burden on society. In terms of city streets it would be virtually impossible to have private enterprise operate the system. Collection costs in these cases are so high as to eliminate the attractiveness of any free market alternatives.

The government, on the other hand, can more easily and cheaply monitor and collect revenue related to the use of vehicles by levying a tax on gasoline. While this is far from a perfect method of collecting the costs of the highways, especially since it does not reflect congestion costs, it is a cheap method of imposing highway costs on the users of highways.

In attempting to formulate policy in this area, the costs of various methods of collecting from users must be kept in mind. Numerous economists and others have suggested fees or tolls for the use of highways during periods of congestion. The difficulty is that the act of collecting the tolls will in itself add to the congestion and be very costly for all concerned.

On the other hand, as Adam Smith says, the cost of providing the infrastructure should not be a burden upon the general revenue of society. Users should pay. To some extent they already do so. But clearly in many cases they do not. Whenever the government licenses or certifies personnel or equipment, the cost of that activity should be paid for by the individuals or the manufacturers.

Whenever possible, fees should be structured so that they reflect the costs imposed on society by the activity. Such fees provide incentives for users to economize on the scarce resources of capacity.

9

Community and
Regional Development
by Robert W. Poole, Jr.

Community and Regional Development, accounting for $9.8 billion in budget authority and $8.8 billion in outlays for FY 1981, encompasses a variety of programs from several agencies. The common themes are three:

- To promote the development or redevelopment of "economically and socially viable neighborhoods";
- To stabilize and revitalize "economically depressed or declining areas"; and
- To provide disaster relief of various sorts.

By far the largest portion of the funding within this function is disbursed as grants and loans by four programs: Community Development Block Grants, Urban Development Action Grants, Economic Development Administration grants and loans, and rural area grants and loans. The first two programs are administered by the Department of Housing and Urban Development (HUD), the third is an agency of the Department of Commerce, and the fourth is administered by the Farmers Home Administration in the Department of Agriculture. All four programs set up criteria defining economically ailing areas, then invite local government agencies in areas which qualify to compete for grant awards.

A diverse assortment of other programs completes the Community and Regional Development function. Included are a number of smaller HUD programs aimed at redevelopment, including the Rehabilitation Loan Program, the Neighborhood Self-Help Office, the Urban Homesteading program, and the Pennsylvania Avenue Development Corporation, as well as HUD grants to state, local, and regional government bodies to engage in the comprehensive planning required by the Housing Act of 1954.

Under the heading of "area and regional development" are grouped not only the Economic Development Administration and the Depart-

175

Table 1
Community and Regional Development
(in millions of dollars)

Major missions and programs	1979 actual	1980 estimate	1981 estimate
OUTLAYS			
Community development:			
Community development block grants	3,161	3,500	3,805
Urban development action grants	73	180	365
Rehabilitation loans	100	170	190
Neighborhood self-help	—	9	10
Neighborhood Reinvestment Corporation .	—	12	13
Pennsylvania Avenue development	29	44	40
Other programs	631	604	539
Subtotal, community development . . .	3,995	4,519	4,963
Area and regional development:			
Rural development and business assis- tance	669	656	784
Economic development assistance:			
Existing law	431	551	802
Proposed legislation	—	16	43
Local public works	1,741	358	200
Coastal energy impact assistance	11	34	53
Inland energy impact assistance	*	10	62
Indian programs:			
Existing law	805	846	856
Proposed legislation	—	—	5
Regional commissions	418	430	458
Other programs	130	199	170
Offsetting receipts	− 305	− 406	− 413
Subtotal, area and regional develop- ment	3,899	2,695	3,020
Disaster relief and insurance:			
Disaster loans	957	626	200
Federal emergency management activities .	617	627	646
Drought assistance and other	36	26	17
Subtotal, disaster relief and insurance	1,611	1,278	863
Deductions for offsetting receipts	− 23	− 25	− 25
Total, outlays	9,482	8,467	8,820
ADDENDUM			
Off-budget Federal entity — Rural Telephone Bank:			
Budget authority	106	156	150
Outlays	101	150	144
MEMORANDUM — Attribution of Federal Financing Bank outlays			
Community development	5	157	264
Rural development	830	992	1,075

*500 thousand or less.
Source: The Budget of the United States Government, FY 1981.

ment of Agriculture grants and loans, but also the Bureau of Indian Affairs, grants and loans to help state and local governments cope with the impact of new energy facilities, and funding for regional commissions.

The final heading is "disaster relief and insurance." Included here are disaster loan programs of the Small Business Administration and the Farmers Home Administration. The largest component, however, is the Federal Emergency Management Agency, established in 1979 to bring together the major federal civil defense, emergency preparedness, disaster relief, and flood insurance programs. The reorganization of these functions into a single agency is still under way.

About 65 percent of the Community and Regional Development funds are accounted for by the four major grant and loan programs noted earlier: CDBG, UDAG, EDA, and Agriculture's rural grants and loans. Accordingly, these four programs will be the focus of this essay.

Community Development Block Grants

The Community Development Block Grant (CDBG) program was created by the Housing and Community Development Act of 1974, one of the manifestations of the Nixon Administration's "New Federalism." It consolidated ten categorical grant programs, including Urban Renewal, Model Cities, and Neighborhood Facilities. Under the former "Great Society" system, the bulk of the money went to large cities, following rather narrow guidelines for each program area. The intent of the 1974 act was to broaden the distribution of funds and permit much greater local discretion as to their use.

A new eligibility formula was included in the act, based on population, housing overcrowding, and poverty. Strict application of that formula would have resulted in a major shift of HUD funds from older central cities to the suburbs, and from the Snowbelt to the Sunbelt. To avoid an abrupt change, the act provided that during its first three years (1975–77) the large cities would be "held harmless"—i.e., guaranteed at least the average amount that they had received during the years 1968–72 under the old categorical programs. But by 1977 a new administration was in office and lobbyists for the large cities succeeded in scrapping the 1974 formula. Eligibility requirements were tightened significantly: a new formula was implemented, based on age of the housing stock, population growth lag, and poverty. This shifted the funding emphasis back toward urban centers. Also adopted was a "principal benefits" test: each applicant would have to demonstrate that the funds would be used in some way that would benefit principally low- and moderate-income persons. Among other requirements, each recipient would have to develop a "Housing Assistance Plan" for such persons. And a requirement for "citizen participation" in developing the CDBG plan for each locality was introduced.

The CDBG eligibility limits were tightened further in 1979. The stricter standards had the effect of reducing the number and size of the areas in each city where CDBG funds can be spent. Another change required that any CDBG funds spent on social services be linked with physical improvements (e.g., housing, sewers, sidewalks). HUD defended the moves by arguing that previously the CDBG funds had been spread too thinly to be effective.

Urban Development Action Grants

The Urban Development Action Grant (UDAG) program began as a $400 million per year effort in FY 1978; it was expanded to $675 million per year as of FY 1980. According to HUD, this program provides discretionary grants to severely distressed cities and urban counties to supplement private and local government funding of private "economic development and neighborhood revitalization" projects. Eligibility is based on six factors: age of housing stock, poverty rate, population growth, per capita income growth, unemployment rate, and employment growth. However, selection is also based on a city's "track record" in providing housing for low-income persons and equal opportunity in housing and jobs, and its immediate ability to leverage private investment. President Carter termed UDAG the "centerpiece" of his urban program.

As of the end of 1979, 333 of the nation's 646 larger cities and urban counties (and 2,500 smaller communities) met the eligibility requirements. At that time, 145 of the larger urban areas and 216 smaller ones had received grants. An expansion of eligibility to permit non-distressed cities to fund projects in local "pockets of poverty" went into effect in 1980. Cities can spend UDAG money in a variety of ways: they may acquire land for a new development, construct roads and sewers to serve it, or lend the developer money at below-market interest rates. Cities are required to demonstrate that the money is needed in order to generate the remaining private investment. HUD claims there is an average of $6 of private money invested for every UDAG dollar awarded.

Economic Development Assistance

The third major program is the Economic Development Administration. EDA was established under the Public Works and Economic Development Act of 1965 "to help generate employment opportunities and improve levels of living in areas that have not shared our national prosperity." EDA provides three principal types of aid: grants to local governments for public works projects, business development loans to private firms, and technical assistance to local organizations.

178

EDA's public works program is intended to assist local governments in providing the infrastructure — roads, water, sewers, etc. — needed to attract industry and encourage business expansion. In order for a local government to be eligible for an EDA grant, it must lie within an EDA-designated area or designated Economic Development Center, based on seven indicators of economic distress (although EDA also makes grants for "pockets of poverty" in affluent areas). In addition, the local governments in the area must prepare and submit to EDA an Overall Economic Development Plan (OEDP) laying out an overall economic planning strategy. The OEDP must be updated annually to maintain the area's eligibility for funding.

In 1971 the act was amended to add the Public Works Impact Program. Under it a percentage of EDA's budget is reserved to provide immediate construction jobs for the unemployed and underemployed in areas with a large concentration of low-income persons, substantial rural outmigration, substantial unemployment, or the closing of a major employer. In these cases the area need not have an OEDP to qualify.

EDA's Business Development Assistance program offers a variety of loans and loan guarantees directly to business firms. The applicant must be located in an EDA-designated area, and the project must be consistent with the approved OEDP for the area. EDA will help a business expand, but will not help finance its total or partial relocation from one area to another if doing so results in a reduction in employment in the former location. In addition to businesses, EDA loans may be made to non-profit organizations, government agencies, and Indian tribes.

EDA technical assistance may be given to the same types of applicants as EDA loans. Such assistance may be in the form of either a grant (to enable the applicant to solve the problem) or as direct services by EDA or a contractor hired by EDA. Unlike other EDA programs, technical assistance is available at any location, and is not limited to economically distressed areas as defined by EDA. Technical assistance may involve a feasibility study of a proposed development project, administrative funds to a local non-profit development organization, or a study of the conversion of a surplus military base to civilian uses.

Rural Development and Business Assistance

The Department of Agriculture's community development programs are administered by the Farmers Home Administration. FmHA was established in 1946 as the successor to the Farm Security Administration and the earlier Resettlement Administration. FmHA has three major program areas: farmer programs (loans to farmers for various projects), rural housing grants and loans, and community programs. Only the latter program is of concern here. It comprises loans and grants for rural water and sewer systems, loans for community facilities, and loan guarantees for business and industrial development.

Over the years the scope of these programs has expanded dramatically. The original (1946) water system program provided only for loans to develop farm water systems in seventeen drought-prone Western states. In 1954 this program was extended nationwide and expanded to include non-farm customers. Five years later, FmHA added loans to assist with local watershed projects. The water systems program was expanded again, in 1961, this time to include entire rural communities up to 2,500 in population. The next year, loans were also authorized for outdoor recreational facilities. And in 1965 the program was expanded once again, to include sewer as well as water systems, and to provide grants as well as loans.

During the 1960s FmHA operated a pilot program in rural redevelopment, aimed at upgrading community facilities to attract industry; it was discontinued in 1969. But the Rural Development Act of 1972 revived and institutionalized it, authorizing FmHA to make and to guarantee loans for business and industry in cities of up to 50,000 population, to make loans and grants for pollution control, to make loans for "essential community facilities" such as fire stations and hospitals, to make grants to improve rural industrial sites, and to increase the population limit for water and sewer projects to 10,000. In the decade from 1965 to 1975 the volume of FmHA loans and grants increased 450 percent, to $3.6 billion. As of 1980, the total of outstanding grants and loans had grown to $44.6 billion.

SHORT-TERM POLICIES

Among the CDBG, UDAG, EDA, and FmHA programs, virtually every part of the country — urban cores, suburbs, smaller cities, and rural communities — is eligible for some sort of large-scale federal grant or loan program, all in the name of economic development and/or revitalization. Since most of the monies are in fact spent in local areas, and on relatively tangible outputs (sidewalks, sewers, parking garages, industrial parks), there is little question that the programs are accomplishing something. The more important question is the cost of their doing so (where cost is considered in the broad sense of foregone opportunities and side-effects, as well as direct expenditures).

There is an inherent dilemma in federal programs of this sort. Because taxpayers' money is at stake, there is a tendency to spell out detailed restrictions on the uses of the funds. As we will see, this tends to shift control from the local to the federal level, and to make the program far less responsive to actual local needs. On the other hand, when discretion is left in local hands, funds tend to be spent in ways far removed from what Congress intended.

Grants as Political Tools

As the brief resume of the CDBG program made clear, there has been intense political battling over the formulas for parceling out these grant funds. To a considerable extent the criteria have shifted in accordance with the power base of the administration in office at the time: suburbs versus central cities, Sunbelt versus Snowbelt. All of these programs are aimed at economically distressed areas. However, since virtually *any* locality of reasonable size contains at least one relatively run-down area (a "pocket of poverty"), UDAG and EDA administrators have been able to award grants even to affluent counties.

The UDAG program is the most openly political of the three. According to *Business Week* (November 12, 1979), UDAG was "proposed after political sophisticates in the Administration and Congress took a searching look at where Carter's votes had come from in 1976." The magazine has described the program as consisting of "grants that can be used to make the President look good."

Indicative of the political nature of the UDAG program is the less than rigorous application of the requirement that the grant money be essential to the participation of private funding in a project. A 1979 General Accounting Office study pointed out that in many instances the money merely goes to subsidize projects that would be built in any case.[1] A $5.8 million grant was given to Montezuma, Georgia, to assist with a Procter & Gamble pulp mill—despite the fact that the grant application was filed six days *after* the company had announced a go-ahead on the project. Likewise, an $8 million grant was given to Boston in 1978 to fund an underground parking garage above which a private developer would build a retail complex and hotel. It turned out that (a) the project had been under way since 1975, (b) the local HUD office economist stated that the project would have been completed without UDAG funding, and (c) the private developer himself had stated that the project was not dependent on receipt of the grant funds.

GAO's evaluation found that over 22 percent of the UDAG projects it examined were questionable. Moreover, *none* of the project files provided adequate identification of the reasons for funding the projects, nor did the files of projects not funded justify those decisions.

GAO has found similar arbitrariness in the CDBG program. An

---

[1] "Improvements Needed in Selecting and Processing Urban Development Action Grants," U.S. General Accounting Office, CED-79-64, March 30, 1979.

early 1978 study found that a number of cities were routinely submitting third-year funding requests for projects whose first and second-year allocations had not been spent.[2] Mount Vernon, New York, for example, was supposed to be building an ice-skating rink (!) with some of its CDBG money. Although nothing had been done with the money approved for the first two years, the city requested and received a third-year allocation. The purpose of the program seemed to be to channel federal money to the city, regardless of results.

That seemingly cynical conclusion is strengthened by two further GAO reports on the CDBG program, released in August 1978.[3] The first points out that neither the grant application forms nor the grantee performance reports provide the kind of data which would enable HUD to measure the extent to which the grants were actually aiding lower-income people. HUD "does not require communities to establish adequate criteria or to provide performance data needed to evaluate community performance and progress." Consequently, HUD's annual reports to Congress "provide very little information on the actual use of block grant funds...[r]eports are based primarily on *planned* program activities and *planned* use of funds...."[emphasis supplied] Once again, the focus seems to be on handing out the money, not on results.

The second GAO study reviewed sixty-seven CDBG grant applications from Ohio and Kentucky communities.[4] Thirty-one (46 percent) "were questionable because the reviewers reached conclusions about project benefits which were not consistent with information contained in the application or without adequately resolving conflicting statements in the application." Of the eight communities to which GAO made site visits, seven "had overstated benefits to low- and moderate-income families and/or had overstated support to expanding or conserving low- and moderate-income housing." HUD officials had visited five of these communities, but in all but one case "they failed to identify the overstated benefit claims"; in the one case where HUD spotted the anomaly, they made no change in their assessment of the value of the project.

GAO found a similar tendency to overstate benefits in the FmHA business and industrial loan program.[5] Using 1974–75 data for six

[2] Letter from GAO's Henry Eschwege to the Secretary of Housing and Urban Development, January 24, 1978.

[3] "Management and Evaluation of the Community Development Block Grant Program Need to Be Strengthened," General Accounting Office, CED-78-160, August 30, 1978.

[4] "The Community Development Block Grant Program: Discretionary Grant Funds Not Always Given to the Most Promising Small City Programs," General Accounting Office, CED-78-157, August 31, 1978.

[5] "Farmers Home Administration's Business and Industrial Loan Program Can Be Improved," Comptroller General of the United States, CED-77-126, September 30, 1977.

states, GAO compared the number of jobs saved and created—based on loans that actually were made—with the number that FmHA claimed were created. Rather than 29,800 jobs, the actual total was 11,100—about one third of what FmHA had told Congress. It seems that FmHA not only had counted the benefits of some loans twice, but included jobs that would have been created by loans that did not go through and by loans not yet granted. FmHA accomplished "little or no verification or analysis" of the job-creation claims of the borrowers.

In both the report cited above and another report on FmHA's water and sewer program,[6] GAO noted the lack of adequate management information—i.e., the lack of a system to provide the kind of information necessary to tell whether the programs are, in fact, accomplishing their ostensible purposes. What is clear is that they are succeeding in spending money; what is far from clear is that they are spending it effectively.

There is a basic conceptual problem with federal grant programs of this sort. In order for each grant to be meaningful, only a fraction of all eligible communities and projects can be funded, given the amounts Congress is willing to appropriate. Yet for political reasons, the eligibility requirements have to be kept flexible enough to allow projects in all 435 congressional districts around the country. The net result is that some communities receive grants and others—quite possibly with equally serious (or equally non-serious) problems—do not. The deciding factors tend to be (a) the communities' relative skills at grantsmanship, and (b) their political connections.

Yet the underlying reality is that *every* community in the nation is paying for these grants, even though only a favored few end up receiving them. Federal outlays on Community and Regional Development for FY 1981 amount to about $40 for every man, woman, and child in the country—$160 for a family of four, or $400,000 for a town of 10,000 people. Yet few towns—or neighborhoods—of that size have much chance of receiving $400,000 from any of these programs.

Needs Versus Waste

In all but the poorest localities, many of the worthwhile projects funded by CDBG, UDAG, and EDA grants would have been carried out anyway, using local resources. But the availability of "free" federal money is an irresistable lure. Yet if there were no federal grant programs, the same projects accomplished locally would cost a good deal less to carry out. The cost difference is due to the inherent "overhead" built into such federal programs.

In addition to paying for the design and construction costs of, say, a

---

[6]"Management of Farmers Home Administration's Water and Waste Disposal Program Needs to be Strengthened," General Accounting Office, CED-78-61, March 13, 1978.

new sewer system, a federal grant-funded project must also cover the following costs:

- A portion of the cost of the HUD, EDA, or Department of Agriculture staff and support system in Washington and the cognizant regional office.
- Interest on the funds for the time they are tied up in the planning process at all levels. (Though not an out-of-pocket cost, this is an opportunity cost, in that money — which would otherwise be spent on the project — is tied up for many months unproductively.)
- The cost of the local planning staff needed to handle grant applications and administration. (Santa Barbara, California, a city of 72,000 people, employs eleven people to administer $1.3 million a year in CDBG projects.)
- Higher project costs due to the necessity of meeting federal requirements. One requirement is the payment of "prevailing wages" (i.e., union scale) required under the Davis-Bacon Act. Another is the preparation of environmental impact reports, even on minor projects. A 1977 GAO study of the CDBG program found that "reviews of about 54 percent of the projects may have been unnecessary."[7] GAO projected the cost of this needless paperwork at $14 million.

Yet another cost-increasing factor is the 10 percent minority business set-aside requirement on EDA grants, and the requirement of affirmative action on the part of grant-funded contractors generally. In 1978–79, GAO found that simply administering the EDA set-aside requirement consumed 25 percent of EDA's $15 million administrative budget.[8] At the local level, GAO found that price quotes from minority firms averaged about nine percent higher than normal prices. Moreover, about 48 percent of rural projects and 51 percent of urban projects had difficulty even *finding* minority firms. In New Hampshire, 57 out of 83 contracts had to be given to out-of-state firms, thereby thwarting the intent of the program. Moreover, GAO found that 32 percent of the supposed minority firms receiving contracts were either fronts for non-minority firms or "brokers" — in either case, not actually eligible.

FmHA programs, too, increase costs needlessly. The water and sewer system program uses the "percentage of construction cost" method of compensating project engineers. As a result, noted GAO,

---

[7] "Environmental Reviews Done by Communities: Are They Needed? Are They Adequate?" Comptroller General of the United States, CED-77-123. September 1, 1977.
[8] "Minority Firms on Local Public Works Projects — Mixed Results," Comptroller General of the United States, CED-79-9, January 16, 1979.

the more expensive the design, the more the engineers are paid — a totally perverse incentive.[9] In its business and industrial loan program, GAO found that FmHA had no criteria for assessing the relative cost per job created.[10] Consequently, in some cases FmHA was ending up paying as much as $200,000 or $300,000 per new job.

But besides inflating the costs of needed projects, grant funding invariably leads to projects which would not have been carried out with local private funding or governmental funds. EDA made a million-dollar loan to set up an aluminum recycling plant in Greensboro, Georgia, despite the fact that existing firms in the industry were running at only 60 percent of capacity.[11] CDBG funds have been used to pay for pet projects of local activists such as community centers, co-op credit unions, food co-ops, and a whole variety of specialized social services.

"Planning" Economic Development

A premise basic to all the federal grant programs under consideration is that central planning is the way to promote economic growth. EDA, in particular, makes this point explicit by requiring local jurisdictions to develop and update annually an Overall Economic Development Plan. CDBG grants, too, can only be awarded if the projects they fund are part of a three-year community development plan.

Yet there is considerable evidence that the most efficient economic growth and development do *not* come about in response to centralized, top-down planning. Economists such as Third World development specialist P. T. Bauer[12] and Alvin Rabushka[13] have shown that the most important correlate of economic development is a climate of incentives — i.e., security of property rights, absence of regulation and bureaucracy, and a minimum of taxation. Under such conditions, investors and entrepreneurs willingly take risks and undertake projects, in the process generating the wealth that makes construction of the accompanying infrastructure possible (whether by government through taxation or directly by the firms themselves). The same observations are historically verified in the United States.

However, the philosophy of economic development via federal grants is totally contrary to this evidence. Rather than encouraging a

---

[9] *Supra*, note 6.

[10] *Supra*, note 5.

[11] "Business Development Loan to Keystone, Georgia Metal Company Inadequately Justified," Comptroller General of the United States, CED-77-111, August 12, 1977.

[12] Peter T. Bauer, *Dissent on Development* (Cambridge, Mass.: Harvard University Press, 1972).

[13] Alvin Rabushka, *A Theory of Racial Harmony* (Columbia: University of South Carolina Press, 1974); and *The Changing Face of Hong Kong* (Washington, D.C.: American Enterprise Institute, 1973).

climate of mobility and flexibility, the grant programs serve to increase the level of local and national bureaucracy, to add new regulations which increase the time and cost of projects, and — to the extent that their accompanying "planning" succeeds — to ossify the local economy rather than encouraging its dynamism.

One of the major factors in economic growth is the mobility of capital. To the extent that investors are free to close down high-cost, obsolete operations and shift resources to modern, efficient ones, short-term costs will give way to longer term benefits. EDA business development assistance works against this principle. EDA funds may not be used to help a business relocate to a lower-cost area, no matter how obsolete its present plant or how costly a local replacement plant might be. Even an expansion which involves *adding* a new plant to supplement an existing one is suspect: according to EDA literature, "EDA will check carefully to determine that employment will not be reduced at the existing place or places of business." This restriction is quite consistent with the central-planning mind-set, in which development is to be forced rather than motivated. It is also consistent with the political nature of the grant-giving process: can one really expect a congressman from State A to vote for a program which would assist firms in his state to move to State B to escape from high taxes and regulation?

EDA guidelines also contain a provision intended to ensure its projects do not stimulate competition: "No financial assistance may be provided for projects that would result in increased production of goods, materials, or commodities, or the availability of services and facilities, when efficient capacity exists to meet estimated demands." In other words, EDA — rather than the marketplace — will determine the appropriate size of each particular industry in the area!

Assistance to the Poor

The CDBG program, as noted earlier, has been aggrandized over time to the point where over 640 communities across the country are automatically "entitled" to these grants, in terms of a formula set down by law. In addition, hundreds of other communities compete for discretionary grants under this program. In a 1978 report to Congress, GAO questioned HUD's process for deciding which communities should receive discretionary grants under CDBG. Discussing the criterion of assisting low- and moderate-income families, GAO concluded that funds were "be[ing] given to some communities which did not have the most promising programs."[14]

The combined effect of automatically dispensing CDBG funds to most larger cities and awarding discretionary CDBG funds to only a few of the smaller cities leads to a rather strange overall pattern. Many

---

[14] *Supra,* note 4.

of the communities being aided are more affluent than many of those not so fortunate. The situation in California illustrates this point. Of 144 incorporated cities in that state, eighty-four were receiving CDBG assistance in FY 1979. Of the remaining sixty communities, five were affluent, with per capita incomes ranging from $11,000 to over $18,000. But aside from those five, fifty-five non-aided cities had an average per capita income of only $6,721. Some—such as Bell Gardens ($3,450), Compton ($3,431), and Paramount ($4,121) are quite poor. Yet 33 of the cities receiving CDBG funds had per capita incomes above $6,721—including such affluent cities as Newport Beach ($11,683), Santa Monica ($8,547), and Mountain View ($8,225).

These results are reinforced by a study by the National Association of Housing and Redevelopment Officials (NAHRO). According to this analysis, about 50 percent of the CDBG money is spent in high-income census tracts. A NAHRO official was quoted in *American City and County* (September 1977) as saying that CDBG money is being used where the short-term investment can be reaped most quickly, and "that's not the slum areas."

It is also worth recalling GAO's finding that HUD itself does not know the extent to which CDBG funds are actually aiding low- to moderate-income persons or housing. This is because no meaningful evaluation system exists; the data are not collected by the recipient agencies and therefore HUD has no basis for assessing results.

With the heavily politicized UDAG program, even the pretense of helping the poor seems largely gone. We have already seen that 333 out of 646 large cities and urban counties have been defined (somewhat arbitrarily, according to GAO) as "severely distressed." In Buffalo, a $4 million UDAG appropriation is helping to build a $17 million Hilton hotel on the lakefront. In Baltimore, two grants totalling $7.8 million are being used to build housing that will be occupied largely by middle- and upper-income people. Similarly, 800 to 900 apartments for middle-to upper-income residents are being built in Chicago's Loop area with the aid of a $1 million UDAG appropriation. Minneapolis and St. Paul have obtained $15.9 million via six grants to finance projects that include a glass-enclosed downtown mall.

GAO has complained that UDAG eligibility criteria do not take into account the degree of severity of the individual factors in the formula —e.g., a city with 6 percent unemployment is just as qualified on this criterion as one with 14 percent unemployment, so long as both figures are higher than the threshhold value.[15] Moreover, three of the six criteria are highly correlated—in effect, the same factor is being counted three times. Several alternative indicators of economic trou-

---

[15] "Criteria for Participation in the Urban Development Action Grant Program Should Be Refined," U.S. General Accounting Office, CED-80-80, March 20, 1980.

bles are not considered at all. Overall, GAO estimates that about fifty of the 646 large cities and urban counties are incorrectly categorized.

FmHA also has problems targeting its water and sewer grants and loans to localities which actually are poor. Its allocation formula distributes $20,000 to each state, then allocates the remaining funds by means of a formula based on each state's rural population, and the number of poverty households in rural areas and small cities. But, as GAO pointed out in 1978,[16] this formula bears no necessary relationship to either the need for or the cost of water and sewer projects in each state. Such factors can only be taken into account at the end of each fiscal year. At that point, if some states have not expended their entire allocations, FmHA can reallocate the excess to those states with unfilled needs. This crude procedure — besides tying up money unproductively for as long as ten or eleven months — often means that low-priority projects in states with large allocations are funded instead of higher-priority projects in states with smaller allocations.

EDA has been criticized for the same lack of care in allocating funds. In response to a complaint by seventy-five members of Congress, GAO undertook a study of the allocation of funds and selection of projects in EDA's Local Public Works Program.[17] They found that communities were taking advantage of a provision of the Public Works Employment Act of 1976 (which set up the program) allowing an applicant to use the unemployment rate from adjoining areas as well as its own, on the assumption that labor for the project might be drawn from those areas as well. Since the project's score in EDA's rating system is based largely on unemployment (55 percent of the total score), "there is a significant incentive for jurisdictions to gerrymander their project areas to increase these factors." As a result of such gerrymandering, GAO found "some areas being assisted that had less severe unemployment problems than others that were not assisted." Also, "in some cases a relatively wealthy suburb was selected on the basis of the unemployment data of an adjoining city while the city itself received little or no assistance."

Affluent Greenwich, Connecticut, managed to report an unemployment rate of seven percent by including data from a neighboring city, whereas its own rate was below four percent. It received a $4.2 million EDA grant (which was 10 percent of the total grant funds given to Connecticut) although it had the second-highest per capita income in the state — $8,283.

A 1978 GAO study pointed out that although EDA's Local Public Works Program had been represented as a way to create jobs in

---

[16] *Supra*, note 6.

[17] "Observations Concerning the Local Public Works Program," Comptroller General of the United States, CED-77-48, February 23, 1977.

depressed areas, it could not really be considered a jobs-creation program:

> The 1976 Act created a public works program, not a job creation program, which is one reason for the low labor intensity during the initial months of many projects. *Public works* projects are designed to construct or renovate useful public facilities and also have the effect of generating *skilled and semiskilled* labor requirements. A typical public works project uses a relatively high percentage of materials in proportion to labor.... The primary objective of *job creation* programs has historically been to provide work for needy unemployed persons, and such programs generally generated *semiskilled* labor requirements. A typical job creation project uses low proportions of materials in relation to labor...."[18] [emphasis supplied]

The same GAO report pointed out that EDA does not have data to assess the extent to which the Local Public Works Program has succeeded in providing jobs to workers who had been unemployed, underemployed, or below the poverty level before being hired for the EDA-funded project.

The projects funded by EDA do not focus on serving those who are poor, any more than do those of UDAG. In affluent Santa Barbara, California, the city's grant writers were able to define a "pocket of poverty" as the basis for a $4 million EDA Round 2 grant to remodel the main downtown library. The building is located in an area famed as a tourist spot, the very antithesis of a "depressed" area. EDA awarded $5 million to Detroit, Michigan, to assist with construction of a new sports stadium for the Detroit Red Wings — a successful professional hockey team, none of whose members or owners could be considered poor.

EDA's Business Development Assistance Program has also come under fire. Although EDA's loans under this program are indeed creating jobs, a 1979 GAO study found that, once again, EDA has not followed up to determine whether or to what extent those jobs are being filled by those who were previously unemployed or underemployed. Moreover, GAO found that about 75 percent of the businesses it examined had not achieved the number of jobs originally projected in their loan applications. Furthermore:

> We found that some jobs were reported as saved and created based on original projections rather than actual results, jobs were still being credited for liquidated loans or bankrupt companies, and certain businesses which received more than one loan had their employment counted twice.[19]

---

[18] Letter from Comptroller General Elmer B. Staats to Representative James C. Cleveland, August 4, 1978.

[19] "Measuring Accomplishments Under the Business Development Assistance Program — More Accurate Verification Recommended," Comptroller General of the United States, CED-79-117, September 6, 1979.

As noted earlier, GAO found the same problem occurring with FmHA's business loans. Borrowers made exaggerated job-creation claims, which FmHA did not bother to investigate. The agency went on to double-count and exaggerate the totals as well.

It is questionable how much of the assistance from these programs — CDBG, UDAG, EDA and FmHA — is actually aiding lower-income people. After reviewing numerous GAO investigations, one gets the distinct impression of the usual political pork barrel, dishing out federal money where it will be visible in a politically advantageous way. While buildings *are* being built and jobs *are* being created, any benefits to the poor are a side effect.

Expanding Control

One aspect of the federal grant programs that is seldom discussed is the steady expansion of federal government control over matters which used to be purely local or even individual matters.

Writing in the April 1975 issue of *The Progressive,* Al Hirshen and Richard T. LeGates complained that local governments were reluctant to undertake activist anti-poverty programs: "Virtually none [of these programs] would have been undertaken by local governments with local money. Many cities refused to undertake them even with 'free' federal funds...." But by 1976 HUD had found a lever to compel nearly all local governments to act. Under the 1974 Housing and Community Development Act, a precondition for receiving CDBG funds is a Housing Assistance Plan (HAP), spelling out how each city intends to meet the housing needs of low- and moderate-income residents (or potential residents). This requirement was not really enforced until after a 1976 court ruling in favor of Hartford, Connecticut; that city had sued seven of its suburbs and HUD for violating the act by participating in the CDBG program without having a HAP in effect.

After that decision, community activists began taking other cities to court — and some thirty of the more than 1300 otherwise eligible cities decided not to participate in CDBG. In 1978, for example, Warren, Michigan, voters rejected a ballot measure calling for low-income housing — thus losing $1.7 million in CDBG funds. Likewise, Manchester, Connecticut, citizens in 1979 voted a two-year moratorium on CDBG grants, so as not to be forced to build low-income housing.

In other cases, cities are contesting with HUD over what type of housing will meet the needs spelled out in their HAP. College Station, Texas, was denied $300,000 in CDBG funds because officials wanted to build public housing for the elderly and handicapped; HUD insisted that the real need was subsidized housing for families. Wauwatosa, Wisconsin, lost $945,000 in CDBG funds over a similar dispute. St. Louis County, Missouri, sued HUD in 1979 because the agency froze

$8.9 million in such a dispute; the county wanted to split the money between building family units and rehabilitating existing units, but HUD insisted that it all be spent on new construction. Alameda County, California, had $1.1 million cut off in 1978 in a similar dispute.

As previously noted, there is still considerable latitude in what CDBG funds can, in fact, be used for. As long as local officials *claim* that low- to moderate-income people are benefitting from a new sewer line, library, or ice-skating rink (and as long as they have an approved HAP on file), they are free to build it, regardless of who the actual beneficiaries might be. But if HUD insists upon requiring documentation of such claims, the cities' options will be severely constrained, and the cost and red tape will increase even further.

Although the UDAG program is notorious for its lack of controls over how the funds can be used, EDA repeats the pattern found with HUD and its CDBG program. The lever for control in this case is the requirement to prepare an Overall Economic Development Plan, discussed earlier. By this means, local government is to intervene into the local business economy to a new and unprecedented extent. We have previously noted the explicit EDA requirement that projects which compete with existing businesses are not to be approved, nor are business relocations aimed at improved efficiency.

In pointing out the lack of data available to assess the performance of EDA's business loans, GAO commended EDA's proposed new reporting requirements:

> Businesses that expect to save or create 15 or more permanent jobs as a result of EDA's assistance would be required to submit annually, for 5 years, employment and payroll data. This information would be used by the Office of Civil Rights to monitor adherence to minority hiring commitments and by the Office of Private Sector Investments to evaluate overall program results.

Thus, those businesses receiving EDA funds will be subjected to increasingly stringent (and long-term) federal controls.

Yet control of this sort is to be expected with a federal grant program. After all, it is taxpayers' money that is being handed out. "It is hardly lack of due process for the federal government to regulate what it subsidizes," wrote Justice Jackson in 1942. Accordingly, questioning of the controls leads inevitably to questioning the existence of the programs in the first place.

Subsidizing Activists

The Housing and Community Development Act of 1974 requires "citizen participation" in planning the use of CDBG funds. Although the precise means for accomplishing this are left to the local governments to decide, the act requires "involvement of low- and moderate-income persons, members of minority groups, residents of areas where a significant amount of activity is proposed or ongoing, the elderly, the handicapped, the business community, civic groups and individuals which are concerned about the program. Where the applicant chooses to establish...a general community-wide citizen advisory committee, there shall be substantial representation of low- and moderate-income citizens and members of minority groups."

This commendable goal – of enabling the persons who are supposed to be helped to have a say in the process – has in some cities been highly politicized. Left-liberal activists, skilled in grantsmanship and politically sophisticated, have seized on these requirements to build a new type of local political machine. A case study will illustrate the process.

In Santa Barbara, California – a CDBG entitlement city – the City Council set up a Community Development Task Force made up of representatives from the five target neighborhoods and various interest groups. Local activists set up a Neighborhood Planning Council in each of the five neighborhoods and convinced the City Council to allow the NPCs to be the neighborhood representatives. To support NPC activities, the city now spends about $60,000 of each year's CDBG allocation plus $25,000 in CETA funds. According to the CETA-funded administrator of Citizen Participation in the Santa Barbara area, "the NPCs have developed a life of their own beyond the purposes of the block grant.... [They] have become a center of community organizing efforts as they hold fundraisers for farm worker families, striking tenants, senior citizen needs, and others." In the spring of 1980 the NPC monthly newsletter – printed with CDBG funds – endorsed a controversial city ballot measure to enact rent control (subsequently defeated at the polls by better than two to one).

No studies have been done to assess how widespread such politicization of "citizen participation" has become. But the example given here is hardly an isolated instance.

LONG-TERM CONSIDERATIONS

Motivating Economic Development

The central thrust of Community and Regional Development is to bring about the development or redevelopment of allegedly depressed areas by channeling federal monies into those areas. There are numerous practical difficulties with this approach, as well as basic questions of equity. Moreover, this approach has been in use for over two decades and has yet to make a measurable dent in the nation's decayed urban centers.

Simply reforming the various programs—CDBG, UDAG, EDA, FmHA, etc.—along the lines suggested by GAO over the years would not alter their fundamental flaws: the impossibility of focusing effort on real needs while simultaneously ensuring fifty congressional delegations of grants to hand out; the high costs built into such programs by overhead and added-on social goals; the continued expansion of federal control over local matters; the tendency of the poor to get lost in the shuffle; and the basic ineffectiveness of top-down central planning as a way of ensuring economic growth and development.

There is no way out of the basic dilemma between, on the one hand, exerting stringent control over how the funds are spent and, on the other hand, ensuring enough flexibility to make sure that the programs truly respond to diverse local needs. Neither can the best of intentions make central planning work, when both economic theory and decades of experience show that it won't.

What is needed, instead, is a fundamentally different approach, one which motivates investment in declining areas rather than attempting to plan and compel it, one which leaves local individuals, firms, and governments free to make their own decisions, one which eliminates political hand-outs so as to undercut the temptation to make the program an end in itself.

Just such an approach has been suggested during the past year: Enterprise Zones. Originally proposed in England by socialist Peter Hall and conservative Sir Geoffrey Howe (now Chancellor of the Exchequer), the idea has been brought to this country by Stuart Butler of The Heritage Foundation. Dr. Butler described the concept in the *New York Times* (June 13, 1980):

> Instead of increasing government support and intervention, enterprise zones eliminate controls, restrictions, and taxes in order to provide an attractive climate for private money and business, and to induce people to stay and raise families and to move in. A zone of about a square mile is chosen in the most depressed part of a city, and in it restrictions and business taxes of almost every kind are removed. Zoning is simplified, property taxes cut dramatically, business taxes reduced significantly....
> A critical element of the approach is that it creates an attractive atmosphere for business in general, rather than attempting to find and subsidize individual businesses.[20]

The key to making such a zone truly attractive is the removal of all the normal bureaucratic and regulatory barriers. Substantial cuts in taxes are also necessary to give it a strong enough economic advantage to overcome the disadvantages which had previously made it unattractive. At a minimum, therefore, this would entail:

---

[20]See also, Stuart M. Butler, *Enterprise Zones: Pioneering in the Inner City* (Washington, D.C.: The Heritage Foundation, 1980).

- Suspending the operation of minimum wage laws, to permit low-skilled people to compete for jobs at pay scales determined by the marketplace.[21]
- Suspending state and local licensing laws which needlessly restrict entry into various fields of endeavor.[22]
- Suspending local zoning ordinances and building codes, which arbitrarily restrict location, and which artificially increase the cost of construction.[23] Only basic life and fire-safety requirements would be retained.
- Cutting local property taxes substantially.

For states and cities willing to create such zones, the federal government would grant substantial cuts in federal corporate, personal income, and capital gains taxes, as well as allowing rapid depreciation of new rental housing and business plant and equipment. (Social Security payroll taxes should not be changed, as reform of this program should be handled separately.)

Two versions of the Enterprise Zone concept have been introduced into Congress. The first, co-sponsored by Reps. Jack Kemp (R-NY) and Robert Garcia (D-NY) is not really an Enterprise Zone, in that it cuts only taxes, leaving regulations intact. It is doubtful that such an approach would succeed in attracting much new investment. A more ambitious proposal has been introduced by Rep. Ron Paul (R-TX). It would require local zoning and land-use ordinances to be lifted, would suspend federal minimum-wage and OSHA regulations, and would cut federal and local taxes considerably. Both bills, however, would cut Social Security taxes as well, thereby creating a whole new set of problems.

Some version of Enterprise Zones should be substituted across the board for the current CDBG, UDAG, EDA and FmHA community development programs, completely reversing the philosophy of how to bring about sound economic development. No longer would cities be competing on the basis of political connections for federal largesse to set up local planning bureaucracies and pad departmental budgets. No longer would they be forced to meet federally-imposed requirements and fill out detailed grant applications and progress reports. No longer would they be required to plan their economies from the top down. Instead, they (and the federal government) would simply be getting out of the way as much as possible, creating a climate in which

---

[21] Walter Williams, "Government Sanctioned Restraints that Reduce Employment Opportunities for Minorities," *Policy Review*, Fall 1977.

[22] *Ibid.*

[23] Dick Bjornseth, "Houston Defies the Planners—and Thrives," *Reason*, February 1978; and Christine Dorffi, "Housing: Tangled in Red Tape," *Reason*, October 1980.

local residents and businesses were motivated to build and invest for their own futures.

In operation, the program would be very straightforward. Under the Kemp-Garcia version, for example, a neighborhood would qualify if its unemployment rate were twice the national average *and* 30 percent of its families were below the poverty level — or if *either* its unemployment rate were three times the national average *or* more than half its families below the poverty level. This kind of standard would focus help on areas that are truly depressed.

What would be the cost of an Enterprise Zones program? Initially, the only cost would be the loss of immediate tax revenue to the federal and local governments. Rep. Kemp estimates this short-term loss at no more than $1 billion (compared with present outlays of $6 billion for the CDBG, UDAG, EDA, and FmHA grant and loan programs). Economists are divided on the long-term effects, some estimating that the increased level of economic activity would generate enough additional revenue — even at the much lower tax rates — to offset completely the short-term revenue loss. But for purposes of budget estimates, it is prudent to count the cost of the substitution of Enterprise Zones as the full $1 billion revenue loss. To make the idea more palatable to local governments accustomed to receiving federal grants, the portion of the $1 billion which represents local revenue loss could be made available as transition grants — solely to cover lost revenue — for those cities setting up Enterprise Zones during the first year.

Earlier approaches, financed and operated by the government, have been conspicuous failures. Innovative programs such as Enterprise Zones, while not guaranteed solutions, show real promise for doing something about poverty in America.

10a

Education

by Eugenia Froedge Toma

The current education budget is of tremendous importance because it is the first to request funds for a Department of Education. Legislation establishing the new Department was enacted late in 1979 following intensive lobbying on the part of the Carter Administration. President Carter had secured political support from the powerful National Education Association (NEA) during his 1976 campaign by promising to create a department dealing solely with education.

According to both educators and the administration, the establishment of the Department would increase efficiency by coordinating programs previously scattered throughout various federal agencies and result in a consistent set of federal policies. This essay will argue that increased efficiency was not the underlying goal of the educators; more importantly, it will not be the actual outcome. Viewing the department from an economic perspective leads to the conclusion that the NEA's efforts stemmed from their desire to reduce competition between schools. Less competition is desired because it enables the educators, and not the students, to reap the benefits from the school system. It is precisely this phenomenon — reduced competition — which is the source of the decline in American education.

A major purpose of this essay will be to examine more specifically how educators benefit and consumers lose from a less competitive system and exactly how federal spending affects the degree of competition. This will be accomplished largely by analyzing the actual spending programs in which the federal government is involved. By contrasting the goals of these programs as stated at the time of their initiation with the actual outcomes, the pernicious effects of a stronger federal role in general, and of the creation of the Department of Education in particular, become obvious.

A Brief History

The establishment of a department which deals only with educational matters marks a formal acceptance of an active federal role in

197

this area. This acceptance is actually the culmination of a relatively recent trend toward greater centralization of educational policy-making and financing. Not mentioned explicitly in the U.S. Constitution, education was previously assumed to be among those powers reserved to state and local governments. While basic provision for education was made in state constitutions, for many years actual control and financing was in the hands of local governments, whether because of geographic necessity, political mores, or simple efficiency. Beginning in the late nineteenth century, states began to assume a more active role by vesting authority in state departments of education, although as recently as 1920, local governments still financed an average of 83 percent of their educational expenditures, with state governments contributing over 16 percent and the federal government accounting for a mere 0.3 percent. After the Great Depression, intervention by federal and state government increased sharply at the expense of local governments, which are now responsible for about 50 percent of expenditures on public education with the federal government's share having climbed to approximately 10 percent.

There are many reasons why financial responsibility has shifted from a traditionally local function to one shared by the three levels of government. Some of the change results from court orders such as *Serrano v. Priest* which required an alteration in the tax base from which school revenues were derived. Additional rearrangements have been more direct, resulting from state legislative and administrative decisions to assume responsibility.

At the same time, as public education was becoming more centralized, the private school was losing its status as the dominant element in U.S. education. Today, public education is revered as the essential ingredient of a responsible, democratic society. Private schools are viewed as an alternative for only a small segment of the population.

The remainder of this section examines in detail the skepticism surrounding centralization of educational decision-making. If, as suggested earlier, centralization benefits producers and not consumers, skepticism on the part of consumers about a move toward more federal financing is an entirely rational response.

Why Federal Funding?

To assess the desirability of a more pronounced role for the federal government in educational matters, it is useful to consider the view presented by its proponents. The argument generally presented by advocates of increased federal intervention is two-fold and to a degree intertwined. At the most basic level, education is considered a public good, or one for which consumption benefits flow not only to the individual consumer but to other members of society as well. These societal benefits are of such a nature that individuals, local governments, or even state governments will fail to account for them fully and thus underprovide the education. Conversely, the federal government, because of its larger perspective, can finance education to a far greater extent and thus generate benefits for the entire nation.

It is also contended that lower income states should be subsidized because (1) the poor are not as likely to recognize the benefits from education and would, in the federal government's absence, underproduce and therefore underconsume, and (2), less patronizingly, the federal government has a responsibility to provide equal opportunities for all citizens. Persons in lower income states will have the same opportunities as those in higher income states only if the federal government helps to equalize spending on education.

Both aspects of the argument contain certain legitimate points. Public finance economists tend to view education as a good with public attributes. For instance, the ability to read benefits not only the individual but others as well; a democratic society depends upon the literacy of its population. The existence of externalities, however, does not provide an automatic justification for federal financing. While there may be benefits from federal involvement, there are also costs. Only if the net outcome is preferable to state and local provision will the federal government's presence be desirable. As will be shown in the remainder of this essay, significant costs are associated with federal financing.

On a similar note, an appropriate role for the federal government may entail aiding in the equalization of opportunity. But, as has been so aptly demonstrated, equality of opportunity does not mean equality of outcome.[1] Advocating equal expenditures for education in all states has been based on the notion that equal expenditures translate into equal opportunity, with opportunity viewed as a proxy for quality of education. But on this note the evidence is clear: spending on education and quality of education are not positively correlated. In fact, as will be argued later, the reverse may be more accurate. Furthermore, mobility factors have resulted in such population changes between states that today there is little reason to believe even the poorest states lack the resources necessary for an adequate public education system.[2]

It must be recognized that federal financing does not entail merely providing money; included is the power to specify how the money will be spent. Initially, from the local school district's perspective, this may

---

[1] Milton and Rose Friedman, *Free to Choose* (New York: Harcourt Brace Jovanovich, 1980), Chapter 5.

[2] For a general discussion of the welfare state, see Roger A. Freeman, *The Growth of American Government: A Morphology of the Welfare State* (Stanford, CA: Hoover Institution Press, 1975).

seem a small price to pay. Problems arise only later, when the one restriction on spending multiplies into numerous criteria which apply uniformly to all states.

Why do federal officials desire to make policy for schools in the fifty states? The answer lies in the very structure of administrative decision-making. As in the case of individuals in private firms, the actions chosen by bureaucrats are determined largely by the constraints they face. The non-profit nature of government requires bureaucrats to seek rewards through activities other than monetary profit-seeking. These activities generally take the form of output or "perk" maximization.[3] A bureaucrat dealing with education gains more status, prestige, and perhaps even a higher salary, the greater the responsibility of his agency. He has an incentive, therefore, to expand the rules and regulations that go with financial aid. Enroute to satisfaction of their own goals, the bureaucrats and their agency gain more control and power over the general provision of education.

To assess the effect of greater federal control, consider first the situation that exists without any federal financing. Suppose local governments finance their own schools and thus possess the power to set their own educational policies. In this case, each local government must provide the schooling most desired by its constituents. If it does not, families will collectively vote out the school committee or individually move to an alternative district. In this framework, competition between school districts increases the likelihood of consumer satisfaction.

Now consider the case in which the federal government finances and constrains programs provided by the schools. Since federal bureaucrats are unable to gear specific policies to different schools, a national policy on education will emerge. As more and more financial control accrues to the federal government, its policy-making powers grow. The effect will be standardized education. Consumers who are dissatisfied with the product of their school district will have few alternatives, because all districts will be similar. Uniformity and greater monopoly power become synonymous. There is no value in creating a monopoly in an industry with such profound impact on the future human capital of the nation.

SHORT-RUN POLICIES

Viewed from the political setting within which educational policy evolves, the desirability of an active federal role is extremely question-

---

[3] See William A. Niskanen, "Bureaucrats and Politicians," *Journal of Law and Economics,* 18 (December 1975), pp. 617–643, for an in-depth discussion of bureaucratic behavior.

Table 1
Education
(in millions of dollars)

Major Missions and Programs	1979 actual	1980 estimate	1981 estimate
OUTLAYS			
Education:			
Elementary, secondary, and vocational education:			
Aid to education agencies:			
Elementary and secondary education:			
Existing law	3,133	3,409	3,631
Proposed legislation	—	—	50
Indian education	292	302	315
Impact aid	912	821	554
Education for the handicapped	589	789	968
Vocational, and adult education	772	855	908
Other...........................	321	394	512
Child development	668	760	822
Subtotal, elementary, secondary, and vocational education	6,688	7,330	7,761
Higher education:			
Student assistance:			
Existing law	3,769	4,882	4,530
Proposed legislation	—	—	91
Higher and continuing education:			
Existing law	588	410	388
Proposed legislation	—	—	—
Special institutions	170	182	196
Subtotal, higher education	4,528	5,474	5,205
Research and general education aids:			
Educational research and improvement .	432	422	362
Unallocated salaries and overhead	131	163	202
Cultural activities	543	629	688
Other...........................	127	182	157
Subtotal, research and general education aids	1,233	1,395	1,408
Total, education	12,449	14,199	14,374

Source: The Budget of the United States Government, FY 1981

able. However, current federal programs are quite varied; therefore, it is appropriate to analyze each individually to determine its desirability.

Elementary, Secondary, and Vocational Education

Currently, the largest portion of federal expenditures, approximately $7.8 billion of the $14.4 billion total, falls in the broad category of elementary, secondary, and vocational education (Table I). In turn, about $5 billion goes to state and local educational agencies to aid low-income students. This represents a rather recent phenomenon.

In the 1950s, spurred by the launch of the Soviet Sputnik satellite, the federal government began to increase its funding for education programs, providing for grants aimed specifically at increasing interest in the technical sciences.[4] However, the most fundamental changes did not occur until 1965. The Elementary and Secondary Education Acts of 1965 began with financial assistance for special programs relating to educationally deprived children. The legislation also included provisions to cover school library resources, textbooks, and other instructional materials, supplementary educational centers and services, educational research and development, and, finally, a measure to strengthen state departments of education. At the time of its passage, it was hailed as the most impressive legislation ever enacted by Congress in the field of education. Its impressiveness, however, may really lie in the ease with which local control over education was diminished. Consider how federal funding was distributed. The legislation allocated over $1 billion to local educational agencies to help the children of low-income families. Although theoretically allocated to local governments, all applications were subject to approval by the appropriate state educational agency. In reality, therefore, state agencies were granted the power to determine where the money flowed within their states. The ability of state agencies to attach their own strings was enhanced by Title II of the Elementary and Secondary Education Acts (1967). Both private and public schools had to meet minimum state requirements in order to receive federal aid. Title II amendments gave further power to state agencies by making them responsible for the development of local programs to meet state requirements. Perhaps the most significant of all these acts from the standpoint of shifting control away from local districts was Title V, explicitly entitled Strengthening State Departments of Education. Forty percent of the accompanying funding had no relationship to income but was apportioned equally among the states to be spent as state agencies desired.

As the federal government's role in education has grown, spending by all levels of government for this purpose has increased, from a total of $6.7 billion in 1950 to approximately $75 billion by 1976.[5] According to studies in educational spending, this outcome was predictable.[6] It is interesting to note that this same period has been one of the bleak-

---

[4] Jay Scribner, "Impacts of Federal Programs on State Departments of Education," in *Education in the States: Nationwide Development Since 1900,* ed. by Edgar Fuller and Jim Pearson (Washington, D.C.: National Education Association, 1969), pp. 513–523.

[5] Frank E. Armbruster, *Our Children's Crippled Future* (New York: Quadrangle/The New York Times Book Co., Inc., 1977), p. 14.

[6] For an analytical description of why increases in spending by higher levels of government will result in further increases by local levels, see Eugenia Froedge Toma, "Bureaucratic Structures and Educational Spending," *Southern Economic Journal,* forthcoming (January 1981).

est in terms of satisfaction with public education. Evidence of growing displeasure with the product of the public schools appears in newspaper editorials, feature articles in magazines, and television commentaries. Continually declining test scores serve as more objective evidence that a real problem exists. For example, mean scores on college board tests (S.A.T.'s) declined from 478 (on verbal) and 502 (mathematical) out of a possible 800 in 1962–63 to 444 and 480, respectively, in 1973–74 and are continuing to decline.[7]

Professional administrators view insufficient funds as the cause of distress and as an argument for additional federal funding, even though the evidence suggests that increased expenditures do not lead to better quality schooling. The request appears quite rational, however, when one recognizes how this spending has enhanced the status of educators and administrators. For example, from 1971–1976, per-pupil spending rose by 58 percent; and although student enrollment *declined* by 4 percent, professional staffs in public schools *grew* by 8 percent.[8] Further evidence that it is the educational bureaucracy that has grown with the increase in spending is available from an earlier period; from 1968–1973, as enrollment declined by 1 percent, total professional staff went up by 15 percent, teachers increased by 14 percent, and supervisors went up by 44 percent.[9]

While administrators blame lack of funds for the poor quality of education, teachers attribute the problem to home environments and parents feel that teachers are responsible. Despite these mutually recriminatory efforts, however, few seem to realize that the real reason the school system has lost its incentive and ability to produce a quality product is that localities and families have lost control over educational decision-making. The fact that expenditures on elementary and secondary education almost tripled between 1950 and 1960 and then more than quadrupled the 1960 amount by 1976–77, although educational test scores continually declined over this period, is a direct consequence of this loss of local control.[10]

Yet the loss of local control over the preceding decade is probably mild compared to that which can be expected over the next ten years. Federal funding has been relatively small and thus, instead of merely bringing about federal control, has worked primarily to enhance the power of state agencies. This has happened only because there has not been a single federal agency to administer the funds; now, however, as state agencies have developed, educational special interests have become more organized and have lobbied successfully for a federal De-

---

[7]Freeman, p. 16, and Armbruster, pp. 4–5.
[8]Friedman and Friedman, p. 156.
[9]*Ibid.*
[10] See Armbruster, p. 3, for further trends in spending and educational scores.

partment of Education. To understand the course of action this agency will likely follow, it is necessary only to examine the general history of state educational agencies.[11]

State legislatures designated formal state agencies to discharge certain responsibilities with regard to elementary and secondary education as early as 1850, but it was not until the 1950s that each state had established a department of education. Initially, when departments were small and often informally organized, their main thrust was the gathering, compilation, and publication of educational statistics. To this was eventually added the exercise of regulatory functions and, increasingly, the direct assumption of power over policy-making. Today, to varying degrees, these departments serve as the locus of considerable pre-emptive power over education, whether in formulating specific regulations, allocating federal and state funds to local districts, or executing the more detailed functions of day-to-day decision-making.

The state agencies gained their power by capturing that which localities previously possessed. Where once each local school district could be considered as a separate school system, there has now evolved a pattern of uniformity in which all school districts in a state closely resemble one another. Today, the American public school system is really comprised of fifty different systems, not thousands as was formerly the case. All schools in a given state have to offer the same required curricula. In California, for example, each public school has to offer more than thirty state-prescribed courses. In many states, textbooks are selected by textbook committees under the jurisdiction of the state educational agency. Furthermore, qualifications and, in some cases, even pay scales for teachers are set at the state level.[12]

To appreciate the outcome of such an arrangement, consider a different example. Even extreme advocates of equal opportunity do not argue for federal financing of automobiles to be distributed by state auto producers. The outcome, nevertheless, would be the same. Differences in consumption would be eliminated. Each state would choose the make and color of automobile for its entire population. Everyone within a state would drive identical cars, but only that portion of the population that independently would have chosen the state-designated automobile would be happy. The remainder of the population desiring bigger, smaller, faster, or even simply different-colored cars would be dissatisfied. Just as this creates a distorted outcome in the area of automobile consumption, so has the loss of local control

---

[11] For a more analytical approach to the actions of state agencies, see Toma, forthcoming 1981.

[12] See Eugenia Froedge Toma, "Economic Organization of Public Education in the United States," Ph.D. dissertation, V.P.I., 1977, Chapter 4, for further evidence of how state agencies have standardized schools in their states.

over elementary and secondary schools encouraged by federal funding created effects precisely opposite to those initially claimed.

While most funding for elementary, secondary, and vocational education falls in the broad category of aid to elementary and secondary education, there are some more specific spending programs that should also be considered:

Impact Aid

The impact aid program had its genesis in the Lanham Act of 1941. During World War II enrollment in many school districts was sharply increased by the children of thousands of relocated military personnel. These districts, however, enjoyed no corresponding increase in revenues since military bases were not subject to local property taxes. While the program began with appropriate intentions, it has blossomed into one which can no longer be justified. Assistance today totals over $500 million; but, more importantly, aid is now allocated to school districts on the basis of how many federal employees live in them, regardless of whether property is taxable by local districts.[13] School districts around Washington, D.C., for example, get the most impact aid even though they are among the wealthiest in the nation. *Impact aid for category "B" districts, those in which parents either live or work on federal property, should be abolished.* The FY 1982 savings would be $325 million.

Indian Education

In 1972, Title IV, the "Indian Education Act," updated and synthesized the numerous laws passed since 1819 to meet the purportedly special needs of the American Indian.[14] The FY 1981 budget anticipated total spending of $315 million. While it may have been desirable 150 years ago, the program now represents inappropriate funding by the federal government. The states with Indian populations show no sign of "needing" federal support to supply a quality education. When the Indian program was begun, its purpose was largely to aid the national territory of Alaska. Alaska, no longer a territorial responsibility, is now the richest state in the Union. There is little reason for the other 49 states to subsidize the wealthiest.

Vocational And Adult Education

Under the Vocational Act of 1963, the federal government authorized grants to states to improve existing programs and to develop new

---

[13] Howie Kurtz, "Impact Aid: Another Fleecing," *The Washington Monthly* (March 1978), pp. 36–37.

[14] Americo Lapati, *Education and the Federal Government: A Historical Record* (New York: Mason/Charter Publishers, Inc., 1975), pp. 44–47.

programs in vocational education so that persons of all ages would have ready access to technical training.[15] As in the case of elementary and secondary education, much of this federal financing required a stronger role by state educational agencies in allocating funds for local and area vocational training. The 1981 budget channels approximately $900 million in this area.

Education for Handicapped

The Education of the Handicapped Act was enacted by Congress in 1970, although certain of its provisions had already been incorporated in several previous enactments during the 1960s. Many of the expenditures under this program result from requirements to provide facilities for the handicapped. While federal financing for compliance with federal rules may seem appropriate, this is another area in which federal funding is likely to bring about unintended consequences. Suppose several states or local jurisdictions have large numbers of handicapped students and want to provide the appropriate facilities. If they can combine to have a law passed requiring such facilities for all schools and simultaneously procure federal money, these areas will be better off. At the same time, however, jurisdictions which have no demand for facilities to serve the handicapped will have to provide them anyway. Such unnecessary expenditures, combined with the likelihood of still more requirements and resultant unneeded outlays, again indicate the need to leave such financing to states and local school districts.

Other Aid

This is a miscellaneous category of expenditures with budget requests totaling $512 million for FY 1981. It includes such areas as assistance for school desegregation and support for greater educational equity for women. Like all the special programs, this one differs from general aid to elementary and secondary education in having as the stated purpose of its funding the accomplishment of federal goals. The effects, however, are the same whether the control is blatant or more subtle; in all cases, decisions requiring all districts to behave identically remove local discretionary powers and thereby reduce competition.

Child Development

The Head Start program differs little from elementary education either with respect to the traditional justifications advanced for federal funding or with regard to its actual effects. At present, it is a voluntary attendance program supposedly designed for low-income children, but its probable future is predictable when considered within

---

[15] Lapati, pp. 105–112.

the context of the main theme of this essay. For example, the budget request for 1981 exceeded that of 1977 by 74 percent; and the program will doubtless continue to grow until it includes all pre-school children regardless of income level, at which point educators can be expected to claim that the program produces so many societal benefits that attendance must be mandatory.

Immediate Changes

Whether one is analyzing special programs or elementary and secondary education in general, the recurring conclusion emerges that federal financing entails federal controls with the subsequent effect of reduced competition. *A necessary first step toward reducing federal funding and control would be abolition of the newly created Department of Education.* The longer the Department continues, the more involved in local educational matters it will become and the more difficult it will be to eliminate.

The remaining expenditures cannot be eliminated immediately. Units of government, schools, and individuals have made plans with the expectation of future funding. *Cuts in the FY 1982 budget could be made by simply allowing no increases beyond the 1981 level.* Beyond this, explicit announcements must be made about plans for future cuts so that school officials can begin making adjustments and plans for future programs. The eventual goal should be the complete elimination of federal funding.

Higher Education

Higher education differs dramatically from elementary and secondary education in a number of ways. The idea of public higher education is not as deeply ingrained as is that of the lower levels. Largely for that reason state universities, although heavily subsidized, are generally not tuition-free. In many states, subsidy levels are sufficiently low that private schools exist as viable alternatives. Although more students attend public institutions of higher education than private ones, 52 percent of the institutions of higher education in 1975 were private schools.[16] However, even in private schools, federal financing has emerged as an important source of funds; in fiscal year 1976, federal financing accounted for an average of 19 percent of their current income.[17]

Another major difference is that no states require attendance for higher education. Continuing education beyond the secondary level

---

[16] Chester E. Finn, Jr., *Scholars, Dollars, and Bureaucrats* (Washington, D.C.: The Brookings Institution, 1978). An excellent description of the federal programs relating to higher education can be found in this book.

[17] Finn, p. 48.

by large segments of the population has occurred only since World War II and especially since the 1960s. Two factors contributing to this increase are a more technologically advanced society which requires more skilled workers and a higher standard of living which voids the necessity of work immediately after high school. Enrollment rates are predicted to decline throughout the 1980s, however, with the passing of the baby boom.

Federal funding of higher education—at least indirectly—has a longer history than that of elementary and secondary schools. The first large step came with the Morrill Act of 1862, which helped establish land grant universities in many states on the condition that they offer instruction in agriculture and the mechanical arts. Today, these institutions are supported by the individual states with supplementary funds from the federal government.

The arguments for federal financial aid for higher education are substantially similar to those for aid in general. Education at higher levels purportedly generates sufficient external benefits to justify the financial encouragement of its consumption. Similarly, opportunities are not equalized unless the federal government insures that lower income persons have access to higher education. Only with federal aid can lower income states produce professionals and, consequently, higher income levels.

These arguments have even less validity than when applied to the lower levels of education. There are societal benefits, as mentioned earlier, stemming from a population which is literate. At least until the last decade, the responsibility of teaching students to read and write belonged to the elementary schools. For external benefits to provide a rationale for federal subsidization, there must be an insufficient incentive for the individual to pursue a higher education as viewed from society's perspective. In other words, if the individual is not a prime beneficiary of the activity, he faces a diluted incentive to partake of it. This situation does not apply to higher education. First, the individual receives numerous nonmonetary benefits in terms of increased awareness, cultural enrichment, etc. Second, and on a more tangible level, monetary benefits flow in the form of increased lifetime earnings. The increased income is the individual's benefit from the services his education allows him to provide for others. Based purely on the public goods argument, there is no reason for the federal government to be subsidizing college attendance.

The second justification, equalizing opportunity, is equally questionable when applied to higher education. The questions here arise, to some extent, from the facts surrounding college attendance. For a variety of reasons, of which current income is only one, more children from middle- and upper-income families attend college than from lower-income ones. In 1976, for example, only 6 percent of all students enrolled in institutions of higher education came from families of less than $5,000 annual income. At the other extreme, over 25 percent were from families considered upper-income, or earning greater than $25,000 a year, and about 60 percent came from families whose income exceeded $15,000. In other words, it is not the poor who receive the benefits from aid to higher education.

At least two studies substantiate the claim that it is middle- and upper-income families who benefit on net from the subsidies to higher education. In a study of four income groups in Florida, a comparison was made of the benefits received from higher education with the costs incurred through taxes. While the top income group received 60 percent more benefits than it paid in taxes, all three lower-income groups paid more than they received.[18] A study of the same type for California revealed that in 1964 families with children enrolled in California institutions of higher education received a positive net transfer equal to approximately 1.5 percent of their average income. However, families who did not have children enrolled in these institutions were on average poorer and incurred a net cost of 8.2 percent of their income.[19] Since, as stated earlier, college graduates on average earn higher lifetime incomes, subsidy programs can actually widen income inequalities. Like the case of elementary and secondary schooling, the present direction of federal financing has been greatly influenced by the Education Acts of 1965.

Financial assistance consists of grants, loans, and loan guarantees and either takes the form of direct student aid or goes to the schools, which in turn give it to the students. There is only one major direct student payment scheme — the basic educational opportunity grants. (GI and Social Security payments are sometimes considered direct payment schemes for education but are administered through other agencies and are based on criteria other than income.)[20] Approximately $2.4 billion is budgeted for the basic grants in FY 1981. The remaining student assistance funds are campus-based. The latter includes supplemental educational opportunity grants (SEOG), college work-study programs, and national defense student loans (NDSL). Federal assistance also comes in the form of insured or interest-subsidized loans made by private lenders.

These subsidized loans are not based on "need." Regardless of the criteria surrounding their receipt, all federal loans include a subsidized

---

[18] Douglas M. Windham, *Education, Equality and Income Redistribution* (Lexington, Mass.: Heath Lexington Books, 1970).

[19] W. Lee Hansen and Burton A. Weisbrod, *Benefits, Costs, and Finance of Public Higher Education* (Chicago: Markam Publishing Co., 1969).

[20] Finn, pp. 67–80.

interest rate. The NDSL programs require the student to pay a 3 percent rate of interest which begins accruing only after graduation. Loans for less needy students generally carry an interest rate of 7 percent with the federal government making up the difference between that and the current market rate of interest.

In neither basic grants nor campus-based programs do all funds go to poorer students. In the SEOG program, 25 percent went to students from families with incomes greater than $12,000 in 1976-77; 38 percent of work-study funds went to the same category of students; and nearly 44 percent of the NDSL funding went to students with family income in excess of $12,000.[21] This indicates that students often are able to obtain loans regardless of actual need. A classic abuse is the "poor" student who secures a loan, buys a parcel of property, and reaps capital gains each year he attends school. In addition to the problem of determining who really "needs" the loans, the sheer mechanics of tracking the loans constitutes a monumental task. Even administrators of the program admit that the current default rate on direct loans exceeds 17 percent.

Further problems, such as devising a method of distributing funds that accounts for differences in schools and states, suggest that it might be more efficient to make individual schools responsible for handling any federal aid. But this method is plagued by its own set of problems. Which schools receive the funds and how much do they receive? Although it is not clear why, about 3 percent of the institutions of higher learning in the U.S. acquire 67 percent of the present federal payments to colleges and universities. A more fundamental problem is the link between financial aid sources and control over decision-making. Control by the government over schools' activities is easier when aid flows directly to schools instead of to students. For example, assistance may be granted only if the schools offer courses of a technical nature or enroll a certain percentage of minority students. Stories abound concerning the costs of complying with federal rules in order to receive funding. A former president of one institution reported that his university received $3 million in federal funds but spent $500,000 to meet federal reporting requirements.[22] At least one school, Hillsdale College, refuses all federal funding for exactly this reason.

The link between federal funding and control is a sufficient argument against either direct or indirect federal aid to colleges and universities; but, like aid to elementary and secondary schools, it cannot be eliminated overnight. *Instead, federal assistance should be limited immediately to its FY 1981 level and, in the future, gradually reduced to*

---

[21] *Ibid.*

[22] James H. Zumberge Jr. was quoted as reporting these facts about his former presidency at Southern Methodist University, *Los Angeles Times*, December 2, 1980.

zero. In the process of phasing out loan programs, changes in their present structure are necessary. Loans should go directly to the students—not to the schools. Furthermore, there is no justification for providing loans at below market rates of interest. Any borrowing done by students should be at the market rate of interest. In other words, if the government has to pay a 12 percent rate of interest for NDSL loans, so should the student who receives the funds, thereby making it the student, as beneficiary, who eventually pays for his schooling. Any repayment could be postponed until graduation, but following that, he would have to repay fully the loan and all accrued interest according to some fixed schedule.

Tax Subsidies

Current tax subsidies apply largely to higher education. Income tax exemptions are available to parents of children over 19 years of age but still in school; income from scholarships and fellowships is not subject to taxation whether its ultimate source be public or private; and contributions to educational institutions are deductions for the donors. These so-called tax expenditures are estimated at approximately $3 billion in FY 1981.

Tax subsidies are one area in which federal "spending" should be increased in the short run.[23] To restore the alternative to public education, tax credits should be allowed for private school tuition payments on the elementary, secondary, and college levels. As public schools have grown increasingly uniform throughout local school districts, states, and, more recently, the nation, private education has emerged as the only option that provides families with some choice over the type of schooling they receive.

While private schools offer the alternatives so necessary for a society premised on individual choice, many persons now fear for their continued existence. At least two major problems plague the private schools. First, all taxpaying families contribute to the support of public schools regardless of whether their children attend these schools. To attend private schools involves an additional tuition payment borne only by the individual family. In this sense, it is only those families who want to pay double for education who have the option of choosing private schools. A second issue concerns the changing demographics in the U.S. Declining birth rates experienced in the recent past translate to declining enrollment rates at both public and private institutions. Although government financing of public schools is determined partially by enrollment or attendance rates, additional across-the-board subsidies enable public schools to continue in spite

---

[23] See Richard E. Wagner, ed., *Government Aid to Private Schools: Is It a Trojan Horse?* (Wichita, Kansas: Center for Independent Education, 1979), for several discussions on government aid to private schools.

of declining enrollments. The same does not hold true for private schools which, being almost wholly dependent on tuition payments, go out of business when enrollments fall.

To illustrate the current bias more pointedly, consider an individual attempting to choose between the private and public school systems. Since his taxes pay for the operation of the public schools, there are no tuition fees. Assume that if he chooses to enroll in a private school, tuition payments will equal $1,000 per year. To choose the latter option, he first must be able to pay both the tax price and the tuition fee. To be willing to do so, he must perceive benefits from attending the private school to be at least $1,000 greater than those he perceives from the public school. In essence, the present financing arrangement says that private schools must not only be superior but must be *far* superior in order to survive.

As a first step, instituting tax credits, which equal private school tuition payments, would remove the double payment dilemma now existing. Such an action would lower the cost of attending private school and thus eliminate the handicap under which private schools now operate. Under these circumstances, taxpayers could choose either the public or private schools on the basis of which provided the better service. In addition to these direct effects, the positive repercussions created by this change might be even greater than the direct benefits. Recall that one of the reasons hypothesized earlier for decline in public school quality is that consumers face few options. Consequently, educators behave more like monopolists and capture many of the potential benefits from the product for themselves. Studies have shown that states with decision-making at the state level and consequently a more uniform system have higher education budgets, *ceteris paribus*.[24] An indication that these budgets were benefits to the educators and not reflections of school quality can be found, for example, in the higher salaries for the professional educators and even in a greater number of administrators per pupil than in other states.[25] If private schools became a more viable option for consumers, the public school monopoly would disintegrate. Subsequently, not only would private school attendees benefit from tax credits, but others would as well since all schools would be forced to provide a better quality education. Ultimately, the entire educational system, both public and private, would benefit from the introduction of private school tuition tax credits.

---

[24] To illustrate, Toma (forthcoming 1981) found that a major determinant of state spending for education was the degree of monopoly power possessed by the state educational agency.

[25] Armbruster, p. 3. Three studies by Eugenia Froedge Toma support this. See Toma (1977); Toma (forthcoming 1981); and "Bureaucratic Regulation of Education," Loyola Marymount University, 1980–81 University Research Grant working paper.

Although tuition tax credits would apply to schooling at all levels, including higher education, further increases in tax subsidies could also be instituted to aid the relatively higher cost post-secondary schools. As mentioned earlier, contributions to public or private educational institutions are tax deductible. *To encourage more private contributions, the existing deductions should be expanded to tax credits. More private scholarships and grants directly to individuals should also be encouraged; this could also be done through tax credits.*

LONG-TERM CONSIDERATIONS

The education system which would provide the product at least cost and greatest satisfaction to consumers would be the one in which each consumer had free choice to select the product. In other words, a competitive market for educational provision establishes the ideal setting.

If government is to be involved to some degree, the question becomes one of how most closely to approximate the outcome generated by the competitive market. Technically, government could finance education but allow private provision and control. In other words, public financing does not theoretically necessitate public provision. As emphasized throughout this essay, however, in practice, the link between the two tends to grow stronger and stronger over time until, ultimately, government finance means government control. If government, in the latter case, included all taxpayers, the finance-control situation would resemble a private market setting. A problem arises in government control, however, because of the cost of direct taxpayer participation, particularly at the federal level. Sheer numbers suggest that the costs of having all taxpayers make decisions would be enormous. This is, of course, why a representative form of government exists. But beyond this, the costs of elected representatives' performing the administrative tasks involved with government financing are also extremely high and, thus, administrative bureaucracies are born. Government decisions, therefore, are not made directly by the taxpaying public and often not even by their elected representatives, but are made indirectly by appointed administrators. The structure surrounding bureaucratic decision-making often results in decisions contradictory to the interests of the public at large. As demonstrated earlier, the bureaucrats' best interest generally translates to more and more power for the agencies and less and less for the taxpayers. It is not likely, therefore, that a centrally financed educational system will be one which approximates a private market setting unless specific constraints are developed which control the behavior of the bureaucrats.

Some budget alternatives suggested by others as a means of moving the system away from government control should be considered.

Block Grants

Concerned about the actual outcome of present federal financing programs, some have argued for a system whereby the federal government grants some given amount of funds to each state to be used at the state's discretion. At least two criticisms of this plan emerge when viewed within the context of this essay. First, although initially funds might flow with no strings, the evidence presented throughout indicates they would not continue to do so. Bureaucracies are not structured so as to permit their members to be content only with disbursing funds.

Second, giving the money to the states enhances a problem which is already enormous. State agencies determine the activities of all schools under their jurisdiction. Giving them more federal money would only perpetuate this tendency. On this basis, any block grants by the federal government should be made to localities. The problem of control by the federal bureaucracy is not removed, but at least that of state control over local districts would be reduced.

A Federal Voucher Plan

If a general subsidy results in centralized decision-making, is it possible that a voucher system could result in an outcome resembling that emerging in a free market setting? Although the specifics vary, a voucher plan works to a great extent like the present food stamp program. The federal government would present all children of school age with a coupon worth $X. The coupon could be used only for purchasing education, but children could redeem them at public or private schools of their choice. A minor problem involves devising a formula which accounts for differences between states.

At first glance, the plan looks perfect. Since the customer (student) receives the money directly, any government control over output appears impossible. Furthermore, the competitiveness of a market system will cause each school to provide the quality product the public desires. Consequently, the education provided by American schools will be as diverse as the population of the nation. Simultaneously, the plan insures that the poor can attend school and promotes competition between schools.

Although this plan offers more benefits than any previously devised, at least some of the benefits exist only on a superficial level. Most important of these is the idea that vouchers would eliminate the potential for government control. At least some minimum criteria will be outlined as necessary for voucher receipt. Requirements concerning acceptable schools will be established even if initially they do no more than refer to students taught at home. Given the built-in propensity for government rules to multiply, eventually schools would have to satisfy a long list of requirements before vouchers could be used. Finally, a national set of policies would emerge and differences between schools would disappear. If this scenario holds true in the end, a voucher plan paid for by the federal government will eventually differ little from the other financing programs. While this is a caution regarding educational vouchers in general, the concern is greatest when considering a federal scheme, for federal control over schools is precisely the outcome to be avoided.

Aside from the fallacious labeling of tax credits as government spending, there is no proper role for the federal government in education. This conclusion rests on both the political setting surrounding government actions and the historical path which educational financing has followed.

As shown in an earlier section, when states assumed more financial control, they also acquired more decision-making powers at the expense of local control. Federal financing at least indirectly seemed to strengthen the state agencies' power even further. The system which has emerged is essentially fifty different school systems — a single system for each state. Although many current problems stem from the fact that there are only fifty producers for all the students of the nation, fifty is preferable to one, which will be the case if the new Department of Education is permitted to continue a greater role in educational decision-making. To the extent that funding of any educational programs continues from the federal level, funneling it through diverse bureaus and thus creating a hodgepodge of policies leads to a more desirable outcome than vesting total authority in a single agency.

The actions taken by a federal Department of Education would prohibit, not promote competition among schools. And yet, competition is the surest method of requiring schools to perform satisfactorily. The gradual removal of the federal government from the educational arena is absolutely necessary: for only if individual schools can make their own decisions will the school system be able to provide the quality education so vital for a better future for all.

215

10b

Employment, Training, and Social Services

by Dave M. O'Neill and June A. O'Neill*

Federal programs dealing with employment, training and social services are recent arrivals to the federal budget. In general terms, their objectives are to help people earn a better living or cope more successfully with handicaps and other problems. Laudable as these goals may be, it is questionable whether the federal government has been an effective agent for achieving them. Nonetheless, federal spending on labor programs and social services has ballooned in the past fifteen years. As shown in Table 2, these programs were fairly insignificant in the early 1960s, accounting for $377 million, which was less than half of one percent of the federal budget. By 1979 expenditures on these programs had reached $17.2 billion and had grown to 3.5 percent of the federal budget.

This essay reviews the often controversial issues surrounding these budget expenditures. Employment and training programs, the larger component, are considered first, and then social services.

EMPLOYMENT AND TRAINING PROGRAMS

This category of programs emerged in the 1960s under the rubric of "manpower programs." It was distinguished from the more familiar categories of education and training because it was specifically focused on remedies for long-term unemployment problems arising from a severe and unexpected imbalance in the labor market. Although the programs have been extensively evaluated, the only question addressed has been whether they have achieved their objectives. The question of whether the government should pursue the objectives or whether there are more efficient mechanisms for achieving them in the private sector has seldom been raised.

This section first presents a brief historical sketch of the development of employment and training programs. The evidence on the ex-

---

*The views expressed in this essay are those of the authors. They should not be attributed to any institution.

Table 1

Training, Employment, and Labor Services
(millions of dollars)

	1979 actual	1980 estimate	1981 estimate
Training and employment:			
General training and employment pro-			
grams	2,450	2,720	2,835
Public service employment	5,041	3,977	4,415
Youth programs:			
Existing law	2,048	2,330	1,844
Proposed legislation	−	−	717
Older Workers	208	238	263
Work incentive program	385	365	385
Federal-State employment service	701	773	841
Subtotal, training and employment...	10,833	10,402	11,299
Other labor services	488	563	602
Subtotal, training, employment, and			
labor services	11,321	10,965	11,901
Social services:			
Grants to States for social and child			
welfare services:			
Existing law	3,091	2,670	2,627
Proposed legislation	−	438	523
Retroactive claims	543	−	−
Aid to the elderly	557	598	726
Services for the developmentally disabled			
and other special programs:			
Existing law	1,016	1,057	1,095
Proposed legislation	−	−	2
Community service programs	594	569	555
Domestic volunteer programs	117	145	175
Other social services	5	21	14
Subtotal, social services	5,923	5,498	5,717
Allowance for youth initiative	−	−	−
Deductions for offsetting receipts	−8	−7	−5
Total, outlays	29,685	30,654	31,989

Source: The Budget of the United States Government, FY 1981.

tent to which these programs have achieved their objectives is then reviewed. Finally, both the meaningfulness of the objectives and various alternative policy solutions are discussed, taking due account of the proper roles of the private and public sectors.

Historical Development

Since the Great Depression of the 1930s, assistance to unemployed individuals has been considered an area of legitimate government in-

Table 2
Federal Expenditures on Employment and Training Programs and Social Services
(millions of dollars)

Fiscal Year[2]	Training and Employment	Other Labor Services	Social Services	Total	Percent of Federal Budget Outlays
1962	194	73	110	377	0.4
1965	534	96	230	860	0.7
1970	1,602	135	1,884	3,621	1.8
1971	1,952	157	2,243	4,352	2.1
1972	2,894	184	3,519	6,597	2.8
1973	3,283	202	3,315	6,800	2.8
1974	2,910	219	3,241	6,370	2.4
1975	4,063	259	3,923	8,245	2.5
1976	6,288	301	4,026	10,615	2.9
1977	6,877	374	4,632	11,883	3.0
1978	10,784	410	5,027	16,221	3.6
1979	10,833	488	5,923	17,244	3.5
1980 (est.)	10,402	563	5,498	16,463	2.9
1981 (est.)	11,299	602	5,717	17,618	2.9

[1]Includes only those programs in function 500 of the budget.
[2]Fiscal year ends June 30 through 1976; ends September 30 starting in 1977.
Source: Office of Management and Budget.

tervention. The large-scale dis-employment of millions of adult workers with families combined with the extensive duration of the resulting spells of unemployment led to the establishment of our federal state unemployment insurance system. It also greatly increased funds allocated to the established system of Public Employment Service offices.

At that time, however, other problems confronting workers — such as the need to obtain new skills, either because of structural shifts in the economy or because of individual low wage rates — were not believed to require specific government action. If government could revive aggregate demand to eliminate the massive cyclical unemployment, than a resumption of normal economic growth would increase real wages at all levels. And with the unemployment insurance system providing unemployed workers with some financial assistance, any structural problems they might have in finding a job would be handled adequately by private market mechanisms.

This was the state of micro labor market policy until the early 1960's. Then, in response to severe structural unemployment among coal miners in Appalachia, Congress passed the Area Redevelopment Act which, among other things, provided for skill training programs

219

run by government to assist unemployed workers in obtaining jobs in other industries and areas. This was probably the first of what subsequently came to be called federal "manpower" programs. Although not stated explicitly, it represented a rejection of the idea that the market mechanism could work well enough to keep structural unemployment at a socially optimal level.

This effort soon expanded as additional population groups came to be considered relevant targets for federal manpower programs. With the passage of the Manpower Development and Training Act (MDTA) and the Economic Opportunity Act in 1964, low productivity workers, chronically unemployed individuals and disadvantaged youth joined structurally unemployed but otherwise job-ready workers as the targets of federal manpower training programs. In the late 1960s with the advent of the Work Incentive Program (WIN), recipients of welfare benefits also became a target group for federally funded and delivered training services.

Until 1970 the major type of service provided was training of various types — classroom training in specific occupational skills; on-the-job training under special contracts with private firms; intensive remedial education combined with vocational training given in residential centers (Job Corps) or in special neighborhood centers. Job placement assistance was another major type of service offered. What was then called "work support" was a minor program area. It consisted of placing individuals in specially funded public jobs in state and local government, the bulk of which were provided for in-school youth during the summer (Neighborhood Youth Corps) and for elderly workers with severe labor market problems (Operation Mainstream).

Beginning in 1971 with the passage of the Emergency Employment Act and continuing with the Comprehensive Employment and Training Act (CETA) of 1973 and the Youth Employment and Demonstrations Project Act (YEDPA) of 1977, the mix of manpower program services has shifted and the direct provision of public jobs has overtaken training as the major approach. Public jobs accounted for none of the employment and training dollars in 1964, while in 1969 they accounted for 21 percent and by 1980 for somewhat more than half.

Evaluation of Current Programs — Have They Worked?

In dollar terms, the increase in the employment and training function of the budget has been enormous, rising almost twenty-fold between 1965 and 1979 (about nine times in dollars of constant purchasing power). Table 3 shows actual federal budget outlays in fiscal year 1979 and estimated outlays for fiscal years 1980 and 1981 for the

Table 3
Federal Outlays on Major Employment and Training Programs[1], by Target Population and Service; Fiscal Years 1979, 1980 and 1981
(millions of dollars)

	1979 actual	1980 estimate	1981 estimate
Programs Serving All Workers			
Public Jobs:	$5,529	$4,430	$4,827
Public Service Employment	4,953	3,906	4,360
CETA Title II-D (Structural)	1,736	2,009	2,411
CETA Title VI (Countercyclical)	3,217	1,897	1,949
Work Experience — CETA Title II	576	524	467
Training:	1,143	1,420	1,544
Classroom — CETA Title II	918	1,085	1,159
On-The-Job — CETA Title II	225	335	385
Programs Serving Only Youth			
Work Experience:	1,567	1,846	2,216
CETA Title IV:			
Summer Jobs (SYEP)	660	794	872
Community Improvement (YCCIP)	91	129	40
General Work Experience (YETP)	480	612	134
Proposed YETP and YCCIP Reorganization	—	—	832
CETA Title VIII:			
Conservation Projects (YACC)	273	256	277
Non-CETA:			
Youth Conservation Corps (YCC)	63	55	61
Training:			
Job Corps — CETA Title IV	380	489	580
Programs for Other Special Groups:			
(CETA Title III and Other)			
Indians (Training and Work Experience)	380	131	124
Migrants (Training and Work Experience) . . .	106	82	79
Older Americans (Work Experience)	208	238	263
Welfare Recipients (WIN, Training and Work Experience)	385	365	385
Other Special Groups[2]	356	481	530
Job and Labor Market Information Services			
Public Employment Service	745	779	888
Labor Market Information	36	39	39
Private Sector Initiatives	7	150	295

[1]Excludes a few minor programs included in the budget 500 functional area and therefore will not sum to the total in Table 1.

[2]Displaced homemakers, the elderly, permanently displaced experienced workers.

Source: The Budget of the United States Government, FY 1981 and Office of Management and Budget, unpublished background information.

major employment and training programs, most of which are administered by the Department of Labor.[1] Have these programs achieved their objectives? Have they reduced structural unemployment below what it would have been in their absence? Have they raised the productive capacities of participants?

With some exceptions (such as the Job Corps) the employment and training programs do not get high marks. The weight of the evidence, however, differs between the major types of program services, and by target group. The strongest negative case emerges for public jobs. The case with regard to training and job placement assistance is much more mixed.

Public Jobs

The objectives for a public jobs program have become more ambitious over time. They are now viewed both as a means of increasing aggregate employment during a business downturn (a countercyclical objective) and as a way of increasing the productivity of disadvantaged individuals (a counterstructural objective).

Proponents of public jobs as a countercyclical program argue that it is superior to other macroeconomic tools since more jobs will be created per dollar of federal spending. This argument, of course, presupposes that fiscal stimulus *is* an appropriate response to any downturn in business activity — a view that has been strongly challenged in recent years by those who question the ability of the government to "fine-tune" the economy and prefer instead a more neutral stance.[2]

Even if one is committed to an interventionist countercyclical policy, however, a temporary public jobs program appears to be a much less sensible policy tool than a temporary general tax cut. State and local officials may use the funds primarily to reduce state and local taxes (or raise them less than otherwise), in which case the program would create about the same number of jobs as a federal tax cut, albeit in a less efficient way. Over the years a number of studies have attempted to estimate the magnitude of this "displacement effect." The range of estimates, although disturbingly large — from approximately 100 per-

---

[1] Some programs are administered by other agencies such as WIN (Dept. of Health and Human Services) and YCC (Dept. of Agriculture).

[2] The classic statement of the non-interventionist view is by Milton Friedman, "The Effects of Full Employment Policy on Economic Stability" in Milton Friedman, *Essays in Positive Economics* (Chicago: The University of Chicago Press, 1953), pp. 117–132. For the pro-interventionist side see James Tobin and Martin Neil Baily, "Inflation-Unemployment Consequences of Job Creation Policies," in John Palmer (ed.), *Creating Jobs: Public Employment Programs and Wage Subsidies* (Washington, D.C.: The Brooking Institution, 1978).

cent to 18 percent — shows the existence of this affect on a significant level.[3]

In 1978, Congress reacted to this evidence by requiring that no individual hired into a slot be paid with federal funds for more than eighteen months and that a large percentage of the slots funded be attached to specially created eighteen-month projects, which presumably "self-destruct" at that time. Actually, the development is ironic, since displacement may be the least disadvantageous of the possible outcomes of the program. If the program truly "worked," in the sense that large scale net additions to state and local government employment in fact occurred, important resource misallocations would likely occur. The reasons for the misallocation lie in the complex nature of cyclical unemployment. The increases in unemployment caused by a recession do not simply involve workers who are temporarily separated from a job to which they know they will return. Many unemployed workers will need to find new long-term job positions and a public job acts as a deterrent to the serious process of job search and accommodation to the changing structure of the market. Massive countercyclical public jobs programs, which successfully create net job additions in state and local governments, are likely to result in resource allocations at the new peak in business activity that are quite different from those desired by households and firms.

To sum up, the following quote from the 1975 Economic Report of the President is apt:

> ... [A] public employment program that is effective as a countercyclical measure would presumably provide jobs that State and local governments would not otherwise create, that can be established quickly, and that can be readily eliminated as job opportunities in the private sector increase. To ensure that jobs are net additions to employment, it may be necessary to create distinct tasks in separate and visible agencies set up for the purpose. To provide productive employment, the jobs have to be suitable for persons of diverse prior training, employment experience, and age; and they must require at most a very short period of training.

To this should be added that they should not distort the desired mix of goods and services in the economy at the succeeding cyclical peak. In short, these conflicting conditions make it impossible to create a successful program. Countercyclical public employment programs appear to be the least defensible of the current manpower program mix. *Title VI of CETA should be phased out over the remainder of fiscal year 1981 and fiscal year 1982.*

---

[3] For an excellent review and critique of this literature see Michael Borus and Daniel Hamermesh, "Study of the Net Employment Effects of Public Service Employment-Econometric Analysis" in *Job Creation Through Public Service Employment,* Vol. III, Commissioned Papers, Report #6, National Commission for Manpower Policy, Washington, D.C., March, 1978.

The counterstructural objective has been pursued in legislation by attempting to target the program more narrowly on particularly disadvantaged workers rather than the average unemployed worker. Despite these efforts, the evidence suggests that the individuals who have been holding public jobs are not the most severely disadvantaged in the labor market. This conclusion is supported by data on the educational attainment of participants in public jobs programs which show that in FY 1978 about 75 percent have completed four years of high school or more, a percentage exceeding that of the average unemployed worker (63 percent).[4]

Additional evidence that the program has been primarily serving mainstream workers who are in the middle of a short or moderate spell of unemployment is given in Table 4 which gives data relating to changes in the amount of long duration unemployment for adults and teenagers at three points in time.

Up to 1973, public jobs for adults and non-summer public jobs for youth were a relatively small effort — about 60,000 slots for youth and 150,000 for adults in 1973. By 1979, non-summer public jobs for youth had mushroomed to about 300,000 and jobs for adults to 420,000. If these jobs had been targeted on the long-term unemployed we might have expected to observe a significant decline in the reported incidence of this unemployment. As Table 4 shows, this did not hap-

Table 4
**Trends in Long Duration Unemployment for Teenagers
and for Adults 25 Years Old and Over
(April of Each Year)**

Year	Long Duration* Unemployment (000)	Total Labor Force (000)	Long Duration Unemployment As Percent of Labor Force
	Adults: 25 Years and Older		
1966	227	62,013	.4%
1973	240	68,360	.3%
1979	414	76,625	.5%
	Youth: 16 to 19 Years		
1973	184	8,460	2.2%
1979	235	9,560	2.4%

*For adults this is a duration of 27 or more weeks. For teens it is 15 or more weeks.
Source: *Employment and Earnings,* Bureau of Labor Statistics (USPS 081-99). May of 1966, 1973 and 1979.

---

[4]See *Employment and Training Report of the President, 1979* and *Employment and Earnings,* January 1980, both U.S. Department of Labor publications.

pen. These two years were both cyclical peaks so that the lack of decline (actually the growth) in long duration unemployment cannot be attributed to cyclical factors. With regard to youth, the extension of coverage of the federal minimum wage that took place in 1977 may explain some of their increased long-term unemployment. It is doubtful, however, that it can account for both the observed growth in long-term unemployment *and* the additional amount that would be required to demonstrate an effect from the increase in public job slots.

Another type of social benefit that could arise from public job creation would be an increase in the earnings potential of those individuals who do pass through the program. Unfortunately, there is little empirical evidence on post-program effects that could be considered conclusive. One careful review of evaluations of youth programs cautiously concluded that work experience programs alone (that is, without any other academic or vocational training services) do not appear to have any perceptible effects on employability.[5]

In sum, while the case against public employment as a counterstructural tool may not be as strong as for the countercyclical objective, there is little positive evidence to support a major role for such a program. A limited program that served as an employer of last resort for long-term unemployed adults with special problems should be substituted. Youth need not be included in such a program since they are covered by their own programs. *It is recommended that Title II-D of CETA be scaled down to the level required by the new target group and that funding be coordinated with the jobs programs for older Americans and for the special groups covered by CETA Title III.* For FY 1982, the savings would be $600 million.

Training

Theoretically, training should be effective in raising earnings capacity. Considerable research shows that individuals do raise their earnings capacity by acquiring additional education and training. However, training *as delivered by federal manpower programs* does not appear to have been highly effective, although the evidence from program evaluations is limited. One conclusion to be drawn is that the efficacy of resources devoted to training are not independent of the pecuniary and other incentives of the users and providers of the training.

A number of studies have attempted to determine whether the training received in manpower training programs raised the post-program

[5] See Ernst W. Stromsdorfer, "The Effectiveness of Youth Programs: An Analysis of the Historical Antecedents of Current Youth Initiatives," in Anderson and Sawhill (ed.), *Youth Employment and Public Policy,* The American Assembly, Columbia University, 1980.

earnings capacity of the participants. Two careful studies of MDTA training by Ashenfelter and Kiefer showed small or no gains for males and modest gains for women.[6] One program, however, that has shown consistently positive post-program effects is Job Corps. Disadvantaged youth attending this intensive program have shown encouraging improvement in their reading and mathematics achievement test scores (compared to control groups). A recent study finds positive net labor market effects as well.[7]

Unfortunately, there have been no substantial impact studies of the CETA training components since the CETA reorganization took place. Under CETA, "decentralization" became the expected cure for what ailed manpower programs. Thus, one cannot be sure that the weak evidence on program effects from the pre-CETA days is still applicable.

A major issue that is often overlooked is the extent to which the efficacy of training may depend on the type of delivery system within which it takes place. Under the approach used in federal programs the individuals receiving the service absorb very little of the cost of training and providers usually have very little pecuniary incentive to worry about the relevance of their skill training in the current labor market. A study of vocational training used by veterans under the GI bill finds significant effects on earnings capacity.[8] Veterans may absorb more of the cost of training (when it exceeds their voucher) and the providers are mainly proprietary schools in which the incomes of school owners can be greatly influenced by the degree to which their training leads students into good jobs.

Recent Growth in Youth Programs

With the passage of YEDPA in 1977 the amount of resources devoted to manpower programs for youth increased dramatically. But perhaps more significant than the growth in total resources was the shift in service mix away from training and toward public jobs. Moreover, legislative mandates to the contrary, many of the youth who occupy these job slots do not receive any supplementary training. A recent survey of youth[9] found that 90 percent of those who had par-

[6] See Orley Ashenfelter, "Estimating the Effect of Training Programs on Earnings," *The Review of Economics and Statistics*, Vol. LX, No. 1, February 1978. And Nicholas Kiefer, *The Economic Benefits from Manpower Training Programs* (Technical Analysis Paper #43), Office of Research and Evaluation, Office of Assistant Secretary for Policy, Evaluation and Research, U.S. Department of Labor, November 1976.

[7] Charles Mallar, *Evaluation of the Economic Impact of the Job Corps Program: First Follow Up Report*. Office of Program Evaluation, Employment and Training Administration, U.S. Department of Labor, December 1978.

[8] Dave O'Neill, "Voucher Funding of Training: Evidence From the GI Bill." *Journal of Human Resources*, Vol. XII, No. 4, Fall 1977.

[9] Michael Borus, *et al., Pathways To The Future: A Longitudinal Study of Young Americans.* College of Administrative Science, The Ohio State University.

ticipated in a government employment and training program after January 1, 1978, had participated in a public job of some kind. Other data in the survey suggest that, at most, only half of these had also been given some training or remedial education while in the public job.

As noted, statistics on changes in long duration unemployment between 1973 and 1979 (Table 4) strongly suggest that these additional public job slots have not been targeted on the teenagers who have the most difficulty in finding a job.[10] Data on changes over time in the summer employment pattern of youth indicate that the same conclusion can be applied to the summer jobs program. Table 5 shows that in the early 1960s, before the existence of federal summer jobs programs, summer employment increases were as large or larger than they were in the late 1970s when federally funded summer jobs programs were made available to about 1 million youths. Although the evidence is highly circumstantial, it does suggest that the federal summer program may have employed those youths who would have found a summer job anyway, either in the regular private sector or in special private sector programs that may have existed before the appearance of the federal effort.

All in all, the vast increase in public jobs for youth appears to have been a giant step in the wrong direction. There are some economically and educationally disadvantaged youth who suffer very long-term unemployment but the number of slots needed for this group is much less than the number now being funded.

Labor Market and Job Vacancy Information

Labor market information (LMI) refers to knowledge about the areas, occupations, and industries that are experiencing brisk demand, slack demand, high wage levels, low wage levels, and so on. Job vacancy information (JVI) refers to information about specific job openings such as the address of the firm or the description of the job.

The public Employment Service (ES) has been performing both of these functions since its inception. And although both of these functions are performed in the private sector, there is general agreement that the socially optimal amount of LMI and JVI may not be generated by the private market mechanism alone. In general, information is costly to uncover — for example, labor market information requires on-going, large-scale surveys — but very cheap to disseminate, once uncovered. Also, the social benefit of widespread and rapid dissemination is very high. Thus, a private firm has little incentive to discover information unless it can charge a high dissemination price, which is

---

[10] Data on the educational attainment of program participants and nonparticipants in the Borus study also suggest this.

Table 5

Teenage Employment and Unemployment Changes During the Summer Months, Males 16–19; Selected Years 1960–1978

Year	May to June Percentage Change In:		June to July Percentage Change In:		July to August Percentage Change In:	
	Employment	Unemployment	Employment	Unemployment	Employment	Unemployment
1960	36.1	93.0	1.0	−27.0	−6.0	−17.0
1961	37.5	82.2	.8	−25.1	−4.3	−22.4
1962	30.2	68.0	1.3	−32.0	−6.5	−19.0
1963	30.1	42.0	4.0	−19.4	−4.7	−29.3
1964	31.2	65.5	3.7	−34.8	−6.1	−15.2
1976	23.3	44.9	9.4	−6.3	−7.0	−18.5
1977	26.2	69.0	5.5	−14.9	−6.8	−17.8
1978	26.4	57.1	6.1	−0.4	−5.9	−24.6

Source: Selected issues of *Employment and Earnings*, U.S. Department of Labor, Bureau of Labor Statistics.

in conflict with the marginal conditions for socially optimal dissemination: that is, the dissemination price should equal the marginal cost of informing an additional user, and this is very low.

To say that government should be performing a function does not guarantee that it will be performing it well. Unfortunately, evaluative evidence on the labor market and job vacancy information functions is sketchy and impressionistic. Whenever sudden and unanticipated dislocations in the labor market take place — such as the stranding of thousands of engineers on the West Coast when many defense contracts were canceled during the 1970-71 recession — the network of ES offices along with the latest labor market information always comes in handy.

With regard to the job vacancy function, it has long been recognized that in American labor markets, formal employment agencies — both public and private — have never played a major role. Survey after survey always finds that informal channels — friends and relatives, associates, applying at the factory gate — are the major networks for disseminating job vacancy information. Two developments in the late sixties and early seventies, however, probably worked to reduce the effectiveness of the ES below what it could be even in American labor markets.

One factor was the shift in the focus of manpower programs and the ES to helping the most disadvantaged in the labor market. The number of job vacancies listed with the ES offices dropped dramatically at that time and it is widely believed that it reflected the fears of businessmen that the ES would no longer be free to give fair weight to their interests as opposed to the interests of the job applicant. The other factor was the institution of the computerized Job Bank system. Although this increased the number of vacancies an applicant could peruse at a single local ES office, it greatly reduced the incentives and ability of any single local ES office to give high quality service to the businesses that were located in its local area. On balance, the overall effectiveness of the system may have declined.

It would appear that if the ES is to improve its performance as an employment agency it may have to consider its old approach, which was essentially that of a private employment agency (without the fee). Those who are the most disadvantaged in the labor market are likely to need some special kind of "job broker" themselves; but the ES is not the best institution to perform this function.

LONG-TERM CONSIDERATIONS:
EMPLOYMENT AND TRAINING

Beyond providing an unemployment insurance system and a job and labor market information system (through a more effective Employment Service), is there a useful role for the government to play in improving the performance of individuals in the labor market? The answer to this question varies according to the particular group considered. Four sub-groups may be distinguished, each with quite different problems: (1) The "job-ready"; (2) Disadvantaged youth; (3) Adults with long-term unemployment problems; and (4) Welfare recipients.

"Job-Ready" Individuals

Most people fit into this category. It contains all those individuals who have enough education and aptitude to make training decisions, to find employment relatively easily, and to make the necessary re-training and re-location adjustments required by structural changes. Although they may make imperfect decisions, given less than perfect knowledge and foresight, it is not likely that government training and employment programs could improve their situations. The one exception may be assistance with the financing of various forms of human capital. It is generally accepted that human capital markets are more imperfect than markets for investment in physical capital. Moreover, the typical investor is young, and would not have ready access to financial capital markets, particularly if parental income is also low. Current federal programs in the area of post-secondary school finance, such as the Basic Educational Opportunity Grants (BEOGs) and the student loan program are applicable to vocational as well as academic education. Program use could be encouraged for individuals who qualify for assistance, but may not be aware of it. *Also, income tax provisions could be modified to allow an unemployed individual who takes occupational training in order to change occupations to deduct some or part of such training expenses as a legitimate business expense.* The current law only allows a training expense deduction when it is for advancement in a current job. Labor Department programs which spend large sums on training and subsidized jobs for job-ready individuals are not effective uses of federal funds.

It is recommended that the federal provision of training and work experience to unemployed, but otherwise job-ready individuals, be scaled down. Revisions and more effective targeting in CETA (Titles II−a, b, c; Title III) and the Youth Conservation Programs (YACC and YCC) would save close to $500 million in FY 1982. Assistance in re-training or re-locating should be given primarily in the form of financing assistance (loans) or in the case of low income individuals, limited direct subsidies (vouchers). In addition, the recently-created Skill Training Improvement Project (STIP) which was supposed to provide re-training to displaced but experienced workers should be carefully evaluated for evidence on this matter.

Disadvantaged Youth

The use of government funds to assist youth from poor and otherwise disadvantaged families in acquiring training and employment is a way of insuring equal opportunity and, hence, an accepted and important role of government. It has, however, proved to be difficult to identify those who need help and to determine the services that would be beneficial.

Most discussions of teenage labor market problems take the high measured rate of teenage unemployment as the main indicator of the problem. More careful analysis, however, suggests that unemployment status *per se* can be a misleading way to diagnose the problem. Much of the high level of teenage unemployment is related to the high incidence of labor force turnover among the young. In 1979, on the average, 68 percent of unemployed teenagers were labor force entrants or re-entrants. Of course, unemployment may be symptomatic of a severe problem if it reduces skill development and leads to low wages and poor economic prospects later on. But employment in a low-wage, dead-end job may produce the same result. How then can policymakers identify the target population and determine its size? Two possible measures are offered. One is the group of teenagers who experience long periods of unemployment during the year. There is some evidence that very long duration unemployment among disadvantaged out-of-school teenagers is related to lower earnings at older ages.[11] In 1977 only 74,000 teenagers (sixteen to nineteen) who were both out-of-school and from poverty families experienced twenty-seven weeks or more of unemployment (0.4 percent of all teenagers.)[12] Another and likely more important correlate of future employment prospects is basic reading and math achievement. Data from various testing surveys indicate that as many as 500,000 sixteen-to-nineteen-year olds from poverty families, and another million from families above the poverty level, cannot read and calculate well enough to fill out forms, read signs and deal with other basic conditions of most adult jobs.[13] Presumably there is an intersection between the long-term unemployed and those with serious educational deficiencies.

These indicators of long-term unemployment and educational disadvantage suggest that probably about 500,000 and at most one million youth are potential targets of federal employment and training

---

[11] See Brian Becker and Stephan Hills, "Teenager Unemployment: Some Evidence of the Long Run Effect on Wages," *Journal of Human Resources,* Vol. 15, No. 3, Summer 1980.

[12] Based on special tabulations from the Current Population Survey, U.S. Bureau of the Census.

[13] Mini Assessment of Functional Literacy (MAFL) from the National Assessment of Educational Programs in 1974. The study was commissioned by the National Right to Read Effort.

assistance. That is, they are likely to be starting out with labor market handicaps and come from families which cannot finance the additional training that they may need.

As discussed earlier, the current set of youth programs emphasizes public jobs as the major service—a misplaced emphasis. A large amount of resources ($4.2 million in fiscal year 1979) have been spent while, on the whole, disadvantaged young people do not appear to have been provided with the basic skills and information needed to make a successful transition from school to work.[14] *It is recommended that the service mix of programs for youth be redirected to emphasize remedial training and informational services. In addition, program resources should be more narrowly targeted on those who are educationally as well as economically disadvantaged.* If the $4.2 million spent in 1979 had been focused on the 500,000 youth with low reading and math achievement and low income, $8,400 of training per person per year could have been provided.

Saying what ought to be done is not, of course, as easy as specifying how to locate the appropriate target population and how to deliver the service in the most effective way. A first step would be to evaluate the entire prolix and literally incomprehensible CETA-Prime Sponsor framework to assess whether it is a well functioning system for youth labor market programs and, if not, to scrap it for a better one.

While not generally considered a "manpower program," the Federal Minimum Wage law probably has had a significant effect on the employment opportunities of teenagers—especially those with the greatest disadvantages. Numerous economic studies of the impact of the minimum wage on employment show a significant *negative* impact for teenagers.[15] *Although it would not cure all teenage labor market problems, elimination of the minimum wage would almost certainly have a salutory effect on the length of time it took a typical teenager to find a job. Moreover, employers would be more willing to provide on-the-job training if the costs could be shared with youth in the form of a lower wage. The minimum wage should be phased out by freezing it at its current level.*

Proposals have been made to provide a lower minimum wage for teenagers while retaining the minimum for adults—the so-called youth differential. Such a change may, however, cause more problems than it would cure. Many adults with low skills could also benefit from removal of this barrier to downward wage flexibility which makes dif-

---

[14] This is not to say that there have been no exemplary programs around the country. For example, Baltimore is said to have developed an excellent one. Lance Gay, "Labor Department Points to Baltimore As Showcase for Job Training Programs," *Washington Star,* September 10, 1980.

[15] See for example, Jacob Mincer, "Unemployment Effects of Minimum Wages," *Journal of Political Economy,* Volume 84, Part 2, August 1976, pp. 87–104.

ferential removal inequitable. There are numerous administrative barriers to implementing a youth differential concerning the age cut-off and the size of the differential. And serious effects on resource allocation could arise. For example, what will happen in a firm that uses a wide age-range of individuals to do essentially the same task? Clearly it will not be possible to pay individuals working side by side different wages for equal work; so there will be powerful incentives to segregate the work force by age, which may be highly inefficient. These factors must be weighed against any potential gain to teenagers.

If it should prove politically impossible to eliminate the minimum wage, a "wage subsidy" approach may be a better alternative than a "youth differential." Under current law, the Targeted Jobs Tax Credit is a program that allows employers a net tax credit of about $1,500 for the first year of employment and $750 for the second year, for each worker hired belonging to certain target groups. The major problem with this particular program is that its use is largely limited to a group designated "economically disadvantaged youth, 18–24." The program has been in place for over eighteen months, but the number of credits filed by business is only a small fraction of the number of these youths known to have been hired over this eighteen-month period. There is a general feeling that the stigma associated with the "economically disadvantaged" label has deterred most employers and prospective employees from using it. *If the program were amended to eliminate any targeting by demeaning socio-economic categories, firms could be allowed to apply it to all hires that were used to fill certain entry level or low-wage jobs, with benefits mainly to teenagers but also to some adults.* However, even a well-designed wage subsidy program is not a perfect substitute for the elimination of the minimum wage in terms of its effects on the efficient allocation of individuals in jobs.

Adults with Long-Term Employment Problems

This group consists of those who experience chronic unemployment either because of basic personal limitations or because they have been stranded in a depressed area and are too old or handicapped to relocate. What should the role of government be toward this group?

The elimination of the minimum wage, or provision of a tax credit wage subsidy, would improve employment opportunities for adults with job handicaps, just as it would for teenagers. Some adults with severe handicaps (either physical or psychological) have proven to be difficult to rehabilitate and are often chronically unemployed. *Although they are usually eligible for income transfer programs such as disability insurance (DI) under Social Security or Supplementary Security Income (SSI), the use of public jobs to provide "employment of last resort" may be appropriate for this group in limited situations.*

233

As noted earlier, the use of public agencies to provide these special employment situations is fraught with difficulties. Improper targeting, lack of any useful output and matching individual personalities and skills are a formidable set of problems. In particular any type of public jobs program with this objective has a very high probability of becoming simply an additional, and socially inefficient, source of revenue for local governments. The administrative system chosen to implement a limited program is crucial and must be designed with these problems in mind.

Welfare Recipients

Since the 1960s, attempts have been made to induce AFDC recipients to substitute jobs for welfare. One approach was to give recipients a financial incentive by modifying the extent by which benefits would fall when earnings increased. The Work Incentive Program (WIN), a result of the 1967 Social Security Amendments, lowered the implicit marginal tax rate — the amount by which benefits would be reduced when earnings increased — by providing that the first $30 of monthly income (net of work-related expenses) be disregarded, after which cash benefits were to be reduced by 67 cents for each additional dollar earned. Even after taking account of additional in-kind benefits (food stamps, medicaid) the tax on total benefits has fallen below that of the pre-WIN era.

Another approach has been to provide AFDC recipients with manpower program services, at first training and later public jobs. WIN II, implemented in 1972, requires all employable AFDC recipients to register for training or placement services as a condition for receiving welfare payments. AFDC recipients aged sixteen or more who are neither disabled nor students under twenty-one years, and women who do not have a child under six years are generally classified as employable. WIN II provides child care services for trainees as well as training, employment placement services, employer subsidies, and public employment. WIN program costs were about $385 million in fiscal 1979.

Despite these efforts, there has been no perceptible change in the work patterns of AFDC recipients. Periodic surveys of women heading AFDC households have shown that the percentage employed has fluctuated between 15 and 16 percent from 1961 to 1975. These are low rates of employment compared to those for all women with children under eighteen years, of whom more than 40 percent were employed in 1975. Perhaps the WIN employment programs have no perceptible effect on work behavior of program recipients because the services tend to be used by those with the highest skills who would find their way off the program anyway. For AFDC recipients with low

234

work skills, the combined benefit from welfare, food stamps, medicaid and possibly housing subsidies is likely to be almost as high as the take-home pay of a job, thus blunting work incentives.

There seems little reason to maintain an extensive employment and training program specifically for AFDC recipients who can be enrolled in other programs. From the point of view of the taxpayer, AFDC may be a less costly alternative to placing a recipient in a subsidized public job where the amount of the subsidy plus child care expenses are likely to exceed the welfare cost. The work requirement and placement services aspect of WIN should be retained and improved, if for no other reason than to assure the taxpayer that AFDC recipients are not simply shirking work. Because many additions to the AFDC rolls are teenage women with children, programs directed at improving the skills of disadvantaged teenagers should include specific programs for them, recognizing the unusual problems they may have with respect to child care. Intensive training for young AFDC women may well have a payoff in terms of reduction in long-term welfare payments.

SOCIAL SERVICES

This area of the budget covers a potpourri of services for people deemed needy because of low income, old age, a handicap, or other special circumstances. While the employment and training programs aim to increase earnings capacity, the social services have a multitude of objectives: physical rehabilitation of the disabled, drug abusers, or alcoholics; mental rehabilitation; comfort and physical care for those presumed helpless; child care for mothers who wish to work; counseling for families and individuals who need advice; protecting abandoned children; and many more. The financing and delivery of the services is similarly diverse. The federal government serves mainly as a fund-raiser for much of the services leaving it to the states to determine target populations and service mix. Other services are specifically chosen by the federal government (e.g., nutrition for the elderly). In some cases the government imposes strict professional standards for the provision of the service (e.g., day care); in other cases amateurs are encouraged to provide volunteer services (ACTION).

While many economists and other analysts have evaluated the employment and training programs, the bewildering array of social services has received little attention of this sort. Yet federal social services programs are expected to spend $5.7 billion in fiscal year 1981. After a brief review of the development and characteristics of these programs, this section turns to the basic questions: should the federal government fund the services, and, if so, what is the most efficient way to do it?

235

Historical Development

Before 1962, the federal government had little involvement with the provision of services to the needy. Such humanitarian activities were largely the work of private philanthropy, which in 1960 accounted for 60 percent of total funding for these purposes, and state and local governments, which provided 34 percent (Table 6). Federal welfare assistance mainly took the form of cash payments to the elderly and disabled, and to fatherless families with children, under the federal-state program established by Title IV of the Social Security Act of 1935.

Although during the 1950s social worker groups has pressed for federal funding of social and rehabilitation services, funding for these services was not actually provided until passage of the Public Welfare Amendments of 1962.[16] Signing the new law, President Kennedy laid out the hope that:

> This measure embodies a new approach — stressing services in addition to support, rehabilitation instead of relief, and training for useful work instead of prolonged dependency.[17]

If reduction in welfare recipience was the goal, it was not achieved, since the number of AFDC recipients increased sharply during the

Table 6
Public and Private Expenditures on Social Welfare Services: 1960-1978[1]

	1960	1965	1970	1975	1978
	Millions of Dollars				
Federal	111	308	2,070	4,162	5,675
State and Local	630	1,140	1,892	3,475	5,088
Private	1,088	1,375	2,000	3,000	4,300
Total	1,829	2,823	5,962	10,637	15,063
	Percentage Distribution				
Federal	6.1	10.9	34.7	39.1	37.7
State and Local	34.4	40.4	31.7	32.7	33.8
Private	59.5	48.7	33.5	28.2	28.5
Total	100.0	100.0	100.0	100.0	100.0

[1]Federal and state social services expenditures are here based on categories compiled by the Social Security Administration (SSA) and are more inclusive than the budget function 500 programs. They correspond to SSA's category of "other social welfare" spending minus child nutrition but plus spending on social services under Title XX of the Social Security Act. Private expenditures are SSA's category for private "welfare and other services". See Alma W. McMillan and Ann Kallman Bixby, "Social Welfare Expenditures in 1978," *Social Security Bulletin,* May 1980.

---

[16] Earlier, the 1956 Social Security amendments had authorized funds for social services, but Congress never appropriated the funds to cover the authorization.

[17] Quoted in Joseph Heffernan, "Public Assistance and Social Services" in *Studies in Public Welfare,* Paper No. 5 (Part 2), Joint Economic Committee of the Congress, 1973.

next few years. The 1967 Amendments to the Social Security Act sought to curb the growth in the AFDC program in various ways. At the same time, however, it added a feature that allowed states to purchase services from private and public agencies which would be matched three for one with federal dollars. Not surprisingly, federal expenditures on social services exploded, rising from $248 million in 1967 to $1.6 billion in 1971. As shown in Table 6, the federal share of all such expenditures in the economy rose from 11 to 35 percent between 1965 and 1970. It may also be noted that while the rate of federal spending accelerated between 1965 and 1970, the rate of state and local funding slowed somewhat (compared with the growth from 1960 to 1965) suggesting that some displacement of state and local government spending may have occurred.

Title XX

The fiscal implications of open-ended matching at a three for one rate were finally recognized when Congress put a cap of $2.5 billion on the federal share of social services effective fiscal year 1973. Currently, our major social services program is Title XX of the Social Security Act, the Social Services Amendments of 1974, as amended. It essentially retains the features of the earlier legislation providing for 75 percent matching funds for most services and retains a limitation on the federal share, which is set at $2.9 billion in 1981 rising by $100 million a year for the next four years.

Title XX now allocates funds to the states based on their total populations regardless of income level. States have considerable freedom in the way they spend their funds and deliver the services. Eligibility for services is not confined to the welfare population; about half of the program's resources are estimated to go to AFDC and SSI recipients. Individuals are eligible for benefits generally if their family income is up to 115 percent of the state median income although fees must be charged when income exceeds 80 percent of the state median. Some services are, however, provided without regard to financial need such as programs related to child abuse. The largest single service is child day-care, which receives about one-fifth of total program expenditures. In the case of child day-care, however, the federal government does impose regulations on the state with respect to prescribing staffing ratios in licensed day care centers. The staffing requirements have been controversial since they make the service more costly, while the benefits to children are debatable.

Other Social Service Programs

Although the limitation on Title XX has curbed spending in that program, it has not curbed spending on social services overall, which have continued to grow in the form of additional categorical programs. The Administration on Aging (AoA), with an estimated budget of $714 million for fiscal year 1981, gives grants to state and local agencies for services to the elderly, most of which are allowable expenditures under Title XX. The situation is similar with respect to the services provided by the Rehabilitation Services Administration, the program of Grants for the Developmentally Disabled and the programs of the Administration for Children, Youth, and Families.

The Community Services Administration (CSA) is another type of activity included in the social services function. It is the successor to the Office of Economic Opportunity, created in 1964 as the "spearhead" of the War on Poverty. CSA's primary function is to provide funds to the approximately 900 local Community Action Agencies which are supposed to involve the poor in planning and delivering services intended for them. Funding for CSA has been held fairly constant for the past few years ($555 million for fiscal year 1981). Another agency, ACTION, supports several volunteer programs, including those involving senior citizen volunteers and the VISTA program, which was intended to be a domestic "peace corps," ACTION is budgeted at $175 million for 1981.

LONG-TERM CONSIDERATIONS: SOCIAL SERVICES

One may question the rationale for providing social services. If someone is in need, why not give cash assistance so that they may choose the type of service they wish? Though such a simple solution might please the beneficiaries, it evidently does not please the donors, since private charities and state and local governments have been providing these services for decades, long before the federal government played a role. Presumably, donors have in mind particular worthy purposes that they fear might not be similarly valued by recipients.

The second question concerns the role of the federal government. The needs of individuals for the array of social services are so diverse that it would be quite impractical to determine what they are and deliver them at the federal level. Indeed, for this reason the federal government's role has been largely that of fund-raiser for the states and local areas. Title XX is essentially a form of revenue sharing earmarked for social services. There are, however, a number of problems with the revenue sharing concept. One is that states may have less incentive to spend funds in the most economical way when they are raised by others. Thus, as long as the federal government is raising the funds it cannot eschew the accountability function, which is difficult to perform, as noted initially, because of the diversity in situations from place to place. These are arguments for having states and localities assume more responsibility in raising their own funds for social service programs.

On the other hand, not all states are equally able to take care of their needy and the federal government could perform the function of enabling the lowest income states to reach a minimum level of service provision. This is not, however, how it is now done since Title XX funds are simply distributed according to population size. *It is recommended that social services funds be allocated according to state income levels as well as population. This can be done using a formula that gives extra weight according to the percentage in poverty and that requires a larger match by the wealthier states.* With this increase in the states' responsibility for raising funds, the basic idea of Title XX, that of allowing the states to choose their own mix of services, is probably feasible.

This still leaves the problem of what to do about the proliferation of additional categorical problems. *It is recommended that all services for the aged, disabled, and youth be consolidated with Title XX (but excluding CSA and ACTION) so that the states would truly have full decision-making responsibility.* Consolidation and the change in formulation (mentioned above) would permit savings of $500 million in FY 1982. *In addition, burdensome regulations, such as staffing requirements for day-care centers, should be dropped.* By giving the states greater responsibility for the mix of services and greater fiscal responsibility by requiring a larger match, it is expected that more efficient use of resources would result. Pressed to economize, states might make more use of delivery systems such as vouchers, which allow the recipient to contract for the service, a practice used in some states (e.g., California), or devise other ways of cutting down on administrative expenditures and providing quality service at the least cost.

The CSA and ACTION present other problems. CSA has been controversial and the subject of numerous investigations for misuse of funds. The network of community action agencies theoretically can serve as outreach centers for federal programs for the poor. Objective evaluation of the actual performance of CSA is needed before determining future funding.

It is difficult to justify the use of federal funds for the domestic volunteer programs under ACTION. Private philanthropy has always offered considerable opportunity for those desiring to donate their time. Moreover, the community action agencies could be advised to encourage the use of volunteers where and when appropriate, and this would avoid duplication of effort between CSA and ACTION (particularly VISTA). Consideration should be giving to phasing out the domestic volunteer programs under ACTION, saving $188 million in FY 1982.

11

Health

by Jack A. Meyer

Federal spending for health care in the U.S. has soared from $5.6 billion in 1965 to an estimated $70.4 billion in 1980, or about 12 percent of the federal budget.[1] While total spending for health was also increasing rapidly over this fifteen-year period ($43.0 billion and $244.6 billion) federal outlays outpaced aggregate spending and, as a result, the federal share of total outlays for health more than doubled, rising from 13.0 percent in 1965 to 28.8 percent in 1980. Moreover, spending by state and local governments for health care rose from $5.1 billion in 1965 to $30.0 billion in 1980 (the proportion of total spending remained about the same — 12 percent), so that by 1980 the public sector as a whole was spending $100 billion for health care, or about 41 cents of the health care dollar. This contrasts with about 25 cents per dollar in 1965.

Ironically, while the federal government complains loudly about rising health care costs, its own policies set the tone for cost escalation. Moreover, the federal government's proposed "cures" for cost increases gloss over the fundamental source of inefficiency in the health care system: indeed, in recent years government's solutions have been a part of the problem. Government policy has centered on a "cost pass-through" approach in which the inefficient delivery of services has been rubber-stamped, if not rewarded, while open-ended federal tax breaks have encouraged the use of resources for health care beyond the point where benefits are commensurate with costs. Then, having contributed to cost increases through such policies, the federal government has vainly sought to contain the inevitable outcome of these

---

[1] See Mark Freeland, George Calat, and Carol Schendler, "Projections of National Health Expenditures, 1980, 1985, and 1990," *Health Care Financing Review*, Winter 1980, pp. 16–17. These figures cover total federal spending for health-related activities, including programs operated by the Department of Defense and the Veterans Administration. The analysis of the FY 1981 budget for health care (Functional Code 550: Health, Budget of the United States Government) focuses primarily on programs run by the Department of Health and Human Services (HHS), and this explains why the estimated federal health spending in the budget for FY 1981 ($61.9 billion) is less than the more comprehensive figure cited here for calendar 1980 ($70.4 billion).

Table 1
Health
(in millions of dollars)

Major missions and programs	1979 actual	1980 estimate	1981 estimate
OUTLAYS			
Health care services:			
Medicare:			
Existing law	29,147	33,540	38,425
Proposed legislation	–	1	– 1,076
Medicaid:			
Existing law	12,491	14,220	15,575
Proposed legislation	–	34	298
Other health care services	3,483	3,802	4,095
Subtotal, health care services	45,121	51,598	57,317
Health research:			
National Institutes of Health	2,698	2,969	3,137
Alcohol, Drug Abuse, and Mental Health Administration research programs	190	200	239
Other research programs	135	170	179
Subtotal, health research	3,023	3,338	3,555
Education and training of the health care work force:			
National Institutes of Health training..	171	190	198
Health Resources Administration training..........................	307	348	265
Alcohol, Drug Abuse, and Mental Health Administration training	105	114	96
Subtotal, education and training of the health care work force ...	583	652	559
Consumer and occupational health and safety:			
Consumer safety	603	645	658
Occupational safety and health	293	337	369
Subtotal, consumer and occupational health and safety........	896	982	1,027
Deductions for offsetting receipts	– 10	– 8	– 8
Total, outlays.................	49,614	56,563	62,449
MEMORANDUM – Attribution of Federal Financing Bank outlays Health care services...................	17	110	134

Source: The Budget of the United States Government FY 1981

policies through an elaborate network of existing and proposed cost controls ranging from existing certificate-of-need programs limiting capital investment projects by hospitals to proposed Hospital Cost Containment legislation. These policies entrench inefficiency in the health care system and foster "cost control" at the expense of considerations of the quality and availability of services. By contrast, greater reliance on market-oriented incentives to economize on the use of

242

Table 2

Percentage Distribution of Total Health Care Outlays by Source of Funds
1965–1980 (calendar years)

Source of Funds	1965	1970	1975	1980
Private	75.1	63.6	57.6	58.9
Direct payments	46.3	35.5	28.7	28.0
Other	28.8	28.0	28.9	30.9
Public	24.9	36.5	42.4	41.1
Federal	13.0	23.6	28.2	28.8
State and local	11.9	13.0	14.1	12.3
Total percent	100.0	100.0	100.0	100.0
Total (billions)	43.0	74.7	131.5	244.6

Source: *Health Care Financing Review,* Winter 1980, pp. 16–17.

health services would encourage health care providers to deliver service of acceptable quality at a lower cost.

The federal government's role in the health care sector is broad-ranging, covering such areas as health care services, research, and the training of health care personnel. Under the Medicare and Medicaid programs, the federal government pays the bills for health care services to the aged, disabled, and poor through entitlement programs. A large portion of the increase in the share of outlays funded by public sources occurred following the initiation of these programs on July 1, 1966. There are also numerous discretionary federal programs providing health services to specific groups such as migrant workers and for specific needs such as alcohol, drug abuse, and mental health. Over 49 million people receive services from federal programs involving the provision of health services, and about 40 percent of national hospital expenditures are financed by programs administered by the Department of Health and Human Services. Of the $62.5 billion estimate for federal health spending in FY 1981, $57.3 billion is accounted for by the provision of health care services.

Health research at the National Institutes of Health (NIH) constitutes 88 percent of the federal government's $3.5 billion health research-oriented expenditures. An estimated $0.6 billion will be spent by the federal government to provide financial assistance to students in a multitude of health professions in FY 1981 and another $1.0 billion will be targeted to programs designed to protect consumers from unsafe and defective products, and workers from occupational hazards.

In addition to the wide variety of federal programs for the health care sector, there are also several federal tax subsidies for health care expenses. The exclusion of employer contributions to health plans from employees' taxable income accounted for an estimated $9.6 billion in foregone federal revenues in 1980. Other tax subsidies include the deductibility of a portion of health care outlays by households ($3.1 billion) and the tax-exempt status of hospital construction bonds ($400 million). Total tax subsidies amounted to an estimated $14.5 billion in 1980.

The reimbursement of health services to the poor, elderly, and disabled is the dominant function of the federal government in the health care sector. The federal government, in effect, influences the type of services provided to these groups through decisions about the proportion of a hospital's total costs that is honored and the fraction of physicians' charges paid for. The greater the extent to which providers' actual charges are assigned to the federal program, the smaller the financial burden on beneficiaries.

In the health services programs, costs are "controlled" through certain limits on program eligibility (particularly in Medicaid), the establishment of limits on the proportion of providers' costs that will be reimbursed (i.e., what charges are "reasonable"), and a combination of peer review programs, designed to ascertain when beneficiaries' care is no longer medically necessary, and patient cost sharing. The latter consists of limitations on coverage, such as a maximum number of days of covered hospitalization, and co-payments and deductibles. All of these cost control devices involve either efforts to squeeze savings out of service providers — doctors, hospitals, or drug manufacturers — or attempts to cut costs by limiting benefits.

Medicare and Medicaid reimbursement policies, along with a comparable Blue Cross, Blue Shield approach, are at the heart of a cost pass-through syndrome underlying trends in health care outlays. The basic problem is that patients with this coverage receive virtually no economic benefit from choosing economical providers. In practice, this means that little benefit is derived from choosing doctors who use hospitalization economically, since most of the apparent savings achieved under alternative plans result from lower rates of hospitalization.[2]

Medicare

The Medicare program was established under Title XVIII of the Social Security Act. Medicare, which became effective on July 1, 1966, was initially intended as a federal insurance plan for acute medical care for the elderly. Permanently disabled workers and their families, eligible for OASDHI disability benefits, along with persons suffering

---

[2]See Harold S. Luft, "How Do Health Maintenance Organizations Achieve Their 'Savings'?" *New England Journal of Medicine*, Vol. 298, No. 24 (June 15, 1978), p. 1337. Luft's estimated range of cost savings attributable to HMOs — 10–40 percent — is based primarily on California comparisons between those enrolled in Kaiser plans and those with conventional coverage.

Table 3

Past and Projected Medicare and Medicaid Outlays
(billions of dollars)

	actual				estimated		
	1967	1970	1975	1979	1980	1981	1983
Medicare	3.4	7.1	14.8	29.1	33.5	38.4	50.8
Medicaid	1.4	2.7	6.8	12.5	14.2	15.5	20.1

Sources: U.S. Department of Health and Human Services, The Budget of the United States Government, FY 1981, and U.S. House of Representatives, Budget Committee, First Resolution for the FY 1981 Report.

from end-stage renal diseases, became eligible for Medicare on July 1, 1973.

The Medicare program provided health care payments for an estimated 25 million aged and 3 million disabled workers in FY 1980. Medicare outlays are estimated at $33.5 billion for FY 1980, compared to actual outlays of $29.1 billion in the prior year. Just five years ago (1975) Medicare outlays were less than half as great as in 1980. The proposed FY 1981 budget projected Medicare outlays under existing law at $50.8 billion for FY 1983 (Table 3).

The importance of hospital care in the Medicare program is illustrated by the fact that in 1978 about three-fourths of benefit payments were reimbursements for hospital care, accounting for about one-fourth of all hospital bills nationwide. By contrast, less than 3 percent of all nursing home expenditures were covered by this program in 1978. Long-term care is reimbursed only if it is skilled nursing care and is required for convalescence.[3]

Medicare is financed by multiple sources, with payroll taxes providing slightly over sixty percent. General revenues provide about one-fourth of Medicare funds, with the remainder accounted for by premium payments by enrollees (or Medicaid on their behalf) and interest.

Medicaid

The Medicaid program was established under Title XIX of the Social Security Act in 1965. A joint federal-state program, Medicaid also became effective on July 1, 1966. It provides medical assistance to people eligible for cash assistance under one of the existing welfare programs established under the Social Security Act — Title IV-A, Aid to Families with Dependent Children (AFDC), or Title XVI, Supplemental Security Income (SSI). Thus, eligibility is extended to low-income aged, blind, and disabled persons, and members of families

---

[3]Robert M. Gibson, "National Health Expenditures, 1978," *Health Care Financing Review*, Summer 1979, p. 10.

with dependent children when one parent is absent, incapacitated, or unemployed. States may also provide Medicaid to a group referred to as "medically needy." This group includes people who fit into a welfare category, but who have sufficient income to cover basic living expenses and therefore are not actually receiving benefits.

Medicaid is administered by the states subject to federal requirements and guidelines. The current federal contribution is based on a formula related to per capita income, and the federal contribution rate ranges from 50 percent to 78 percent.

All state Medicaid programs must cover the following basic health services: in-patient and out-patient hospital services, laboratory and x-ray services, skilled nursing home services for those 21 years of age or older, home health services for individuals eligible for skilled nursing services, physicians' services, family planning services, rural health clinic services, and early and periodic screening, diagnosis and treatment services for individuals under 21. States may also provide, on an optional basis, such services as drugs, eyeglasses, private duty nursing, intermediate care facility services, in-patient psychiatric care for the aged and persons under 21, physical therapy, and dental care.

Since states have wide latitude in determining welfare eligibility criteria, they indirectly exercise control over income eligibility levels for Medicaid. The extent of this discretion can be depicted by noting that the annual income ceiling for initial AFDC eligibility of $1575 in Texas contrasts with a corresponding level of $7050 in Michigan. Similarly, Tennessee's Medicaid-Medically Needy annual income ceiling for eligibility is $2400, while Connecticut's is $6000. States with medically-needy programs may establish the income level for eligibility at any point between the AFDC income cutoff line and a level 1.33 as great as this amount.

States may also affect the scope of services under Medicaid by limiting days of hospital care or number of physicians' visits covered, as well as by determining the reimbursement rates for some services. As a result of these differences in benefits offered, coverage, income standards for eligibility, and provider reimbursement rates, Medicaid programs, in practice, vary widely across states.[4]

In the five years ending in 1980, outlays under Medicare and Medicaid more than doubled, rising from about $22 billion in 1975 to roughly $48 billion in 1980. Projections of outlays under current law suggest that this total will soar to a little over $70 billion in 1983. Moreover, when the federal health spending in other programs (Department of Defense, Veterans Administration) and the revenue drain from health-related tax subsidies are also considered, it is likely

[4]U.S. Department of Health and Human Services (HHS), Health Care Financing Administration, *Data on the Medicaid Program: Eligibility, Services, Expenditures* (Baltimore, MD, 1979), pp. 1–2.

that the overall federal budgetary commitment to health care will exceed $100 billion dollars in about three years. What forces are causing these sharp and seemingly inexorable upward trends?

Federal Policy, Inefficiency, and Cost Escalation

Medicare pays for covered hospital services on the basis of cost reimbursement and for covered physician services on the basis of fee-for-service. While there is some incentive for patients to seek out doctors with low fees since Medicare pays 80 percent of physicians' fees for covered services up to 80 percent of "reasonable charges," such an incentive is largely absent for hospital services. After a modest "per-spell" deductible, Medicare pays the full cost of covered hospital services for the first 60 days. As a result, Medicare pays more on behalf of patients choosing doctors who perform more services and order more hospital services for a given medical condition. Professor Alain Enthoven reports that one study, comparing Medicare enrollees receiving fee-for-service care with a group matched by medical need served by six pre-paid group practice plans, indicated that Medicare paid 36 percent more on behalf of the fee-for-service beneficiaries.[5]

A further indication of the inefficiency of the Medicare program emerges from a study by Professor William Hsaio of Harvard University. Hsaio compared administrative expenses per unit of output (number of claims processed) under a public (Medicare) and a private (Federal Employees Health Benefit Plans—FEHBP) health insurance plan. After controlling for differences in expenses associated with auditing of providers, inspections and certifications to assure quality of services, and enrollment, Hsaio found that the administrative cost per claim was 35 percent greater in Medicare than in FEHBP in FY 1971 and 18 percent greater in FY 1972.[6]

The Medicaid program follows a similar cost-reimbursement policy with the additional factor that no extra billing of patients for charges in excess of the government-determined reimbursement level is permitted.

The Basis of Inefficiency

In trying to explain the sharp increase in health care spending over the past three years, many observers have pointed to the enormous

[5]Alain C. Enthoven, "The Politics of NHI," in Cotton M. Lindsay, ed., *New Directions in Public Health Care: A Prescription for the 1980s* (San Francisco, CA: Institute for Contemporary Studies, 1980), p. 230.

[6]William Hsaio, "Public Versus Private Administration of Health Insurance: A Study in Relative Economic Efficiency," *Inquiry*, Vol. XV, No. 4 (December 1978), pp. 379–387.

growth in insurance coverage. The growth in insurance coverage *per se* has frequently been designated as the culprit responsible for the escalation of costs and charges in the health care sector of the economy. Insurance, it is claimed, has led consumers to demand a quantity and quality of health care services that exceeds the level where the benefits derived from these services justify the costs.[7]

While the enormous growth in insurance coverage has led consumers to purchase more health care services than they would otherwise be inclined to choose, the explanation for rising health insurance costs goes beyond a simple assessment of the proportion of costs covered by insurance and the problem of "moral hazard" (the propensity of consumers to spend the insurer's money with more profligacy than if they were spending their own). Moral hazard is not unique to health insurance; it is an inherent problem in the insurance business generally. And insurers in other fields (e.g., auto insurance) have recognized the need to combat this tendency through such means as insurance adjusters, multiple estimates, and fixed cash benefits.[8] Thus, as Havighurst and Hackbarth contend, moral hazard cannot by itself explain the steep increase in health costs.

> The primary cause of the persistent rise in health care costs is not moral hazard itself, but the unwillingness of providers and insurers to experiment with new techniques to control its impact. Health insurance is now too comprehensive, and it features administrative approaches and claims policies that indulge, rather than counteract, moral hazard.[9]

In fact, the growth of health care costs is inextricably linked to the nature of insurance reimbursement plans. Most health insurance plans reimburse patients on the same basis irrespective of whether they choose efficient or inefficient providers. Under many health insurance policies, consumers who deal with extravagant providers will be reimbursed on the same basis as those who search out economical providers.[10]

Doctors who are careful not to hospitalize patients when ambulatory care is an effective substitute, who avoid over-testing their patients, who are careful about prescribing too many drugs, and who would be reluctant to put their patients in a hospital on a Friday for

---

[7]Martin Feldstein, "Quality Change and the Demand for Health Care," *Econometrica,* Vol. 45, No. 7 (October 1977), pp. 1681–1702; and Feldstein, *The Rapid Rise of Hospital Costs* (Washington, D.C.: U.S. Council on Wage and Price Stability, January 1977), pp. 29–38.

[8]Clark C. Havighurst and Glenn M. Hackbarth, "Private Cost Containment," *New England Journal of Medicine,* June 7, 1979, p. 1299.

[9]*Ibid.*

[10]Enthoven, "The Politics of NHI," p. 228.

procedures which are not scheduled to begin until Monday are not rewarded under this prevailing health care reimbursement system in ways that efficient providers who conserve resources are normally rewarded in other markets.

Until this aspect of the health care system is reformed, both in public and private reimbursement policies, we will not make meaningful progress against the sharp escalation of health care costs. As Enthoven has correctly observed, the normal rules rewarding buyers and sellers for economy in the use of resources are violated by institutional arrangements whereby hospitals are rewarded for generating more costs under Medicare, Medicaid, and many Blue Cross plans and doctors are rewarded for providing more services in higher cost settings.[11]

Under prevalent Medicare and Medicaid reimbursement policies, not every item of cost incurred by providers may automatically be passed through to the government. For example, the Department of Health and Human Services may refuse to allow hospitals to pass their bad debts through to the government, or HHS and hospitals may wrangle over whether all R&D outlays can be included in the cost base. But, subject to such limitations which might operate to exclude a few components of total cost, the federal health services programs essentially operate on a cost pass-through basis, with a concept of average daily in-patient cost over a particular time period as the basis of reimbursement. Thus, while HHS may negotiate with a hospital over whether to reimburse 90 or 95 percent of average daily cost, it is unlikely to question the hospitalization of a patient who could be treated satisfactorily on an out-patient basis or the ordering of more laboratory tests or ancillary services.[12] In other words, the practice patterns of providers are typically not questioned by the third-party payor — in this case the federal government. While the government may question some expense category such as bad debts (i.e., there will always be accounting squabbles), it will not typically question efficiency (creating a "license" to be indulgent or inefficient), and it is this phenomenon that distinguishes the health insurance market from other insurance markets.

The concept of the cost-conscious claims adjuster, so common to insurance in general, is largely absent from federal health programs. To some extent, this may be a reflection of the peculiar nature of health care services and the agency relationship between providers and consumers. In the case of Blue Cross, Blue Shield, where the approach to reimbursement is similar to that used in federal programs, the spe-

---

[11]*Ibid.*

[12]Mark Perlman, "Prices, Technological Change, and Productivity in the American Health Care Industry," in William Fellner, ed., *Contemporary Economic Problems 1980* (Washington, D.C.: American Enterprise Institute, 1980), pp. 235–237.

cial relationship between Blues and providers[13] may partially explain the "free choice of doctor" policy which lacks the bottom line discipline of other insurance markets.

But it is not clear that reimbursement of inefficient providers on a no-questions-asked basis is inherent in medical markets. Indeed, there is recent evidence that dental insurers practice cost control measures similar to those used in non-health-related insurance markets even where this involves second-guessing or challenging the dentists.[14]

It is hardly surprising that some health care providers are lax about conserving resources since the predominant insurers practice an "everybody wins" policy. If doctors are going to "discipline" patients by discouraging wasteful tests, drugs, or hospital visits, and hospitals are going to avoid the purchase of expensive, redundant equipment or unneeded beds, the federal government and the Blues must first discipline these providers.

Equity Considerations

The present structure of Medicare and Medicaid promotes not only inefficiency but also inequity. First, large numbers of poor people are ineligible for Medicaid even as many people whose incomes are above the poverty threshold receive Medicaid benefits. Second, there is significant horizontal inequity on a geographic basis, i.e., unequal treatment of potential Medicaid recipients across states.

Low-income persons in two-parent families and single persons under age sixty-five typically do not qualify for Medicaid. They are ineligible for Medicaid because their family status makes them ineligible for other federal welfare programs — AFDC and SSI. The systematic exclusion of most families headed by an employed male and of non-aged singles has led to a disparity between the use of medical services by Medicaid recipients and by ineligible poor and near-poor persons.[15]

---

[13] The influence of physicians on Blue Cross, Blue Shield policies has been the subject of considerable controversy. There has been concern over whether doctors exercise direct influence through participation on Blue Cross/Blue Shield boards, as well as indirect influence operating in more subtle ways. See Clark C. Havighurst, "Professional Restraints on Innovation in Health Care Financing," *Duke Law Journal*, Vol. 1978, No. 2 (May 1978), pp. 303–387; David I. Kass and Paul A. Pautler, *Physician Control of Blue Shield Plans: Staff Report of the Bureau of Economics to the Federal Trade Commission*, November 1979; and William Lynk, "Physician Influence on Blue Shield Plans: A Reexamination of the Findings." *Socio-economic Issues of Health 1979*, pp. 129–142.

[14] Warren Greenberg, "The Evolution of the Relationship of Professional and Provider Organizations and Third Party Reimbursement," American Enterprise Institute Conference, *Health Care — Professional Ethics, Government Regulation, or Markets?*, September 1980.

[15] Thomas W. Grannemann, "Reforming National Health Programs for the Poor," in Mark V. Pauly, ed., *National Health Insurance: What Now, What Later, What Never?* (Washington, D.C.: American Enterprise Institute, 1980).

Table 4

Estimated Coverage of Persons Below the 1980 Federal Poverty Level (in millions)

Total with some protection		24.9
Medicaid	11.3	
Medicare	4.0	
Group health insurance	5.3	
Individual health insurance	3.4	
Miscellaneous Government programs	.8	
Total with no coverage (includes persons eligible for but not utilizing Medicaid)		7.4
TOTAL		32.3

Source: Senate Finance Committee "Low-Income Coverage Issues" staff report.

An estimated 32.3 million people (14 percent of the population) had incomes below the federal poverty level ($7,500 for a family of four) in 1980. Approximately 11.3 million (35 percent) of these individuals received Medicaid benefits (Table 4). While many of the remaining families have some other form of insurance coverage (Medicare, group health insurance, etc.), an estimated 7.4 million low-income persons — or 23 percent of the poverty population — had no health benefit protection in 1980.[16] An unknown fraction of this group is eligible for Medicaid but not utilizing the program. The remaining people are ineligible either because they are not in one of the welfare program eligibility categories or because their income exceeds state-established limits.

Furthermore, while many people below the poverty line are not receiving Medicaid, many above this line are enrolled. In addition to the 11.3 million poor people receiving Medicaid in 1980, an estimated 11.1 million near-poor people received Medicaid benefits during the year.

The relationship between the Medicaid and poverty populations varies widely by state. Although the most recent state-by-state data are for 1970, they show that in that year Medicaid recipients were only 10 percent of the total state low-income population in Arkansas, 16 percent in Mississippi and South Carolina, and 17 percent in Alabama and South Dakota. By contrast, the corresponding figures for California and New York are 174 percent and 156 percent, respectively.[17]

There is also wide variation by state in outlays for Medicaid, correcting for variations in income levels. For example, in New York, total Medicaid expenditures (including the state's share) per million dollars of personal income amounted to $22,684 in FY 1977; the cor-

---

[16]U.S. Senate, Committee on Finance, "Low-Income Coverage Issues," staff report, October 26, 1979, p. 1.

[17]DHHS, *Data on the Medicaid Program*, pp. 62–63.

Table 5
Inter-Regional Distribution Effects of Medicaid
(millions of dollars FY 1977)

	Benefits (Federal Payments)	Cost (Federal Tax)	Difference	Benefit/Cost Ratio
Northwest	$3,066	$2,171	+ 895	1.41
North Central	2,136	2,530	− 394	0.84
South	2,251	2,510	− 259	0.89
West	1,432	1,693	− 261	0.95
District of Columbia	59	40	+ 19	1.48
NOTE: Figures exclude Puerto Rico and the Virgin Islands.				

Source: Medicaid Statistics Fiscal Year 1977, Health Care Financing Administration, Department of Health and Human Services, April 1978.

responding figure in Wisconsin was $16,064; in Georgia, $10,945; in Colorado, $6,443; and in Wyoming, $2,733. Thus, total Medicaid outlays were more than eight times as great per dollar of income in New York as in Wyoming.[18] And, while California and New York were providing one-half of the total Medicaid outlays in their states, Arkansas and New Mexico were providing about one-fourth of total outlays.

A recent study by Thomas Grannemann of Mathematica Policy Research, Inc. reveals that high-income states are receiving more federal Medicaid dollars than low-income states, the opposite result of that which would be dictated by considerations of equity. The twenty-five high income states received an average of $45.04 per capita in federal Medicaid payments in FY 1977, as compared to $33.67 for the twenty-five low-income states.[19] Of course, high-income states also pay more taxes than low-income states, and there is no net redistribution of income toward high-income states after taking relative tax burdens into account. But there is a sharp net redistribution of income from West, South, and North-Central regions to the Northeast (Table 5).

Grannemann concludes:

> The observed interregional redistribution is arbitrary and is probably not necessary for the attainment of health policy goals. There is no evidence that Medicaid has been effective in providing greater federal assistance to low-income states where the needs of the poor are greater and state taxpayers are less able to support the program alone.[20]

Another aspect of the inequity in the Medicaid program involves the nature of the limits on covered services. Not only is there considerable

---

[18]Grannemann, *op. cit.*, pp. 3–4.

[19]*Ibid.*, p. 106.

[20]*Ibid.*

variation from state to state in the scope of covered services, but also the limits imposed by some states are quite restrictive, arbitrary and operate to deny care to those who need it most. The wide variation in covered services is illustrated by the fact that while Alabama and Tennessee limit covered in-patient hospital days to 20 per year, Kentucky and Missouri allowed 21 days per *admission*, Texas 30 days per spell of illness, and Ohio 60 days per spell. At the same time many states, including Montana, New York, Massachusetts, and Minnesota, have no limitations on in-patient hospital services. Similarly, some states require pre-authorization for skilled nursing and intermediate care facilities while others do not, and there are a variety of restrictions placed on covered physicians' services.

In summary, as low-income states with disproportionately low levels of federal aid wrestle with the problem of using their limited resources to provide health care assistance to a large number of poor people, they are faced with a difficult choice. They can either limit the number of eligibles or restrict the scope of services provided to a larger group. These options are necessitated by both the arbitrary nature of the federal matching formula and the absence of cost control measures which would reduce the costs associated with a given level of benefits, rather than reduce costs by limiting benefits or beneficiaries.

Although the benefit limitations are less severe in Medicare than in Medicaid, both programs suffer from a combination of inadequate coverage for major illnesses and insufficient incentives to economize on the use of resources. Medicare enrollees have good coverage at the "front-end" (e.g., relatively low deductibles, full coverage of hospitalization beyond deductibles for 60 days), but the program lacks a full-scale catastrophic feature.[21] This means that patients requiring relatively routine treatment are well covered, while the extremely complicated cases may not be. In addition to this equity problem, there is also considerable disparity between the generosity of coverage for hospital care and the quite limited coverage for convalescent and long-term nursing care.

SHORT-TERM POLICIES

Regulatory Strategies — A Deceptive "Cure"

For the past three years, the Carter administration has sought to moderate hospital costs through enactment of its Hospital Cost Con-

---

[21] Between 61 and 90 days of hospitalization, the patient is responsible for a copayment of $45 per day. In addition, there is also a "lifetime reserve," but when this is exhausted, the patient would then be vulnerable to high medical bills. Thus, the real "cost-sharing" is at the "back-end."

tainment legislation. The most recent version of this proposed legislation involves a mandatory cap on allowable hospital in-patient revenue increases that would be triggered by hospitals exceeding a guideline for expenditure growth.[22] The expenditure guidelines are based on the inflation rate for goods and services purchased by hospitals, population growth, and an intensity-of-service factor. If total national hospital expenditures exceeded the national guideline, the performance test would be applied to hospitals on a state-by-state basis. If total expenditures in a state exceeded that state's guideline, the performance test would be applied to individual hospitals within the state which are not covered by one of the several exemptions included in the bill.

The Congressional Budget Office estimates that the original version of the Hospital Cost Containment Act of 1979 would produce $24.6 billion in savings over the 1980–84 period. Of this total, $9.8 billion represents cumulative federal savings—$8.4 billion in Medicare and $1.4 billion in Medicaid. The bill reported by the Senate Committee on Labor and Human Resources is estimated to save more than the Carter proposal because of a tougher penalty for exceeding the voluntary guideline. The cumulative savings for this Senate version are estimated at $28.6 billion, the Medicare savings at $9.7 billion, and the Medicaid savings at $1.6 billion.[23]

There are two reasons why these expectations are unlikely to be fulfilled, even should the hospital cost containment legislation be enacted.

First, the particular form of the recent proposal seems so riddled with exclusions, exceptions, and contingencies as to make it unlikely that it would have any bite. Three triggers must go off before any hospital can possibly be in jeopardy. Labor costs, now accounting for about 50 percent of total costs for the average hospital, are in effect exempt from the cap. There are numerous ways in which hospitals could unbundle services or spin off functions to evade the intent of the proposal. There also is wide latitude for the Department of Health and Human Services to grant special adjustments or exemptions for various special circumstances.

Second, and more generally, the proposal would seem capable of producing only short-term results and some of these results would be likely to take the form of undesired cutbacks in service or reductions in quality. Since the system of financial incentives and reimbursement mechanisms would essentially remain unchanged, there is little reason

---

[22]For an analysis of earlier proposals to restrict the rate of increase in hospital costs, see American Enterprise Institute, *Proposals for the Regulation of Hospital Costs*, Washington, D.C., 1978.

[23]Congressional Budget Office (CBO), *Controlling Rising Hospital Costs* (Washington, D.C.: Congress of the United States, September 1979), pp. 29–38.

to believe that the legislation would spur hospitals to eliminate inefficiencies rather than to redefine, relocate, or simply cut services.

A closely-related strategy for containing hospital costs in the Medicare and Medicaid programs is incorporated in a series of proposals such as the one offered by Senator Herman Talmadge in the 96th Congress (S. 2885). This bill would regulate differences in hospital expenditures from group norms rather than increases in expenditures from past levels as in the Hospital Cost Containment approach. Hospitals are grouped on the basis of such criteria as beds, size, metropolitan or non-metropolitan location, and type (e.g., community). A target rate of increase for per diem routine operating costs would be established for each hospital. Hospital expenditures in excess of this targeted rate by more than a specified amount would not be reimbursed by Medicare or Medicaid, while hospitals with routine costs below their target rates would receive bonus payments.

Although the Talmadge proposal is intended to *save* federal outlays, CBO estimates that this bill would actually *increase* federal outlays by \$710 million, cumulatively, over the FY 1981–1985 period (\$610 million for Medicare, \$100 million for Medicaid).[24] Bonus payments under this legislation would increase Medicare outlays by an estimated \$700 million (more than offsetting the \$90 million in Medicare savings associated with penalty provisions). Most of the incentive payments probably would go to hospitals which would have been below their target rates anyway (thereby limiting bonus-induced cost reductions). The bonuses could then be used to purchase new equipment or spent in areas exempt from the target, thus leading to higher Medicare and Medicaid outlays in future years.[25] The penalties under this proposed bill would become more restrictive over time, and CBO argues that as the penalties become more severe, they could impair hospitals' ability to improve quality.[26]

There are several levels of danger in this type of legislation. First, to the extent that the unrefined techniques or criteria for grouping hospitals are too limited in scope, some hospitals will be penalized unfairly for cost "excesses" which are actually attributable to uncontrolled characteristics rather than poor management. Second, there is an implied premise that in response to a rigid revenue ceiling, hospital administrators would root out waste and inefficiency and thereby reduce costs without cutting quality. But, with the forces generating such inefficiency still intact, it is equally likely that the practical result of this legislation would be to foster a deterioration in service quality. Third, there is evidence from other kinds of control programs in the health

---

[24] Paul B. Ginsburg, Congressional Budget Office, letter to Jack A. Meyer, August 29, 1980.

[25] *Ibid.*

[26] CBO, *Controlling Rising Hospital Costs*, p. 54.

care area that controls on one type of hospital spending are associated with corresponding increases in other categories of spending.[27]

Incentives Strategies — A Realistic Promise

An alternative approach to moderating health care cost increases and holding down federal outlays for health involves a very different set of ingredients from the cost lids, revenue formulas, and capital expenditure limits featured in the "controls" approach. This approach is based on the following principles: (1) a more rational system of consumer cost-sharing that encourages people to economize on the use of routine health services while at the same time offering better protection for expenses associated with serious illnesses; (2) federal aid that increases with increasing need, and vice versa; (3) fixed dollar instead of open-ended federal subsidies to aid those who are unable to purchase adequate health insurance; and (4) fair competition among alternative health care plans for the consumers' dollar. In the long-run, incorporating these changes into government policy will require a major overhaul of federal programs, and the broad contours of such a change will be sketched in the final section of this essay. First, it may be useful to propose some shorter-term steps based on the principles of competition that would at least lead us in the right direction and lay the groundwork for more fundamental changes in the future.

Improved Cost Sharing Provisions

Both the Medicare and Medicaid programs would be improved by introducing rational and equitable systems of cost sharing. A combination of greater deductibles and co-payments for routine services, coupled with catastrophic illness or stop-loss provisions assuring that greater cost-sharing imposes no burden on those with the most serious medical problems, should be implemented. Catastrophic illness protection need not increase *net* federal outlays if it is coupled with sufficient cost-sharing for routine services. It makes little sense to make routine doctor appointments virtually costless to a Medicaid recipient, but to terminate that recipient's coverage after 21 days in the hospital when this individual is seriously ill. Furthermore, cost control measures such as Medicare's lifetime reserves, which can be exhausted by serious or lingering illness, exposing patients to financial burdens at the most inopportune times, should be replaced by more significant cost-sharing for routine services (through greater deductibles or co-payments). Cost-sharing should be restructured not only in the inter-

---

[27]See, for example, David S. Salkever and Thomas W. Bice, *Hospital Certificate-of-Need Controls: Impact on Investment, Cost, and Use* (Washington, D.C.: American Enterprise Institute, 1979), and Frank A. Sloan and Bruce Steinwald, "Effects of Regulation on Hospital Costs and Input Use," *The Journal of Law and Economics,* April 1980, pp. 81–109.

est of greater fairness, but also to encourage beneficiaries and their providers to economize on the use of resources in non-critical medical situations.

Revising Medicaid Matching Rate Formula

The current formula for computing the federal share of Medicaid payments is arbitrary and inequitable. Grannemann has argued that this formula reflects only a desire to have the federal government pay at least 50 percent of Medicaid costs. It is not designed to foster the achievement of any particular policy goal.[28] *The matching rate formula should be revised either to equalize the effective tax burden of the program across states or to equalize Medicaid benefits across states.*

Other short-term steps needed to conserve resources include the encouragement of local health planning agencies to "deregulate" as much as possible, the reduction of fraudulent claims in federal health services programs, and antitrust activities designed to increase the competition in the health sector.[29] In the 1979 health planning amendments Congress manifested its intent to rely on competitive forces to allocate health services wherever this step would be consistent with quality assurance, cost effectiveness, and access to care. While not a wholesale turnabout, the statutory modifications included in these amendments provide a foundation for expanding the role of competition (and reducing the scope of regulation) in the future.[30]

Fair Competition From HMOs for Federal Subsidies

Only about 1 percent of all Medicare enrollees are served by Health Maintenance Organizations (HMOs)[31] which offer comprehensive medical care to patients for a fixed annual fee. HMOs are believed to hold down utilization since providers — who receive a fixed fee — have no financial incentive to increase utilization. The low incidence of pre-paid plan care for the elderly is rendered almost inevitable by the fact that Medicare often pays substantially less on behalf of beneficiaries who join HMOs than on behalf of those who obtain care from fee-for-service providers. Medicare does not pay HMOs on their customary fixed prospective periodic payment basis. Rather, Medicare typically forces fee-for-service payment on HMOs which would serve the elderly. Thus, Medicare discourages beneficiary participation in HMOs

---

[28]Grannemann, *op. cit.*, p. 119.

[29]Some experts believe anti-trust enforcement would also be a vital component of a long-run strategy, functioning as a necessary adjunct to competitive reforms in financing mechanisms. See Havighurst, *op. cit.*, pp. 384–387.

[30]See Clark C. Havighurst and Glenn M. Hackbarth, "Competition and Health Care," *Regulation*, May/June 1980, pp. 39–48.

[31]Department of Health and Human Services, Health Care Financing Administration.

as there is no financial incentive for either party to reach out to the other. Current legislative proposals would enable Medicare beneficiaries to direct the Medicare program to pay 95 percent of the average cost to the program of serving their actuarial category to an HMO as a prospective payment. This would benefit both Medicare enrollees and the federal government.

How much could be saved by this step? The answer is very uncertain despite ample evidence that HMO enrollees have lower medical care expenditures than people with conventional insurance coverage. If the 10–40 percent savings reported to be associated with HMOs were portable to enrollees in federal health programs, it could be possible to save anywhere from $6–25 billion in FY 1982 outlays. But it is important not to jump from evidence of relatively lower health expenditures for current HMO enrollees to the conclusion that an expansion of the market share of HMOs would generate proportionate savings. Before one even can be sanguine about the potential for HMO growth to generate cost savings, one must be able to assert that HMOs save money through real efficiencies — the same services at lower costs — rather than through (1) providing lower quality services or (2) serving a group of enrollees healthier or less inclined to utilize medical services. Consumers may be concerned with the pace of rising health care costs, but they are also concerned with the availability and standards of health care services.

There is considerable doubt about whether HMOs reduce outlays by avoiding unnecessary treatments, and indeed there is evidence of a self-selection bias in which people who join HMOs tend to be relatively low utilizers.[32] Clearly, the elderly are typically not low-utilizers, and their entry into HMOs in large numbers could reduce the apparent HMO cost advantage.

Furthermore, there is no doubt about the extent to which the market share of innovative plans would swell in response to altered incentives. First, observations about the growth of HMOs in a few regions of the country may be a misleading guide to a potential nationwide spread of innovative health plans, as factors indigenous to those regions may be largely responsible for the substantial HMO presence.

Second, changes in incentives may be unable to overcome the dominant position of Blue Cross and Blue Shield in certain market areas. The widespread exemption of Blues from state premium taxes paid by commercial insurers confers an estimated 30 percent cost advantage on Blue Cross plans; the corresponding figure for Blue Shield is 20 percent.[33]

---

[32]See Harold S. Luft, "Health Maintenance Operations, Competition, Cost Containment, and National Health Insurance," in Pauly, *op. cit.,* pp. 294–295.

[33]See H. E. Frech, III, "Blue Cross, Blue Shield, and Health Care Costs: A Review of the Economic Evidence," in Pauly, *op. cit.,* p. 252.

Third, there may be legal and regulatory barriers to the development of various types of innovative health plans. Legal barriers include the vulnerability of closed panel arrangements to legal challenges by excluded providers and the availability of various legal defenses to antitrust litigation that could allow boycotts of innovators or more subtle forms of pressure to go unpunished.[34] Regulatory barriers include the potential backfire effect of unduly comprehensive minimum coverage requirements for HMOs.

Although the 1973 Health Maintenance Organization Act was intended to foster the development of HMOs, some observers believe that the legislation was drawn much too narrowly. Frech and Ginsburg suggested that the legislation has been ineffective, if not counterproductive.

> The immediate problem with regard to HMOs is to reverse current policies that discourage them. There is a long history of state laws hostile to the development of HMOs, and while federal policy became officially favorable with the passage in 1973 of the Health Maintenance Organization Act, one may suspect that the law was written by interests hostile to HMOs. Little help has actually been rendered and some provisions of the law are, indeed, harmful to the continued existence of HMOs.[35]

The chief barrier to HMO development emerging from the legislation seems to involve the very high minimum standards of comprehensiveness of insured services which, in some cases, exceed those typical in private health insurance policies. The HMO act, however, has helped stimulate competition among delivery systems by requiring that employers offer qualified HMOs, where available, to their employees, and has more recently been amended to relax the rigid requirements. *If federal policy becomes neutral regarding the choice among HMOs, conventional fee-for-service, and alternatives combining some features of each, it is possible that HMO enrollment would increase. But the factors cited above suggest that in order to breathe some life into the expansion of the market share of HMOs, federal policy changes aimed directly at HMOs would have to be supplemented by state tax changes, regulatory reform, and perhaps antitrust activities to assure that all plans compete on a truly equal basis.*

Broader Plans to Increase Competition

A broader version of the principle of equal contributions to all health plans is incorporated in several legislative proposals designed to restrain health costs on a nationwide basis. Shunning the regulatory

---

[34] Havighurst, "Health Care Financing," *op. cit.,* pp. 343–374.

[35] H. E. Frech, III, and Paul B. Ginsburg, *Public Insurance in Private Medical Markets: Some Problems with National Health Insurance* (Washington, D.C.: American Enterprise Institute, 1978), p. 67.

approach, these proposals would attempt, instead, to improve incentives to economize on health spending (1) by imposing a limit on the tax-free premium that an employer could contribute to a health plan, (2) by requiring employers to offer a range of options, and (3) by allowing employees who selected a low-cost plan to reap the savings and forcing those selecting a high-cost plan to pay the excess premiums over a fixed employer contribution.

These principals should be incorporated into our health care system. Ending the open-ended nature of federal tax-subsidies would put pressure on insurers to practice their own brand of cost containment, and this approach makes more sense than the arbitrary formulas for cost containment through federal government controls.

This approach has a realistic chance of slowing the increase in health care costs. At least it recognizes that a major reason for the increase in costs is the combination of broader insurance coverage and the lack of incentives to select a low-cost insurance plan. Moreover, this strategy would economize not simply by fostering consumer cost sharing, but primarily by stimulating competition among alternative health care plans — and delivery systems — so as to hold down the cost level itself, irrespective of how that cost is shared between workers and firms. Finally, with the incentives approach, it would be in the interest of providers to hold down costs (for example, by avoiding unnecessary hospitalization of patients) because people who chose efficient providers would ultimately reap the benefit. The incentives approach is preferable to one that tries to wring the waste out of the system through controlling providers' fees and charges — but leaves the forces driving costs upward largely intact.

CBO has estimated that legislation incorporating these principles introduced by former House Ways and Means Committee chairman Al Ullman in 1979 would reduce consumer health care expenditures by $5–8 billion in FY 1985 and would increase federal revenues by $4–6 billion in FY 1985. According to the CBO, the program would have little effect on federal outlays.[36]

LONG-TERM CONSIDERATIONS

In the long run, we have a choice between two fundamentally different cost containment strategies. One targets health care providers and imposes direct controls on physician fees, hospital revenues, and hospital capital expenditures. The other seeks to change the incentives among different insurance arrangements and health care delivery

[36]Statement of Alice M. Rivlin, Director, Congressional Budget Office, Hearing before the Subcommittee on Health of the Committee on Ways and Means, U.S. House of Representatives, on H.R. 5740, February 25, 1980, pp. 24–30.

mechanisms—in effect, financing added benefits by reducing "waste." This reflects a basic division of opinion among health care experts regarding the nature of the market for medical services. Those who favor more regulation of providers stress inherent "market failure" in medical markets and believe that supply creates its own demand; the answer, then, is to control supply. Those who favor tax reform and incentives to induce consumers to shop for health insurance stress "regulatory failure" and argue that the alleged excess spending on health care is best contained by altering the system of signals to which providers, patients, and insurers all respond.

This argument is, in a sense, a microcosm of the controversy over government attempts to clamp economy-wide controls on suppliers while simultaneously stimulating demand in the overall economy. And the result—rapid cost and price increases, shortages, and quality problems—is likely to be the same. Past attempts to increase the rate of growth in a nation's money supply above the pace that would otherwise be considered prudent, relying on wage and price controls to ensure that this excessive growth improves production and employment without accelerating inflation, have typically resulted in various supply shortfalls and black markets and ultimately caused a spurt in inflation as controls are relaxed.

Similarly, if a National Health Insurance (NHI) program substantially increases the demand for health services while supply is constrained through controls on hospital beds and charges as well as on physician supply and fees, the result will be a combination of longer waiting times for treatment, a deterioration in the quality of service, and an explosion in costs when consumers ultimately insist on a restoration of the kind of services to which they had grown accustomed.

Efforts to freeze the share of gross national product (GNP) accounted for by health care expenditures through negotiating or legislating "acceptable" fees and charges seem to fly in the face of free consumer choice. It would be more prudent to alter those forces that distort consumer choice and feed wasteful spending so that such growth as occurs in the health care share of GNP is simply a sign of consumer preferences for more health care—in return for which the consumer is willing to sacrifice some other goods and services. Surely we do not want to freeze permanently the shares of the economic pie accounted for by food, health, housing, etc.

There is growing evidence, both from studies of controls on hospitals[37] and from general evaluations of cost-plus regulatory interventions, that a regulatory approach to cost containment will not provide the anticipated results. Indeed, the increasingly complex body of fed-

---

[37]See Salkever and Bice, *op. cit.*, and Sloan and Steinwald, *op. cit.*

eral and state regulations is beginning to be viewed as much as a part of the health cost problem as it is as a cure. Given this mounting evidence, it is important that we think carefully about the need for either NHI or further federal controls on spending. Surely many Americans have inadequate coverage for certain health care expenses, particularly in the catastrophic illness category, at the same time as many others have first-dollar coverage for relatively minor health problems. But to what extent is this problem receding as people become more aware of the availability of low-cost catastrophic insurance? To what extent could those people who fall between the cracks of public and private insurance be helped by modifications in current programs (e.g., reform of Medicaid or Medicare) or through the establishment of either a voucher system or a pooled-risk fund to serve those otherwise deemed uninsurable?

We need a plan to help those who are victims of "adverse selection" so that people are not slapped with exorbitant penalties for being in a medically-needy situation, for being out of work temporarily, or for being members of an intact family headed by a working male. We do not want the sick subsidizing the well in our society.

Some observers have advocated solving this problem by substituting community rating of insurance premiums (under which individuals or employee groups with varying risk profiles pay the same premium) for experience-rating (where premiums vary with expected outlays based on past experience). Community rating is unlikely to stop adverse selection and represents an inefficient answer to this legitimate concern. *Far better would be a system which allows experience rating to bring premiums in line with costs, but uses a system of vouchers, tax credits scaled to income and age, or assigned risk pools to assist those whose experience-rated premiums would be beyond their financial means.*

Medicare

To accomplish these objectives, we do not need an elaborate new set of federal controls or a network of new federal agencies, boards, or institutes. Instead, we should begin by cleaning up our present house. *This entails converting the Medicare program to a program of fixed dollar premium subsidies equal in real value to the average cost to Medicare of serving people in each major demographic category.* This proposal broadens the short-term step designed only to encourage HMOs, fostering the choice of a variety of plans falling between classical HMOs and solo practice, fee-for-service arrangements. For example, independent practice associations (IPAs) incorporate some features of the pre-paid group practice form of an HMO, but they frequently retain fee-for-service payments made by an HMO to physicians operating in their own offices. Because they are less radical departures from traditional insurance plans, IPAs may raise fewer

262

concerns about quality and attract some people who are skeptical of HMOs, but dissatisfied with solo practice, fee-for-service arrangements.[38] Another type of innovative plan is the Health Care Alliance. This concept is a little closer than an IPA to conventional solo practice, fee-for-service arrangements. The primary distinction is that under an Alliance, only a specific group of participating providers are reimbursed. Participating physicians are office-based and do not assume the financial risks which those in an IPA typically undertake. The latter, even if they are reimbursed on a fee-for-service basis by an HMO, are at risk because patients pay a fixed prospective fee to the HMO, which in turn may limit the amount of funds available for physician reimbursement.

This action would encourage all types of plans to bid for the right of providing a basic package of health care services to the elderly. The fixed fee, in effect, would be paid on behalf of the Medicare enrollee to the plan of his choice. In such a competitive environment, efficient providers would find it profitable to serve the Medicare population and could offer savings to Medicare enrollees who, in turn, would then benefit from this relative efficiency. By contrast, those choosing inefficient providers would pay a penalty.

Medicaid

Medicaid should be replaced by a system of sliding scale premium subsidies in which the very poor would be fully subsidized (the subsidy would equal 100 percent of their actual cost). The subsidy, which could be paid to alternative health plans as in the case of Medicare, could be phased out either at the poverty line or a little above the line, subject to budgetary constraints. The subsidies could also vary across demographic categories so that health plans would receive higher premiums for serving higher-risk people without penalizing the people themselves for being in such categories.[39]

The combination of open-ended tax subsidies and cost-pass-through reimbursement mechanisms is distorting consumer health care choices and fostering purchases of costly health services. Removing these distortions might moderate consumer spending increases if a variety of barriers to an operational competitive environment are overcome, but this would not occur overnight. Whatever cutback in spending increases did occur, however, would be consistent with consumer preferences, and it is this outcome, rather than some fixed percentage of GNP for health spending, that should be sought.

---

[38]Havighurst and Hackbarth, "Private Cost Containment," p. 1302.
[39]Enthoven, *op. cit.,* pp. 324–236.

263

12

Income Security

by Charles D. Hobbs

The Question of Welfare

More than one-third of the federal budget, $220.0 billion in 1981, is allocated to income security, a collection of costly and controversial wealth redistribution programs. These programs present unmatched opportunities to change the course of federal spending. They also contain the greatest pitfalls.

To try to reduce overall expenditures by nibbling away at the individual budgets of these programs, considering each in isolation and making detailed adjustments in design and administration, has not worked and will not work. These programs constitute the major portion of an enormously complex social engineering system, which supports a large and thriving industry. Only when the system is restructured and the industry redirected can income security costs be brought under control.

The twenty-one programs which make up the income security function are essentially welfare programs: that is, programs designed to alleviate poverty through wealth redistribution. Among them are the aging giants born of the Great Depression—aid to families with dependent children (AFDC), unemployment compensation, public housing, and the retirement and disability elements of social security—as well as the programs of the '60s and '70s—food stamps, child nutrition, rent and mortgage interest subsidies, earned income tax credits, low-income energy assistance, and assistance to refugees—many of which duplicate or supplement the benefits of the earlier programs. The federal civil service retirement program, with its generous benefits and large unfunded liabilities, is also included in the income security function.

All of these programs involve the federally-controlled transfer of purchasing power from one group to another: from wealthy and middle class to poor, from young to old, from workers to non-workers, and from citizens to aliens. Revenues come mainly from workers' wages and are distributed as either dollar or in-kind transfers, on the basis of assumed need. Put succinctly, these programs tax earned incomes to provide unearned incomes.

Table 1
Income Security
(in millions of dollars)

Major missions and programs	1979 actual	1980 estimate	1981 estimate
OUTLAYS			
General retirement and disability insurance:			
Social security (OASDI):			
Existing law	102,595	117,927	137,020
Proposed legislation	—	− 14	− 99
Railroad retirement:			
Existing law	4,279	4,748	5,227
Proposed legislation	—	—	− 70
Special benefits for disabled coal miners ..	1,610	1,968	1,994
Other	8	12	12
Subtotal	108,492	124,641	144,084
Federal employee retirement and disability:			
Retirement and disability:			
Existing law	12,192	14,305	16,686
Proposed legislation	—	—	22
Federal employees workers' compensation.	187	252	381
Subtotal	12,379	14,556	17,089
Unemployment compensation	10,742	15,610	18,752
Public assistance and other income supplements:			
Supplemental security income:			
Existing law	5,471	6,374	6,908
Proposed legislation	—	—	17
AFDC and other:			
Existing law	6,611	7,127	7,681
Proposed legislation	—	− 79	− 249
Earned income tax credit	773	1,696	1,570
Food stamps	6,822	8,678	9,656

Characteristics of Income Security Programs

Income security programs have been characterized by high and accelerating expenditure growth rates and extensive duplication of benefits and beneficiaries.

Total 1981 income security expenditures are $220.3 billion, 35.8 percent of total federal outlays and 7.8 percent of the GNP. Ten years ago, in 1971, income security expenditures were $55.7 billion, 26.3 percent of federal outlays and 5.2 percent of the GNP. Twenty years ago, in 1961, income security expenditures were $21.2 billion, 21.7 percent of federal outlays and 4.1 percent of the GNP. From 1961 to 1981 income security expenditures increased nine-fold, an average annual growth rate of 12.37 percent. In the same period federal outlays grew at an average annual rate of 9.61 percent, the GNP at 8.73 percent, and the cost of living at 5.82 percent.

Not only has the growth rate of income security expenditures been

Table 1 (Cont.)
Income Security
(in millions of dollars)

Major missions and programs	1979 actual	1980 estimate	1981 estimate
WIC food supplements:			
Existing law	542	735	860
Proposed legislation	–	–	43
School lunch and other nutrition programs:			
Existing law	3,423	3,955	4,240
Proposed legislation	–	–	–432
Housing assistance	4,367	5,318	6,606
Refugee assistance:			
Existing law	141	419	228
Proposed legislation	–	–	296
Low-income energy assistance:			
Existing law	186	1,660	–
Proposed legislation	–	–	2,400
Other:			
Existing law	252	259	214
Proposed legislation	–	–	22
Subtotal	28,586	36,143	40,060
Deductions for offsetting receipts	–2	–2	–2
Total, outlays	**160,198**	**190,948**	**219,982**
ADDENDUM			
Off-budget Federal entity:			
Pension Benefit Guaranty, Corporation:			
Outlays	–38	–37	–44
MEMORANDUM			
Attribution of Federal Financing Bank outlays:			
Housing assistance	–	1,557	–50

Source: The Budget of the United States Government FY 1981.

extremely high, but that rate has also been accelerating at a pace equal to that of other federal outlays and faster than the GNP. From 1961 to 1971 income security expenditures rose at an average annual rate of 10.36 percent; from 1971 to 1981 that rate increased to 14.41 percent, a 40 percent acceleration rate. Comparable acceleration rates for all federal outlays and the GNP were 40 percent and 36 percent, respectively.

Individual program growth rates have varied widely, but invariably a relatively low growth rate in one program has been offset by high growth rates in other programs with duplicative benefits. Expenditures for aid to families with dependent children grew, between 1971 and 1981, at an average annual rate of 9.0 percent, only slightly higher than cost of living growth (8.6 percent) and considerably below the average of income security programs (14.4 percent). Yet during the same period AFDC recipients were able to take advantage of the high average annual growth rates of programs whose benefits duplicated those of AFDC: food stamps (19.9 percent), earned income tax credits (21.1 percent), mortgage interest subsidies (23.6 percent), rent subsidies (62.6 percent), and special supplemental food (WIC, Women, Infants, and Children) (79.0 percent).

In another example, expenditures for food donations (commodities) actually declined, from 1971 to 1981, to 40 percent of their 1971 level. However, it had been the intent of the Department of Agriculture, as long ago as 1969, to phase out the food donations program entirely and replace it with food stamps, a program which grew between 1971 and 1981 at an average annual rate of 19.9 percent. Food donations expenditures dropped from the late '60s until the mid '70s, but are now rising again, from $7.9 million in 1976 to $126 million in 1981. The program that was to have been replaced has taken on new life, while its replacement grows at a rate more than twice that of the cost of living.

Each of the twenty-one income security programs provides benefits that are duplicated by at least one, and in many cases by several other programs.[1] Social security, old age and survivors insurance (OASI), disability insurance (DI), and supplemental security income (SSI) provide food benefits that are duplicated by food stamps and food donations, and housing benefits that are duplicated by public housing, rental subsidies, or mortgage interest subsidies. AFDC has the same housing benefit duplications, and its food benefits are duplicated by food stamps, WIC, and child nutrition. Earned income tax credits and low income energy assistance duplicate the benefits of AFDC, SSI, and OASI and DI, as well as the smaller cash assistance programs for refugees, coal miners, and retired railroad workers. There are also substantial overlaps in unearned benefits among programs such as OASI and the civil service retirement program, and unemployment compensation and food stamps.

The fiscal impact of benefit duplications cannot be estimated accurately, mainly because recipient record-keeping is structured so as to thwart such calculations. Based on the proliferation of programs with duplicatory benefits—seven of the twenty-one income security programs have been adopted since 1960—and the expenditure growth rates, which in per-capita terms have greatly exceeded cost of living growth in the past 20 years, it can be assumed that at least 20 percent, and perhaps as much as 50 percent of all income security expenditures duplicate other expenditures to meet the same needs for the same recipients.[2]

---

[1] See Charles D. Hobbs, *The Welfare Industry*, (Washington, D.C.: The Heritage Foundation, 1978), pp. 18–20, and notes 36–38, p. 80.

[2] An admittedly rough estimate, but one which can only be refined by a major analytical effort of a current administration, excluding the federal bureaucracy.

A smaller but significant portion of welfare expenditures goes to those who are not "needy" in any commonly accepted sense. Examples abound. Families who become eligible for AFDC because of unemployment remain eligible for AFDC-tied grants and services even after their bread winners are re-employed and their incomes are far above the poverty level. Children in the summer feeding portion of the child nutrition program are eligible for free meals simply because they live in a "target" area, regardless of their familial economic circumstances.

Again, the extent of these unnecessary expenditures cannot be estimated accurately, especially when they are combined with benefit-duplicating expenditures, but it is not unlikely that they constitute another 5 to 15 percent of all income security expenditures.[3] Thus it is conceivable that anywhere from 25 to 65 percent of current income security expenditures could be eliminated from the federal budget without reducing the benefits of these programs to less than the need standards for the recipients set by federal and state governments.

Reform: Complicating Factors

The central policy and, therefore, budget questions are whether, to what extent, and for how long, the federal government should continue to redistribute income.

Three factors complicate any discussion of these questions. The first is that it has been so long since anyone in power has asked them other than rhetorically; for the past fifty years, even among responsible critics of the welfare system, the answers have been taken for granted to be "of course", "to the extent necessary to meet the needs of the 'poor' ", and "forever". Since the mid-'60s the welfare system has grown 50 percent faster than the GNP,[4] yet opponents of an expansive welfare state have had to content themselves with negotiated "tinkerings" to keep the system from growing even faster. Only in the past few years, as the public's dissatisfaction with both government and welfare has finally reached the attention of the nation's leaders, has it become possible to question seriously the federal role in welfare. Even now, such questions generate open hostility throughout the federal bureaucracy.

The second complicating factor is that not all of welfare is in the income security function, and not all of income security expenditures are necessarily welfare. Many other earnings redistribution programs favoring the poor are spread throughout the federal budget: programs related to jobs, health, education, community development, legal assistance, and other similar services, as well as welfare programs for veterans and Indians. On the other hand, an argument can be made

---

[3] Another rough estimate but, based on the California welfare reforms of the early 1970s, probably conservative.

[4] GNP figures are taken from various editions of the U.S. Statistical Abstract.

that some income security programs, notably social security and the civil service retirement system, provide a partial return on investment, in the form of insurance and pension payments, and therefore are not totally redistributive.

The result of this diffusion and ambiguity is that Congress and the Executive, in their budget deliberations, have apparently found it too costly to examine total welfare spending, and thus seem unaware of the magnitude and impact of the federally-controlled welfare system. In 1981 total public welfare expenditures — for earnings redistribution programs designed, managed and, for the most part, operated by the federal government — will approach $300 billion, or about 11 percent of the estimated 1981 GNP.[5]

The Welfare Industry

The third complicating factor, and the most important in preventing productive debate on questions about the federal role, is the welfare industry.

Before the passage of New Deal social legislation in the '30s, welfare had been almost exclusively within the province of local governments and private charities. Efforts were concentrated on self-reliance and the reduction of dependency on the "dole". Public assistance administrators were neighbors both of those who provided it and those who received it, and clearly the less spent, the better.

But federal programs created a national market, and spawned a national industry led by federal bureaucrats who feel no pressure to contain welfare spending. The organization of the industry is, like the system itself, extremely complex; decisions are made informally, in an atmosphere of philosophical agreement that welfare should be forever expanded. Like a half-filled balloon with a very tough skin, the organization is virtually impenetrable. Outsiders are uncertain about who belongs to it and who controls it, since its products seldom leave a clear audit trail. Insiders often know less: they shift positions rapidly and lack the perspective to judge what is going on and how they fit into it. There is no conspiracy to control, only a common commitment to self-interest, without any countervailing political force.

That self-interest lies in more people becoming more dependent on government, the result being goals that expand welfare and enhance the federal role. These goals are: growth of welfare expenditures at a pace faster than national economic growth, centralized control, ever-increasing complexity, and ever-expanding welfare industry employment.[6]

The industry has met these goals to a remarkable degree: expenditures are growing at 1.5 times the pace of the economy; virtually all

---

[5] U.S. Department of Commerce estimate, August 1980.
[6] See Hobbs, *The Welfare Industry*, especially pp. 63–69.

national welfare programs are controlled by the federal government, and most are administered directly by federal agencies; the programs are so widely dispersed, the interactions among them so complex, and the duplications of benefits among them so common, that neither Congress nor the Executive can comprehend their combined effects; and the industry now employs more than 5 million public and private workers.

But the industry may now be falling victim to its own success. In its zeal to meet its own goals—goals in conflict with the public's desire to keep welfare to a necessary minimum—it has expanded programs and duplicated benefits to the point where many welfare families are better off financially than are the families of workers.

Ten years ago the Congressional Research Service demonstrated that a family in Portland, Oregon, consisting of a mother and four children could theoretically compound AFDC cash payments with benefits of fourteen other programs to a total untaxed income three times the median income for families headed by female workers. Since then, expenditures-per-recipient have grown faster than wages, making the disparity more common, if not more acute.

Forcing workers to subsidize non-workers at standards of living higher than their own, the ultimate absurdity of wealth redistribution, has created tax burdens that the public is no longer willing to bear. Intensified public dissatisfaction with the costs and policies of the federal welfare system, expressed in the last four years through the nationwide taxpayers' revolt, has created a climate in which radical revisions of income security programs and practices—revisions which would progressively and dramatically reduce welfare spending and the federal role in its administration—can now be seriously considered.

And none too soon. A look at the history of income security programs shows that attempts to cut back on unnecessary benefits or remove non-needy recipients from the rolls have been largely ineffective, due to the welfare industry's control of the writing and administering of welfare laws and regulations and its demonstrated ability to defend itself against even the most modest proposals to reduce or restructure these programs. Food stamps and rent subsidies, two programs with benefits almost totally duplicated by other programs, have not only survived but actually grown more rapidly because the industry has so successfully drawn attention to the "needy" they serve, albeit redundantly.

To try to adjust the details of such programs to make them more responsible fiscally is an exercise in futility: the industry, through its control of program design and administration, simply readjusts such proposals to meet its own expansionary goals. Only a conceptual and organizational restructuring of the welfare system can bring fiscal and social sense to these programs.

271

Restructuring Income Security

To say that it is technically possible to reduce income security expenditures by at least 25 percent and still meet the needs for which these programs were established is a far cry from saying that it is politically practical. While the poor may not be harmed by such reductions if applied to benefit duplications and aid to those who are not really poor, the welfare industry can be counted on to fight any reduction in its "sales" volume. At the first indication of the smallest reduction in the least defensible program, special interest groups created and supported by the welfare industry will descend on Congress to protest. They will appear either as helpless victims of a vindictive cutback, or as a political power group whose welfare "rights" have been violated.[7]

Income security expenditures can be controlled only through a restructuring of the welfare system — a restructuring accomplished through changes in process rather than program. And since the welfare industry controls the design and administration of the system, it is the industry itself whose processes must be changed.

The principles for industry redirection are simply the reverse of the industry's own goals. The size and power of the federal welfare bureaucracy must be drastically reduced and control of welfare budgeting taken out of its hands. The welfare system must be simplified to the point where it can be understood and revamped by Congress and the President without industry assistance or interference. Control of welfare benefits and expenditures must be decentralized to those levels of government where individual needs can be determined accurately and met humanely. The growth in welfare expenditures must be controlled, and federal wealth redistribution reduced to the lowest level necessary to meet locally determined welfare needs.

In the short term — three to five years — these principles can be applied to the restructuring and rebudgeting of income security programs through three process-oriented techniques. While these techniques are logically valid and technically workable, they have the potential, if mishandled, to be politically explosive and should be approached with great care, organization, and precision, or not at all.

The first of these techniques, and a precursor to the other two, is the separation of the "earned" benefit component of programs which are not pure welfare — principally OASI, DI, civil service retirement, and unemployment insurance (UI) — from the "unearned", or welfare, component. More than half of OASI and DI expenditures, for example, are for benefits in excess of the original "contributions" plus normal interest, and it is these unearned benefits which are slowly

---

[7]See Hobbs, *The Welfare Industry*, pp. 63-73.

272

bankrupting social security.[8] Removing these unearned benefits, together with their costs, and placing them in pure welfare programs, such as SSI and AFDC, will leave a residue of earned benefits and the revenues to pay for them, which can be used to set up individual annuity accounts in the retirement programs, such as OASI and civil service retirement, and actuarially sound insurance funds in the insurance programs, such as DI and UI. The result of this process will be increases in SSI and AFDC budgets, offset by decreases in the budgets of OASI, DI, UI, and civil service retirement. With these pension and insurance programs self-supporting, attention can be turned to revamping the operations of the pure welfare programs.

The next step is to consolidate the welfare programs and eliminate the massive duplications of benefits among them. AFDC and SSI, as the most universal programs for, respectively, families and adults without children, should absorb the budgets allocated to potentially duplicative benefits in the other programs. Since AFDC incorporates a housing component in its grant, for example, it should absorb the portions of the public housing, rent supplements, and mortgage interest subsidies budgets that cover AFDC recipients. Potential benefit duplications should then be intensively analyzed, in federal and state regulations and in actual benefit distribution practices, to determine the extent of actual duplication and the budgets for those benefits reduced accordingly. The result of this process will be slightly expanded AFDC and SSI budgets, more than offset by greatly reduced budgets for the food, housing, and other pure welfare programs.

The final step is to remove the federal strings from the expenditures for pure welfare and assign the money to the states in the form of block grants for welfare purposes. All of the pure welfare money would go to the states: the entire AFDC and SSI budgets plus the budgets for the other welfare programs. These monies would be used to supplement social security and UI payments up to state-determined need standards and to create community-based welfare programs sponsored and monitored by the states.

Timing and Budget Goals

The three steps outlined above must be carried out in the order presented. If welfare money is sent to the states before the duplications of benefits are eliminated, the current bloated welfare system will continue to expand. If there is an attempt to eliminate benefit duplications before earned and unearned benefits are separated, the present confusion over income security purposes and operations will be exacerbated, to the benefit of the welfare industry.

---

[8] Estimates of the size of the welfare component of social security were done by Douglas R. Munro in his "Welfare Component and Labor Supply Effects of OASDHI Retirement Benefits" (Ph.D. dissertation, Ohio State University, 1976).

It will take, at the very least, three years, and perhaps more realistically a minimum of five years, to complete the process of earned-unearned benefit separation, elimination of benefit duplications, and assignment of block welfare grants to the states, and even a three-to-five-year schedule will require dedicated, bi-partisan political support in Congress and sincere cooperation between the executive and legislative branches.

Budget goals should be extremely conservative. In the first year the goal should be no more ambitious than current expenditures plus cost of living growth. In the second year the goal might be to hold the line at current expenditures. In the third to fifth years the goals might be progressive annual reductions, adjusted to cost of living, ranging from 10 to 20 percent, depending on the level of benefit duplications uncovered. A change in expenditure pattern, from growth to reduction, will be more important than the amount of the reduction.

The difficulty, as well as the necessity, of basically restructuring the processes which govern income security expenditures is clearly demonstrated by examining a sampling of the programs.

Social Security: Old Age and Survivors Insurance (OASI)

OASI is the original social security program enacted in 1935 to provide income protection for retired workers and their surviving dependents. The program pays beneficiaries through a trust fund fed by taxes on workers' wages. Frequent amendments, most of them in election years, have substantially expanded both the benefits and the recipient population. Thirty-one million persons now receive benefits, which average about one-half of earnings prior to retirement. OASI taxes have risen substantially faster than benefits, particularly in recent years: in 1971 the first $7,800 of each worker's earnings were taxed at $631.80; in 1981 the first $29,700 of earnings will be taxed at $2,554.20, a 300 percent tax increase in ten years. Despite the higher taxes, the trust fund is now expected to be depleted, and the program unable to pay its beneficiaries, by 1983 unless Congress enacts still higher taxes.

OASI is at once the most expensive, the most politically difficult, and the most seriously flawed of the income security programs. Its current outlays are one-fifth of the entire federal budget, 5 percent of the GNP, and growing faster than either.

In the last 10 years annual OASI outlays have increased from $32.3 billion to $121.2 billion, an average annual growth rate of 14.1 percent, 1.6 times the average annual cost of living increase and 1.4 times the average annual GNP increase.[9]

OASI's 31 million beneficiaries, together with their relatives, consti-

---

[9] See Note 2.

tute a powerful and highly sensitive special interest group, quick to react negatively to any program change except direct benefit increases. Yet the program is designed to fail. With its "social insurance" rhetoric peeled away, it is nothing more than a gigantic, government-operated Ponzi scheme, in which earlier, smaller investors (workers now retired) are paid off with the receipts from later, larger investors (currently active workers). Continuation of the program depends upon ever-larger numbers of new workers paying ever-higher taxes, and inflation accelerates this need. Yet current tax rates have reached levels which are generating resistance among younger workers, and the pool of new workers needed to sustain the program is dwindling instead of getting larger.

Politically difficult as it may seem, the only way to cure the fiscal dilemma of OASI is through a fundamental redesign of the social security system. There is no need to change social security's original goal — retirement income protection for workers and their families — nor its basic premise — that it is in the public interest to compel individuals to provide for their retirement years — nor its basic product — a monthly retirement check reflecting the return on the social security investment made by each worker.

There is a need, however, for public recognition that social security cannot be sustained as an intergenerational wealth redistribution scheme, but must instead gradually be converted to what most Americans have always assumed it to be — an actuarially sound individual annuity program. With this recognition the program can be redesigned to live permanently within reasonable fiscal means. Basic to any redesign must be the separation of the "earned" component — the composite of tax investments plus interest for all participants — from the "unearned" component — current and future benefit commitments which are above and beyond the value of tax investments plus interest. *The unearned component should be integrated into pure welfare programs, such as supplemental security income (SSI), where it can be dispensed on the basis of need at the local level and after elimination of redundancies with other welfare programs. The investment component should be structured into individual annuity accounts to make an actuarially sound OASI program which can sustain itself even through severe demographic and economic fluctuations.*

The transition should take place over at least a three-year period. Expenditure reduction goals should be those associated with other welfare programs providing benefits which duplicate those of the unearned portions of OASI. OASI tax rates should be reduced to the level necessary to fund the annuity program. The unearned benefits should be funded from general funds through SSI.

Social Security: Disability Insurance (DI)

DI benefits were added to social security in 1956 to replace lost wages of disabled workers. Benefit levels are the same as those of OASI and, like OASI, DI pays beneficiaries through a trust fund fed by taxes on workers' wages. Currently 4.7 million disabled workers and their dependents receive benefits. DI tax rates are only about one-seventh of OASI rates, but DI tax increases have averaged 35 percent annually over the last 10 years: in 1971 the first $7,800 of each worker's earnings were taxed for DI at $85.80; in 1981 the first $29,700 of earnings will be taxed at $386.10. The faster increases have made the DI trust fund temporarily more solvent that the OASI trust fund.

In the last 10 years annual DI outlays have increased from $3.6 billion to $17.4 billion, an average annual growth rate of 17.1 percent, twice the average annual cost of living increase and 1.7 times the average annual GNP increase.

Like OASI, DI is designed to fail, because it is tied to OASI and operated under the same fiscally unsound social insurance concept. OASI benefit increases automatically become DI benefit increases, driving DI costs and taxes upward in the same Ponzi-like spiral that afflicts OASI. Since disability is more uncommon than retirement, DI tax rates will remain lower than those of OASI; but the rate of cost increases will remain at least as high and probably higher, due to constant recipient pressure to liberalize eligibility requirements.

The long-term solution to the fiscal insolvency of DI is to separate it entirely from OASI and make it an independent, actuarially-based insurance program. In the meantime, DI should be incorporated in the redesign of OASI, with separation of the earned and unearned components and assignment of the unearned component to other welfare programs where redundancies of benefits can be eliminated and remaining benefits assigned on the basis of need.

With the separation, DI tax rates should be lowered to the level necessary to fund the earned component of the insurance. The cost of unearned benefits should be borne by SSI and AFDC through general funds.

Civil Service Retirement and Disability Benefits

The federal bureaucracy has handsomely feathered its own nest by applying welfare program development techniques to federal civil service retirement and disability benefits. It has successfully resisted joining social security since the inception of that program. Instead, it has created and lobbied into law its own welfare-laden retirement program, in which any unfunded liability resulting from legally enacted benefit increases must be financed from general funds. The unfunded liability will require interest payments from the general fund in 1981 of $11.6 billion, while the payments into the fund by federal civil service employees will amount to only $3.7 billion.

In the last ten years annual outlays for civil service retirement and disability benefits have increased from $3.3 billion to $16.8 billion, an average annual growth rate of 17.7 percent, twice the average annual cost of living increase and 1.8 times the average annual GNP increase.

Federal civilian employees should be required to join social security and to pay the unfunded liability of their own retirement program. They are one group whose "welfare" expectations should not have to be met, since those expectations are the result of the self-serving use of their power to control the federal legislative process.

Unemployment Insurance (UI)

The UI program was enacted in 1935 to replace wages lost during periods of unemployment. Weekly cash payments, averaging 65 percent of previous net wages, are provided to members of the work force who are "involuntarily unemployed" and who are able and available to work. The program has been amended frequently, especially during periods of high unemployment, to expand eligibility and increase benefits and length of benefit period. The program is financed by state payroll taxes on employers, and administered through a federal trust fund fed and drawn on by the states.

In the last ten years outlays for UI benefits have fluctuated with the economy, but the general trend has been upward. In 1971 outlays were $6.1 billion; in 1976, $17.7 billion; in 1978, $11.1 billion; and in 1981, $18.7 billion.

The major problem with UI is that it collects too much money during periods of high employment and dispenses too much money during periods of high unemployment, necessitating periodic infusions of federal general funds. Like the other social insurance programs, it is actuarially unsound. *UI should be restructured to live strictly within its means—a reasonable tax on employers to support an actuarially sound insurance fund—with the remainder of the necessary benefits, if any, paid from pure welfare programs.*

A secondary, but growing, problem with UI is that in recent years the courts and state legislatures, following the federal lead, have liberalized eligibility requirements so that many people who have never worked, or have not worked recently, have been defined as part of the work force and thus made eligible for UI benefits. *Only those who were working immediately prior to applying, and who were laid off because of lack of need for their work, should be eligible for this insurance program.* Restoring it to its proper scope will require actions by state legislatures and correct interpretation of those actions by the courts, but a restructured federal program based on actuarially sound insurance principles is the best way to stimulate both.

The period of unemployment benefits should remain fixed at thirteen weeks. Under no circumstances should general funds be used to supplement the UI trust fund, and federal unemployment benefits should be tightened up to reflect the practices of the more conservative states.

Supplemental Security Income (SSI)

SSI was originally enacted, as part of the Social Security Act of 1935, as two separate federal-state matching programs to provide cash assistance to the impoverished aged and blind. The disabled were added in 1957, just after DI was added to social security. The welfare industry engineered the merger of the aged, blind, and disabled programs into SSI in 1974, in part to gain more federal control and in part to hide, within a larger program, the extraordinary growth of expenditures for the disabled due to liberalized definitions of disability. There is significant overlap between SSI and other welfare programs, particularly social security. Three-quarters of aged SSI recipients and one-half of all SSI recipients also receive social security payments.

In the last ten years annual federal SSI outlays, which constitute about 80 percent of combined federal and state SSI expenditures, have increased from $2.3 billion to $6.9 billion, an average annual growth rate of 11.6 percent, 1.34 times the average annual cost of living increase and 1.15 times the average annual GNP increase.

Since 1974 SSI has increasingly become associated with social security, both in the way it is administered and in the minds of its recipients. Administration of the program was purposely placed in the Social Security Administration to achieve social security-like precision in payment distribution. For 1.1 million of the 1.5 million aged SSI recipients, monthly SSI checks are simply supplements to OASI checks. Considering that OASI payments are mostly welfare, the public perception of the consonance of the two programs is correct. And, because the programs operate so closely together, there is little or no duplication of benefits between them.

There is, however, considerable duplication of benefits between SSI and other welfare programs. SSI is the basic program for adults without dependent children and thus, like AFDC, an entry point into the welfare system for new recipients. Its growth has been held somewhat in check because duplicating benefits have been incorporated in programs, such as food stamps, commodities, and rent subsidies.

SSI should become the focal point for the consolidation and analysis of all adult welfare benefits, wherever they appear in the federal budget. A given benefit to meet the need of a given recipient must be assigned to only one program. *For adults without dependent children, welfare benefits for cash assistance (including the unearned component of social security), food, housing, health, education, employment and work training, and other services, together with the federal outlays to provide those benefits, should be assigned to the SSI program.*

Outlays should be reduced by the amount that represents elimination of benefit duplications in other programs, principally health, housing, food, and social services. Then the outlays should be returned as block grants to the states, along with the authority to use those grants to create community-based welfare programs in which eligibility and levels of assistance are determined locally.

Aid to Families with Dependent Children (AFDC)

AFDC was enacted as part of the Social Security Act of 1935, to provide cash assistance to impoverished families. It has been amended frequently to expand benefits and eligibility standards. The period of greatest growth was from the mid-'60s to the mid-'70s, reflecting the effects of 1967 amendments which required the states to deduct more than one-third of earned income in determining eligibility for payments. This change allowed families with gross incomes far above the poverty level to receive AFDC payments and, as a result of AFDC eligibility, to qualify for other welfare programs.

In the last ten years annual federal AFDC outlays, which constitute slightly more than one-half of combined federal and state AFDC expenditures, have increased from $3.2 billion to $7.7 billion, an average annual growth rate of 9.2 percent, 1.06 times the average annual cost of living increase and .91 times the average annual GNP increase.

Growth has slowed in the last few years as the welfare industry, thwarted in its attempts to make AFDC the basis for a guaranteed annual income, has turned its attention to expanding such duplicative-benefit programs as food stamps, WIC, child nutrition, rent and mortgage subsidies, earned income tax credits, and low-income energy assistance.

As the basic family welfare program, and therefore the entry point for most recipients, AFDC has received more than its share of public scrutiny and legislative attention. In fact, most welfare popularizers and reform proposals have treated AFDC as if it were the only welfare program, whereas in reality it is only one of forty-six and its expenditures are less than 5 percent of total welfare expenditures. All of the attention, most of it unfavorable, that AFDC has received has tended to obscure its complex interrelationships with other programs and the extensive duplication of benefits and beneficiaries among them. As a result reform proposals, ranging from turning AFDC into a guaranteed annual income program to distributing AFDC funds as block grants to the states, have addressed only a small part of the welfare policy and expenditure problems.

Reform cannot be limited to AFDC, or to AFDC and a few other programs. Wherever they appear in the federal budget, all must be assessed together to eliminate program redundancy and duplication of benefits. As with SSI, a given benefit to meet the need of a given recipient must be assigned to one program, and to one program only. *Family welfare benefits for cash assistance, food, housing, health, education, employment and work training, and other services, together with the federal outlays to provide those benefits, should be assigned to the AFDC program.*

Outlays should be reduced by the amount that represents elimination of benefits in such other programs as health, jobs, housing, food, and social services. Outlays should then be returned as block grants to the states, along with the authority to use those grants to create family-oriented, community-based welfare programs in which eligibility and levels of assistance are locally determined.

Food Stamps

Enacted in 1964 as a part-subsidy, part-welfare program to allow low-income families to increase their food purchasing power with stamps purchased at less than redemption value, the program has been amended several times to expand eligibility, reduce the purchase cost to recipients, and increase the bonus value of the stamps. In 1977, the requirement that recipients pay for a portion of the value of the stamps was dropped altogether, thereby reducing recipient participation cost to zero. The easy negotiability of the stamps and restriction of their use to food products has fostered an extensive black market.

In the last ten years annual food stamp outlays have increased from $1.6 billion to 9.7 billion, an average annual growth rate of 19.8 percent, 2.3 times the average annual cost of living increase and twice the average annual GNP increase.

The food stamp program has been out of control since its inception. Its benefits are totally duplicative of the food benefit allowances in AFDC and SSI, which supply three-fourths of food stamp recipients, and partially duplicative of other food programs, such as child nutrition and WIC. Created to replace the food donations program (which is still thriving, and which is the only food welfare program *not* duplicative of food stamps), this program has established its own strong bureaucracy and an even stronger lobby, both of which have successfully resisted all attempts to curb it or incorporate it in other programs. Proposals for welfare "reform" in the last three administrations would have added the cash value of food stamps to the guaranteed annual income, thus fixing in perpetuity the double food benefit.

In a redesign of welfare expenditure programs, food stamps should be eliminated for all AFDC and SSI recipients and for recipients whose incomes are above the AFDC and SSI eligibility levels. The remaining outlays should be incorporated in SSI and AFDC block grants to the states.

Child Nutrition

Better known as the "school lunch" program, the child nutrition program was enacted in 1946 as a general subsidy for school lunches. Since then it has been increasingly infused with welfare through a series of amendments, especially those in 1966, 1968, and 1970, which expanded the program to cover breakfasts and other meals in child care institutions and established reduced-price and free meals for children of low income families.

In the last ten years annual child nutrition outlays have increased from $0.5 billion to $3.5 billion, an average annual growth rate of 21.0 percent, 2.4 times the average annual cost of living increase and 2.1 times the average annual GNP increase.

Three-fourths of this program's expenditures are for welfare benefits duplicated by AFDC and food stamps. The remaining one-fourth subsidizes meals for children who are, by definition, not needy. *The welfare portion of the budget should be integrated with AFDC and reduced by the actual amount of duplication. The remainder should be cut from the budget on the ground that the federal government should not subsidize meals for school children whose parents can afford to pay the full price.*

Special Supplemental Food Program for Women, Infants, and Children (WIC)

Enacted in 1966 and "discovered" by the health faction of the welfare industry in 1974, WIC provides fortifying foods to undernourished or low-income mothers and children. Despite its relative youth, WIC has achieved almost untouchable status as a reducer of infant mortality; promoted by health care facilities as well as welfare agencies, WIC is one of the fastest growing of all welfare programs.

Since 1974, when the WIC program first began to gather momentum, its outlays have grown from $15 million to $913 million, an average annual growth rate of 79.0 percent, 9.0 times the average annual cost of living increase and 7.9 times the average annual GNP increase.

WIC's benefits are duplicated by the food component of AFDC, and the same foods can be purchased with food stamps. Also, child nutrition provides duplicate benefits for children in child care facilities. Thus at least two, and for some recipients three, other programs provide for the same nutritional benefits. *Despite its semi-sacred status, WIC should be folded into AFDC and its budget reduced by an*

281

amount equal to its duplication of benefits with AFDC, food stamps, and child nutrition.

Section 8: Subsidized Private Rental Housing

Enacted in 1974 to expand availability of low-rent housing as well as to bolster supposedly inadequate subsidies in earlier programs, Section 8 has become one of the fastest growing income security programs and a windfall for landlords. It provides direct rent subsidy payments to landlords on behalf of low-income tenants, thus removing, for the landlord, the uncertainty of the rent's being paid and, for the tenant, the leverage of not paying the rent if the dwelling is not maintained.

Since 1976, when Section 8 was first funded, its outlays have increased from $269 million to $3.1 billion, an average annual growth rate of 62.6 percent, 7.3 times the average annual cost of living increase and 6.2 times the average annual GNP increase.

Benefits are, in large part, duplicated by the housing component of AFDC. *Section 8 should be integrated into AFDC and its budget reduced by the amount of this duplication.*

Challenge and Opportunity

Despite the almost insurmountable difficulties associated with restructuring such politically-favored programs as social security, rent subsidies, food stamps, and school lunches, it is clearly better to make the attempt than to let the current situation continue. The income security programs, with their enormous costs and fantastic individual and collective expenditure growth rates, constitute a severe and unwarranted drain on the nation's economy. They are also colossal failures, benefitting mainly the welfare industry that spawned and nourished them and those recipients who are shrewd enough to collect benefits from three or four programs to meet the same need.

Up to now these programs have spread like cancers without a cure, and those who would control them have been reduce to the use of the equivalents of band-aids and aspirin. The taxpayers' revolt provides the opportunity for radical surgery, not only on the programs but also, more importantly, on the welfare industry itself. The greatest pitfall facing those who see the need for reducing wealth redistribution is that they will continue to tinker in the mistaken belief that they can "work with" the welfare industry to accomplish their goals.

It cannot be done. The welfare industry is too firmly entrenched and too committed to its own growth-oriented goals to be "worked with." Instead, the power of the budget must be used to dismantle the welfare bureaucracy and to overhaul the processes it has used so successfully to meet its goals.

While the challenge is great, so are the rewards. The welfare system has failed the nation, the taxpayers, and those in need. Only the welfare industry has benefitted. The radical rebudgeting of the income security function will refocus welfare to its true purpose: helping those, and only those, who cannot help themselves.

13

Veterans Benefits and Services

by Cotton M. Lindsay

President Carter's FY 1981 budget proposed to spend $21.7 billion for veterans' benefits and services. The Veterans Administration coordinates a variety of programs on behalf of roughly 30 million exservicemen. These are meant to "recognize and...meet the special needs of veterans and their dependents and survivors that result from the sacrifices that veterans have made in military service to this country." These needs are as follows:

- To meet the nation's obligation to compensate veterans disabled while in military service for their loss of earning power.
- To provide medical care to veterans for disabilities incurred while in military service.
- To compensate the families of veterans who are killed in service or who die from service-related disabilities for the reduction in the family's earning power.
- To help veterans of warfare and draft service return to civilian life on a social and economic basis comparable to their peers who did not perform military duty.
- To provide psychological readjustment services and extended training opportunities to Vietnam-era veterans with special needs.
- To provide financial assistance to needy veterans and their survivors.

Three distinct veteran populations are the chief beneficiaries of these programs. Much of the discussion below will concern these distinctions and the differing justifications for providing benefits to each group. It is, therefore, important to distinguish one group from another and to be able to associate the appropriate set of benefits with each. The first group contains newly discharged servicemen whose needs are principally concerned with readjustment to civilian life. Benefits available to these veterans are comprised mainly of counseling, training and education, and are financed under Veterans Education, Training and Rehabilitation (Table 1). As entitlement to and demands

Table 1
Veterans Benefits and Services
(in millions of dollars)

Major missions and programs	1979 actual	1980 estimate	1981 estimate
OUTLAYS			
Income security for veterans:			
Compensation and pensions:			
Service-connected compensation:			
Existing law	6,743	7,411	7,471
Proposed legislation	–	–	846
Non-service-connected pensions	3,522	3,712	4,032
Burial and other benefits	177	185	190
Insurance programs:			
National service life insurance trust fund	785	803	931
U.S. Government life insurance trust fund	71	69	64
All other insurance programs	– 60	– 62	– 54
Insurance program receipts	– 458	– 458	– 445
Subtotal, income security for veterans	10,780	11,660	13,034
Veterans education, training, and rehabilitation:			
Existing law	2,760	2,226	1,750
Proposed legislation	–	–	193
Subtotal, education, training, and rehabilitation	2,760	2,226	1,943
Hospital and medical care for veterans:			
Medical care and hospital services:			
Existing law	5,159	5,926	6,101
Proposed legislation	–	– 45	– 353
Construction	251	274	381
Medical administration, research, and other	201	226	242
Subtotal, hospital and medical care	5,611	6,380	6,370
Veterans housing:			
Loan guaranty revolving fund	207	– 32	– 195
Direct loan revolving fund	– 65	– 175	– 107
Other (HUD participation sales trust fund)	12	22	2
Subtotal, veterans housing	154	– 184	– 300
Other veterans benefits and services:			
Undistributed VA overhead and other:			
Existing law	598	654	655
Proposed legislation	–	–	– 1
Non-VA support programs	29	32	32
Subtotal, other benefits and services	627	687	686
Deductions for offsetting receipts	– 4	– 3	– 3
Total, outlays	19,928	20,766	21,731

*$500 thousand or less.
Source: The Budget of the United States Government, FY 1981

for these benefits have been dramatically curtailed in the post-Vietnam era, this category of expenditure will decline sharply over the next decade.

Most of this essay will concern the remaining two groups. These both are composed of older veterans with disabilities. The distinction between them involves the source of those disabilities: (1) Veterans whose disabilities developed during, or as a result of, military service; and (2) those whose disabilities are unrelated to that service. This distinction applies to the services and benefits received by these two separate groups. Those veterans in the first category are entitled to "service-connected" benefits; those in the latter may receive only "non-service-connected" benefits.

A careful reading between the lines here reveals two distinct functions being served by the sets of benefits received by each group. Although the benefits themselves are essentially the same (at least qualitatively), the underlying rationale for each is different. Benefits provided to veterans with "service-connected" conditions are regarded as a form of delayed compensation for those disabilities. Participants in combat face risks of injury or death which are not borne by workers in civilian jobs. The Veterans Administration provides income as well as medical services for the disabled and their survivors in recognition of these risks and sacrifices. Income payments received under this program are called compensation. (Item 1 of Table 1.)

A second function served by the Veterans Administration has nothing to do with "compensation" as such. The VA plays a custodial role to many indigent members of society whose "need" for such assistance is not traceable to their performance of military service. Income payments and medical care are also provided to veterans and their survivors with "non-service-connected" disabilities, though income payments received under this program are called pensions to distinguish them from compensation payments. (Item 2 of Table 1.) The rationalization for benefits to these veterans is fundamentally paternalistic. As such they clearly duplicate benefits extended to the population at large under the Social Security, Public Assistance, and Medicare and Medicaid programs. As entitlements to "non-service-connected" disabilities are uniformly more generous than benefits extended under these other programs, questions may be raised concerning both the equity and appropriateness of what appears to be a redundant, anachronistic, and perhaps wasteful program.

Although the present interpretation and scope of the concept "service-connected" for the purposes of qualifying for these benefits may be challenged, there can be no question that the federal government has the responsibility to provide income and needed medical attention for combat casualties. Indeed, some evidence exists that benefits to veterans and their survivors with combat-related disabilities fall far short of adequate "compensation." Criticism here is aimed chiefly at benefits provided to veterans with "non-service-connected" disabilities. For the purposes of comparing the validity of

287

the first with the possible redundancy of the second, we will examine benefits extended to both groups in detail.

SHORT-TERM POLICIES

Service-Connected Compensation

One of the first acts of the Continental Congress was to call for pensions to be paid to soldiers and sailors incapacitated in battle during the American Revolution. Disabled veterans of every war since have received some form of compensation from the federal government, and the claim of such war casualties to compensation is undeniable. Wartime service is offered for the most part out of a sense of patriotic duty. Performance of this duty, therefore, implies the reciprocal responsibility of the nation to care for those who have been struck down. If service-connected compensation were limited, as it was originally, to cases involving battle-related injury, budgetary examination of these entitlements would be limited to assessing the adequacy of the benefits.

It is the revised interpretation of the phrase "service-connected," extending compensable disability far beyond the bounds of battle wounds, which raises questions concerning the equity and appropriateness of current "compensation" policy. Those veterans injured in literal defense of their country are no longer a distinguishable group compensated for extraordinary sacrifice. In order to examine this merging of two separate areas of benefit, it is necessary to assess the current criteria for eligibility.

Members of the armed services are assumed to be "on duty" continuously: an injury or illness suffered at home or on vacation qualifies a claimant for compensation just as if it were received in battle. A spinal cord injury is equally compensable whether it is received on the battlefield or in diving into a resort swimming pool. Qualification for compensation makes no distinction between tropical diseases contracted in Vietnam and chronic bronchitis developed during stateside assignment. An incapacitating stroke suffered while in bed may entitle a serviceman to the same compensation received by a soldier with a serious head wound. No attempt is made to relate compensable disabilities to the performance of a job, much less to participation in hostilities.

Whether these non-combat-related disabilities warrant compensation or not, it is clear that the ultimate justification for honoring these claims cannot lie in a simple extension of the argument for compensation for war wounds. Civilians are at risk for most of these same diseases and injuries, yet few employers stand ready to "compensate" their workers for conditions having no relation to job performance. A comparison to state "workmen's compensation" laws is instructive here. Workmen's compensation may be regarded as a form of insur-

288

ance against the risk of disability suffered in the performance of private sector jobs. Workmen's compensation does not honor claims for off-the-job injury or even illness contracted while at work. Civilian employees wishing to extend their "insurance" coverage to these risks must supplement job-related compensation with additional private insurance and retirement plans. Many do.

It might be argued that such generous treatment of non-combat-related disabilities merely represents a part of an efficient "fringe-benefit" package offered to attract military manpower. This argument would have to show that inclusion of this "fringe" is valued by military volunteers more than a simple pay raise of equal cost. Assessment of the validity of such an argument would require a great deal of information unavailable at this writing. We do not even know, for example, the amounts paid and the percentage of claims falling into the category of non-combat-related compensation. Available evidence raises serious doubts about the plausibility of such a justification, however. That the cost in terms of "foregone" pay is substantial is suggested by the fact that in 1979 service-related compensation paid by the VA represented 25 percent of the total Defense Department outlays for military manpower. If non-combat-related disabilities accounted for only one-fifth of all service-related claims, eliminating these payments would have permitted military pay increases of 5 percent across the board.

Furthermore, evidence suggests that such broad-gauged disability "insurance" is an inefficient way to reward servicemen. Most claims are for partial disability involving small monthly payments. The cost of qualifying for and administering these payments represents a substantial part of the cost of the total package. Each claim must be verified by a physical examination (paid for by the VA) and considered by a VA rating board which establishes the validity of the claim and the extent of disability. Yet 40 percent of all claims honored are for disabilities rated at 10 percent or less. The average monthly value of all such claims in 1978 was only $185 per claim, and the value of disabilities judged to be 10 percent was only $41. Clearly, the cost of qualifying for and administering these small payments consumes much of what otherwise would be paid as salary.

Finally, if such insurance were part of an attractive "fringe benefit" reimbursement package, we would expect to see it widely replicated in the private sector. The risk of non-combat-related disability is present to an approximately equal extent in most private employment. We should, therefore, expect civilian workers to demand similar "fringes" from their employers if they are cost-effective. The rarity of similar provisions in private employment contracts raises serious doubts concerning the efficiency of this practice as a means of paying our military manpower.

Compensation payments should be limited to veterans and survivors of veterans whose disabilities are traceable either to combat or job-performance as defined under workmen's compensation regulations.

Advocates of the current compensation fear that the reduction of veterans' benefits would make military service less attractive, thus making the enlistment of adequate numbers into the armed services more difficult. Veterans, by serving their country, have earned these benefits, and to withhold them would be callous and ungrateful.

Private employers experience little difficulty in attracting workers without these extraordinary benefits. As the risks of disability of this type are essentially equal in civilian and military employment, the difficulty of attracting adequate recruits should be approximately equal also. All men and women serving in the military are entitled to our gratitude, not merely those who are disabled during that service. Fairness requires expressing that gratitude through adequate pay for all, rather than through benefits limited to those whose disabilities have no connection with performance of military duty.

We lack data on the relative shares of compensation going to those who would be excluded and those who would continue to receive benefits under this program. Without this information only the sketchiest estimates of expected savings can be made. It must also be recognized that some veterans dropped from the compensation program would be entitled to increased payments from other sources, at least partially financed by federal dollars, such as public assistance. Total compensation is budgeted at $9.2 billion for FY 1982. Assuming that adoption of this recommendation would delete 20 percent of the present recipients from the rolls, we would find a savings of roughly $1.8 billion in that year and similar savings in subsequent years.

Non-Service-Connected Pensions

For every 100 disability cases judged to be service-connected, the VA finances pensions to 45 veterans whose entitlement has no connection whatever to their military service. Eligibility for a pension requires prior service of a specific length (normally 90 days or more) during a war period together with a permanent disability and an income below specific limits. Those veterans reaching the age of 65 are assumed to be disabled without physician examination. Nearly a million veterans (980,000) are projected to receive pensions under this program in fiscal year 1981, averaging $2,602 per claimant. Total pensions to veterans under this program are projected to cost $2.5 billion.

In addition to payments of pensions to veterans with non-service-connected disabilities, the VA also pensions widows and children of deceased veterans. Widows qualify on the basis of need alone. Chil-

290

dren of deceased veterans may continue to receive these benefits up to age 23 if they remain full-time students and indefinitely if they become disabled while pensioned. A total of 1.2 million survivors of veterans are projected to receive these benefits in FY 1981, averaging $1,309 per recipient. Indeed, there are more than three times the number of survivors receiving pensions under this program than are receiving compensation as survivors of servicemen who died "in the line of duty." Although the latter benefits are typically more generous, total expenditure for "pensions" to survivors of this category is projected to be $1.55 billion, exceeding the amount projected for "service-connected" compensation to survivors ($1.33 billion).

The cost of these pensions will escalate rapidly in the 1980s if they continue to be granted as liberally. This cost increase will result from two trends which will converge in the early part of this decade. The first of these is a product of the age distribution of veterans. This distribution reflects the varying extent of mobilization into the armed forces in the recent past. Nearly half of all war veterans served in World War II, the remainder are scattered among other war periods of this century. The average age of these veterans is 60 years, yet most have not reached the age of 65. Indeed, in 1978, 43 percent of all war veterans were between the ages of 50 and 65 and thus can be expected to reach 65 before the year 1994.

The second of these factors is the relation between age and qualification for VA pensions. Few veterans qualify before the age of 65, due to the requirement that disability must be established by a physical examination before that age. In 1978, for example, only 6.6 percent of veterans from ages 60–64 were receiving pensions. At age 65, however, the granting of pensions increases significantly, and the incidence of pensions grows dramatically with age thereafter (Table 2). According to these data, the likelihood that a veteran will receive a pension within the first ten years after reaching 65 is nearly one in five.

Let us assume that only 15 percent of the 11.5 million veterans reaching the age of 65 during this period qualify for pensions. This would add 1.7 million additional veterans to the pension roles, increasing our pension obligation over the next thirteen years by 189 percent! Assuming that these benefits continue to be extended at current levels,[1] real costs of non-service-connected pensions will rise from the projected level of $3.8 billion in 1981 to $11.0 billion in 1993.

Non-service-connected pensions could easily become the most costly single item in the VA budget during this decade. Although total service-connected compensation currently accounts for more outlays than any other program, these costs are likely to rise much less dramatically

---

[1]The Veterans and Survivors' Pension Improvement Act of 1978 indexed these pensions to provide automatic cost-of-living increases comparable to annual social security increases.

Table 2
Veterans Receiving Non-Service-Connected VA Pensions as a Percentage of Eligible Veterans by Age: September 1978

(1) Age	(2) Eligible Vets[1] (thousands)	(3) Pensions (thousands)	(4) (3)/(2)
60–64	2,300	151	.066
60–69	1,019	141	.138
70–74	455	87	.191
75–79	190	46	.242
80–84	420	150	.357
85 up	170	83	.488
65 up	2,252[2]	508[2]	.226

Source: Veterans Administration: Annual Report 1978 and author's computations.

[1]Eligible veterans: total war veterans minus those receiving service-connected pensions.

[2]Individual age groups do not sum to total due to rounding error

than pensions during the next decade. Few veterans are awarded service-connected compensation after more than two years have elapsed since their discharge. For particular age cohorts, the percentage of veterans receiving compensation is, therefore, unlikely to change from year to year. Most of those who will qualify for compensation already receive it. As this large group of middle-aged veterans moves into the post-65 year category, we will not observe the increasing incidence of benefits which characterizes the pensioner group. Only 7.3 percent of eligible under-65 veterans currently receive compensation benefits, and there is little reason to expect a larger proportion of this group to qualify during the 1980s. Compensation outlays will thus remain static in real terms at roughly $8.4 billion, while non-service-connected pensions will grow to exceed this level by nearly one-third by 1993.

In view of the budgetary importance of this item, serious thought must be given to its underlying rationale. Veterans and their survivors qualifying for pensions do so on the basis of need alone. This need bears no relation to military service, and may, therefore, be thought of as a separate income security program operated exclusively for ex-servicemen. Furthermore, benefits under this program are far more generous than similar public assistance programs operated by many states.[2]

The maintenance of a separate and preferential welfare system for

[2]For a detailed comparison of benefits under veterans' pensions and public assistance (although prior to the Veterans' and Survivors' Pension Improvement Act of 1978), see S. A. Levitan and K. A. Cleary, Old Wars Remain Unfinished (Baltimore: The Johns Hopkins University Press, 1973), p. 60ff.

Table 3
Economic and Educational Performance of
Veterans and Non-veterans 1977–1978

	War Vets	Male Non-Vets
Unemployment Rate (FY '78)	3.8	6.6
Year of Education (Mar '78)	12.6	12.5
% with H.S. Degrees (Mar '78)	86.8	65.0
% with College Degrees (Mar '78)	18.0	18.0
Median Income by Education Level (1977)		
Less than high school	$ 7,450	$ 5,370
Some high school	10,930	7,450
High school graduate	13,620	10,440
Some college	15,270	8,750
College graduate	20,990	15,550
Family Income (1977)	$19,800	$15,540

Source: Veterans Administration: *Annual Report 1978*

veterans is questionable on equity grounds. It cannot be convincingly argued that veterans who have not suffered service-connected disability have been disadvantaged by their military duty. Indeed, veterans as a group typically outperform their non-veteran counterparts in the civilian economy. Table 3 presents some comparisons of the economic and educational performance of veterans and non-veterans.

Veterans typically experience less unemployment. Only 15 percent of all male veterans failed to work in 1977, compared to 20.3 percent of the non-veteran men. Educational attainment is slightly higher among veterans than non-veterans, and earnings by education level are from 30 to 75 percent higher for veterans.

Vietnam era veterans, particularly the very young veterans of this conflict, do not compare as favorably with their non-veteran cohorts. Family income for these veterans exceeded that of non-veterans by only 8 percent. This supports the argument that veterans face transitional problems entering the civilian economy. Finding the right job and accumulating skills and experience are tasks that require time. The VA offers many programs to ease this transition, however, and evidence suggests that they are, for the most part, successful.

The premiums earned by older veterans appear to more than compensate for these initial hurdles. Doubtless VA-financed education and on-the-job training play a role here. To single out this group for preferential dispensations of public assistance, therefore, appears merely to add yet another economic advantage to the many already enjoyed by veterans.

A tradition of pensions for "old soldiers" existed long before the enactment of the New Deal legislation which provided Social Security to the elderly. The introduction of that program has seriously eroded the rationale for a non-service-connected pension system. As long ago as 1956 a presidential commission was convened to study veterans benefits in light of the apparent duplication of many services and benefits newly extended to the civilian population. This commission chaired by General Omar N. Bradley concluded:

> The non-service-connected benefits are the lowest priority among veterans' programs. Their justification is weak and their philosphy is backward looking rather than constructive. Our society has developed more equitable means of meeting most of the same needs and big strides are being made in closing remaining gaps. The non-service-connected benefits should be limited to a minimum level and retained only as a reserve line of honorable protection for veterans whose means are shown to be inadequate and who fail to qualify for basic protection under the general Old-Age and Survivors Insurance system.[3]

Though this advice has been ignored for a quarter of a century, it seems as valid today as it did in 1956.

Congress should eliminate all pensions for veterans and survivors of veterans which are not compensable as "service-connected."

Non-service-connected pensions are justified on two grounds: Pensions are a method of honoring those who fought to defend our liberty. Withdrawing these pensions would be to dishonor those to whom we owe this debt. Secondly, withdrawing these pensions would merely shift the burden of providing for this indigent population onto states and local governments who can ill afford it.

Military service should be adequately compensated at the time it is performed. Those who are not disabled in combat suffer no disadvantage as a result of that service and, when otherwise disabled, should receive no special treatment not extended to the rest of the American public. Federal resources can be made available to states and local governments to finance income maintenance on an equitable basis for all citizens.

Although some of those currently receiving pensions will make larger claims on other funding sources which are at least partially federally sponsored, the extent of this shifted requirement is unlikely to exceed 20 percent of current appropriations. Deletion of the total pension program will, therefore, save at least $3.38 billion in FY 1982. Due to the important demographic factor discussed above, adoption of this recommendation is projected to save $8.8 billion per year by FY 1993.

Hospital and Medical Care

One of the gaps which remained to be closed in 1956 was a program to extend medical care, when needed, to members of the population unable to obtain it themselves. The operation of VA hospitals, once

---

[3]President's Commission on Veterans' Pensions, *A Report on Veterans' Benefits in the United States: Findings and Recommendations* (Washington: GPO, 1956), p. 138.

needed as a welfare service for indigent veterans, is now redundant. As the Bradley Commission foresaw, this problem would be dealt with, as was the problem of economic security during old age, with a government program broadening access to medical care. The passage of the Medicare-Medicaid bill in 1965 provided both medical and hospital care to the two sizable populations in American society who could not reasonably be expected to provide it for themselves: the aged, because private insurance companies would not insure them, and the poor, who could not afford to pay insurance premiums.

The existence of these two programs raises serious doubts about the need for the costly health care system operated by the Veterans Administration. This system consists of 144 VA general hospitals, 28 VA psychiatric hospitals, 16 domiciliaries, 97 nursing homes and 229 outpatient clinics, scattered throughout the various states to reach the veterans population. Nearly 200,000 employees representing 88 percent of the entire staff of the VA are associated with one of these medical care facilities.

The operation of such an extensive health care system is justified by the Veterans Administration on two bases: the first is the obvious responsibility to provide care for those suffering disabilities arising directly from combat. However, the VA sees an important responsibility to provide medical care to medically indigent veterans whose conditions bear no connection with past military service. As was the case with veterans pensions, the extension of medical care to indigent ex-servicemen began early in our history, before the federal government acknowledged a responsibility to provide these benefits to the civilian population in general. Here an additional argument may be added to the objections raised above concerning pensions. The VA is now duplicating, at great expense, existing health care programs. Provision of special hospitals for veterans of either category is an inefficient way of extending health care benefits.

When the federal government chose to provide hospital and medical benefits to the elderly and medically indigent, they did not attempt to organize a separate hospital system for this purpose. The U.S. already had a robust and growing hospital sector amply financed through private insurance reimbursement and federal Hill-Burton construction grants. Today, our economy boasts more than 7,000 non-federal hospitals, and most governmental energies are being directed toward eliminating redundant hospital beds rather than adding to the stock.

The veteran population is widely dispersed. With only the existing 144 general hospitals in place, it would be impossible to supply veterans with the sort of neighborhood service and protection which each already has in the existing non-federal hospital sector. Currently, there is only one VA general hospital for every 21,000 square miles in the 48 contiguous states and none in Alaska or Hawaii. Almost one-third of all veterans live more than 50 miles from a VA hospital and one in ten lives more than 100 miles from such a facility. With such distances involved it is not surprising, therefore, that 85 percent of all veteran hospitalizations take place outside the VA system. Indeed, according to a 1971 survey, nearly three out of four veterans on the compensation and pension rolls (and thus with the greatest priority to VA hospitalization) found it expedient to enroll in some form of medical insurance.[4]

These data tell us that for many veterans the use of VA medical attention is inconvenient, and that most seek that attention elsewhere. One is, therefore, led to question the basis on which the Veterans Administration and Congress justify its continued supply. One seemingly promising explanation is that care of veterans requires special skills and talents which can only be fully exploited by collecting many veterans under one roof. The treatment of war-related injuries might be thought to require the services of specialists not typically found in community general hospitals. Examination of case-load data fails to support such an explanation.

In the first place, few veterans in VA hospitals actually suffer from war-related or even service-connected disabilities (Table 4). Of the 72,034 patients in these institutions in 1978, only one in six was being treated for a service-connected condition. Less than one in ten discharges involved such a disability. Well over two-thirds of these patients were neither being treated for nor had ever had any disability associated with their military duties.

Table 5 lists all those diagnostic categories in which the VA was treating more than 1,000 patients on a sample day in 1978. One scans this list in vain in search of cases of battlefield trauma or disease contracted in the fetid jungles of southeast Asia. Most of these problems are routinely treated in every general hospital in the country.

Two out of five patients are suffering from mental disorders or alcoholism, but even here it is difficult to trace a link to past performance of military duty. The average age of patients with mental disorders reported here is 54; the average age of those patients suffering from alcoholism is 48. Only 37 percent of all psychoses were reported to be even 10 percent service-connected. Drinking may indeed be, as John Dryden wrote, "the soldier's pleasure," but it is certainly not a problem found only in military life. If the VA health system is to be justified on the basis of economies of scale in the treatment of war-related injuries and diseases, then patients in these two categories represent a slender reed on which to base such a justification.

---

[4]Levitan and Cleary, *op. cit.*, p. 75.

Table 4
VA Hospital Patients Remaining and Discharges
By Disability Status, 1978

	Patients Remaining	Percent	Discharges	Percent
All patients	72,034	100.0	942,070	100.0
Service-Connected Conditions	12,241	17.0	93,053	9.9
10% or more disability	11,599	16.1	91,316	9.7
less than 10%	642	0.9	1,737	0.2
Condition Not-Service-Connected, but patient with S.C. Disability	8,358	11.6	144,377	15.3
No Service Connection	51,060	70.9	693,260	73.6
Pension	19,101	26.5	210,027	22.3
Other	31,959	44.4	483,233	51.3
Non-Veterans	375	0.5	6,750	0.7

Source: Veterans Administration: *Annual Report 1978.*

Table 5
Diagnostic Categories Containing more than 1,000 Patients
Remaining in VA Hospitals, October 4, 1978

	Number	Percent
All diseases and conditions	72,034	100.0
Cancer of digestive organs and peritoneum	1,000	1.4
Cancer of respiratory system	1,536	2.1
Diabetes mellitus	1,234	1.7
Psychosis with organic brain syndrome (excluding alcohol and drug dependence)	2,846	4.0
Psychosis not attributed to physical condition	15,036	20.9
Alcoholism	5,120	7.1
Non-psychotic organic brain syndrome	3,394	4.7
Other non-psychotic mental disorders	2,660	3.7
Diseases of the central nervous system	1,783	2.5
Chronic ischemic heart disease	1,510	2.1
Other forms of heart disease	1,093	1.5
Other cerebrovascular disease	2,243	3.1
Other diseases of arteries, arterioles, & capillaries	1,076	1.5
Other diseases of liver, gall bladder and pancreas	1,012	1.4
Arthritis and rheumatism	1,045	1.5
Symptoms and all other ill-defined conditions	2,569	3.6

Source: Veterans Administration: *Annual Report 1978.*

A second argument for government-organized hospitals for veterans might be made on the basis of cost. Private sector hospitals have not distinguished themselves in the past two decades by being conspicuously cost conscious institutions. Defenders of the VA hospital system might, therefore, seek to justify direct provision of such services as an economy measure. Indeed, a simple comparison of per diem costs of treatment in VA and private sector hospitals from 1969 to 1973 suggests that costs per patient day are from 30 to 55 percent

297

lower in the former hospitals than the latter.[5] Unfortunately for this argument, these economies in daily treatment cost vanish when costs are compared by number of cases treated. Bureaucratic incentives influence the retention of VA patients for longer stays. Comparisons of lengths of stay for VA and private hospital patients consistently show that stays in VA hospitals are about twice as long as those in private hospitals. Appropriate comparisons of costs reflecting this difference will, therefore, indicate higher costs per case treated by VA hospitals.[6]

Therefore, it is recommended that the present VA health care system be dismantled. VA hospitals and other facilities should be turned over to local governments or private groups where their continued operation is economically viable. Those veterans with legitimate claims for medical attention of service-connected conditions may obtain that care on a reimbursable basis from community facilities as do present Medicare-Medicaid patients.

Defenders of the present system argue that disabled veterans in VA hospitals will be turned over to crowded community facilities which have no space for them and little understanding of the special health care problems of veterans. Treating those veterans with non-reimbursable disabilities will seriously drain community resources already pressed by the fiscal demand of financing Medicaid.

Most community facilities are not crowded today. Recent legislative initiatives of the Carter Administration have sought to encourage these hospitals to reduce the number of active beds. All but a handful of VA patients suffer from conditions contracted in civilian life with which most community facilities deal on routine bases. This change would permit those veterans with compensable disabilities to be treated nearer home by a physician of their choosing. For those veterans whose conditions are not related to military service (83 percent of those currently being treated in VA hospitals), there seems no reason to treat their cases any differently from civilians whose circumstances are similar. The federal Medicare program currently provides generous medical benefits for the elderly, and the Medicaid program provides similar coverage for the indigent. Veterans with non-service-connected medical needs who are not covered by either of these programs should look to their own resources for this care just as do the great majority of their fellow Americans.

Savings

Total spending for hospital and medical care by the VA is budgeted at $6.8 billion for FY 1982. Elimination of direct provision of health

---

[5]Cotton M. Lindsay, "A Theory of Government Enterprise," *Journal of Political Economy,* 84 (October 1976), pp. 1061–1077.

[6]*Ibid.,* p. 1073.

Table 6
Cost Savings Attributable to VA Health Care Recommendations
FY 1982 (millions)

VA Health Care Budget FY 1982			$6,766
Continuing Federal Spending for Health Care for Veterans:			
Care for Service-Connected Conditions (17 percent of existing budget)		$1,150	
Increase in Medicare Costs:			
Care for NSC over 65	$1,685		
Less Deductibles and Copayments	(388)	1,297	
Increase in Medicaid Costs:			
Care for NSC 65 and under	$3,931		
Less Cost of those not Qualifying for Medicaid	(1,376)		
Less State Share of Medicaid	(1,277)	1,277	3,724
Net Savings to Federal Budget, FY 1982			$3,042

services by the VA will not, of course, lead to a net reduction in federal spending of this amount. The VA will continue to have the responsibility for the financing of needed care to those with service-connected conditions. Some of those who qualified as indigent under the more liberal standards applied by the VA will qualify for Medicaid care financed on a matching fund basis by the federal government and the states. Those elderly patients now treated by VA hospitals will presumably seek coverage of their care under the Medicare program. Substantial savings should nevertheless result from implementing this recommendation.

Calculation of these savings is presented in Table 6. The current budget for FY 1982 provides for $6.8 billion for health care. Seventeen percent of those patients treated by the VA have service-connected conditions and must continue to be treated. The cost of this treatment in community facilities is assumed to be equal to its cost in VA facilities; hence, this care is budgeted at 17 percent of the health care budget, that is, $1,150 million.

Slightly under 30 percent of all non-service-connected patients in VA hospitals are over 65 years old. As these patients will automatically qualify for Medicare, implementing this proposal will increase the costs of this program by the federal share of these costs. Assuming that 30 percent of non-service-connected medicine is devoted to this population, and that 23 percent of these costs will be borne by patients in the form of deductibles and co-payments, results in a federal outlay of $1,297 million.

Means tests for admission to VA hospitals are somewhat more lenient than for Medicaid programs in most states. It is, therefore, estimated that 35 percent of those under 65 qualifying for admission to VA hospitals would not qualify for Medicaid. Deducting these costs and also

Table 7
Currently Budgeted Outlays for
Veterans Benefits and Proposed Changes FY 1982
(millions)

	Budgeted	Proposed Change	New Budget*
1. Service-Connected Compensation	$ 9,202	($1,800)	$ 7,402
2. Non-Service-Connected Pensions	4,230	(3,380)	850
3. Hospital and Medical Care	6,766	(3,042)	3,724
4. Veterans Education, etc.	1,534	(none)	1,534
5. Other	1,430	(none)	1,430
Total	$23,162	($8,222)	$14,940

the state share of half of all Medicaid appropriations leaves a net increase of Medicaid expenditure of $1,277 million. Total continuing federal spending for health care for veterans would thus be $3,724 million, leaving a savings of $3.0 billion for this fiscal year.

LONG-TERM CONSIDERATIONS

President Carter's budget for 1981 expressly limits VA benefits to the meeting of "special needs of veterans and their dependents and survivors that result from the sacrifices that veterans have made in military service to this country." Medical care and rehabilitation of those disabled in combat clearly represents such a "special need." Hospitalization for diabetes does not. Compensation payments to the widows and minor children of soldiers killed in action recognizes the larger risks associated with military duty. Pensions to elderly ex-servicemen and their survivors serves a need which is shared alike by civilians with no former military service. Education and training for those pressed into service in time of national emergency merely compensates for interrupted preparation for other careers. A preferential income maintenance program for veterans fails to recognize that, as a group, veterans are not permanently either educationally or economically disadvantaged by having performed military service. On the contrary, they earn considerably more than their non-veteran counterparts.

The Veterans Administration has been a pathbreaker in the introduction of social welfare programs in this country. Long before the New Deal, elderly veterans were provided a measure of income security through the granting of pensions. Those who required custodial care were placed in National Homes. Hospitals organized expressly for the treatment of veterans were opened after World War I. However, many of the needs first recognized for veterans are now being served for a much larger population by more modern and better designed systems. Income security for retired veterans as well as non-veterans is provided through OASI. Financial support for the indigent veteran and non-veteran is available through federally supported state public assistance payments. Medical care for the elderly and the indigent is available through Medicare and Medicaid to veteran and non-veteran alike.

It is time to return to the drawing board with a sharply circumscribed view of the mission for the Veterans Administration in the 1980s. Veterans do have special needs. Many of these are admirably served by the VA together with the host of voluntary organizations with which it works. Serving those special needs will doubtless be more easily accomplished when those non-essential and redundant functions discussed above no longer occupy the attention, energies, and financial resources of this agency.

14

Federal Aid to State and Local Governments

by Richard E. Wagner

President Carter's initial budget proposal for 1981 allocated $96.3 billion for federal aid to state and local governments. The actual programs financed through the federal government have been treated in this volume under the appropriate budget functions: transportation (highway construction, urban mass transit), community and regional development (community development block grants, urban development action grants), education, training, employment, and social services (elementary and secondary education, employment and training assistance), health (medicaid), and income security (low income energy assistance, child nutrition, public assistance). This essay is concerned not with these expenditures *per se*, but with the implications of these expenditures for the character of our federalist system of government. Programs of federal aid, in other words, are examined with respect to how they strengthen or weaken the functioning of that system.

A federalist system of government is closely related to a free enterprise system of economic organization, for both are decentralized systems in which people face options among which they can choose.[1] Just as people can choose among producers of goods and services in a market economy, so can they choose among units of government in a federalist political system. In both cases, it is competition for peoples' support, not monopoly power, that guides the organization of production. While some governmental actions are capable of strengthening the federalist system (just as they are capable of strengthening the market system), other actions are capable of weakening this system (just as they can weaken the market system by strengthening

---

[1] On federalism and the consent of the government, see Martin Diamond, "The Federalists' View of Federalism," in *Essays in Federalism* (Claremont, Ca.: Institute for Studies in Federalism, Claremont Men's College, 1961), pp. 21–64. See also, Vincent Ostrom, *The Political Theory of a Compound Republic* (Blacksburg, Va.: Center for Study of Public Choice, Virginia Polytechnic Institute and State University, 1971).

303

the forces of monopoly). Accordingly, programs of federal aid can also be assessed in terms of whether they strengthen or weaken the ability of our federalist system to provide effectively for those wants that are most effectively provided for through government. The first section of this essay describes briefly the scope and variety of programs of federal aid to state and local governments. The second evaluates these programs from the perspective of whether they strengthen or weaken our federalist system. The third and final section discusses possible options for future reform that are consistent with strengthening our federalist system.

A Brief Description of Federal Aid

The $96.3 billion initial budget proposal for federal aid to state and local governments represented a four-fold increase from the $24.1 billion of aid outlays in 1970, and represented a more than thirteen-fold increase from the $7 billion of aid in 1960. During an era of rapidly expanding federal budgets, programs of federal aid have been expanding even more rapidly. In 1960, federal aid accounted for 7.8 percent of federal expenditures. Ten years later federal aid had increased to 12.2 percent of federal outlays. President Carter's initial 1981 budget proposed a level of federal aid equal to 15.7 percent of proposed federal outlays. A more dramatic and telling measure of the federal government's expansion is the share of state and local government spending financed through federal assistance. In 1950, federal aid amounted to 10.4 percent of state and local spending. By 1960 this percentage had risen to 14.7. During the decade 1960–1970, federal assistance expanded to 19.4 percent. For the current fiscal year it is expected to reach 25.3 percent. Thus, over a thirty-year period, the locus of responsibility for financing of the activities of state and local government has shifted dramatically in the direction of federal responsibility.

Programs of federal aid, while present in all cabinet departments and budget functions, are of course concentrated in departments and functions in which the activities undertaken are largely of a state and local nature. Nearly one-third, $30.8 billion, of the proposed 1981 assistance was to be spent by the Department of Health and Human Services. The Departments of Transportation and Labor were each to spend more than 10 percent of the total amount of aid, with the respective amounts being $11.6 and $11.1 billion. Other significant programs are administered by the Departments of Housing and Urban Development ($8.8 billion) and the Treasury ($8.2 billion, mainly for revenue sharing). With respect to budget functions, nearly two-thirds of total aid expenditures occur in three functions: education, training, employment, and social services ($23.2 billion), income security ($20.3 billion), and health ($17.8 billion). When transportation ($12.3

billion) and general purpose fiscal assistance ($9.4 billion) are added, over 85 percent of all federal aid is represented.

The picture that emerges is one of substantial and rapidly expanding programs of federal aid to state and local governments, concentrated in a few areas of activity that have traditionally been under the aegis of state and local governments. The largest federal aid program, for instance, is Medicaid, which was initially proposed for $15.8 billion in 1981. A few other of the particularly large programs are those for highway construction ($7.7 billion), public assistance ($7.4 billion), revenue sharing ($6.9 billion), construction of sewage treatment plants ($4.0 billion), community development block grants ($3.8 billion), elementary and secondary education ($3.7 billion), child nutrition ($3.0 billion), urban mass transit ($2.6 billion), block grants under the Comprehensive Employment and Training Act ($2.0 billion), low income energy assistance ($1.7 billion), and anti-recession fiscal assistance ($1.0 billion).

Programs of federal aid are customarily separated into three main categories: categorical grants, block grants, and general purpose grants. In the initial 1981 budget proposal, categorical grants were allocated $76.7 billion, block grants $10.0 billion, and general purpose grants $9.6 billion. It is commonly suggested that this separation classifies programs of federal aid according to the stringency of federal control over state and local governments.[2] Categorical grants, which are sometimes referred to as conditional grants, to indicate that their receipt depends upon the fulfillment of conditions specified by the grantor, would have the most stringent requirements. A frequently used condition is a requirement that state or local recipient governments match with their own funds their receipt of federal aid. Block grants cover a wider range of activities, so they might seem to involve less stringent federal control over state and local activities. Indeed, some block grant programs were created by consolidating several categorical grant programs into a single, broader program. For instance, the block grant program for community development resulted from a consolidation of such former categorical grants as urban renewal, model cities, neighborhood facilities, water and sewer facilities, and rehabilitation loans, among others. General purpose grants, primarily revenue sharing, are typically portrayed as contrasting sharply with categorical grants, for the recipient governments are able to spend the grants largely as they see fit, or at least without detailed supervision.

---

[2]See, for instance, George F. Break, "Intergovernmental Fiscal Relations," in *Setting National Priorities: Agenda for the 1980s* (Washington: Brookings Institution, 1980), pp. 247–81.

An Assessment of Federal Aid

Although categorical grants account for more than three-quarters of federal aid expenditures, they have been declining in relative importance over the past decade. Thus it might seem that grant programs have been evolving in the direction of reducing federal control over state and local governments. It is erroneous to infer that the decline in the relative importance of categorical grants implies a reduction in the extent of federal control over state and local governments, i.e., an increase in the extent to which government is based on the "consent of the governed." For the most part, however, programs of federal aid to state and local government weaken rather than strengthen the consensual elements in our federalist system, for reasons to be explained below. *A combination of reduction in federal taxation and federal aid would make a substantial contribution to strengthening our federalist system;* conversely, further expansions in federal aid will drive our system of government yet farther away from being grounded in the consent of the governed.

Categorical Grants

As noted above, requirements for matching are a prominent type of control over state and local governments exercised by the federal government. Such grant programs have also been used to exercise control over the decisions of state and local governments about hiring and compensation, as, for instance, when these governments have been forced to pay union wages on construction projects. The receipt of federal health grants depends on the creation of agencies empowered to regulate the decisions of hospitals on such things as expansions in the size of their facilities and their purchases of major equipment. The extension of unemployment insurance to public employees has been made a condition for states to qualify for employer tax credits under the unemployment insurance program. To receive aid for highway construction, states are required to comply with federal safety standards in constructing their highways. Likewise, state conformity to the 55 m.p.h. speed limit was imposed as a condition for receiving federal highway aid. Numerous other illustrations of federal controls imposed as a condition for receiving federal grants could be presented; federal aid always carries with it strings or conditions of some kind, so an expansion in federal aid will increase the extent of federal control over state and local governments.[3]

Some have argued that this centralization is necessary if our govern-

---

[3]For a description and discussion of these controls, see *Federal Constraints on State and Local Government Actions,* Congressional Budget Office, Background Paper (Washington: U.S. Government Printing Office, 1979).

mental institutions are to cope with the increasing complexity and pace of contemporary life. The centralization that categorical aid entails is regarded as necessary to maintain the consent of the governed. In contrast, others have argued that the increasing centralization reflects not a consensus among the governed, but the outcome of a process in which power is used to benefit some at the expense of others. These widely divergent attitudes about categorical grants were epitomized during a 1965 congressional hearing in an exchange between Charles E. Goodell, then a member of the House of Representatives from New York, and Anthony J. Celebrezze, then Secretary of Health, Education, and Welfare: " 'What makes me tear my hair in frustration is when you say there are no controls', Mr. Goodell said. 'Mr. Goodell, you call it controls, I call it objectives,' Mr. Celebrezze replied quietly."[4]

Efforts have been made to rationalize categorical grants by arguing that they represent a type of contract. According to this line of rationalization, the federal government offers grants to state and local governments in exchange for their agreement to act in specified ways, perhaps by constructing interstate highways or by constructing plants for the treatment of sewage. Categorical grants are viewed as being necessary to inject considerations of national interest into the decisions of state and local governments. Without such an incentive, it has been argued, state and local governments will consider the interests of only their own residents when making their budgetary decisions. A state will invest in the construction of highways or sewage treatment plants, for instance, only so long as the benefits to its citizens are at least equal to the costs they bear. But what if residents of other states travel upon this state's highways? Or what if this state's less thoroughly treated sewage travels downstream to other states? If the interests of the residents of these other states can be taken into account, it is argued, there will result a pattern of expenditure on such things as highways and sewage treatment plants that is both larger and more beneficial to all parties involved. A categorical grant, it is claimed, allows the residents of one state to express their interest in another state's actions. Accordingly, categorical grants would represent the consent of the governed. They are a contract between a recipient government and the citizens of other units of government with the fed-

---

[4]As reported in the January 23, 1965, issue of the *New York Times*. The citation is taken from George F. Break, *Intergovernmental Fiscal Relations in the United States* (Washington: Brookings Institution, 1967), p. 79.

[5]The literature that attempts to rationalize categorical grants along contractual lines is voluminous. Two major works, each of which contains further references, are Wallace E. Oates, *Fiscal Federalism* (New York: Harcourt Brace Jovanovich, 1972); and Albert Breton and Anthony Scott, *The Economic Constitution of Federal States* (Toronto: University of Toronto Press, 1978).

eral government acting as an agent for the citizens of these other units of government.[5] In this regard, the various specific conditions that are attached to grants, such as state compliance with the 55 m.p.h. speed limit to qualify for federal highway grants, are portrayed merely as contractual conditions necessary to fulfill the objectives of the contract between the recipient state and the other, grantor states.

Contract implies consent among the contracting parties; it implies a *quid pro quo* relationship in which all gain from the contract. For example, if each state acts independently of the others in constructing highways or in similar endeavors it has been argued that underprovision of the service will result.[6] In this view, a program of categorical grants for highway construction may be looked upon as a vehicle by which the states reach agreement with each other to deal with the external effects of their actions. Under such circumstances, the grant program would be beneficial, so each state would prefer to participate in the grant program rather than withdraw from it, have its payments refunded and the program dissolved.

It is not appropriate to regard categorical grants from a contractual perspective. The manner of finance and the conditions under which decisions on the awarding of grants are made make it unreasonable to view grants as reflecting a contractual relationship between the federal and state and local units of government. The relationship seems more properly regarded as a coercive one, much along the lines of the "contract" offered by the armed robber: "Your money or your life."

Grant programs are neither based upon nor reflect a consensus among states. States have no choice but to participate in grant programs, for taxes will be extracted from their residents in any event. Grants are equivalent to people being taxed to finance tickets to the Super Bowl, and being eligible to apply for a ticket grant, but being unable to choose not to participate and to pocket the money instead. It is stretching notions of contract beyond credibility to claim that notions of contract are appropriate in such contexts as these. A grant to aid mass transit in New York financed by making the same tax extractions from residents of Arizona or Texas as from residents of Connecticut or New Jersey can hardly be characterized as reflecting a contractual agreement. What is dominant is not a contractual process, in which there results a consensus among the affected parties, but a process of levying taxes on some people, with the proceeds used to subsidize others.

This point can be illustrated quite simply. Suppose a nation is divided into three equally populous states, with two developed primarily

[6]For a development of this general line of argument, though with respect to the provision of education, see Burton A. Weisbrod, *External Benefits of Public Education* (Princeton, N.J.: Industrial Relations Section, Princeton University, 1964).

before the automobile and the third after. Assuming a situation in which mass transit is a state function, suppose national legislators in the first two states propose a program of federal grants for the construction of mass transit facilities, with these grants to be financed by taxes apportioned throughout the nation. Most, if not all, of the demand for mass transit will reside in the older states. Yet the grant program enables the politically dominant states to place one-third of the cost of their mass transit expenditures onto the third state. The grant program reduces by one-third the cost borne by residents of the dominant states, so, these states will support an expansion in grant spending to a level beyond that which they would support if they had to finance the expenditures themselves.[7] Categorical grants that distribute expenditures in concentrated fashion among the winners in a political process accomplish both a transfer of wealth from the losers to the winners and a wastage of resources because projects are pursued for which the costs exceed the benefits. Because of the disincentives and the malincentives that are created, any such tax-transfer process involves the destruction of wealth, in addition to any transfers that are achieved.[8]

It is a simple task to rationalize categorical grants as representing the federal government's acting in effect as an agent of the states to create the necessary quasi-contractual relations that would allow the interests of affected external parties to be incorporated into the decisions of any particular state or local government. In the presence of a system of majority rule in which taxes are apportioned over the entire population despite the concentration of benefits among subsets of the population, however, it is practically impossible to argue that the rationalization is an apt explanation of what is truly taking place. On the contrary, grants are predominately devices for subsidizing winners in the competition for grants at the expense of losers, as well as for enabling legislators to build supporting constituencies based on government spending.

The outcomes of the categorical grant are a reduction in the effectiveness with which resources are used and a strengthening of the role

---

[7]As one illustration of how politics, redistribution, and grants are tied together, urban renewal grants were, before they were replaced by the Community Development Block Grants, found to be highly concentrated in those congressional districts whose members sit on the committees that are responsible for urban renewal. See Charles R. Plott "Some Organizational Influences on Urban Renewal Decisions," *American Economic Review* 58 (May 1968), pp. 306–21.

[8]On different aspects of the ability of a network of taxes and transfers to destroy wealth, see, for instance, Terry L. Anderson and Peter J. Hill, *The Birth of a Transfer Society* (Stanford, Ca.: Hoover Institution Press, forthcoming); Gordon Tullock, "The Welfare Costs of Tariffs, Monopolies, and Theft," *Western Economic Journal* 4 (June 1967), pp. 224–32; and Richard E. Wagner, "Capital, Consumption, and Tax-Transfer Politics," *Policy Report* 1 (February 1979), pp. 1–7.

of the federal government in the allocation of resources to the activities of state and local governments.[9]

General Purpose Grants

Categorical grants began to some extent to be replaced by block grants in the 1960s. At about the same time, there developed a growing interest in revenue sharing.[10] Such general purpose grants were perceived by different groups as a means of accomplishing different and occasionally contradictory objectives. Some saw general purpose grants as a vehicle for promoting greater decentralization within our federalist system. As general purpose grants replaced categorical grants, the strings attached by the federal government to state and local governments would dissolve, it was thought. Indeed, general purpose grants were often referred to as unconditional grants, indicating a belief that such grants could actually be given without any strings at all. And even should the strings be few, it would seem that general purpose grants would permit greater state and local autonomy over expenditures.

In contrast, others saw general purpose grants as a means of increasing the relative share of government in the economy. This vision was couched in terms of such notions as fiscal drag, in which the primary budgetary problem of the federal government was seen as one of its ability to spend its revenues as rapidly as they accrued.[11] It was, for instance, noted that under a progressive tax system a 10 percent increase in national income would elicit approximately a 17 percent increase in federal tax revenue, while creating only about a 10 percent increase in state and local revenues. These proponents of revenue sharing did not wish to see these revenues returned to individuals as tax reductions, nor did they favor increased defense spending. They favored increased government spending, but they wished to see this increase devoted primarily to transfer payments, social services, and the like, much of which had been the direct responsibility of state and local governments. Revenue sharing was seen as a way of accomplishing this increased federal participation in state and local affairs while appearing to promote state and local autonomy.

[9]See Richard E. Wagner, *The Fiscal Organization of American Federalism* (Chicago: Markham, 1971), pp. 41–46.

[10]For a survey of pertinent options at the time, see Charles J. Goetz, *What is Revenue Sharing?* (Washington: Urban Institute, 1972). On block or consolidated grants, see George C. S. Benson and Harold F. McClelland, *Consolidated Grants* (Washington: American Enterprise Institute, 1961).

[11]For discussions of fiscal drag and proposals for revenue sharing, see Joseph A. Pechman, "Financing State and Local Government," in *Proceedings of a Symposium on Federal Taxation* (New York: American Bankers Association, 1965), pp. 71–85; and Walter W. Heller, "Strengthening the Fiscal Base of our Federalism," in *idem, New Dimensions of Political Economy* (Cambridge: Harvard University Press, 1966), pp. 117–72.

An alternative to general purpose grants is federal tax reduction. Tax reduction, however, would enhance the autonomy of individuals and of state and local governments in decisions about the use of resources. In contrast, general purpose grants diminish this autonomy. It is also erroneous to think that general purpose grants are free of strings or controls over state and local governments. Since revenue sharing disbursements are tied to state or local revenues, the program favors those governments that impose taxes over those that use prices and fees. It also favors states that make relatively heavy use of income taxes over states that use other taxes. Recipient governments are required to hold public hearings on how revenue sharing funds are to be spent, and they must also conform to federal requirements about such matters as nondiscrimination and financial management. Revenue sharing clearly possesses strings or conditions, only they take a different form from those that commonly characterize categorical grants.[12]

Revenue sharing has sometimes been advocated as preferable to federal tax reduction because it can help state and local governments overcome the tax competition that keeps their revenues lower than otherwise. It is, of course, true that tax competition results in lower taxes than does fiscal monopoly. It is similarly true that a monopoly bakery would yield higher prices than would result from competition among bakers. It is, however, quite peculiar to adopt what results under monopoly as the ideal when it comes to government. The problem would seem to be not the competition among states that keeps taxes lower than they would otherwise be, but the absence of competition faced by the federal government, which results in taxes being higher than they would otherwise be. Competition within our system of government is something that needs to be encouraged, especially with respect to the federal government, not discouraged through revenue sharing. General purpose grants are not a substitute for categorical grants; the former do not promote state and local autonomy while the latter promote federal suzerainty. Rather, both categories of grants are complementary means of enhancing federal control over state and local affairs, so both infuse monopolistic elements into our federalist system, thereby weakening the extent to which our system of government reflects the consent of the governed.

Block Grants

Block grants are commonly thought to represent a compromise between categorical and general purpose grants. They are awarded for a broader range of activities than are categorical grants. At the same time, block grants for, say, community development do not cover

---

[12]See Robert D. Reischauer, "General Revenue Sharing — The Program's Incentives," in *Financing the New Federalism,* ed. by Wallace E. Oates (Baltimore: Johns Hopkins Press, 1975), pp. 40–87.

education, so block grants would seem to entail less flexibility than general purpose grants. While this common perception may seem valid upon a casual look, a more careful inspection shows that a block grant, so long as its size is less than what the recipient would spend on the activity in question in the absence of the grant, is indistinguishable from a general purpose grant.

To illustrate, suppose a state spends $1 billion each on education and health, and further assume that one-quarter of increases in disposable income within the state are spent on public services, with this increased spending distributed evenly between education and health. If the state receives a general purpose grant of $200,000, net public spending will rise by $50,000, $25,000 for each function. While the state's accounting system will show it spending the entire $200,000 grant, with $100,000 each being spent for education and health, the grant actually will lead to only a $50,000 increase in spending. Under the postulated conditions, the federal grant will also lead to a $150,000 reduction in state taxes.

Now suppose instead that the $200,000 is given as a block grant for education. The grant does nothing to change the desire of state residents to devote one-quarter of increases in disposable income to the provision of state services and three-quarters to the provision of personal services. Consequently, the $200,000 grant will lead to a $50,000 increase in state spending and a $150,000 increase in personal spending, with this latter coming about through a $150,000 reduction in state taxes. Furthermore, the block grant has done nothing to alter the desire of state residents to spend equally on education and health. Accordingly, while the state's accounting records will in the end show it spending the entire $200,000 on education, it will actually increase its spending on education by only $25,000, and will also increase its spending on health by $25,000. So long as the amount of the block grant is less than what the state would spend on the activity in the absence of the grant, the block grant will be indistinguishable from a general purpose grant in its impact on state spending.[13]

For block grants to alter the pattern of state spending, the federal government must impose restrictions of some type on how the state spends its own revenues and on how heavily the state taxes its residents. One way of doing this is through the imposition of matching requirements, but such requirements are suitable for categorical grants

---

[13]For some examination of the possible scope for nonmatching grants to alter the spending patterns of recipient governments, see Paul N. Courant, Edward M. Gramlich, and Daniel L. Rubinfeld, "The Stimulative Effects of Intergovernmental Grants: Or Why Money Sticks Where it Hits"; and Wallace E. Oates, "Lump-Sum Intergovernmental Grants Have Price Effects," both in *Fiscal Federalism and Grants-in-Aid,* ed. by Peter Mieszkowski and William H. Oakland (Washington: Urban Institute, 1979), pp. 5–21 and 23–30 respectively.

and not for block grants. Another restriction, suitable for block grants, is through some requirement of expenditure maintenance, under which a state would be required, in one way or another, to demonstrate that it did not reduce its own spending on the activity for which the grant was awarded. In terms of the previous illustration, the state would have to show that it maintained its own expenditures on education at $1 billion. The state could, of course, escape this effort at federal control by directing disproportionate shares of increases in state spending to health until the desired balance between health and education is attained once again. The ability of states to choose how to allocate increases in their budgets means that a requirement of expenditure maintenance ultimately will be ineffectual. The only way expenditure maintenance could possibly be made binding would be by having the national government specify for future periods both the size and the composition of the state's budget, something that would fully nationalize our system of government. Block grants, then, do not really represent a compromise or intermediate position between conditional grants and unconditional grants. If expenditure maintenance is not required, block grants are essentially indistinguishable from general purpose grants. If expenditure maintenance is practiced effectively, block grants degenerate into a particularly oppressive form of categorical grant, in which our federalist system will be destroyed.

There are only two main types of grant programs, not three. And even the distinction between categorical and general purpose grants threatens to vanish in light of the general fungibility of money. An increase in categorical grants for highway construction, for instance, will, depending on the nature of such revenue maintenance features as matching provisions, bring about a reduction in the state's own spending on highway construction. The released funds will be directed to other activities, in much the same way as would have happened with a general purpose grant. The ability of a grant to induce recipient governments to act differently depends on the creation of a sufficiently binding network of strings and conditions. All federal grants are accompanied by strings, and these strings seem to multiply with the passage of time. In contrast to a program of tax reduction, which would allow state and local governments to raise more revenues on their own, federal grants seem almost invariably to erode the polycentric nature of our federalist system, creating more of a monopolistic, hierarchical-type system in its place.

Future Options

Federal aid to state and local governments has served as a major vehicle for the centralization and nationalization of our federalist system of government. While federal grants supply only about one dollar in four of state and local spending, the federal government has been able to use these grants to insinuate substantially greater control over the activities of state and local governments. It is often suggested that an increased emphasis on general purpose grants would strengthen the federal aspects of our system of government, while an increased emphasis on categorical grants would strengthen the national aspects.[14] For reasons already explained, however, this portrayal of the options does not conform to our experience.

All grants have conditions attached, and these conditions tend to become more stringent over time in response to political pressures. Perhaps all that can be said about a shift from categorical to general purpose grants is that it might temporarily slow down the rate of effective centralization of our system of government.

A major and relatively painless step toward establishing a competitive federalism can be taken by eliminating federal aid, along with a concomitant reduction in federal taxes. On the average, state and local governments would be in the same position as before, absent only the federal strings and controls.[15] That the major effect of such a change is only a reduction in the ability of the federal government to exercise control over state and local governments is easily seen by using a line of reasoning introduced above. Suppose for illustrative purposes that 25 percent of changes in disposable income go to provide state and local services, with the remaining 75 percent for personal use. A $100 grant program, then, would actually increase state spending by $25, with state taxes being lowered by $75 to finance increased personal spending. Should the grant be eliminated and taxes reduced, state taxes and spending would rise by $25, and the remaining $75 still would be for personal use. There is no essential difference between the two programs, other than the promotion of monopolized government under a program of grants. By replacing federal aid with federal tax reductions, individual state and local governments will come to exercise more autonomy in our federalist system, thereby nurturing the efficiency and pluralism that have been eroded through federal programs of federal aid.

A second option might be to require the approval of, for instance, 75 percent of the state legislatures before a grant program might be implemented.[16] Under the current arrangement, each state finds itself

---

[14]See, for instance, the concluding remarks in Break, "Intergovernmental Fiscal Relations," in *Setting National Priorities.*

[15]Since some states receive more in grants than they pay in taxes and since other states are in the reverse position, a combination of grant and tax reduction will entail some redistributions among the states. States in which federal taxes exceed grants received will gain by the combination of grant and tax reduction, while states in the reverse position will lose.

[16]For a discussion of the central conceptual issues involved here, as well as the presentation of a specific proposal, see William A. Niskanen, "The Prospect for Liberal Democracy," in *Fiscal Responsibility in Constitutional Democracy*, ed. by James M. Buchanan and Richard E. Wagner (Leiden: Martinus Nijhoff, 1978), pp. 168–74.

in a large-number analogue to the prisoners' dilemma. Each will have contributed tax monies to finance the grant, and the only way a state can recoup its losses is by participating in the grant program. States are individually motivated to accept the grant, yet all states taken together might be better off if they reject it, or at least succeed in modifying its terms. The federal government is, as it were, a monopsonist with respect to state and local governments. The imbalance can be redressed through some form of collective bargaining among the states, in which a consensus would be necessary before grant programs could be adopted. If this were done, grants would come to reflect a truly contractual relationship among the states, with the federal government serving merely as agent. The general principle that is involved here is that the maintenance of an effective federalist system requires that the states possess some means of checking those actions of the federal government that, while individually acquiesced to by the states, ultimately transfer responsibility from the states to the federal government, thereby transforming a polycentric system of government into a hierarchical one.

15

Tax Policy

by Stephen J. Entin

The Need for Tax Reform

The whole area of tax policy and tax theory is undergoing a sea change, and rightly so. Major errors in tax theory and practice have led, despite the best of intentions, to a tax code which has hobbled the economy in ways economists are only just beginning to understand. It now seems apparent that the tax code has caused large quantities of labor and capital to become misdirected or withdrawn from the market. The result has been a growing shortfall of skill and capital, costing the economy as much as $500 billion *annually* in permanently lost output.

A thorough reform of the tax code and its underlying philosophy should be the top priority of tax policy. Instead of focusing solely on business cycles and how to get GNP up to its existing potential, tax policy should be aimed at letting capacity itself reach its true "potential." Instead of analyzing tax changes in terms of abstract concepts of "horizontal and vertical tax equity," we should be looking at the economic consequences of the tax system. There is no equity in perpetually depriving the economy of several million jobs and several hundred billion dollars a year in lost production. Growth of GNP, rather than its redistribution, should be the goal of tax policy and tax reform in the 1980s.

A restructured tax code can bring major benefits. While full realization of the gains will not be instantaneous, substantial progress can be made within a decade. A few numbers will illustrate the potential for economic recovery and expansion. From 1973 to 1979, the U.S. economy grew in real terms at a rate of only 2.5 percent a year, barely two-thirds the 3.7 percent annual growth rate the U.S. achieved between 1950 and 1973 and well below the 4.4 percent growth rate realized from 1962 to 1969.

If, after the current recession, the economy continues to grow at the recent rate of 2.5 percent, real Gross National Product (GNP) will barely reach $3.1 trillion by 1990. But if the economy regains the

317

growth rates of the 1960s, GNP will reach $3.7 trillion by 1990, nearly 20 percent higher.

With this kind of growth, incomes and living standards would be substantially higher. Jobs would be plentiful. Fewer people would be dependent on welfare or unemployment compensation. Federal revenues in 1990 would be nearly $120 billion higher than otherwise, enough to provide for a balanced budget, adequate funding of health, education and social spending, and substantial improvements in military preparedness. Payroll and income taxes could be cut rather than increased. Economic growth would generate price stability as the expanding economy eliminated budget deficits and reduced pressure on the Federal Reserve to create more money. Obviously, the social gains from growth would be enormous.

Fortunately, the required policy changes are affordable. There are four ways that these tax changes can finance themselves without inflation. First, the initial revenue impact of reductions in tax rates could be offset by broadening the tax base, reducing the quantity of exemptions and deductions. To a significant extent, this will occur naturally, as reduced tax rates make tax shelters and the underground cash economy relatively less attractive than before. It must not be done by closing so-called loopholes whose chief function is simply to offset the multiple taxation of savings. Second, economic growth will provide a substantial additional cushion of revenue reflows. Third, a more prosperous economy will mean reduced demands on government for spending on income security. Fourth, and of major importance, the restructured and simplified tax code will induce large increases in private sector saving. Even if net tax reduction were part of the restructuring process, the jump in saving would be enough to pay for sharply higher private investment, with enough left over to cover any residual government deficit without inflationary money creation by the Federal Reserve.

Tax Policy: Conflicting Theories

For centuries, tax theory consisted primarily of searching for ways to divert private resources to public use without damaging the willingness or ability of the private sector to produce and grow. This emphasis was wiped out by the Depression and the emergence of Keynesian economics.

In Keynesian theory, tax reduction is assumed to increase private spending by giving people more disposable income. As spending increases, producers rush to meet orders and spend their sales receipts hiring labor and capital. It is assumed that ample capital and labor are available and willing to work. Demand for goods automatically calls forth supply.

The initial rise in the government deficit, from either a tax cut or an increase in government spending, is supposed to have a ripple effect on the economy, as each person who receives a dollar spends part of it in turn. However, in a Keynesian model the ripple effect from a tax cut is always less than that from a government spending increase of the same size because the individual will save a portion of the tax cut. This biases Keynesian policymakers against saving and tax reduction and in favor of consumption and government spending.

Furthermore, it supposedly does not matter very much what kind of spending or type of tax cut is involved. To fight a recession, all a Keynesian really need know is how far the economy is from full employment GNP and how big the ripple effects are. He then chooses either a rise in spending or a cut in taxes to start off the ripples that will carry total spending up to capacity.

Since Keynesian demand theory holds that all types of tax cuts affect the economy in roughly the same way, it is quite compatible with the theory of tax "equity," which has as its goal the redistribution of income. This union has produced countless efforts to use the tax system to redistribute income from rich to poor, capital to labor, young to old, industry to industry, and region to region. Almost all these efforts have either failed or achieved a portion of their aims at the cost of enormously expensive economic side effects.

In the name of "equity," and on the assumption that labor and capital are always willing to work, both have been overtaxed. The earnings of capital in particular have been subjected to repeated taxation at federal, state, and local levels, on both corporate and personal tax returns, and both labor and capital have had to face high tax rates that have discouraged their full participation in the economy.

Supply-Side Economics

The twin concepts of demand management and "equity" are falling victim to the realities of our economic conditions. Two alternative principles of tax policy rapidly gaining prominence are classical or "supply-side" economics and a theory of "neutrality" as the goal of a restructured tax system.

The supply-side or classical view focuses on the profit and income incentives that motivate people to work, save, and invest. All the demand in the world is useless if the after-tax rewards to labor and capital are insufficient to induce them to work. In the classical view, tax reductions that improve the after-tax wage and rate of return are assumed to increase the supply of labor and capital and the desire to hire them. As they are hired, they receive wages, interest, and dividends sufficient to allow them to buy up the output they produce. Supply generates its own demand.

319

Supply-side economics rejects the entire demand-side approach. The Keynesian idea that taxation is harmless as long as the proceeds are spent is judged unrealistic in light of the disincentive effect of taxes on labor and capital. Furthermore, the Keynesian notion that tax cuts increase disposable income and encourage spending (demand) is sharply questioned.

Suppose the government creates a $10 deficit by raising spending or cutting taxes $10. How does the deficit get paid for? By borrowing the difference. But if the government borrows $10 that someone else would have borrowed and spent, it "crowds out" $10 in private spending to finance $10 in public spending. Why should that raise total national "demand"? Why should that cause an increase in the supply of labor, capital, or production? Fiscal policy may move spending around but not enlarge it. The money received from the tax cut will simply be lent back to cover the government deficit, with no real impact.

In fact, no real increase in income, spending, or demand can occur unless there is a change in real output. No change in real output can occur unless there is a change in the supply of labor or capital. Tax cuts alone cannot change real disposable income and spending unless and until they first affect the incentive to supply labor and capital.

However, supply-side economists do not give up on fiscal policy. They have found another use for it. If fiscal policy does not do much for short-run *demand,* perhaps fiscal policy can be used to encourage long-run *supply.* If fiscal policy can create incentives to steer more existing production and income into saving, capital goods, and higher productive capacity, and if tax changes can encourage more people to take jobs and work longer, we can achieve real growth and more employment through fiscal policy.

The supply-side view looks at the way the tax structure has affected capacity itself, and how changes in the tax structure might affect long-term capacity by influencing the long-term supply of labor and capital. People respond to prices, and taxes can change prices. For example, a tax on butter raises the price consumers pay for butter and lowers the price producers receive for it. A subsidy on margarine does the opposite. Thus, a tax on butter and/or a subsidy on margarine would cause people to consume and produce less butter and more margarine.

Similarly, a rising tax rate on interest and dividends makes it more "expensive" to save (or defer consumption). The taxpayer will increase current consumption or seek out tax-sheltered investments. A rising tax rate on the use of equipment causes investment and output to fall. A rising tax rate on earnings causes a drop in hours worked by making leisure less "expensive" in terms of after-tax wages given up. In other words, taxes discourage the supply of labor, capital, and output. They do so by affecting the relative prices of labor vs. leisure and future consumption vs. current consumption.

Suppose that an increase in income has pushed a taxpayer from the 30 percent tax bracket to the 50 percent tax bracket. Before the increase, $10 earned with one hour of overtime yielded $7 after taxes. Now it yields $5. A $100 bond paying 10 percent interest yielded $7 after tax. Now it yields $5. The incentives to work and save have dropped. In each case, it is *marginal* tax rates, the rates on the last and next few dollars of earnings, that are critical to the decision to work or invest a little bit more or a little bit less.

If tax cuts are to succeed in expanding production, jobs, work effort, saving, and investment, they must reduce the marginal tax rates on each activity. Such changes include: cuts in the marginal personal income tax rates in all brackets, either on all income or on interest, dividends, and capital gains; exclusion of a proportion of capital gains or savings income from tax, with no limits; cuts in corporate tax rates, fast depreciation or larger investment tax credits. Tax changes *not* generally at the margin would include: increases in personal exemptions or standard deductions; limited savings exclusions; tax rebates; cuts in a few lower brackets only.

Classical theory holds that tax changes differ markedly in their impact depending on how they affect incentives to engage in some activity, such as work effort and saving for future consumption, as opposed to others, such as leisure and current consumption. When this is the case, tax reductions ought to be structured to reduce the distortions, biases, and disincentives in the current tax code against work effort, saving, and growth. Reducing these biases would partially restore "neutrality" to the tax code, a situation in which marginal tax rates are as even and as low as possible across all activities. Thus, just as "equity" emerges as a logical normative rule in Keynesian theory, "neutrality" emerges as a logical normative rule in classical theory. The full extent of the non-neutrality of the current tax system will be explored in a later section.

Tax Neutrality

If taxes are applied at high marginal rates, a significant amount of output is lost as labor and capital are discouraged from participating in the economy. If taxes are applied unevenly across various industries, regions, or types of labor and capital, the pattern of output will be altered. Labor and capital will flee the high tax activities and either be lost or reappear in another use. Either way, efficiency and output fall.

Thus, output and income will be least damaged by taxes when the burden and its disincentives are low and evenly spread (neutral) across activities.[1] From an economic standpoint, neutrality should be one of the major goals in design of the tax code. The current income tax is not at all neutral or efficient. It is widely regarded as complex, uneven in its burden, riddled with loopholes, and a major cause of misallocation of resources.[2]

In 1977 the Treasury released *Blueprints for Basic Tax Reform,* a study of possible changes in the U.S. tax code. One of the proposals contained in the *Blueprints* was a "comprehensive income tax" (c.i.t.), which would reduce the complexities and "loopholes" in the tax code. By eliminating many existing tax deductions, the c.i.t. would broaden the tax base, expanding the amount of income subject to tax by enough to permit significant reductions in the marginal income tax rates compared to current law. The c.i.t. would also move the tax code closer to the concepts of horizontal equity (equal taxation of people with equal current incomes) and vertical equity (higher taxation as a percent of income of those with higher current incomes), which are part of the Keynesian school of thought.

The c.i.t., while superficially appealing, has serious drawbacks. Neutrality is not simply the closing of loopholes and a patching up of the existing income tax, as is frequently advocated by those aiming at "equity." Neutrality means equal taxation of all activities, not equal taxation of all current measured income. In particular, neutrality includes the even-handed treatment of leisure versus effort and current consumption versus saving for future consumption. No income tax, not even a broadly-based, low-tax-rate income tax, is neutral with re-

---

[1]Ture and Sanden state:

> "Every tax increases the cost of something to someone in the private sector. The less neutral a tax is, the greater it changes the cost of something relative to the cost of all other things. A perfectly neutral tax or tax system would increase the cost of all goods, services, and activities to the private sector in the same proportion. It would increase the cost of leisure in the same proportion as the cost of effort, the cost of consumption in the same proportion as the cost of saving, the cost of any one consumption good in the same proportion as the cost of all others, of the use of one production input in the same proportion as all others, etc." See research study and report prepared for the Financial Executives Research Foundation entitled "The Effects of Tax Policy on Capital Formation," by Norman B. Ture, president, Norman B. Ture, Inc., and B. Kenneth Sanden, partner, Price Waterhouse & Co. (1977), p. 59.

[2]"The dominant complaint made about the present tax system is that it does not tax all income alike. This complaint reflects concern about equity: taxpayers with the same level of income bear different tax burdens. It reflects concerns about efficiency: taxation at rates that differ by industry or by type of financial arrangement leads to misallocation of resources. Finally, it reflects concern about simplicity: the enormously complex tangle of provisions the taxpayer confronts in ordering his affairs and calculating his tax leads to differential rates of taxation." See *Blueprints for Basic Tax Reform,* a study published by the Department of Treasury (January 17, 1977), p. 21.

spect to these choices. Many so-called loopholes are merely steps toward restoring neutrality.[3]

Leisure is not taxed, while income earned through the efforts of labor and capital is taxed. Furthermore, income taxes fall at least twice as heavily on income that is saved as on income that is consumed. Income is taxed when earned. If it is spent on consumption, it is not taxed again, except perhaps for a small sales tax. However, if it is saved, the earnings on the savings are taxed again at rates ranging from 14 to 70 percent, plus capital gains taxes, if any, plus state and local income and property taxes, if applicable. These rates are in addition to whatever corporate taxes were paid on the earnings before they reached the saver.

A tax code which was as neutral as possible across all activities, including the choice between consumption and saving, would have to eliminate the multiple taxes on saving. In particular, either the amount of income saved each year would have to be tax deductible, or the interest, dividends, and capital gains from saving would have to be tax-exempt. The tax should fall either on income saved or on its earnings, but not on both.[4]

The Tax Bias Against Saving

Any income-based tax imposes a double burden on saving, the purchase of a stock, bond, savings account, capital good or any other asset, such as a home, which yields services over time. The market

---

[3]According to *Blueprints:*

"An especially serious drawback of an accretion income base is that it leads to what is sometimes called the 'double taxation' of savings: savings are accumulated after payment of taxes and the yield earned on those savings is then taxed again. This has been recognized as a problem in the existing tax law, and many techniques have been introduced to make the tax system more neutral with respect to savings. The investment tax credit, accelerated depreciation, special tax rates for capital gains, and other provisions are examples. Also, tax deferral on income from certain investments for retirement purposes is an example of how current law attempts to offset the adverse effects on savings of using an accretion income base. Significantly, this last example is also viewed as desirable for reasons of equity.

"All these techniques have the same practical effect as exempting from tax the income from the investment. *To this extent, this is equivalent to converting the base from accretion income to consumption.*" (See p. 23.)

[4]Ture and Sanden explain the problem as follows:

"...the bias against saving in the present U.S. tax system stems primarily from the fact that, for the most part, neither the part of income which is saved nor the return on such saving is excluded from the base of the income tax, the principal source of revenue. Since saving is the capitalized amount of the future income purchased by the saving, this characteristic of the income tax subjects the part of current income used to buy future income to a double tax, whereas the part of current income used to buy consumption goods and services is taxed only once." (See "The Effects of Tax Policy on Capital Formation," p. 71.)

price of these assets is simply the current value placed on the anticipated future earnings or services of the assets. To tax both the money used to acquire the asset and the future earnings of the asset is to tax the same item twice. To be neutral between saving and consumption, the tax code should exempt from tax either the amount of income saved or the earnings of the asset. Any income tax based on current measured income is non-neutral and severely biased against saving, capital formation, and economic growth.

Financial Assets

Since saving is the deferral of consumption to a future date, the double or multiple taxation of saving raises the effective price of goods bought in the future with today's income (which has been "stored" as savings in the interim) relative to the price of goods bought today with today's income.

Interest is the service one gets from owning a bond. Good music is the service one gets from owning a stereo. Compare the purchase of a $1,000 bond now, at 5 percent interest, to be cashed in to buy a $1,000 stereo in ten years, with the immediate purchase of the stereo. If the stereo is bought now, the next ten years will be filled with music tax free. If the bond is bought now, ten years of silence will be compensated by $50 a year in interest, after which the stereo will be bought. The cost of the ten years of music is the $50 a year foregone by not buying the bond, and the cost of the $50 income stream is the musical enjoyment given up.

Now let us impose a 50 percent income tax on a person who was having trouble deciding between buying now or buying later, and allow no deductions for either the saving or the interest. To buy a $1,000 stereo, the taxpayer will need to earn $2,000 before taxes. To acquire $50 in interest after taxes, the taxpayer will need $100 in interest before taxes. For that, he will need to buy two bonds, for $2,000. But to buy two bonds, he will need to earn $4,000 in pre-tax income. The cost of the ten years of music has doubled. The cost of the ten years of $50 in interest has quadrupled.

If the taxpayer has only $2,000 to spare, he can only afford a $1,000 bond and will only receive $25 in after-tax income. If the decision to save or buy was a toss-up before the tax was levied, he will clearly prefer to buy the stereo after the tax is imposed. However, if the $2,000 used to buy the bonds were made tax deductible, two bonds could be bought to earn $50 after tax, and the choice would still be a toss-up. Alternatively, the $2,000 in savings could be taxed and the $50 earned on a $1,000 bond be made tax free to produce the same result.

324

Physical Assets

In the case of investment (saving by buying a physical asset, such as a machine or an apartment building), the double taxation is offset, although only partially, by the depreciation deduction allowed by the tax code. The machine is bought in year one. The tax write-offs stretch over several years. The delay in receiving the full deduction costs the buyer the interest which could be earned or the consumption which could be enjoyed if the taxes saved by the deduction were available right away for saving or spending. Only first-year expensing of investment purchases restores neutrality completely between investment and consumption.

Corporate Income Tax

Having a separate tax on corporate income adds another layer to the double taxation of capital, a sort of triple tax. Income is first taxed at the corporate level. Then, any dividends paid out are taxed again as income to the shareholder. This extra taxation of dividends hits hardest at low-income shareholders.

Suppose a large corporation earns $100 and pays a tax of $46. If it distributes the remaining $54 to a shareholder in the 70 percent tax bracket, the shareholder will pay another $37.80 in tax, for a total tax of $83.80. If the shareholder were in the 14 percent bracket, the extra tax would be $7.56 for a total of $53.56.

If the corporate tax were not present, and the corporate earnings were attributed directly to the shareholders whose earnings they really are, the tax burden would be very different. The total tax paid on the $100 by the upper income shareholder would be $70 instead of $83.80, a $13.80 decrease. The tax paid by the lower income shareholder would be $14 instead of $53.56, a $39.56 decrease.

Eliminating the corporate income tax by attributing corporate earnings directly to the shareholders is called "corporate and personal income tax integration." It is considered a major step toward tax neutrality and simplification.

Capital Gains

Capital gains are not income in the ordinary sense and ought not to be taxed as such. All other types of income represent payment to labor and capital for their services in current production. Capital gains represent a price increase of an existing asset, not the production of a new machine, building, consumption good or service. That is why capital gains are not counted as part of GNP or national income.

This price increase may simply be due to inflation, in which case there is no real gain at all, and there certainly should be no tax. Or the price increase may exceed inflation. If so, the real increase is due to

325

the market's perception that the asset is now "worth more" because it is earning more income or profit than before, or to the market's hope and expectation that increased income is likely in the future. In either case, the added income or profit will be taxed if and when it occurs by other provisions of the tax code, and there should be no capital gains tax on the asset price increase. Taxation of capital gains, even at reduced rates, is double taxation of the earnings of a capital asset.

Estate and Gift Taxes

The imposition of estate and gift taxes is another tax on capital. Again, the market value of an asset is the current worth of its future earnings. Since the future earnings will be taxed, a tax on the current market value is a double tax on that income.

There are other effects. Ture and Sanden state that these taxes

> ...not only increase the cost of saving but the cost of transferring the accumulated savings as well. In this respect, they set up strong incentives for arranging the property transfers in ways aimed at minimizing the tax liability, not at maximizing the efficiency with which the property is used.
>
> The objective of such taxes, presumably, is to prevent the concentration of wealth ownership by breaking up large estates. Whether or not this is deemed to be a socially desirable objective, reducing the efficiency with which the property is used certainly is not. Yet premature disposition of property, fragmentation of the ownership interest in family businesses, limitations on the ownership and use of the property in ways which reduce the productivity of the transferred capital are commonplace results of efforts to reduce the impact of these taxes.[5]

An "Ideal" Tax

Numerous tax proposals under discussion in Congress and among economists would provide partial reform of the tax system or offset the tax increases that are occurring due to inflation. How should they be judged? Before turning to them, it would be useful to describe a sort of "ideal" tax system which is as neutral as practical. Tax changes which move toward the ideal could then be favored over those which move further from it.

If we were to go all the way to a neutral tax code, what would it look like? In its simplest form, it would require the taxpayer to report his income for the year, subtract whatever portion of income he saved, and be taxed on the difference. Very few other exemptions would be allowed.

How does this concept of neutrality relate to the desire for equity, efficiency, and simplicity in the tax system? Neutrality and economic

---

[5]"The Effects of Tax Policy on Capital Formation," p. 66.

efficiency are practically synonymous. As for simplicity, a neutral tax would eliminate the double taxation of saving, and with it most of the complex special provisions now in the tax code which provide partial relief to savings, depreciation, and capital gains.

A completely neutral tax code would not discriminate against the supply of labor or capital services from any source. This would mean moving to a very simple flat rate tax. A progressive tax structure taxes suppliers of large amounts of capital and labor services at higher rates per unit of service than suppliers of smaller amounts. This brings up the question of "vertical equity"—should high-income individuals be taxed at a higher rate than low-income individuals?

While a total elimination of progressivity and a sharp easing of the tax burden on capital may appear shocking and inequitable, bear in mind the increased wages and wealth that society would have at its disposal if a major expansion of productivity and income occurred. Is it equitable to continue with a tax code which is sharply depressing the income of the whole society, including those with the lowest earnings?

The idea that progressivity and high taxes on capital obviously shift the tax burden to the rich to the advantage of the poor has little in the way of empirical evidence to support it. It is based on a superficial analysis which neglects the detrimental effects of such a tax system on the quantity of capital, the real wage, employment, prices and output. The ultimate burden of the tax system is far different from the apparent burden based on who writes the checks to the IRS. In any event, major steps toward efficiency and neutrality can be taken without significant change in the progressivity of the tax code.

Toward that end, the *Blueprints for Basic Tax Reform* offered a second type of tax system. The alternative is the "cash flow tax" (c.f.t.), which is based squarely on the principle of neutrality. Like the comprehensive income tax, it would be a broad-based tax with few deductions and markedly reduced tax rates. However, it would eliminate the fundamental double taxation of saving.

Under the c.f.t., there would be two methods of dealing with saving. To be neutral between saving and consumption, an income tax must exclude from the tax base either the amount saved or the earnings on the saving. The *Blueprints* suggest that both options be made available. Such a tax would work as follows:

Financial Assets

To use the savings exclusion method, each taxpayer would set up a "qualified account" for excluded assets to measure his net saving or dis-saving during the year. The account would record the purchases and sales of stocks, bonds, and equipment for the taxpayer's unincorporated business, and net additions to savings deposits. Net purchases would be tax deductible. Net sales or withdrawals of interest, dividends or principal would be added to taxable income, but would be tax deferred if rolled over. The deduction of the purchase price of an asset and the inclusion of the sales price would automatically include capital gains and losses in the tax base with no need for separate accounting. Pension contributions, including social security, would be tax-exempt. Pension benefits, including social security, would be taxed unless saved. Borrowing by the account would be a withdrawal for consumption and would be added to taxable income. Repayment of a loan would be considered saving.

Because borrowing is taxable under the saving exclusion method, taxpayers would probably choose the earnings exclusion method for home buying. The purchase price of the home would not be tax deductible, but any mortgage money borrowed would not be taxed, and there would be no tax on imputed rent or capital gains from the sale. In fact, this is very much like the current treatment of home ownership. If for some reason the taxpayer chose this method for other asset purchases, too, the same exemption of any earnings or gains on the asset would apply. (See the section on owner-occupied housing.)

Physical Assets
(Other Than Home Ownership)

Purchase of a physical asset such as rental property or a machine, whether by a proprietorship, partnership or corporation, would be treated much like financial assets. All investment in structures, plant and equipment would be deducted in the year purchased. Purchase of a capital good is saving and hence would be deductible. This would end the need for depreciation allowances and their complicated tax rules and accounting problems.

It would also put a stop to rarefied theoretical disputes among accountants about the proper measurement of depreciation and the matching of depreciation to the economic earnings of the asset. None of that is meaningful when the tax code is shifted from a tax based on current measured income to a tax based on neutral treatment of saving and investment versus consumption.

Corporate Income Tax

Corporate earnings would not face a separate tax. They would be passed on to the shareholder, enormously simplifying the tax code. The corporation would deduct all investment in plant and equipment in the year purchased, while retained earnings would be counted as saving. Only dividends not reinvested would be taxable to the shareholder. These would be taxed only once, at the shareholder's level, thus eliminating the double taxation of dividends and the tax bias against equity finance found in current law.

328

Owner-Occupied Housing

Because borrowing is taxable under the savings exclusion method, this method would be inconvenient for the purchase of a home. Homebuyers would probably prefer the earnings exclusion method, under which the purchase price of an asset is not deductible, nor borrowing taxable, and the earnings or capital gains on the asset are not taxed.

The current tax code is often criticized for giving more favorable treatment to owner-occupied housing than to other forms of saving or other types of housing. This could be viewed more accurately in reverse: The tax code does not treat home ownership too leniently; it treats other forms of saving and investment too harshly.

Imputed Rent

Only in the context of an income tax in which most saving is double taxed does the current treatment of imputed rent on owner-occupied housing, which is no treatment at all, appear to be inequitable compared to rental housing or other forms of saving and investing.

A neutral tax code, such as the c.f.t., would remove the double tax on saving and investing by one of two methods. It would permit either a tax deduction for the purchase of an asset while taxing all returns on the asset, or no tax deduction for the purchase while exempting from tax all returns on the asset, including services in kind and capital gains.

The earnings exclusion method closely describes the current treatment of owner-occupied housing. Under current law, there is no deduction for the down payment or mortgage principal payments made in buying a house. However, most of the returns on the house — the in-kind service it provides and at least some of the capital gains — are not taxed. That is, the homeowner is not required to pay tax on the imputed rental value of the house. As for capital gains on the home, they are tax-exempt if they are rolled over (used to buy another house), and there is a one-time $100,000 exemption for each taxpayer on capital gains from sale of a home after age 55.

On the other hand, the owner of rental property must pay taxes on the net service of the property, which is measured by rental income. The depreciation allowances are a partial deduction of the present value of the purchase price of the property, and accelerated depreciation brings the value of the amount written off nearer to that of first-year expensing. This is an approximation of the first method of restoring neutrality, but the offset is not complete.

Under the cash flow tax in the *Blueprints*, the owner of rental property would expense his building the first year, thus bringing the tax treatment of rental housing into line with that of owner-occupied housing. Purchasers of any other type of financial or physical assets would also receive deduction for the amount of purchase, thus bringing the tax treatment of all other forms of saving into line as well.

Under a truly comprehensive income tax, on the other hand, the homeowner should be forced to pay tax on the imputed rental value of the house, thus imposing a double tax on home ownership as on rental housing and other assets. However, this is such a complex administrative problem that the *Blueprints'* comprehensive income tax continues the present practice of not taxing imputed rent.

Deduction of Local Property Tax

The *Blueprints* would not allow a deduction of local property taxes on owner-occupied homes because a deduction discriminates in favor of owner-occupiers. When property taxes rise, rents rise by an equal amount. The renter is worse off. The landlord is no better off and no worse off. He deducts the property tax but must pay more income tax on the higher rent. The owner-occupier, on the other hand, pays no added rent and no added tax on the added rent, and he deducts the property tax and saves something on his income tax.

Deductibility of Mortgage Interest

This is allowed by the *Blueprints'* comprehensive income tax. To deny it would discriminate in favor of those who buy a house by drawing down their savings, and hence have less interest income than before and pay less tax, and those who must borrow to buy a house. Borrowing is also dis-saving, but if the interest is not deductible, there is no drop in taxes.

Under the cash flow tax, if the proceeds of the loan are added to taxable income as in the savings exclusion method, the principal and interest payments are tax deductible. However, if the earnings exclusion method is used, principal and interest payments are not tax deductible.

Tax Base and Tax Rates Under the Cash Flow Tax

Individuals would be taxed on their total income (including their share of corporate income), less net saving in qualified accounts (or by the corporation), and less any gains on assets purchased without claiming the savings deduction. This would involve a tax deduction for all contributions to retirement plans, including social security taxes, which are not now tax-deductible by individuals. However, the benefits received from such plans, including social security, would be taxable unless saved. Capital gains and losses would be included as ordinary income. However, the up-front deduction of the purchase price of capital assets, the deferred taxes on the reinvested earnings of capital assets, and the reduced tax rates made possible by the cash flow tax, would more than make up for the loss of separate tax treatment.

This tax base is broader than the current tax base. Even with retention of some amount of personal exemptions to assist lower income individuals, plus medical and casualty loss deductions, this tax system could raise as much revenue as the current system with lower tax rates, particularly as the capital stock and GNP increased with the elimination of the distortions in the current code. The c.f.t. in the *Blueprints* (1977) would have had only three tax brackets, with a bottom rate of 10 percent, a middle rate of 26 or 28 percent (for single or joint returns), and a top rate of 40 percent. Using 1977 figures, the top rate would have started at $30,000. This dollar starting figure for the 40 percent top bracket would be higher now after inflation.

The Treasury arrived at these tax brackets and rates by assuming little or no change in economic behavior from the conversion to a neutral tax, and with the goal in mind of keeping the tax liabilities distributed much as they are now by the progressivity of the current tax code. In fact, the reduction in tax rates from a top rate of 70 percent to a top rate of 40 percent, coupled with the elimination of the tax bias against saving, would probably cause a considerable reduction in the use of tax shelters and the underground economy. It could substantially boost the rate of growth of saving and investment. In all likelihood, the c.f.t. would yield sufficient revenue to permit further rate reduction than assumed by the Treasury.

The *Blueprints* points out that this neutral tax base is not so different from the current tax base as it might appear. The current treatment of homeownership and pensions is close to the "ideal" tax method. Other savings and investment incentives, such as the capital gains exclusion, the investment tax credit, and accelerated depreciation, move in that direction. The *Blueprints* suggests that the current tax system might more easily be moved closer to this ideal base than to a pure income tax system.

Practical Tax Changes

Radical overhaul of the tax system in one sweeping motion is probably impractical. However, there are many intermediate steps which could be taken which would move the tax code closer to neutrality.

Indexing

An immediate but strictly stop-gap measure would be to index the tax code. Such a step, it must be emphasized, will not reverse or obviate the flaws of our tax system, but merely prevent inflation from further exacerbating them.

Personal Taxes

The reason inflation is a tax problem for individuals is that the tax system treats every increase in income as if it were real income. The progressive rate structure and the exemptions are defined in dollars and are not adjusted for inflation. Inflation pushes people into higher tax brackets, even when their incomes have just kept up with the cost of living. Their average tax rate rises, which means that their tax burden rises faster than inflation, and they have less to spend. In fact, every 10 percent increase in wages and prices produces a 16 percent increase in federal tax receipts. This extra 6 percent inflation windfall to the government is in excess of what the government needs to keep up with inflation. Even after adjusting the fiscal year 1980 tax levels for inflation, this extra 6 percent will push the level of taxes above fiscal year 1980 levels by $15 billion in FY 1981, $39 billion in 1982, $65 billion in 1983, $95 billion by 1984, and $129 billion in 1985, for a total inflation windfall to Washington of $343 billion over five years.

It is often pointed out by demand-side economists that much of the inflation-related tax increases since 1965 have been offset by tax cuts. Taxes from all sources were 17.8 percent in 1965 and approximately 20.1 percent in 1979. The average tax burden would have risen by far more had tax cuts not been enacted. However, there is an added effect, which demand-oriented economists tend to overlook, which changes the whole picture.

Inflation raises the average tax rate by raising the *marginal tax rate*. As nominal incomes rise, the government takes a larger slice out of the last few hundred dollars of earnings. Incentives to work, save, and invest are reduced, since any added income will yield less after taxes than before. Marginal tax rates have risen sharply on most taxpayers since 1965.

A good real-world example of the problem is the way in which inflation and rising tax rates have crippled saving. In 1965, a saver might have been in the 25 percent tax bracket, earning 4 percent interest at a time of 2 percent inflation. Of the 4 percent, about 1 percent went for taxes and 2 percent went to protect the principal from inflation. The saver earned 1 percent real after-tax interest.

In the spring of 1980, that same taxpayer might have been in the 32 percent tax bracket, earning 12 percent interest at a time of 14 percent inflation. Of the 12 percent, almost 4 percent went for taxes, and 14 percent was lost to inflation. The saver had a real loss of 6 percent on his savings after taxes and inflation.

In the late 1960s and early 1970s, people saved about 7 percent of their after-tax income. In late 1979 and 1980, people saved between 3 and 4 percent. The drop in the real after-tax interest rate is a major reason for the halving of the personal savings rate.

To make matters worse, what reduced saving is still being done is directed away from ordinary businesses and sent into tax-exempt bonds and other low-productivity tax shelters. Married taxpayers who earned $20,000 in taxable income in 1964 were earning the equivalent of roughly $50,000 in today's dollars. In 1964, these taxpayers with $20,000 were just entering tax brackets (with tax rates of 32 percent and higher) that made tax shelters look attractive. They were upper income people who filed only 2 percent of the tax returns, but they reported 10 percent of the country's income and were responsible for at least 15 to 20 percent of the county's personal saving. Today, after only minor changes, the same tax rates apply to just over $21,000 in taxable income. Now, eight to ten times as many people earn that much. They file 16 to 20 percent of the tax returns, report 40 percent or more of the country's income, and do 50 to 80 percent of the country's personal saving. Many of them were not using tax shelters sixteen years ago. They are now. By 1986 or 1987, unless the tax code is restructured or indexed, people filing 25 percent of all tax returns and doing 80 percent or more of the country's personal saving will be considering or using tax shelters.

Labor also responds to rising marginal tax rates. Wage demands have to outstrip inflation to keep pace with rising taxes as well as prices. Overtime becomes less rewarding, and several major strikes have occurred in recent years over the issue of mandatory overtime. Workers bargain for more days off and non-taxable fringe benefits in lieu of bigger wage increases. A spouse may have second thoughts about accepting a job if the primary breadwinner is in a higher tax bracket, since the first dollar of the second paycheck would be taxed starting at the top bracket rate reached by the primary worker.

To completely offset the affect of inflation on the income tax, the personal exemption, standard deduction (now called the "zero tax bracket"), and all the income levels which divide one tax bracket from another should be adjusted each year for inflation.

Corporate Taxes

In the case of business, inflation depresses growth by interfering dramatically with the tax treatment of depreciation and inventories. The tax code only permits a tax deduction for the historical cost of plants, equipment, and inventories. When inflation increases the cost of a new plant and equipment, the firm finds that the money it has set aside for replacement is inadequate. It must use taxable income to supplement its depreciation allowances just to maintain its productive capacity — just to stand still. Thus, actual economic depreciation is understated, and corporate profits are overstated. Inflation "disallows" the deduction of a real cost of doing business, increases the firm's tax liability, and reduces its ability to grow.

The effects of inflation on corporate tax liability and the rate of return on investment are dramatic. Inflation has increased the effective tax rate on real profits from about 40 percent in 1965 to between 50 and 60 percent, on average, in the last few years. When the true cost of depreciation is counted, some industries pay heavy taxes when they are really losing money on continuing operations. The effective tax rates on many utilities, railroads, and steel companies exceed *100 percent* of *real* earnings!

In 1979, the capital consumption adjustment and inventory valuation adjustment, government measures of the understatement of depreciation and inventory replacement costs, were in excess of $17 billion and $42 billion, respectively, for the corporate sector alone. This $59 billion in overstated income was in excess of 25 percent of unadjusted profits and increased corporate tax liabilities by $20 to $30 billion. This was at a time when investment was falling more than $10 billion short of replacing worn-out equipment and providing tools for new entrants into the labor force.

The consequences of underdepreciation range from falling productivity and declining average weekly spendable earnings (which have fallen, after taxes and inflation, back to 1964 levels) to reduced competitiveness and loss of jobs in major U.S. industries, such as autos and steel.

One method of correcting the tax treatment of depreciation, called "indexed depreciation" or "replacement cost depreciation," would let the firm adjust each year's depreciation installment upward by the amount of inflation. Suppose a firm was writing off a $100 machine at $10 a year under current law. With indexed depreciation, the firm would compensate for 7 percent inflation by writing off $10 the first year, $10.70 the second, $11.45 the third, and so on, each installment 7 percent larger than the last.

The other method, accelerated depreciation, allows the firm to write off its equipment faster than it really wears out, so that the deductions are taken before inflation can reduce their real values. This is the principle behind the Capital Cost Recovery Act, also known as the 10-5-3 bill.

Capital Gains

Changes in the price of an existing asset are not payments to labor and capital for current output of goods and services. Thus, capital gains are not income in the economic sense. Nonetheless, the current tax code treats capital gains as income (and capital losses as negative income) and taxes them whether they are real or fictitious, although at reduced rates.

Inflation makes matters worse. Even at reduced rates, any tax on

334

nonexistent profits is pretty steep. In fact, it is a capital levy, partial seizure of an asset.

Martin Feldstein of the National Bureau of Economic Research, Inc., testified at a hearing of the Joint Economic Committee on July 11, 1978, on the magnitude of the problem:

> In a recent study at the National Bureau of Economic Research, we found that in 1973 individuals paid capital gains tax on $4.6 billion of nominal capital gains on corporate stock.[6] *When the costs of these shares are adjusted for the increase in the consumer price level since they were purchased, this gain becomes a loss of nearly $1 billion.*
>
> The $4.6 billion of nominal capital gains resulted in a tax liability of $1.1 billion. The tax liability on the real capital gains would have been only $661 million. *Inflation thus raised tax liabilities by nearly $500 million, approximately doubling the overall effective tax rate on corporate stock capital gains.*

Not only did inflation make for excessive capital gains taxes, but the distribution of the real gains and losses across individuals, with statutory limits on the deduction of losses, would have produced a tax liability even if the gains and losses had been adjusted for inflation before being taxed!

If capital gains and losses are to be kept as part of the tax base, the losses should be fully deductible, and the gains and losses should be adjusted for inflation. The taxpayer would multiply the purchase price of each asset by a number (provided in the tax tables) reflecting the amount of inflation since the year of purchase. This inflation-adjusted purchase price would be compared to the sales price to determine real gain or loss. For example, suppose that prices have doubled between 1969 and 1980, and a house bought for $40,000 in 1969 is sold for $90,000 in 1980. The taxpayer would turn to the table of adjustment factors and read 2.00 beside the year 1969. He would multiply $40,000 by 2.00 and claim $80,000 as his purchase price. His real taxable capital gain would be $10,000. This inflation adjustment with full deduction for losses is the very minimum that a real tax reform program should do for capital gains.

Across-the-Board Personal Income Tax Rate Reductions

Indexing would simply keep the current biased income tax structure from getting worse due to inflation. It would be better first to reduce tax rates to more reasonable levels, and then to index them. Reductions in marginal income tax rates on personal income increase the rewards of working in the market system compared to leisure or work

---

[6]Martin Feldstein and Joel Slemrod, "Inflation and the Excess Taxation of Capital Gains," National Bureau of Economic Research (published in the *National Tax Journal*, June 1978).

in the underground economy, and would cut the cost of saving and investing compared with immediate consumption. These incentive effects would induce increases in the amounts of labor and capital services employed, hence increases in total output and income compared with the levels otherwise attained. In turn, the increases in income would lead to additional saving and capital formation. While this expansion of production would enlarge tax bases compared to their size in the absence of the tax reductions, the resulting revenue reflow would fall short of completely replacing the revenues lost by the rate reductions. Nonetheless, the additional saving undertaken in response to the rate reductions would be sufficient to finance the incremental government deficit as well as substantial gains in capital formation.

These results are in sharp contrast with those from reducing *effective* or *average* tax rates rather than *marginal* tax rates. Rebates, for example, provide no incentives whatsoever for expanding the supply of labor services or for undertaking additional saving and investing. This form of tax cut primarily is allocated to financing the deficit it generates. Increases in personal exemptions or in the zero-rate brackets, although they have modest effects on marginal tax rates, principally reduce effective rates of tax. Accordingly, they have little effect in increasing incentives for productive efforts and saving.

Marginal rate reductions can, of course, be concentrated on particular brackets or income levels, but equal percentage across-the-board rate reductions avoid discrimination among taxpayers at differing income levels in pursuit of an elusive redistribution of measured income. Concentrating rate cuts at the low end of the income scale is not justifiable in terms of desired effects on saving and effort; any such pattern of tax reductions aims at income redistribution, not economic growth and efficiency.

Top priority in restructured tax policy should be given to substantial across-the-board marginal rate reductions. The rate cuts provided in the Kemp-Roth bills afford an excellent model for this basic tax revision.

Personal Savings Incentives

The importance of saving is the major theme of this paper, but saving has not been treated as important in the United States. Over the last thirty years, the U.S. has viewed saving as a drag on the economy, as a luxury item to be tacked onto other income to push it into the highest tax brackets, and as discretionary income of the rich which should be redistributed to the poor.

Other major industrial nations have treated saving as a national resource. Their personal savings rates have exceeded that of the U.S. by two, three, even four to one over the same time span. Many of these

Table 1
Personal Saving, Incentive, Productivity

	Percent of Disposable Income Saved, 1973–77	Ratio of Gross Fix Capital Formation to GNP, 1975–79	Cumulative Percent Increase in Output Per Hour in Manufacturing, 1973–79
Japan	22	31	27
France	17	22	33
Italy	25*	24	24
Germany	14	21	35
Canada	10	23	16
U.K.	14	18	4
U.S.	7	17	10

*Italy, 1975–77.
Source: OECD.

nations have encouraged saving by people of all income levels with special tax incentives. The result has been increases in capital formation, productivity, wages, and industrial strength much in excess of those scored by the United States. In fact, within a few years, several Western European nations will exceed the U.S. in real per capita income. (Table 1.)

Savings incentives may be divided into two classes — those that reduce marginal tax rates and increase incentives, and those that do not. The latter are a waste of money.

Reducing the existing tax bias against personal saving should be a top priority objective of tax policy. This objective could be served by excluding some part of personal saving from the tax base, by excluding some part of the return on saving from tax, or by reducing the rate at which these returns are taxed. These would all be partial steps toward the savings exclusion or earnings exclusion treatment of savings in the unbiased cash flow tax.

Reducing the Rate of Tax on Savings Income

Any income tax subjects savings to double taxation, as described above. Our progressive tax code makes this bias even worse. For most individual taxpayers, returns on saving — e.g., interest, dividends, capital gains — are marginal income; as such, this income is on top of the taxpayer's principal source of income, hence taxed at the top marginal rate to which the taxpayer is exposed. This accentuates the basic bias against saving.

One way to moderate this additional bias is to decouple, for tax purposes, returns on saving from wage and salary income. Savings income should be taxed separately, starting in the 14 percent tax

337

bracket, just like earned income. It should face a top tax rate of no more than 50 percent, just like earned income.

Under the current law, earned income and savings income are added together for tax purposes. An added dollar of either type of income is taxed at the taxpayer's top tax rate. However, earned income faces a maximum tax rate of 50 percent, while for savings income the maximum rate is 70 percent. Decoupling would move savings income down from the top brackets to start over again in the bottom brackets, and leave the marginal dollar of either type of income facing a lower tax rate. This is the approach of the Brown, Rousselot, Roth bill (H.R. 6400 in the 96th Congress).

The tax computation would be simple. The taxpayer would take his standard deductions and personal exemptions against whichever type of income was larger, or split them between the two, and would compute the tax due on each type of taxable income and add the two taxes together. Table 2 illustrates the change in tax computation and shows the resulting drop in the marginal tax rate on both earned income and savings income.

Table 2
Example of Tax Computation with Separation of
Earned and Unearned Income

Wage and Salary Income	$25,400	
Interest Income	2,200	
Dividend Income	2,200	
Tax Under Proposal		
Gross Earned Income	$25,400	
Less 4 Personal Exemptions	4,000	
	$21,400	
Less Zero Bracket Amount	3,400	
Equals Taxable Earned Income	$18,000	
Gross Unearned Income	$ 4,400	
Less $400 Exclusion	400	
Equals Taxable Unearned Income	$ 4,000	
Tax on Earned Income	$ 3,609	(top rate 28%)
Tax on Unearned Income	598	(top rate 16%)
Total Tax	$ 4,207	
Tax Under Current Law		
Gross Income	$29,800	
Less 4 Personal Exemptions	4,000	
	$25,800	
Less $400 Exclusion	400	
	$25,400	
Less Zero Bracket Amount	3,400	
Equals Taxable Income	$22,000	
Total Tax	$ 4,761	(top rate 32%)

Most taxpayers have only a few thousand dollars of interest, dividends, or capital gains a year. For such taxpayers, decoupling would move their savings income down to the lowest three or four tax brackets and sharply raise the after-tax yield.

This proposal would sharply reduce incentives to use present tax shelter arrangements and to rearrange income to lower tax liabilities. Current regulations prohibiting such activity would still be required, however, as would similar regulations to ensure proper compliance and enforcement under an income decoupling plan. And, of course, the details of this tax provision would have to be drawn so as to minimize opportunities for tax avoidance.

Because the proposal would create two categories of income, there would exist difficulties in identifying income by type for tax purposes to minimize avoidance. For the self-employed or proprietors, some method would have to be devised to determine what portion of income should be considered "earned" and what portion "return on saving." This would also arise in the case of small corporations, although to a far smaller degree.

The proposal does not seek to limit the taxpayer's choice of which income type to apply itemized deductions against, although some simple restrictions on the use of certain types of interest deductions may be advisable. In general, however, this flexibility is important to allow the taxpayer to receive maximum benefit from such socially important deductions as charitable contributions, medical costs, home mortgage and consumer loan interest, and state and local taxes.

This is a very powerful savings incentive, second only to outright exemption of all savings income, but much less expensive. The change in marginal tax rates and incentives would be very large for a small initial tax cut. It is very likely that this approach would generate savings increases substantially larger than the cost in revenues, enough to cause "crowding in," lower interest rates, and substantial increases in investment, resulting in no permanent revenue loss to the Treasury.

Excluding a Percent of Savings Income from Tax

Another revision for reducing the marginal tax rate on savings income would exclude some percentage of interest or dividend income from tax. A (say) 30 percent exclusion would be "at the margin" for all savers if there were no dollar limit. It would lower the effective marginal tax rates or savings income from a range of 14 to 70 percent down to a range of about 10 to 49 percent. A 60 percent partial exclusion would be similar to current treatment of capital gains. This proposal also creates two categories of income, and the same regulations would be needed as in the decoupling plan described above.

In contrast to the percentage exclusion described here, the tax code will permit limited deductions in 1981 and 1982 of small fixed dollar amounts of interest and dividends, $200 for a single return and $400 for a joint return. Such limits sharply reduce the effectiveness of the deductions. For the vast majority of savers, who already earn more than $200 or $400 in savings income, no added incentive to save is generated. The ceilings would have to be raised to several thousand dollars for such an approach to generate substantial incentives at the margin, an expensive undertaking.

Deferring Tax on Interest and Dividends

So-called rollover accounts would permit a taxpayer to accumulate interest, dividends, and/or capital gains without tax as long as they were reinvested and remained in the rollover account. There would be no deduction for savings used to buy the assets placed in the account, but the tax on the earnings would be deferred, although not eliminated.

Limited Deductions for Saving

In lieu of deferring, reducing, or eliminating tax on the returns to saving, some limited deduction for current saving could be afforded. The present-law Keogh and IRA plans could be liberalized and made more widely available, with fewer restrictions on the saving objectives and with higher limits on the amount of excludable saving allocated to such plans.

Increases in the present ceilings would be needed if any such tax revision were to be effective in providing incentives for additional saving. For those who already save the maximum amounts allowed by the plans, no added incentive would be created unless the ceilings were raised. The tax rate would not be cut at the margin.

The Marriage Tax

If two single working people get married, their tax burden rises for two reasons. First, instead of getting two standard deductions of $2,300 each, they get one standard deduction of $3,400. Second, and more importantly, their incomes are added together for tax purposes. When they were single, each income started in the 14 percent tax bracket. After marriage, one income in effect starts off paying tax in the bracket where the other income left off. Any time two incomes are added together in a progressive tax system, the tax burden rises.

To compensate, the marginal tax rate structure for married couples has been reduced at each income level. Thus, a single taxpayer faces a 30 percent tax rate on taxable income above $15,000, while a married couple faces a 21 percent tax rate at $15,000. The compensation is not complete, however.

The Senate Finance Committee has proposed that the lower-paid spouse be allowed a 10 percent exclusion of income up to $30,000 to reduce the marriage penalty further. This is a sensible approach. It effectively reduces the 21 percent tax rate in the example by one-tenth, to 18.9 percent. It not only returns money, it changes the marginal tax rate to restore incentives. It would be better without the $30,000 ceiling, but it is far superior to other proposals to give such couples an extra personal exemption, which has no marginal impact.

Why not eliminate the marriage penalty entirely? It cannot be done as long as the tax system remains progressive (as long as there are rising tax rates instead of one flat rate for all income).

If the tax rates for *all* joint returns were lowered substantially, including those for one-worker families, the marriage tax on two-worker families could be eliminated. However, this would lead to a severe bias against single workers in favor of married workers in one-worker families. Currently, a single worker pays a much higher tax than a married worker with the same salary whose spouse does not work. The married worker filing jointly splits his income with his spouse and pays a lower tax. If the tax rates on joint returns were lowered further, single workers would protest.

The solution has to come either by giving an exemption to two-worker families, preferably at the margin, or by reducing the progressivity of the tax rates, or by giving married taxpayers the option of filing as single individuals. ("Married filing separately" does not accomplish this last proposal. It simply splits the joint return brackets and standard deduction in half.)

Corporate Tax Changes

Capital Cost Recovery

The most important corporate tax reform to reduce the bias against saving would be to move as closely as possible toward expensing (first-year write-off) of purchases of plant and equipment, as in the cash flow tax. This can be done by shortening the tax lives of the various classes of plant and equipment or by increasing the investment tax credit. Either method would increase the present value of the tax saving associated with buying and depreciating a capital asset. Note that the concept of "useful life," now embedded in the tax code, is a useful concept only in the context of an income tax where neutrality is not an objective. Even here, "useful life" is an artificial "guestimate" of the decline in value of a machine from one year to the next. Machines may become technologically or competitively obsolete long before they fall apart.

While expensing may be deemed to be too drastic for any near-term program of tax changes, it should nevertheless be the goal toward which tax revisions in the area should be directed. A number of current legislative proposals represent major steps in the right direction. The 10-5-3 approach of Congressmen Jones and Conable (see above, pp. 15–18) would greatly reduce the classes of durable physical capital for which separate write-off schedules would be afforded, provide far shorter write-off periods than the present "useful life" and specify highly accelerated write-off schedules for the three classes of property. The Senate Finance Committee bill specifies four classes of machinery and equipment, for each of which an open-end account would be set up, with write-off periods far shorter than those assigned to the respective property types under present law. A 200 percent declining balance method would be used to compute the annual allowance for each account. This approach would afford enormous simplification of capital recovery by eliminating "recapture" of the excess of sales or other disposition proceeds over adjusted bases of the assets, as well as separate accounts for each year's capital acquisition as under present law and the 10-5-3 proposal. However, it would do so at the cost of incomplete write-off of the amounts invested in the property.

Each of these approaches is subject to technical modification to deal with the various relatively minor objections which have been voiced. Each, however, represents a substantial improvement over the present-law system. Without going into a detailed and extensive examination of their respective virtues and disadvantages, some such revision should be given very high priority on a tax reform agenda.

One approach to faster depreciation which should be avoided was that suggested by the Carter Administration. It proposed a complex depreciation plan with thirty categories of assets, even less complete write-off off the amounts invested, and a disturbing element of Treasury control over investment decisions. Treasury would have discretion to change the write-off periods differentially across the thirty asset categories, thus potentially directing investment money out of one industry into another. There would also be a special investment tax credit for revitalizing declining areas obtainable through a "certificate of necessity," potentially directing investment money out of one region into another. The possibility of political considerations distorting economic decisions would be substantial.

Corporate Tax Rates

To reduce the corporate tax rate is to reduce one of the multiple layers of taxation of the earnings of capital. Corporate rate cuts therefore would reduce the tax bias against saving and capital accumulation in general, and use of the corporate form in particular. Corporate tax rate reduction is a strong, neutral, nondistorting tax change "at the margin."

Ideally, the corporate tax would be eliminated by integrating it with the personal tax and passing corporate income on to the shareholder. This is far more difficult if the personal tax system remains based on income than if it is remodeled to exclude net saving.

With a fully integrated income tax, retained earnings would be taxable to the shareholders even though they are a form of saving, yet the shareholders would receive no cash with which to pay the tax. Also, retained earnings would increase the value of the shares, but since the retained earnings had already been taxed, some means would have to be found to exclude an amount equal to retained earnings from taxable capital gains when the shares were sold.

Short of total integration, it is possible to eliminate the double taxation of dividends by allowing the firm a tax deduction for dividends paid out, just as it receives for interest paid out. Alternatively, shareholders could be given a tax credit of an appropriate amount for the tax paid by the corporation. Both of these approaches have received serious consideration at one time or another in the past. To date, progress along either line has been interrupted by diverse and somewhat shortsighted objections from the corporate business community. The more substantial the reductions in corporate income tax rates, the less important would be eliminating or reducing double taxation of dividends. But for the foreseeable future, this remains a serious deficiency in the tax law, and its remedy should be a major concern of tax policy.

Savings, Productivity and Economic Growth

Anyone hoping for more rapid economic growth must be concerned with savings. Only that part of national income which goes into savings (and which is not borrowed by government to fund its deficits) is available to finance investment. Thus, investment depends on savings, and growth depends on investment. The amount of GNP devoted to investment basically determines the country's growth rate. Only by increasing savings can the real growth rate be raised.

Saving and growth are not just an end in themselves. Professor Michael Boskin recently told the Joint Economic Committee:

> Private saving is important for two reasons: It is a major form of funding available to finance new investment, and it is *the* way in which our citizens transfer resources from one part of their lifetime to another, especially from their peak earning years to retirement.[7]

Saving for retirement is not just storage of cash. It provides funds for investment to expand the capacity of the economy to produce goods in the future. The retiree can draw on that increased production

---

[7]See "Taxation, Inflation, Social Security, and Economic Growth," Testimony of Michael J. Boskin, professor of economics, Stanford University (July 30, 1980), p. 3.

without taking goods and services away from future workers. The U.S. population is aging. The ratio of retirees to workers will climb sharply over the next few decades. Only by increasing the growth rate can we be assured of an adequate capacity to produce goods in future years to allow for both increasing numbers of retirees and a rising standard of living for future workers.

Economic growth is particularly critical to the solvency of the Social Security System. The social security tax increases now taking effect are drawing sharp protests. In fact, these tax increases are just the tip of the iceberg. Benefits currently promised will require increases in the social security tax rates by more than 30 percent, from over 12 percent of payroll to over 16 percent of payroll, over the next 50 to 70 years, if real wages grow only as rapidly as the Social Security Administration predicts (1¾ to 2 percent per year) under its "intermediate" assumptions about demographics and productivity. Under its "pessimistic" assumptions, which grow more likely as productivity continues to falter, the tax rates will jump by nearly 90 percent, to almost 24 percent of payroll! It is widely assumed that the next generations will be unwilling to pay such taxes. Some have suggested reducing benefits or raising the retirement age to 68 for workers just entering the System. However, if wages could be encouraged to grow faster, revenues could rise without a tax rate increase. An increase in the annual growth rate of productivity and wages by only 0.75 percent above the intermediate assumption would raise wages by enough to forestall most of the projected tax rate increases, at the same level of benefits.

The government could help growth by reducing government spending to lower the deficit. This would reduce federal borrowing and free up savings to finance investment. However, a tax rate increase to reduce the deficit would also reduce saving by reducing the after-tax return to saving and would be counterproductive. Contrary to the old canon, it is not the deficit per se that determines the degree of crowding out or inflation, it is the relationship between the deficit and the supply of saving to finance it without inflationary creation of new money. In fact, a tax change that induced a bigger jump in saving than it cost in revenue would produce "crowding in," lower interest rates, and less inflation.

There are only three sources of domestic saving for an economy (aside from foreign capital). These are depreciation allowances and other retained earnings of firms, the personal savings of households, and government budget surpluses (which add money to the capital markets by repaying government debt). Other nations have saved and invested more than the U.S. by wide margins over the years.

The following shows how serious the problem is.

In 1979, gross investment was $387 billion, but $114 billion went for housing and $18 billion for additions to inventory. Only $254 billion went into plant, equipment, and other production-oriented private sector investment. Of that, $188 billion went to replace worn-out plant and equipment, leaving only $66 billion. Of that net investment, some $25 to $30 billion went for pollution control and safety, leaving $40 billion or less.

With only $40 billion in net investment, it was not possible to maintain the same ratio of heavy manufacturing to GNP of earlier years. Approximately 2.5 million people entered the labor force in 1979. Had they sought employment in basic industry in the same ratio as the total labor force, instead of going heavily into the less capital intensive service sector, each new worker would have required about $20,000 in plant and equipment, or $50 billion, just to be as productive as existing workers! We would have had an investment gap of at least $10 billion just to keep productivity standing still.

In reality, productivity fell 0.9 percent in 1979. Even worse, the average weekly spendable earnings (adjusted for inflation and taxes) of the average worker have now declined for several years and have fallen to *1964* levels! It is hard to tell how much of this decline was due to inadequate capital formation, how much to inadequate education and training, and how much to an increase in the number of young workers and women in the labor force who wanted only light or part-time work in the less productive service sector. The basic point is that workers in all sectors of the economy would be more productive and better paid if they had more capital with which to work.

Clearly, both corporate and personal savings and the resulting investment must be encouraged, and soon. In view of the gains that are possible from economic growth, and the affordability of the necessary tax reforms, the Administration should work with the Congress to design and implement a comprehensive multi-year tax policy as soon as possible.

16

Credit Programs

by Ron Boster

A budget, it has been said, is a mathematical confirmation of your suspicions.[1] The federal budget process, politicized by both the Executive and Legislative branches, has sought to avoid such direct confirmation and therefore evokes even more suspicion.

This essay is concerned with federal credit programs and how they are treated (and mistreated) in the budget of the United States government. Federal credit programs and federally-sponsored credit activities — extensive in scope, size, variety, and growing dramatically — constitute the single most important source of distortion in the budget. The focus here is on how broad categories of credit programs are handled in the federal budget, what problems result from their treatment, and what solutions there are for these problems.[2]

Budgeting is taken here to be synonymous with fiscal or financial planning and, as such, is concerned with two main problems:

- determining the size and impact of government as a share of the domestic economy; and,
- determining the distribution (allocation) of resources among government programs and activities.

The present treatment of federal credit activities in the budget thwarts both of these objectives. By understating the size of the federal establishment, credit programs make the government appear smaller and less significant than it is. And, since the distortions fall

---

[1] Attributed to A. A. Latimer.

[2] At best, this chapter can be little more than a cursory treatment of what is a significant area of public policy. Many important topics must, of necessity be glossed over. More extensive work has been done, however, and the reader may want to consult other studies for a more complete analysis. These include the various references noted throughout this chapter. A bibliography of reports and studies dealing with federal credit programs is contained in the recent Congressional Budget Office study, "Federal Credit Activities: An Analysis of the President's Credit Budget for 1981," Congressional Budget Office, February 1980 (Appendix A).

disproportionately in the various program areas, the budget presents a misleading picture of the distribution of federal resources.

Because they can be understated within the budget or hidden outside the budget, credit programs in general enjoy a certain political advantage over non-credit programs which are more directly and openly accounted. A variety of means of meeting national policy goals by direct expenditures — grants, contracts, in-house — may be more efficient than credit programs, but may not be selected because their costs are more obvious. The ability to hide or understate program levels thus creates a built-in tendency for bigger government. In addition, at least in part because of their budgetary treatment, credit programs generally receive less legislative and budget-related oversight than do non-credit programs.

The number of individual credit programs is both large and a matter of definition. A detailed, but unofficial 1978 Office of Management and Budget count pegged the number of active direct loan programs at eighty-one, the number of loan participation and purchase programs at ten, non-cash credit extension programs at five, and loan guarantees and insurance programs at forty-six. Within the Farmer's Home Administration alone, an on-budget agency, there are more than fifty distinct, direct loan programs.

The Scope, Magnitude, and Impact of Federal Credit Programs

Federal credit involvement constitutes a significant component of the federal establishment and fiscal policy. Federal and federally-sponsored credit programs have grown dramatically over the past few decades, far faster than the federal budget (Figure 1). Between 1970 and 1979, federal outlays (including off-budget spending) increased 151 percent.[3] Over that same period, direct loans outstanding increased 250 percent, guaranteed loans increased 171 percent, net direct loans (gross new lending less repayments from previous lending) increased 436 percent, and net guaranteed loans increased 459 percent.

An excellent indication of the size and scope of federal credit programs is to compare their level to the total U.S. capital market. In terms of the total $410.7 billion advanced in U.S. credit markets in 1979, participation by the federal government (either by government agencies or by government-sponsored entities) amounted to 17.8 percent, above the average of 13.7 percent for the past 10 years (Table 1); federal participation varied from a low of 10.6 percent in 1976 to a high of 18.6 percent in 1970.

---

[3] Throughout this essay, extensive use will be made of data for fiscal year 1979. At the time of this writing, fiscal year 1979 represented the latest year for which full-year (actual) data were available. Because of the high volatility of credit program activity, the use of estimates for 1980 or 1981 was deemed unwise.

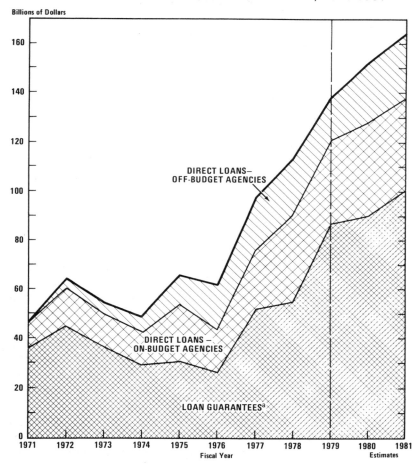

Figure 1.

Growth of Total New Commitments for Federal Credit, 1971-1981

Billions of Dollars

DIRECT LOANS—
OFF-BUDGET AGENCIES

DIRECT LOANS –
ON-BUDGET AGENCIES

LOAN GUARANTEES[a]

1971 1972 1973 1974 1975 1976 1977 1978 1979 1980 1981

Fiscal Year   Estimates

SOURCE: Budget of the United States Government, Special Analysis on Credit,
Fiscal Years 1973-1981.

[a] Primary guarantees: excludes secondary guarantees and guaranteed loans
acquired by on- and off-budget agencies.

By law, most federal credit activities are excluded from the budget. As a result, the unified budget understates both the extent of government involvement in money markets and the government's credit activities. Nevertheless, owing to qualitative differences between facilitating or even making credit and making an "exhaustive" (never to be seen again) cash payment, legitimate questions have been raised as to whether federal credit activities should be in the budget. This question is analyzed below, with the conclusion that federal credit activities should be included in the budget.

Table 1
Federal Participation (Funds Advanced) in U.S. Capital Markets
(dollars in billions)

Year	Total Funds Advanced in U.S. Capital Markets	Total Funds Advanced Under Federal Auspices	Federal Participation Rate
1970	$ 93.6	$16.1	17.2%
1971	125.7	16.5	13.1
1972	163.5	22.9	14.0
1973	207.7	27.2	13.1
1974	193.4	25.5	13.2
1975	181.3	27.0	14.9
1976	251.8	26.8	10.6
TQ*	66.1	6.7	10.1
1977	314.4	37.2	11.8
1978	385.3	58.7	15.2
1979	410.7	73.3	17.8

*Transaction Quarter

Source: Budget of the United States Government, FY 1981, Special Analysis F (Federal Credit Programs), GPO, Washington, January 1980, p. 144.

The very nature of credit programs introduces major distortions in the capital market. Federal credit programs induce resource allocations that would not otherwise occur in the absence of federal involvement. Resources are shifted, maintained, or otherwise utilized in a manner different from how they would otherwise be employed. This means that certain individuals and segments of society are favored at the expense of others. "By directing credit toward some uses, and implicitly away from others, the federal government significantly influences almost every facet of economic life."[4] These distributional impacts translate into structural effects over time.

Government credit programs, create a deliberate "crowding out" in the credit market. The government substitutes its credit standing for that of the favored activity or industry. Credit-worthy private sector customers are thus either closed out of the capital market or required to pay higher prices (interest rates) and/or receive less favorable terms and conditions than they would be able to obtain in the absence of the federal intervention. For example, the Chrysler bailout took that company from the bottom of the credit line to near the top. In the process, other companies and individuals were relegated to a lower credit priority.

The rationale for credit programs is found in the budget:

Credit programs, much like Federal expenditures on goods and services,

---

[4] "Federal Credit Activities: An Analysis of the President's Credit Budget for 1981," Washington, Congressional Budget Office, February 1980, p. xxii.

tax expenditures, or transfer payments, can be used to change the allocation of resources and the distribution of income. In this regard, they can be used to overcome market imperfections, to provide additional liquidity for investors, and to furnish funds to maintain stability in a particular sector of the economy during business cycle fluctuations. Credit programs have been designed to fill perceived needs in private capital markets by providing credit to certain classes of borrowers, or on special terms or conditions or for special activities. An element of subsidy is involved in any Federal credit program since assistance is given on terms or conditions more favorable than would have occurred in private capital markets.

A subsidy is provided, in general, because the Federal Government is willing to accept risks that lenders in private capital markets are unwilling to bear or would bear only at higher interest rates than the Federal Government would charge.[5]

It is wrong to assume that all activities undertaken with the aid of federal or federally-sponsored credit programs would not occur in the absence of government programs (e.g., veterans would still buy houses). It is, however, difficult to estimate what portion of subsidized credit activities would be discouraged if the subsidies were eliminated. Thus, it is difficult to measure the degree of resource misallocation.

In like manner, reduction in federal credit programs would not necessarily result in a reduction in money-market activity. To the extent federal credit programs "crowd out" private borrowing, a drop in activity could be mitigated by new, private borrowing; to the extent federal programs increase liquidity (capital rollover velocity) by providing well-organized and specialized secondary markets,[6] a reduction could be offset by new, private arrangements that would raise trading activity. A more certain result of a reduction in government credit activity would be a different allocation of capital resources.

Forms of Federal Credit Programs

Federal credit activities consist of direct loans and guaranteed loans. These are taken up below, followed by an examination of off-budget credit activity, and a commentary on the Federal Financing Bank (FFB), currently the major actor in the federal credit arena. Because of the FFB's prominent role, the important topics of loan asset sales and purchases of guaranteed loans are examined with the FFB. The essay concludes with a treatment of government-sponsored,

---

[5] *Budget of the United States Government, Special Analyses,* Fiscal Year 1981, Washington, GPO, p. 141.

[6] Whether federal or federally-sponsored credit programs increase *total* credit liquidity is a worthy — if heroic — question. Total liquidity may be more independent of federal credit programs than is commonly assumed.

351

Table 2
Direct Federal Loans by Agency or Program, Fiscal Year 1979
(dollars in millions)

Agency or Program	Outstanding	Percent of Grand total	New Loans	Percent of Grand total
On-Budget				
International security assistance	$1,790	8%	1,308	3%
International development assistance	1,001	5%	3	*
Agriculture:				
Farmers Home Administration	3,896	18	14,448	28
Commodity Credit Corporation	0		6,104	
Public Law 480 long-term export credits	0		778	
Other	0		0	
Commerce:				
Economic Development Administration	63	*	73	*
National Oceanic and Atmospheric Administration	80	*	27	*
Maritime Administration	0		29	
Education:				
Student Assistance	466	2	310	1
Other education programs	468	2	349	1
Health and Human Services:				
Health programs	18	*	63	*
Housing and Urban Development:				
Housing programs	841	4	1,196	2
Government National Mortgage Association	5,529	25	2,053	4
Community planning and development	118	1	333	1
New Communities Administration	0		0	
Interior	37	*	47	*
Transportation:				
Railroad programs	264	1	73	*
Other	158	1	12	*
Treasury	8	*	*	
Veterans Administration:				
Housing loans and default claims	9	*	394	1

yet privately owned enterprises which engage in major loan programs.

Direct Loans

Direct loans are cash payments secured by a promise to repay (an

Table 2 (Continued)
Direct Federal Loans by Agency or Program, Fiscal Year 1979
(dollars in millions)

Agency or Program	Outstanding	Percent of Grand total	New Loans	Percent of Grand total
Insurance policy and other loans	*		181	*
To: District of Columbia	0		141	*
Export-Import Bank	4,204	19	3,367	7
Federal Home Loan Bank Board	0		32	*
National Consumer Cooperative Bank	0		0	
National Credit Union Administration	0		17	*
Small Business Administration:				
Business and investment loans	94	*	541	1
Disaster loans	446	2	1,288	3
Tennessee Valley Authority Fund	0		21	*
United States Railway Association[1]	0		708	1
Other agencies and programs	2	*	28	*
Subtotal, on-budget agencies	19,489	88%	33,924	66%
Off-budget				
Rural electrification and telephone revolving fund	2,124	10	1,250	2
Rural Telephone Bank	449	2	131	*
Pension Benefit Guaranty Corporation	0		0	
Federal Financing Bank	0		16,045	31
United States Railway Association	0		53	*
Subtotal, off-budget Federal entities	2,573	12	17,479	34%
Grand total	22,062	100%	51,402	100%

*Less than 0.5 percent or less than $50 million, totals may not add due to rounding.
[1]Includes both debentures and repayable preferred stock of Conrail.

Source: The Budget of the United States Government for Fiscal Year 1981, Special Analysis F (Federal Credit Programs) January 1980, GPO, Washington, Table F-2, p. 146.

IOU). Such loan programs occur in many program and policy areas (Table 2). Direct loans are recorded in the budget as net of repayments. Treatment of direct loans on a net basis produces an accurate cash flow and financial statement — certainly an important criterion — but also serves to conceal the magnitude of direct loan activity. Net figures are of no use for comparing the sizes of various direct loan programs; a very large and active loan program can look quite innocuous if loan repayments are significant relative to loan originations. Because lending is commonly reported on a net basis, lending and outlays are understated in the 1979 budget by $25.9 billion (the amount of repayments of previously-made loans). In the same manner, off-budget spending is understated by $2.7 billion.[7]

Should Direct Loans be in the Budget?

The budgetary status of direct loans is controversial. In 1979, 70 percent of direct federal loans were off-budget. Some, including the Federal Reserve Board and Congressional Research Service specialist Allen Schick, have argued for excluding direct loans.[8] Others, including the President's Commission on Budget Concepts and the Congressional Budget Office, have argued for inclusion.

Because loans are made in exchange for a promise to repay, and because these IOUs are, in fact, marketable, the making of a direct loan constitutes an exchange of assets. This, it is argued, has an economic impact different from a direct payment; a person on the receiving end is likely to behave differently than if he did not have to pay it back later, with interest. Direct loans are excluded from the government expenditure accounts of the national income accounts (NIA). This dovetails with business practice, wherein loans owned are counted as assets rather than expenditures.

A more compelling case exists for inclusion. No one budget can accomplish all purposes generally sought for budgets. This is why there are capital or dividend budgets, NIA-based budgets, administrative budgets, full-employment budgets, and various kinds of unified budgets.

The President's Commission on Budget Concepts (1967) recommended a unified budget that would include "all programs of the Federal Government and its agencies." Loan programs were to be included, though the Commission recommended separate loan accounts within the expenditure side of the budget. In this way, the budget would not only include all government activities, but would better facilitate the measurement of the economic impact of the fiscal policy embodied in the budget. The Commission sought a federal budget that

---

[7] Loan repayments are not actually "hidden"; rather, they are simply not readily apparent (or available) to people unaccustomed to dealing with budgets. Specifically, lines 11 and 14 of federal budget program and financing statements ("P & Fs" in budget parlance) have always shown loan repayments.

[8] See statements by Governor Nancy Teeters, representing the Federal Reserve System, and Allen Schick in: *Control of Federal Credit Program,* House Committee on the Budget, Hearings before the Task Force on Budget Process, November 13 & 14, 1979, Washington, D.C., 1980.

would increase public understanding and be "thought of as a part of a broad financial plan."

These objectives are difficult to reach if billions of dollars of direct loans are systematically excluded. The Commission recognized fully the likely behavior-induced differences between non-loan (exhaustive) direct expenditures and direct loans, but felt that including loan activities in the budget, in separable accounts, was the best way to meet the objectives of a federal budget.[9] The Commission also recognized the importance of recording loan activity on a net basis, but recommended that gross new loans and total loans outstanding be displayed prominently.[10]

Including direct loans in the budget better serves the objectives of including all government activities in the budget, increasing public understanding, and making the budget a financial plan and summary. An additional argument for the inclusion of federal credit programs stems from the political reality of the almost singleminded public focus on budget margins (deficits or surpluses). The President's Commission on Budget Concepts did not want the unified budget to become the political focal point it has become; the Commission sought to de-emphasize the viewing of the federal budget so narrowly. Nevertheless, so long as this fascination persists, it is clearly better to present budget margins that represent what most people expect — namely, *all* the activities of the federal government.

Federal Loan Guarantees

Federal loan guarantee programs have grown dramatically in recent years (Figure 1).[11] Loan guarantees can be a very flexible policy tool, yet widespread misconceptions about their economic and budgetary impacts have contributed to their rapid growth and abuse. Histori-

[9] *Report of the President's Commission on Budget Concepts,* GPO, 1967.

[10] When the government makes a loan, it expects to get the money back with interest. But not always; some government programs operate under the guise of loan or credit programs, but probably would be more accurately classified as transfer payment or direct expenditure programs. Traditional non-recourse loans (before the inception of the Farmer Owned Reserve), whereby a farmer posts commodities as collateral, are probably closer to transfer payments. This type of "loan" is really an expenditure in the form of a deferred purchase of commodities by the Commodity Credit Corporation, and is so treated in the national income accounts (*Report of the President's Commission on Budget Concepts,* p. 51). In addition, many foreign loans are made on non-commercial terms. For example, Food for Peace (P.L. 480) loans provide twenty-to-forty-year terms, 2–3 percent interest, and five-to-ten-year grace periods.

[11] For more detailed information, see: "Loan Guarantees: Current Concerns and Alternatives for Control," Washington, Congressional Budget Office, August 1978; and, "Loan Insurance and Guarantee Programs: A Comparison of Current Practices and Procedures," in: *Loan Guarantees: Current Concerns and Alternatives for Control, A Compilation of Staff Working Papers,* Washington, Congressional Budget Office, January 1979.

Table 3
Federal Loan Guarantees by Program or Agency, Fiscal Year 1979
(dollars in millions)

Agency or Programs[1]	Outstanding	New Loan Guarantees
Funds Appropriated to the President:		
Energy security trust fund	0	0
International security assistance	5,670	1,207
International development assistance	852	49
Callable capital contributions	11,545	883
Agriculture:		
Farmers Home Administration	37,078	8,857
Commodity Credit Corporation	136	136
Rural Electrification Administration	7,535	2,650
Commerce:		
Economic development assistance	883	636
National Oceanic and Atmosphere Administration	106	58
Maritime Administration	5,703	266
Education:		
Guarantees of SLMA debt issues	1,275	530
Student loan insurance fund	8,302	1,477
Other education programs	1,305	− 21
Energy:		
Geothermal resources development fund	14	1
Energy Conservation	0	0
Energy production, demonstration, and distribution	0	0
Energy Security Reserve	0	0
Energy Security Corporation	0	0
Health and Human Services:		
Medical facilities guarantees	1,321	− 26
Health programs	167	32
Housing and Urban Development:		
Subsidized low-rent public housing	15,050	483
Federal Housing Administration	110,051	11,922
Community development grants	12	12
Urban renewal	466	− 325
New Communities Administration	141	− 2
GNMA: Mortage-backed securities	70,558	17,594
Interior:		
Indian programs	49	− 3

cally, loan guarantees have been used primarily for housing assistance (e.g., FHA, VA insurance programs). More recently, other areas — notably agriculture and foreign trade assistance — have carved out portions of the growing loan guarantee pie. The diversity of policy areas in which guaranteed loan programs operate is even greater than for direct loan programs (Table 3).

The government guarantees a private loan when it agrees to "stand behind" that loan in the event of a default. The guarantee may be for the entire loan amount or some specified fraction of the principal.

Table 3 (Continued)
Federal Loan Guarantees by Program or Agency, Fiscal Year 1979
(dollars in millions)

Agency or Programs[1]	Outstanding	New Loan Guarantees
Transportation:		
Rail programs	1,102	40
Washington, D.C. METRO bonds	997	0
Aircraft loans	190	−19
Treasury:		
Guarantee of New York City notes	500	500
Chrysler Corporation loan guarantee program	0	0
NASA: Long term satellite leases	423	186
Veterans Administration (housing)	89,158	8,364
Export-Import Bank	6,586	1,179
General Services Administration	1,242	30
NCUA: Credit Union share insurance fund	12	4
Small Business Administration:		
Business loan guarantees	7,621	720
Lease and surety bond guarantees	596	93
Lease guarantees	228	−32
Disaster Loan fund	7	−2
Pollution control bond guarantees	55	40
TVA: Seven State Energy Corp.	0	0
Other agencies and programs	238	−49
Subtotal, guaranteed loans (gross)	387,172	57,469
Adjustments		
Less secondary guaranteed loans:[2]		
GNMA guarantees of FHA/VA pools	70,558	17,594
DEd guarantees of SLMA debt issues	1,275	530
DOT guarantees of USRA debt	537	85
Subtotal, guaranteed loans (net)	314,801	39,260
Less guaranteed loans held as direct loans:[3]		
By budget agency (GNMA)	3,105	−137
By off-budget Federal Financing Bank	47,100	13,282
Subtotal, primary guaranteed loans	264,596	26,115

[1]Includes off-budget loan guarantees.
[2]Secondary guarantees by the Export-Import Bank of the debt of the Private Export Finance Corporation have not been estimated and are excluded from the table.
[3]When loan guarantees are acquired by a budget account, they are direct loans. However, in this instance, GNMA is acquiring a guaranteed loan not only from different accounts, but different agencies.

Loan insurance programs, such as FHA and VA-insured mortgages, are forms of government loan guarantees.

Loan guarantees have an unparalleled attraction as a vehicle for carrying out government policies. The common perception is that they are almost free — that aside from modest administration costs, only in the event of default does the government pay (in accordance with its commitment to stand behind the loan). Thus, there is a widespread belief that guaranteed loans offer tremendous leverage in terms of the size of a program that can be supported relative to its costs.

This perception is illusory. One reason is that the resulting inefficient distribution of resources, although admittedly difficult to measure, is rarely considered. Another reason is that guaranteed loans are often converted to off-budget direct loans through purchase by the off-budget Federal Financing Bank.

Some direct loans start out as private loans guaranteed by the government. A circuitous accounting route is initiated when a government agency guarantees a private (non-government) loan. If this private loan is purchased by the government or one of its sponsored entities, thereby replenishing the original lender's lendable cash reserves (i.e., a loan portfolio "rollover"), the original government loan guarantee is converted into a direct government loan.

An outrageous example is the operation of the Student Loan Marketing Association (SLMA, or Sally Mae). Sally Mae purchases loans from private lenders made to students and guaranteed by the U.S. Department of Education. Although the SLMA is legally under private ownership, its unique relationship with the federal government permits it to borrow all of its operating funds from the government, through the Federal Financing Bank. SLMA thus purchases guaranteed loans with funds borrowed from the FFB, which in turn, borrows from the Treasury (which, in turn, borrows from the public). In the process, privately generated loans are converted into "extra-budget" government direct loans.

The logical question is why jump through so many hoops; why not operate the student loan program as an on-budget, direct loan program? This would make it much easier to understand and to compare and contrast with other federal education programs, whether loan or non-loan in nature. In fact, the Carter Administration proposed in its higher education legislation that Sally Mae's activities be assumed in 1982 by the Department of Education and that they be included in the budget totals. Congress has ignored the proposal.

Guaranteed loans are routinely purchased by the federal government — usually by the Federal Financing Bank. The vast majority have been guaranteed not by private lenders, but by government entities. Because the FFB is off-budget, the resulting direct loans are excluded from the totals of the unified budget. In such cases, the FFB acts as the lender on behalf of the federal government; the FFB originates (makes) the loan. This is similar to the FFB purchasing loan assets (discussed below).

Why are guaranteed loans purchased? One reason is to advance the objectives of the guaranteed loan programs by keeping the interest rates lower than private market rates. For the borrower, the "liquidity premium" that would otherwise be faced is eliminated. Even though a loan may be backed by the full faith and credit of the federal government, it is nevertheless distinct from normal Treasury offerings, and will therefore attract a smaller pool of buyers. For this reason, the market demands a higher yield on the loan.

If, for example, the Chrysler guaranteed loans had been purchased by the FFB (as was originally provided for in the legislation) Chrysler would have been able to borrow at about 10.5 percent, the rate which government securities of equal maturities were going for at the time. However, an eleventh-hour provision of the Chrysler legislation prohibited government purchases of the loans, and as a result, Chrysler paid 11.4 percent.[12]

In lieu of purchase by the government, guaranteed loans must compete with other government issues. Therefore, it is in the government's self-interest to assume the posture of a monopolist (becoming in effect, the sole provider) in order to reduce competition and, therefore, total borrowing costs. By substituting a government direct loan for a government-guaranteed loan, the government eliminates a "competition premium." The government, in effect, is exchanging a current lump-sum payment (the purchase price of the loan) for a time stream of lower interest charges on all government credit offerings.

Current budgetary treatment excludes most purchases of government-guaranteed loans because they are made by the FFB, an off-budget agency with unlimited authority to finance such purchases through Treasury borrowing. Bringing the FFB on-budget would correct the problem of not reflecting all direct loans (including guaranteed loans converted into direct loans) in the budget totals. This poses a political problem because both the spending side of the budget and the budget deficit would increase by the amount of the loan purchase price. This would not, however, alter the economic impacts of guaranteed loan programs unless this change significantly reduced loan guarantee activity.

Off-Budget Federal Credit

When a unified budget was first adopted for fiscal year 1969, the intent was to follow one of the main recommendations of the President's Commission on Budget Concepts — that the "budget should include all programs of the Federal Government and its agencies." Yet, by law,

---

[12] In dollar terms, the Treasury estimated that had Chrysler been permitted to sell its bonds to the FFB, the company "could have saved about $2 million in underwriting fees and about $26 million in interest costs in the next ten years" (*Wall Street Journal*, August 24, 1980, p. 3). The political/rhetorical subtleties associated with the purchases of guaranteed loans should not go unnoticed. Rarely is there a straightforward request for government direct loans; usually, the request is couched in terms of guaranteed loans (which, more often than not, just happen to be eligible for purchase — conversion to direct loans — by the federal government).

Table 4

Activity Levels of Federally-Owned Off-Budget Entities, Fiscal Year 1979
(dollars in thousands)

Off-budget Federal Entity	Direct Loans Outstanding	New Loans Dispersed	Repayments of Principle	Net Outlays
Federal Financing Bank	$47,100,400	$15,459,492	$2,763,035	$12,586,422
Rural Electrification & Telephone Re-volving Fund	7,534,641	1,690,757[1]	313,786	589,285[1]
Rural Telephone Bank	739,310	130,540	5,329	100,719
Pension Benefit Guarantee Corp.[2]	N/A	N/A	N/A	– 38,848
Postal Service Fund[2]	N/A	N/A	N/A	– 890,748
U.S. Railway Assoc.	387,252	53,068	22,885	88,938
U.S. Synthetic Fuels Corp.[3]	–	–	–	–
Total	$55,761,603	$17,333,857	$3,105,035	$12,435,768

Source: Budget of the United States Government, GPO, Washington, January 1980.
[1]These numbers have been adjusted to reflect the $585,525 thousand in sales of CBOs by the revolving fund to the FFB. The figure has been subtracted from the FFB row and added to the revolving fund row in order to more accurately reflect program activities of the revolving fund.
[2]These entities do not conduct loan programs; however, the Administration has proposed future credit activity for the Pension Benefit Guarantee Corp. to provide financial assistance to insolvent pension programs in the form of direct loans.
[3]U.S. Synthetic Fuels Corp. began operations in 1980.

the spending of off-budget agencies is excluded from the budget totals. The existence of federally-owned off-budget agencies (apart from the government-sponsored, yet privately-owned enterprises discussed below) clearly flies in the face of this recommendation and the Commission's concept of a unified budget.

Table 4 shows the agency distribution and magnitude of off-budget loan programs by loans outstanding, new loan disbursements, repayments of principal, and net outlays for 1979. Five of the seven off-budget agencies conduct credit programs. Only the Pension Benefit Guaranty Corporation and the Postal Service do not. The major off-budget agency — the Federal Financing Bank — is discussed in detail in the next section.

The number of off-budget agencies outside of the unified budget has fluctuated from none in 1969 through 1973, to a high of eight in 1976, to the present seven (including the new Synthetic Fuels Corporation which began operations in 1980). While the number of entities has fluctuated, total off-budget activity has grown dramatically (Table 5). Both actual dollar increases in off-budget deficits (column 2) and the increasing ratio of off-budget deficits to on-budget deficits (column 5) are cause for concern. Except for 1976, off-budget spending has been

Table 5
Off-Budget Deficits and the Unified Budget
(dollars in billions)

(1)	(2)	(3)	(4)	(5)
			Percent of	Percent of
	Off-Budget	Percent	Unified	Unified
Fiscal Year	Deficit	Increase	Budget Outlays	Budget Deficit
1969–1972	$ —	—	— %	—
1973	0.1	—	0.02	0.4
1974	1.4	1300.0%	0.5	30.9
1975	8.1	478.6	2.5	17.8
1976	7.3	9.9	2.0	11.0
1977	8.7	19.2	2.2	19.3
1978	10.3	18.4	2.3	21.1
1979	12.4	20.4	2.5	44.8
1980	16.1*	29.8	2.8	26.4
1981	21.7*	34.8	3.4	72.8

*Administration estimates of July 1980.

climbing steadily as a percent of unified budget outlays (column 4). As a percent of the unified budget deficit, the rise has been startling, though erratic — totalling almost 45 percent in 1979, and projected to rise to nearly 73 percent in 1981.

Credit programs clearly dominate off-budget activity. In fact, 1979 credit-related off-budget outlays are actually higher, by nearly a billion dollars, than the $12.4 billion total because of offsetting receipts of the Pension Benefit Guaranty Corporation and a rare surplus in the Postal Service fund.

Off-budget status need not mean less oversight or more independence in carrying out assigned tasks. Neither is off-budget status necessarily incompatible with strict financial control. Off-budget status does, however, make financial control more complicated and confusing.

The best example is provided by the latest pledge to the off-budget fraternity — the Synthetic Fuels Corporation. Descriptions of the financial/budgeting requirements for the Corporation constitute an unnecessary set of accounting pylons that must be negotiated in order to understand the relationship of the corporation to the United States government and the budget. There are no compelling arguments for the off-budget status of the Corporation. The establishment of a new off-budget entity eleven years after the adoption of the unified budget concept is a step away from honest budgeting.

It is important to note that off-budget loans are no different than on-budget loans in terms of their economic impacts and government involvement. But, as noted above, returning off-budget spending to the unified budget poses political problems because of the resulting highly visible impact on total outlays and the deficit.[13]

The Federal Financing Bank (FFB)

The Federal Financing Bank (FFB), an off-budget, federal agency quartered in the Treasury Department building, was established in 1973 and is authorized to purchase: 1) agency debt; 2) agency-guaranteed loans; and 3) agency loan assets (agency-owned loans, pools of loans, or shares in pools of agency-owned loans).[14] To finance these operations, the FFB borrows exclusively from the Treasury, from which it has unlimited borrowing authority.[15] The bank passes on to its agency customers a one-eighth percent charge to cover administrative costs; any excess over its costs are paid as dividends to the Treasury.

Although the FFB conducts no government loan programs itself, it originated $15.5 billion in direct loans in 1979 on behalf of on-budget agencies (Table 4). FFB loans accounted for 92 percent of all new off-budget loans in 1979. Loans outstanding tell much the same story; the FFB holds 84 percent of the $56 billion in off-budget loans outstanding at the end of 1979. Table 5 shows the growing amounts and proportions of direct loans that are off-budget.

Since its inception, the bank's holdings have grown dramatically (Table 6). The FFB is easily the largest (some would also say the most infamous) off-budget agency; its outlays swamp those of the other six off-budget federal entities.

The FFB plays the dominant role in government loan asset and guaranteed loan transactions. The budgetary treatment of agency loan asset sales to the FFB results in major outlay understatements in the unified budget. Yet, for all its notoriety, the FFB is a scapegoat. The bank's outlays do not result from programs it runs; the bank serves only as a financial conduit for other federal agencies and their programs.

---

[13] In his final budget (FY 1978), President Ford showed the off-budget deficit and the total deficit in the first budget summary tables, on pages 3, 4, 5, and 7 of the budget. This courage—which, it should be noted, came after the election—has yet to be repeated.

[14] For more detailed information about the FFB see: "The Federal Financing Bank: A Primer," in *Loan Guarantees: Current Concerns and Alternatives for Control,* Congressional Budget Office, Washington, January 1979; also, *The Federal Financing Bank: Background Operations and Budget Status,* Library of Congress, Congressional Research Service, February 2, 1979, (H.J. 8045 U.S.).

[15] Public Law 93-244 (The Federal Financing Bank Act of 1973), 12 U.S.C. 2281. The FFB also has authority to borrow directly from the public (not to exceed $15 billion outstanding) but has done so only once, early in its history, wherein the bank learned it was cheaper to borrow from the Treasury. Thereafter, the bank's policy has been to borrow exclusively from the Treasury.

Table 6

Holdings of the Federal Financing Bank, End of FY 1979

(in millions of dollars)

Program	September 30, 1979
On-Budget Agency Debt	
Tennessee Valley Authority	$ 7,125.0
Export-Import Bank	7,952.9
Off-Budget Agency Debt	
U.S. Postal Service	1,587.0
U.S. Railway Association	445.7
Agency Assets	
Farmers Home Administration	31,080.0
DHEW-Health Maintenance Org. Loans	77.3
DHEW-Medical Facility Loans	160.1
Overseas Private Investment Corp.	35.8
Rural Electrification Admin.-CBO	1,223.2
Small Business Administration	94.4
Government Guaranteed Loans	
DOT-Emergency Rail Services Act	37.4
DOT-Title V, RRRR Act	92.7
DOD-Foreign Military Sales	5,270.9
General Services Administration	359.7
Guam Power Authority	36.0
DHUD-New Communities Admin.	38.5
DHUD-Community Block Grant	5.4
Nat'l. Railroad Passenger Corp. (AMTRAK)	432.3
NASA	420.3
Rural Electrification Administration	5,926.5
Small Business Investment Companies	336.4
Student Loan Marketing Association	1,275.0
Virgin Islands	21.6
Wash. Metro. Area Trans. Auth.	177.0
Total	$64,211.0*

Source: Federal Financing Bank
*Totals do not add due to rounding.

FFB Purchase of Agency Debt

One of the main objectives of the FFB is to act as the coordinator of agency borrowing. Not long ago, several government agencies borrowed directly from the public, but, with the creation of the FFB, this practice has virtually ceased. In 1979, more agency debt was repaid than was borrowed (net borrowing was − $1.6 billion) while agency borrowing from the FFB totalled $2.9 billion.[16] Only two programs have been authorized to undertake their own financing since the mid-sixties.[17]

---

[16] Agency borrowing from the FFB (which borrows from the Treasury, which, in turn, borrows from the public) is not considered borrowing from the public. Thus, the $2.9 billion in agency borrowing from the FFB is not included in the − $1.6 billion net agency borrowing from the public. This distinction explains why new agency "borrowing from the public" has been almost nonexistent since the FFB began operations.

[17] These are the FHA debenture program to pay off mortgagors for defaulted FHA-insured mortgages which went into operation in 1965, and the more recent National Credit Union Central Liquidity Facility to increase the loanable reserves of credit unions which began in 1979.

Individual agencies now market their securities to the FFB instead of directly to the public. The advantage of this centralized approach is the FFB's ability to market the securities at a lower interest rate (the Treasury's rate). The lower rates arise from the market's greater familiarity with Treasury offerings as well as the likely lower costs to the public of doing business with the Treasury rather than several individual agencies. There is also an expected savings in administrative costs. The purchase of agency debt by the FFB is an example of a government activity that works well and saves money.

Furthermore, FFB borrowing has no impact on budget totals because government borrowing and repayment of borrowings are properly considered a means of financing rather than as income and outlays. If borrowing were considered income, the budget by definition would always be balanced. To record agency borrowing from the FFB as outlays would double count since the funds will be scored as outlays on the agency's books when expended by the agency.

FFB Purchase of Guaranteed Loans

If coordinating agency borrowing was the FFB's only duty, the FFB's budget status would be an academic argument. However, the bank's other functions — purchasing loan assets and guaranteed loans — have profound budgetary impacts.

When the government purchases a loan made by a private lender, the expenditure is scored (properly) as an outlay; the government, in effect, makes the loan. This would not present any budgetary problem were it not for the fact that the primary lender is the FFB; its off-budget status means that the FFB's purchase of guaranteed loans — or, put another way, its making of direct loans — is recorded outside the totals of the unified budget. In 1979, the FFB purchased more than $5 billion in guaranteed loans.[18] Offsetting repayments from new purchases, net FFB outlays for the purchase of guaranteed loans totaled $3.9 billion in 1979; thus, the unified budget (and the deficit) is understated by $3.9 billion from this source alone.

The only other government agency in the business of purchasing loans from private lenders (other than defaulted guaranteed loans) is the Department of Housing and Urban Development's (HUD) Government National Mortgage Association (GNMA, or Ginnie Mae) which, in 1979, bought $1.5 billion in guaranteed mortgage loans. But because Ginnie Mae is an on-budget agency, its purchases are included in the unified budget.

---

[18] 1979 was a slow year; in 1978, the figure was $6.6 billion and, at the time of this writing, preliminary estimates for 1980 are $10.8 billion.

FFB Purchase of Loan Assets

The IOU created when a government loan is made may be in the form of a bond, promissory note, or debenture. These IOUs are loan assets and are marketable.[19] Often, shares in pools of loan assets — called participation certificates — are sold; the Department of Agriculture terminology is certificates of beneficial ownership, or CBOs (not to be confused with the Congressional Budget Office). The purchase of loan assets constitutes a major activity of the FFB (51 percent of its portfolio at the end of 1979) and results in significant budget distortions.

In terms of financial and accounting principles, the purchase of loan assets differs significantly from the purchase of guaranteed loans. At issue is whether loan asset sales constitute agency borrowing or income (repayments of loans). If a government-owned loan asset is sold to a buyer in the private sector, as far as the government is concerned, the loan has been repaid; offsetting loan repayments against new loans presents a fair financial picture. This is analogous to the budgetary treatment of offsetting receipts which are recorded as negative outlays rather than revenues.

But, what happens when loans are sold, not to investors in the private sector, but to the off-budget FFB? Laws permit the selling agencies — in particular, the Farmer's Home Administration (FmHA) and the Rural Electrification Administration (REA) — to record the proceeds of such sales as repayments, thereby rolling-over their loanable funds and reducing agency outlays by the amount of the sale. However, the government still owns the loans; the government has not been repaid; spending has merely been moved off-budget. When agency loan assets are sold to the FFB, the selling agency, in effect, is borrowing against the future income stream of the loan repayments.

Currently, the FmHA and the REA are the major marketers of loan assets;[20] the only other active seller of loan assets to the FFB is the Health Maintenance Organization Loan and Loan Guarantee Fund ($21 million, net, for 1979) designed to help establish health maintenance organizations (HMOs).

It is axiomatic that one way to reduce a highly visible and politically embarrassing deficit is to reduce outlays. One way to reduce outlays is to net out as repayments the proceeds from loan asset sales to the FFB. If these sales were treated properly — as borrowing — the offsets

---

[19] For an in-depth treatment of loan asset sales, see: "Loan Asset Sales: Current Budgetary Treatment and Alternatives, *Loan Guarantees: Current Concerns and Alternatives for Control,* Congressional Budget Office, January 1979, pp. 71–109.

[20] The REA is an off-budget agency, so in a narrow sense, there are no unified budget distortions when the REA sells CBOs to the FFB, since both agencies operate outside the unified budget.

to outlays would not be allowed; total 1979 outlays and the 1979 deficit would be higher by $9.4 billion. Predicting large future loan asset sales has become a convenient way to show a lower (unified budget) deficit.

If the FFB were on-budget, and if its purchases were recorded within the same sub-function as the selling program, the transactions would have no effect on functional totals. Sales receipts would be offset exactly by the outlays used to purchase the loan assets. This would, of course, remove any incentive to use loan assets to understate spending. Sales to the public, however, would escape control, because they would (properly) be recorded as loan repayments (offsetting new loan outlays). However, sale to the public would undermine the objective of keeping total government borrowing costs as low as possible. The solution is to require agencies who could otherwise sell their loan assets directly to the public to market their assets only through an on-budget FFB.

The most flagrant budget distortions originate with the Farmers Home Administration (FmHA). Of the total $9.4 billion in FFB loan asset purchases, $8.8 billion (94 percent) stem from the sale of CBOs by the FmHA in the conduct of the Agricultural Housing Insurance Fund (in the Commerce and Housing Credit budget function), the Agricultural Credit Insurance Fund (in the Agriculture function), and the Rural Development Insurance Fund (in the Community and Regional Development function).

The Commerce and Housing Credit, Agriculture, and Community and Regional Development budget functions are not large, but the distortions are significant (Table 7). Proper attribution of FFB purchases of FmHA CBOs would increase the proportion of the budget that these functions comprise from 3.7 to 5.4 percent, a distortion of 46 percent.

Two of these three functions show major distortions. Under conventional accounting, the Agriculture function showed outlays of $6.2 billion, comprising 1.3 percent of the total unified outlays. However, if CBO sales were recorded as borrowing instead of offsets to outlays, the Agriculture function would show outlays of $11.3 billion, or 2.2 percent of the budget, a distortion of 78 percent. The Community and Regional Development function is understated by $2.9 billion and is distorted by more than 100 percent; instead of comprising one half of one percent of the budget, a more accurate reflection would be 1.1 percent.

Credit Activities of Federally-Sponsored Enterprises

Federally-sponsored enterprises are privately-owned financial intermediaries that perform specialized credit functions by either serving as reserve facilities (sources of funds) or as makers of secondary markets

(Table 8). While excluded from the unified budget, government-sponsored enterprises are not classified as "off-budget"; that distinction is reserved for the FFB and six other government-owned entities. "Extra-budget" is a more appropriate term.

Despite their non-budget status and their private ownership, these entities share many of the same characteristics of government agencies, whether on- or off-budget. They are subject to federal supervision and they interact with the Treasury in much the same way as do federally-owned agencies. Unlike other privately-owned entities, they enjoy special tax preferences which enable them to operate profitably in selected corners of the U.S. credit market.

Federal authority over the activities of government-sponsored enterprises is more significant than commonly assumed. In the case of Fannie Mae (the Federal National Mortgage Association), the President appoints five of its fourteen directors, the Secretary of the Treasury must approve all of its debt issues, and the Secretary of Housing and Urban Development has specific authority to set FNMA's debt-to-equity ratio (in effect, the power to place limits on its portfolio). In addition, the HUD Secretary has "general regulatory power" over Fannie Mae.[21] Sally Mae borrows exclusively from the Federal Financing Bank.

The feature most often put forth as the reason for their being outside the unified budget is their private ownerships. Yet no one seriously doubts that the government would not bail out any government-sponsored enterprise in the event of impending failure, its private ownership notwithstanding. Including government-sponsored enterprises in the totals of the unified budget need not affect their private ownership. Any so-called federal credit budget would be inadequate without them.

RECOMMENDATIONS

In this final section, the various problems associated with the budgetary treatment of federal credit programs are linked to recommendations and solutions. These recommendations and solutions are grouped into two broad problem areas corresponding to the two main purposes of a government budget — determining size and resource allocation.

By misrepresenting both the size of government and the allocation of the resources employed by the government, the entire budgeting, or fiscal planning process is damaged. At the practical level, agencies that are able to move substantial portions of their activities off-

---

[21] Title III, Section 309(h), the Federal National Mortgage Association Act.

Table 7

Budget Distortions Resulting from On-Budget Agency Loan Assets Sales to the Federal Financing Bank, Fiscal Year 1979[1]
(dollars in millions)

Budget Function	Program Description	Unified Budget		Loan Asset Sales to FFB	"True" Outlays[2]	Percent "true" Outlays are of Adjusted Total Outlays[3]	Distortion[4]
		Outlays	Percent of total				
International Affairs	Foreign military credit sales	$ 6,091	1.2%	$ 1,293	$ 7,384	1.5%	18.8%
General Sciences, Space and Technology		$ 5,041	1.0	184	5,225	1.0	1.5
Agriculture	Agriculture Credit Insurance Fund	6,238	1.3	5,045	11,283	2.2	77.2
Commerce and Housing Credit	Rural Housing Insurance Fund and Small Business Investment Co.	2,565	0.5	3,016	5,581	1.1	113.1
Transportation	Amtrak and other RR programs	17,459	3.5	−25	17,434	3.5	−2.2
Community and Regional Development	Rural Development Insurance Fund and other community development	9,482	1.9	835	10,317	2.0	6.6
Health	HMOs	49,614	10.1	20	49,634	9.8	−2.1
Undistributed by function							
TOTAL, on-budget		$96,490	19.5%	$10,368	$106,922	21.2%	8.5%

ADDENDUM (other asset sales to FFB)		Appropriate On-budget Function	Loan Asset Sales to FFB
Off-budget	REA, CBOs, and new organizations	Energy	2,321
Extra-budget	Sally Mae (SLMA)	Education, Training, Employment, and Social Services	530
Undistributed	By on-budget functions or off-budget or extra-budget status.	N/A	64
	(loan asset sales to FFB; equal to total 1979 FFB outlays exclusive of $110 million in interest, transfer of surplus, and administrative expenses)		
GRAND TOTAL			$13,283

Source: Unpublished OMB data and the *Budget of the United States Government for Fiscal Year 1981*, GPO, Washington, page 331.

[1] The Energy and Income Security functions showed no loan asset sales to the Federal Financing Bank in 1979, and are therefore not reflected in this table. For a multi-year perspective, see table on p. 331 in the 1981 budget.

[2] Unified budget outlays plus sales of loan assets (including CBOs) to off-budget Federal Financing Bank.

[3] The $10.4 billion in sales of loan assets by on-budget agencies to the off-budget Federal Financing Bank was added to total unified budget outlays before computations so as not to create an upward bias on the column entries.

[4] Percent differences between nonrounded figures of the fourth and seventh columns.

Table 8
Activity Levels (Funds Advanced) of
Government-Sponsored Enterprises, 1979
(dollars in millions)

Entity	Loans Outstanding	New Loans	Net Lending
Student Loan Marketing Association	1,239	627	529
Federal National Mortgage Association	49,174	11,129	7,983
Farm Credit Administration:			
Banks for cooperatives	7,222	17,027	1,101
Federal intermediate credit banks	16,407	11,975	2,370
Federal land banks	29,871	7,558	5,057
Federal home loan bank system:			
Federal home loan banks	41,486	28,425	9,853
Federal Home Loan Mortgage Corporation			
Corporation accounts	2,528	6,453	1,305
Participation certificate pools	15,648	4,903	3,731
Subtotal, lending (gross)	163,575	88,100	31,930
Less Adjustments:			
Loans between sponsored enterprises:			
Federal home loans banks to FHLMC	2,799	662	400
Secondary funds advanced from Federal			
sources: SLMA from FFB	1,275	530	530
Guaranteed loans held as direct loans			
by Student Loan Marketing Assoc.	1,239	527	529
Federal National Mortgage Association	33,971	3,384	3,069
Federal home loan banks	91	21	15
Federal Home Loan Mortgage Corporation	1,189	–	– 155
Total	123,012	80,876	27,542

Source: Budget of the United States Government, FY 1981, Special Analysis F
(Federal Credit Programs), GPO, Washington, January 1980, p. 178 (Table F-6).

budget — some would say out of sight — enjoy a competitive advantage over agencies which must rely on less creative accounting to support their funding requests. In the extreme, there can be no meaningful comparisons; budgeting becomes an adding-up instead of a zero-sum process and difficult choices are avoided.

These recommendations and solutions are neutral with respect to individual credit programs. Nor is there any attempt to make normative judgments on federal credit programs *per se* except as to how they ought to be treated in the budget in order to fairly represent their activity levels (while nevertheless recognizing their qualitative differences from direct expenditures and other government activities).

If implemented, these recommendations would make the government appear larger than it now appears because, under the present budgetary treatment of credit programs, the government is made to look smaller than it is.
smaller government.

Problem 1: Understating the Size of Government

The existence of off-budget entities results in the budget being understated by billions of dollars each year. The lion's share of off-budget spending is for credit programs.

Therefore, all off-budget agencies, including the FFB, should be brought within the unified budget.[22] It should be noted that the Office of Management and Budget is sympathetic:

> . . . [T]he exclusion of the FFB (Federal Financing Bank) from the budget is unequivocally contrary to the principles recommended by the President's Commission on Budget Concepts. The exclusion reduces the significance of the budget totals and the validity of presentations in the budget documents.[23]

Federally-Sponsored Enterprises

In 1979, net direct loan activity of federally-sponsored enterprises totaled $27.5 billion, $80.9 billion in new loans were made, and loans outstanding stood at $123.0 billion. If net loan activity of federally-sponsored enterprises were included in the budget totals along with off-budget spending, the 1979 aggregates would take the following appearance:

	Outlays	Deficit
	(dollars in billions)	
Unified budget total (before adjustments) .	$493.7	$27.7
Add:		
Net off-budget agency spending	12.4	12.4
Subtotal	$506.1	$40.1
Net Loans by Government-sponsored		
enterprises	27.5	27.5
TOTAL	$533.6	$67.6

Inclusion of federally-sponsored enterprises in the budget aggregates would be strong political medicine considering the singular emphasis on deficits. This accounting would, however, be consistent with and analogous to making taxes both painful and obvious. Separate credit accounts within the expenditure side of the budget may offer some comfort and would provide analytical flexibility.

In view of the overall behavior and characteristics of these entities,

---

[22] In 1976, the House Budget Committee adopted a report recommending that all off-budget agencies, except the FFB, be brought on budget. The Committee was not, however, recommending retention of off-budget status for the FFB, only deferring judgment. FFB's marketing of agency debt, the purchase of loan assets, and the purchase of guaranteed loans could be handled just as efficiently by an on-budget FFB.

[23] Tech. Paper Series BRD/FAB 76-1, 2026-76; also see "Government Agency Transactions with the Federal Financing Banks Should be Included in the Budget," Comptroller General, Washington, D.C., PAD-77-70, August 3, 1977.

the arguments for extra-budget status less than compelling. *Accordingly, the activity levels of these entities should either be reflected in the unified budget, their private ownership notwithstanding, or their ties to the government severed by cancelling their federal charters. If the former, they should also be included in any federal credit budget.*

Problem 2: Misstating the Activity Levels Within the Budget

In the competition for funding, appearance can be more important than reality; programs which can be made to appear less costly stand a better chance for funding.[24] Budgetary accounting practices place many credit programs in a special position.

Eliminating off-budget status solves the problem of understating the size of government, but may do nothing to correct the allocation distortions at the program or functional levels. Proper attribution of credit program activities within the budget is also needed.

Strategy for an On-Budget FFB

Much of the distortions caused by the treatment of federal credit programs stem from the off-budget status of the Federal Financing Bank. However, it does not follow that, even with on-budget status for the FFB, the best way to eliminate the distortions is to focus control on the FFB. The problem is not uncontrolled FFB financing, but instead uncontrolled agency financing.

Placing the control on the FFB rather than on an individual program could lead to several undesirable results and may not solve the allocation distortion problem at all. The solution is to make the FFB the "frictionless conduit" originally envisioned by properly attributing to the agencies and to their respective subfunctions their dealings with an on-budget FFB.

Despite a strong conclusion by the President's Commission on Budget Concepts, and others, that the sale of participation certificates constitutes agency borrowing, the Congress enacted into law provisions that, in effect, require CBO sales to be treated as repayments. The sale of CBOs does not constitute transfer of equity, since the government still owns the loans. There is general agreement (at least outside the Department of Agriculture) that CBO sales constitute agency borrowing and, as such, the proceeds should not be recorded as repayments that offset outlays. *These provisions of law should be repealed to require the proceeds from CBO sales to be recorded as borrowing by the selling agency.*

---

[24] This statement would be more forceful if the dominant budgeting mode was "two-step" rather than "adding-up." But an ever increasing budget "pie" resulting from the addition of new programs and the expansion of existing programs (adding-up) rather than a predetermined, stable "pie" whose slices are rearranged to accommodate changing priorities diminishes the competitive advantage argument.

372

Net vs. Gross Lending

The issue is how to accurately represent the financial picture (net vs. gross lending) while at the same time showing activity levels (gross lending and loans outstanding). Recording loan activity on a net basis may introduce a bias, but this bias results from defendable accounting. Separating repayments from direct loans in the budget — for example, showing repayments in a separate function — would simply introduce another distortion into the allocation picture.

The best approach is to continue showing loan activity on a net basis while at the same time developing a separate credit section that is an integral part of the budget. A meaningful credit budget is the best way to establish a control framework for federal credit programs.

A Related Problem: Control of Federal Credit Programs

The main thrust of this essay has been the treatment of federal credit programs within the budget. Actual control of federal credit programs — which are the least controlled programs in the budget — has been a peripheral topic throughout. Accordingly, control of federal credit programs is an appropriate concluding topic.

Federal credit programs have evolved to be relatively uncontrolled by Congress.[25] Generally, Congress has not chosen to exercise its authority through annual limitations. Except for entitlement-like credit programs, credit programs often permit considerable administrative discretion. Presidents, too, have generally not sought to exercise tight control over program activity levels. This lack of control by both the Executive and the Congress has certainly contributed to the dramatic growth of federal credit programs in recent years.

The issue of control of federal credit did not really surface until 1978 when the House Budget Committee's Task Force on Budget Process began looking into this question. To date, the most Congress has mustered is a non-binding credit "limitation" in the equally non-binding first concurrent budget resolution for 1981. A bipartisan congressional proposal would restrain new loan guarantee commitments to amounts provided for in appropriation acts.[26] The proposal should be extended to include a similar control on direct loan obligations.

The Carter Administration proposed a control system that included both loan guarantees and direct loans, with the "control points" on commitments and obligations, respectively.[27] At first, the Administra-

---

[25] All federal spending is, of course, controllable. In budget terminology "controllable" refers to spending that requires legislative action. Most spending — about three-quarters of the budget — occurs under authority contained in current laws.

[26] H.R. 5683, The Federal Credit Program Control Act of 1979.

[27] Placing control on actual loan disbursements or guarantee extensions (both of which follow obligations and commitments, often by significant time periods) would be much less effective because once committed, the federal government cannot back out of a credit agreement without consent from the other party.

373

tion's proposal covered only about 45 percent of total net direct loan obligations and 40 percent of total loan guarantee commitments for 1981.[28] The loan obligation was subsequently raised to almost 75 percent by bringing Ginnie Mae and FHA mortgage insurance programs into the limitation sphere. The direct loan limitation amounts to $28.5 billion, or 4.5 percent of total unified budget outlays. The limitation on loan guarantees cannot easily be reduced to a single figure because different limitations are attached to primary and to secondary loan guarantees, and also to loan guarantees held as direct loans. After adjustment, the limitation on loan guarantee commitments total $112.7 billion, so that the total proposed federal credit budget for 1981 is $141.2 billion. For comparison purposes (since guarantees are not scored as outlays), this figure is about one-fifth of total estimated government outlays.[29]

The Administration's cautious proposal to attach dollar restrictions on federal credit program activity levels in annual spending bills is sound—a major step in the right direction. Unfortunately, the proposal has not been met with an outpouring of enthusiasm on Capitol Hill.

Apart from whether Congress will include limitation language in appropriation bills is the issue of how control of federal credit programs should be approached within the precarious and weak congressional budget process. H.R. 5683 sought to amend the 1974 Budget Act to add gross new lending obligations and gross new loan guarantee commitments to the two budget aggregates currently subject to "ceilings" (total new budget authority and total outlays). Legislation that would breach either of these ceilings could be halted by a simple point of order. However, this would have no effect on curtailing commitments and obligations arising from on-going and previously funded programs. In lieu of enactment of legislation that would strengthen the budget process (e.g., making credit aggregate ceilings subject to points of order when threatened), the best to be expected is a continuation of non-binding language in non-binding budget resolutions.[30]

---

[28] For an analysis of the Administration's credit proposals, see: "Federal Credit Activities: An Analysis of the President's Credit budget for 1981," Congressional Budget Office, Washington, February 1980.

[29] Such a comparison belies an important analytical problem. Although both direct loans and loan guarantees are measured in dollars, they are not commensurate in terms of their likely economic impact. Just as a dollar of direct expenditures will differ in economic impact from a dollar of direct loans, so too will a dollar of direct loans differ in economic impact from a dollar of loan guarantees. The tendency is to add direct loans to other direct expenditures as if they were commensurate. This presents much less of a problem than if direct expenditures were added to loan guarantees.

points of order when threatened), the best to be expected is a continuation of non-binding language in non-binding budget resolutions.[30]

The author wishes to thank Ed Brigham of the House Budget Committee staff, and John Shillingburg of the Congressional Budget Office for having generated and generously shared so much of the useful factual information on the operation and accounting of credit programs.

[30] However, budget resolution ceilings have been more of a nuisance than a restraint to the Congress. The Budget Act, is, in large part, a rewrite of the operating rules of the House and Senate. This means that the law is frequently violated by simple resolutions which waive or change provisions in the Budget Act. In three of the past five years, binding second resolutions have been supplanted by binding third resolutions.